NIGHTHAWK RISING

A Biography of Accused Cattle Rustler
Queen Ann Bassett of Brown's Park

To Mike

Nighthawk Rising

A Biography of Accused Cattle Rustler
Queen Ann Bassett of Brown's Park

Diana Allen Kouris

High Plains Press

The background art on the cover is a photograph by the author.
The portrait of Ann Bassett was colorized by Laura McCormick.

The Wyoming bucking horse and rider trademark in our logo is federally registered by the State of Wyoming and is licensed for restricted use through the Secretary of State.

Library of Congress Cataloging-in-Publication Data

Names: Kouris, Diana Allen, author.
Title: Nighthawk rising : a biography of accused cattle rustler queen Ann
  Bassett of Brown's Park / Diana Allen Kouris.
Description: Glendo, WY : High Plains Press, [2018] | Includes index.
Identifiers: LCCN 2018017720| ISBN 9781937147150 (hardcover : alk. paper)
  | ISBN 9781937147167 (paperback : alk. paper) | ISBN 9781937147174 (ebook)
Subjects: LCSH: Bassett, Ann, 1878-1956. | Women
  ranchers--Colorado--Biography. | Ranch life--Colorado--History--19th
  century. | Outlaws--Colorado--Biography. | Frontier and pioneer
  life--Colorado--Biography. | Ranchers--Colorado--Biography. |
  Women--Colorado--Biography. | Brown's Park--Biography. | LCGFT:
  Biographies.
Classification: LCC F781 .K68 2018 | DDC 978.8/02092 [B] --dc23
LC record available at https://lccn.loc.gov/2018017720

HIGH PLAINS PRESS
403 CASSA ROAD
GLENDO, WYOMING 82213

CATALOG AVAILABLE

WWW.HIGHPLAINSPRESS.COM

ORA HALEY.

P. O. address, Laramie City, Wyo.; ranch P. O., Lay, Routt Co., Colo.

Range, Snake and Bear Rivers, Colo.

Horse brand ♡ on left shoulder.

HOY BROTHERS.

Represented by V. S. HOY.

P. O. address, Brown's Park, Uinta County, Utah; also Fremont, Neb.

Range, Brown's Park, Wyo., Colo. and Utah.

Other brands, ᴴ on left shoulder, and ᴶᴴ some of our old cattle have ᴶᴴ on left side.

Horse brand, **HOY** on left shoulder, some of which have ᴶᴴ on left shoulder.

4

above from the Wyoming Stock Growers Association
Brand Book of Mike Shoney, 1885

Bassett, Samuel, Ladore, Colo

On left hip.

On left thigh.

McKnight, Ladore, Colo

Cattle.

Horses.

Haley, Ora, Laramie, Wyo.
H.H. Bernard, Mgr, Craig, Colo

Cattle, right hip.

Horses, left shoulder also

Cattle, left side

Bassett, Elbert, Ladore, Colo

On left ribs.

Rash, Madison M., Ladore, Colo

Cattle, left side

Ayer, C. E., Dixon, Wyo.

Cattle, left hip.

Doty Bros., Willows, Wyo.

Cattle, left hip or side. Horses, left shoulder; also numerous Utah brands

above from Snake River Stock Growers Brand Book, 1890
(Craig Stock Growers section)

Isam Dart,
Brown's Park.

E.B. Thompson,
Maybell.

above from the State Brand Book of Colorado *January 1, 1894*

CONTENTS

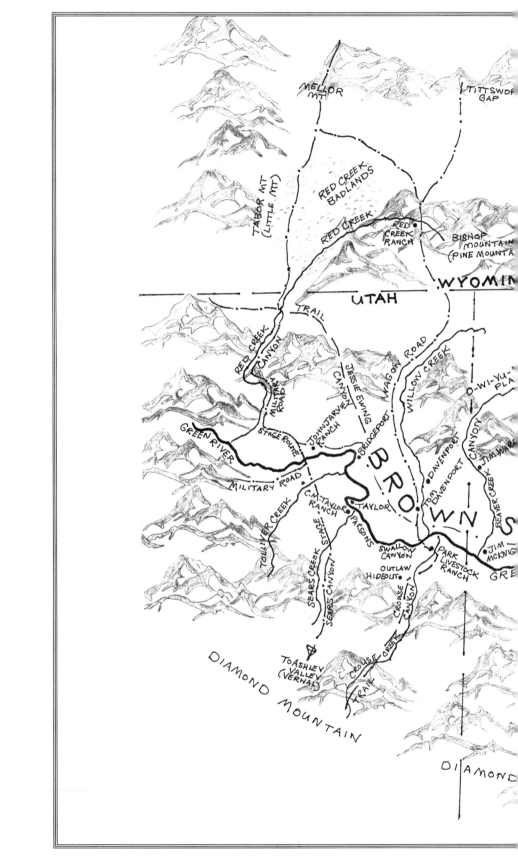

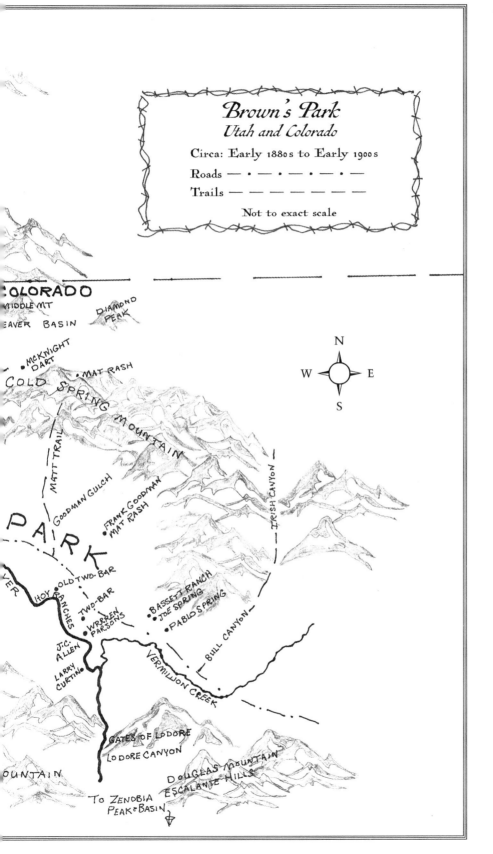

Brown's Park
Utah and Colorado

Circa: Early 1880s to Early 1900s

Roads — • — • — • —

Trails — — — — — —

Not to exact scale

COLORADO
MIDDLE MT
BEAVER BASIN
DIAMOND PEAK

McKNIGHT DART
MAT RASH

COLD SPRING MOUNTAIN

MATT TRAIL

GOODMAN GULCH

FRANK GOODMAN MAT RASH

IRISH CANYON

PARK

OLD TWO-BAR
HOY RANCHES
TWO-BAR
WARREN PARSONS
PABLO SPRING
BASSETT RANCH
JOE SPRING

RIVER

J.C. ALLEN
LARRY CURTIN

BULL CANYON

VERMILLION CREEK

GATES OF LODORE
LODORE CANYON

MOUNTAIN

TO ZENOBIA PEAK & BASIN

DOUGLAS MOUNTAIN
ESCALANTE HILLS

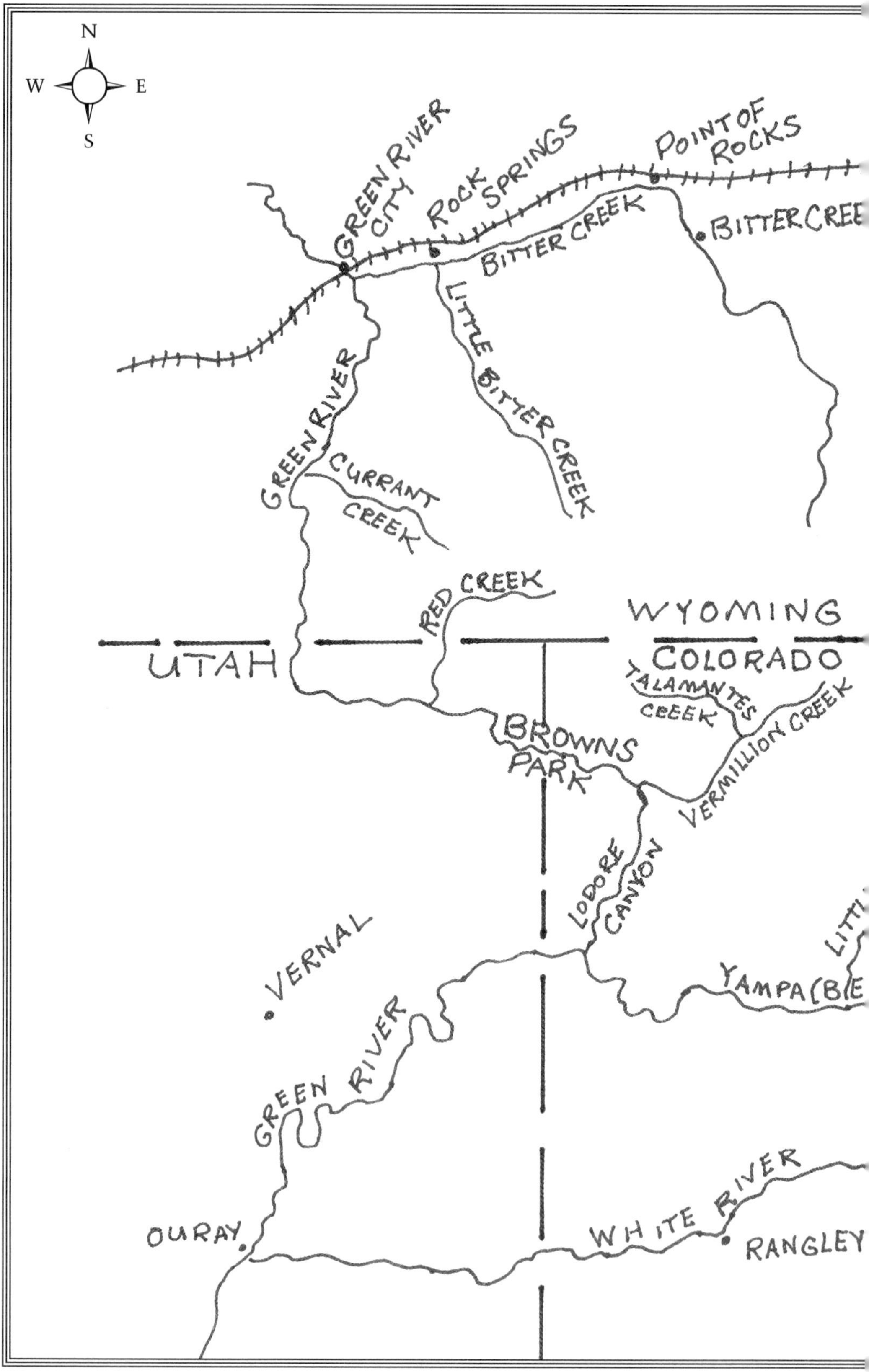

N
W
E
S
GREEN RIVER CITY
ROCK SPRINGS
POINT OF ROCKS
BITTER CREEK
BITTER CREEK
BITTER CREE
LITTLE BITTER CREEK
GREEN RIVER
CURRANT CREEK
RED CREEK
WYOMING
UTAH
COLORADO
TALAMANTES CREEK
VERMILLION CREEK
BROWNS PARK
LODORE CANYON
VERNAL
GREEN RIVER
YAMPA (BE
OURAY
WHITE RIVER
RANGLEY

UP RAILROAD

RAWLINS
FT STEELE

Overview of Brown's Park Area
Utah, Wyoming, Colorado

Locations Established Between
1862 and 1907

First Transcontinental Railroad 1869

Not to exact scale

POWDER SPRING

BAGGS
DIXON
SAVERY

LITTLE SNAKE

VDER
SH

E RIVER

HAHNS PEAK.

ELK RIVER

IVER

MAYBELL

LAY

CRAIG

HAYDEN

STEAMBOAT

JUNIPER SPRINGS

YAMPA RIVER
YAMPA

MEEKER

PREFACE

A PRELUDE

I grew up enfolded in history in the legendary valley of Brown's Park, and I share the intricate texture of the valley's narrative with many notable history-makers. Some include Butch Cassidy, Tom Horn, Kit Carson, Snapping Annie, John and Nellie Jarvie, Isam Dart, and the compelling subject of this book, Queen Ann Bassett.

Queen Ann and I both received the rare providence of being the daughters of Brown's Park cattle ranchers. My family's ranch house sat just across the river from the meadow on Willow Creek where Ann was born. Although our ages were seven decades apart, we rode the same trails, breathed the same ancient fragrances, admired the stately mountains that surrounded us, and each formed a selfish love for our valley home. We tasted identical hints of dust, sage, cedar, and pine when we worked cattle on the range. At dusk, after long days in the saddle, we were both escorted home by the grace of nighthawks flying overhead as they fed upon the insects stirred into the twilight by the rhythmic beat of horse hooves.

❧ ❧ ❧

Ann Bassett's parents—and twenty-eight years later my grandparents—traveled by wagon to the valley of Brown's Park to realize a dream of building a cattle ranch in the West and raising their children there. The Bassetts and Taylors likely agreed with the descriptive words written by adventurer Rufus Sage, for they were all captivated by Brown's Park.

> Few localities in the mountains are equal to this, in point of beautiful and romantic scenery. Every thing embraced in its confines tends to inspire the beholder with comingled feelings of awe and admiration.
> *Rufus B. Sage, Brown's Park, 1842*

Queen Ann first met my grandmother, Nina Taylor, in July 1906 when Ann was twenty-eight-years-old and Grandma was about to turn twenty-four. Queen Ann's most treasured heroes throughout her life were the pioneering women she lived among. She welcomed Nina into her life and they became friends. Nina, my grandfather C.M. Taylor, and their son Jess held affection for Queen Ann from the moment they met her when she had lunch with them at their covered wagon on the trail to Brown's Park. Grandma Taylor told me some of her memories of laughter and sorrow that she shared with Ann. Uncle Jess was over eighty years old when he talked to me at length about the cattlewoman he had loved and admired from the time he was five years old. He spoke in a wistful voice when he said, "Queen Ann was a lady."

My mother and beloved idol, Marie Taylor Allen, was Uncle Jess's youngest sister. She grew up a top-hand cowgirl on the Taylor Ranch in upper Brown's Park. She and my father, Bill Allen, were cattle ranchers and raised six kids on the Brown's Park Livestock Ranch. Mom was passionate in her devotion to Brown's Park, and my siblings and I had the great delight of being immersed in her stories of the past. In the 1800s a young cowboy had been knifed to death in what became our ranch house. He is buried nearby. Butch Cassidy lived there when, as a teenager, he worked for Charlie Crouse, the founder of our ranch. When Butch was an outlaw on the run, he sometimes hid out in a small cabin near a spring that we often used for drinking water. Butch rode getaway horses from Charlie Crouse's herd of thoroughbreds that once grazed in the same pastures where our saddle horses grazed. Mom's stories about Brown's Park were intriguing and, because they happened in our domain, each one felt personal.

Mom, as did Queen Ann, found it hurtful when books and articles written about our valley brimmed with untruths. Mom gathered research, gave talks and tours, and corresponded with and interviewed some of the descendants of Brown's Park's historical figures. She wrote newfound details on whatever paper might be available at the time including napkins, scraps of paper, envelopes, and tablets. Mom's efforts resulted in the Dr. Parsons cabin and the Lodore School both being placed on the National Register of Historic Places. The Parsons cabin, built in the 1870s, was Mom's childhood home for several years before her parents, Grandma and Grandpa Taylor, built a new ranch house.

Mom had not realized her dream of writing the history of Brown's Park when she passed away in 1975. She gifted that aspiration to me. I found a sanctuary from my sorrow when I was surrounded by her research. Her passion became mine, and I discovered my life's work.

❧ ❧ ❧

My family owned some of the most historically important places featured in this book including the Brown's Park Livestock Ranch, the Joe Tolliver Ranch, the Parsons place, the Bridgeport Ranch, the Jarvie Ranch, the Red Creek Ranch, and land on Cold Spring and Douglas Mountains. I wrote about these locations from intimate knowledge.

I am grateful that I had my family's perspective on both Queen Ann and her sister, Josie, as I composed this book. Not only did my grandparents, uncle, and mother know them both, but my aunt, Isabelle "Belle" Mac-Knight Christensen, was Queen Ann's niece and Josie's granddaughter.

This biography reveals Ann Bassett to be complex and fascinating. She dwelled within the danger and splendor that her valley and time period presented. She was confident—arrogant at times—about her abilities on the back of a horse and while working cattle. It's where she felt most alive. At a young age, though, she was devastated by family tragedy. A few years later, the deadly repercussions of range war changed her life.

However, before the book moves fully into Ann's life, some side trails must be explored. The painting of Ann's life would be incomplete without them. The mountain men and the Ute people made up some of Ann Bassett's underpinnings; her foundation was interrelated with Brown's Park's history. Outlaws and shootings were part of her surroundings. The Meeker Massacre occurred when Ann was a toddler, but it had a major impact on her life. Not only did her family have to flee to safety, but also if the uprising had *not* occurred, the Bassett Ranch would have probably been built elsewhere, if it was ever built at all. The endurance of the women who were taken captive after the massacre undoubtedly influenced Ann's life in the years to come, for she drew strength from the bravery of women. I used painstaking research and direct testimony to convey the events of the Meeker Massacre through the female point of view.

It is an awesome responsibility to write the lives of those who came before and I take it most seriously. I, in a sense, time-travelled into the era of Ann Bassett, Mat Rash, Isam Dart, Herb and Elizabeth Bassett, and so many others who embroidered the fabric of Ann Bassett's life. I came to know them. Sometimes I cried, other times I smiled, but all the while I strived to write the truth about them and dispel falsehoods that sear reality.

It has been a long, gratifying voyage since Queen Ann whispered in my ear and asked me to write her story. I consider it my privilege.

CHAPTER ONE

THE WELCOMING

Cowgirl Queen Ann Bassett was a stunning portrait when on the back of a horse, but the trails she rode were rugged and dangerous and took her headlong into the storms of the times. She knew outlaws including Butch Cassidy and his partner Elzy Lay. They shared her valley and called her friend. However, stock detective Tom Horn infiltrated her life and wrecked her dreams. Grim-faced and enraged, Queen Ann moved with the rhythm of the loping horse beneath her, a rifle strapped to her saddle and at the ready. She rode hard, moving against the wind that swirled through the pinions and cedars, to defend her valley and avenge the man she loved.

Queen Ann was a cattlewoman, arrested and tried for rustling. She was declared to be a terror and a wildcat but also a heroine.[1] About herself she said, "I was a mangy coyote and loved it."[2] In Brown's Park, in the spring of 1878, her journey began.

Deep within the wilds of the American West on May 12, 1878, a spring storm unleashed from a sky of overcast chill. Soon water laden snowflakes made mounds upon the roof of a windowless cabin and melted silently into the silver ripples of nearby Willow Creek. The plaintive sound of a newborn began drifting through the walls of log and into the whiteness beyond. Anna Maria Bassett[3] whimpered and cried for nourishment her mother could not provide. Never before had a white child been born to this valley that now cradled Anna's tiny life. Even as she was born, destiny entwined this child with the narrative of the charismatic valley of her birth.

As the years passed, the valley of Brown's Park nurtured this girl called Ann to perfection. Anna Maria, a feral-like beauty with cinnamon red hair and eyes the green of sagebrush after a sweetening rain, came into bloom as a cowgirl. Ann loved this valley with a devoted, aching passion, even as it steeped her in tragedy and sorrow.

Brown's Park, an offspring of the Rocky Mountains at the eastern tip of the Uintas, lay in the secluded northwest corner of the new state of Colorado and northeast corner of the Territory of Utah. Ann's parents Herb and Elizabeth Bassett, recent arrivals at this faraway place, found themselves a long way from everything familiar, except perhaps their dreams. Courage and optimism were their valuable companions from the time they ventured west. Those tenets must have wavered a bit with the reality of this unanticipated situation with their infant daughter. Their little one, named after Herb's mother, was in peril. However, Ann came from resilient breeding and both her father and mother well knew the meaning of perseverance.

❧ ❧ ❧

Amos Herbert (Herb) Bassett had been born to Samuel Clark and Ann Mariah Bassett on July 31, 1834, in Brownsville, Jefferson County, New York. Herb's younger brother, Samuel Clark Bassett, was born three years after Herb in Mohawk, New York. Samuel played a major role in Herb and Elizabeth's destined place in history.

In the summer of 1862, a few years before Herb knew Elizabeth, he was an educated musician teaching school and farming in Sweetwater, Illinois. Standing five feet six inches tall, Herb was not athletic or even very physically strong, but he was a handsome young man with bluish grey eyes and black hair that revealed a thickness of natural curl. Though his life had been mostly a quiet one, he was deeply worried about his country and its political crisis.

A year earlier on April 12, 1861, Confederate warships bombarded Union soldiers at Fort Sumter, South Carolina. After thirty-four hours of assault, Fort Sumter fell. Three days later President Abraham Lincoln issued a proclamation "to call forth the Militia of the several States of the Union to the aggregate number of seventy-five thousand." Many, including Herb, believed the rebellion would be squelched and the conflict would be over quickly; very soon they realized that was not to be. Herb along with the rest of the nation watched the American Civil War burst into actuality.

A year after the fall of Fort Sumter, President Lincoln made the call for three hundred thousand more men to join the Union cause, to serve for an enlistment period of three years. On August 14, 1862, Herb volunteered.

Herb and other volunteers from his home county of Menard trained briefly in Lincoln, Illinois, before they were organized into Company K, Illinois of the 106th Regiment. On September 18, 1862,[4] Herb mustered into Federal service as "musician," a rank beneath corporal but above private. Both Union and Confederate Armies depended on their musicians to entertain troops, lift morale, position soldiers in battle, and when critical times came, to emotionally and physically rouse the men and help spur them onward into battle. Sometimes musicians assisted the surgeons in their work. Drummers and buglers often served on the battlefield and sometimes took casualties. While considered noncombatant, musicians held important and dangerous duties.[5]

The following June, en route to join the siege at Vicksburg, Mississippi, the steamboat transporting Herb's regiment came under Confederate fire. The 106th had little ability to effectively return fire and Herb saw several of his fellow soldiers killed. At least twenty-five more lay wounded by the time the steamboat reached Vicksburg.

Eventually Herb and the 106th were assigned to keep the peace throughout Arkansas while also guarding posts against any Confederate counter-attacks. Unimaginable joy, anger, and sorrow must have laced sunset on the evening of the day of April 9, 1865. The staggering war halted. Finally, it was over.

According to the Adjutant General Report of Illinois, Herb was mustered out of the Army on July 12, 1865, at Pine Bluff, Arkansas. The report states: "Except the siege of Vicksburg, the Regiment was not in any of the most noted battles, but, nevertheless, it performed well its part in putting down the rebellion and it suffered many privations and hardships marching through swamps and bayous, guarding railroads, government property, fighting and foraging, as is proved by its long list of casualties."[6]

Herb decided to stay in Arkansas and live in Hot Springs County. He, like other soldiers, was attracted to the soothing and healing properties of the thermal waters of the Hot Springs Reservation. Yes, he survived the war, and he served admirably, but his health had not fared well. Two-thirds of the 620,000 soldiers who perished in the war died from disease.[7] Besides enduring the inner pain and scarring-over of mental wounds, doctors treated Herb for liver and heart trouble. He described having awful fevers and chills that were, at times, uncontrollable. He had also developed asthma.

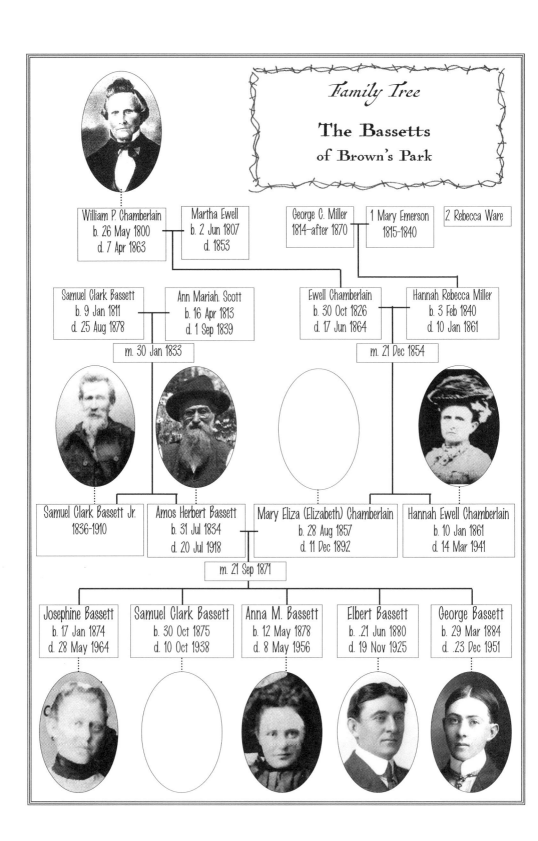

Family Tree

The Bassetts
of Brown's Park

William P. Chamberlain
b. 26 May 1800
d. 7 Apr 1863

Martha Ewell
b. 2 Jun 1807
d. 1853

George C. Miller
1814–after 1870

1 Mary Emerson
1815–1840

2 Rebecca Ware

Samuel Clark Bassett
b. 9 Jan 1811
d. 25 Aug 1878

Ann Mariah. Scott
b. 16 Apr 1813
d. 1 Sep 1839

Ewell Chamberlain
b. 30 Oct 1826
d. 17 Jun 1864

Hannah Rebecca Miller
b. 3 Feb 1840
d. 10 Jan 1861

m. 30 Jan 1833

m. 21 Dec 1854

Samuel Clark Bassett Jr.
1836–1910

Amos Herbert Bassett
b. 31 Jul 1834
d. 20 Jul 1918

Mary Eliza (Elizabeth) Chamberlain
b. 28 Aug 1857
d. 11 Dec 1892

Hannah Ewell Chamberlain
b. 10 Jan 1861
d. 14 Mar 1941

m. 21 Sep 1871

Josephine Bassett
b. 17 Jan 1874
d. 28 May 1964

Samuel Clark Bassett
b. 30 Oct 1875
d. 10 Oct 1938

Anna M. Bassett
b. 12 May 1878
d. 8 May 1956

Elbert Bassett
b. .21 Jun 1880
d. 19 Nov 1925

George Bassett
b. 29 Mar 1884
d. .23 Dec 1951

Herb's nature compelled him to do his best to lead a low-key but productive life surrounded by books and music. He served a short stint as postmaster at the Rockport Post Office in the summer of 1869.[8] Herb didn't know, though, that in the near future he was going to meet an enchanting young girl who would alight on the stage of his life. The paradigm shift that would take him and Elizabeth headlong into a far-off and adventurous world was, for now, still just whispering its secrets into nighttime dreams. However, the journey was waiting.

❦ ❦ ❦

Mary Eliza (Elizabeth) Chamberlain, who would eventually marry Herb Bassett, move to Brown's Park, and become the mother of Ann and her siblings, came into the world at Hot Springs, Arkansas, on August 28, 1857. Elizabeth's lovely mother, Hannah Miller Chamberlain, was just seventeen at the time of Elizabeth's birth and her husband, Ewell Chamberlain, was fifteen years older. The two had known each other as close neighbors most of Hannah's life. The custom during that time in Arkansas allowed for young girls to wed older men.[9]

Hannah's father and Elizabeth's grandfather, George Crawford Miller, was born at Valley Forge, Virginia. He was a leading member of the Hot Springs, Arkansas, community. Aided by the labor of some twenty slaves, he farmed cotton and raised thoroughbred horses. Hannah's mother, Mary, died from complications of childbirth when Hannah was born, so Hannah never had the chance to know her. Instead, her father and his second wife, Rebecca, raised Hannah.

Hannah's husband, Ewell Chamberlain, had been born in Tennessee but his family moved to Arkansas not long after and farmed near Hannah's family. Both Hannah and Ewell had known contentment and prosperity and their daughter Elizabeth's entry into the family was surely a joyful time for them. However, just four years later, on January 10, 1861, a sorrowful and haunting past revisited when Hannah went into labor with her second daughter. At the age of twenty-one Hannah died, just as her own mother had, giving birth to a healthy little girl. Hannah's grief-stricken family named the baby Hannah Ewell Chamberlain, after both her mother and father.

Even as Elizabeth's father Ewell was being crushed by tragedy, the Civil War came crashing into their southern world. Elizabeth and her baby sister, Hannah, went to live with their grandfather George Miller and step-grandmother Rebecca when four months after his wife's death, the young father, Ewell, went to war.

Ewell joined a group of local volunteers, the Hot Springs Hornets, the very day it was formed on June 20, 1861.[10] Ewell traveled with his company to Lynchburg, Virginia, where the company was assigned to the Third Arkansas Regiment Infantry, Confederate States of America.[11]

Within the year, Ewell was promoted to fourth sergeant. On September 17, 1862, he was wounded at Sharpsburg, Maryland. Then in the spring, he received the horrible news that his sixty-three-year-old father, William Chamberlain, had been killed on April 7, 1863. Family stories passed through the generations claim that William Chamberlain was murdered in the barn of his home place, not by Union soldiers but by marauding bushwhackers which included Cherokee Indians.[12]

The following year in February, Ewell was promoted to third sergeant. However, three months later on May 6, his time on the battlefield abruptly ended in Virginia at the Wilderness, a seventy square-mile tangle of trees, thick undergrowth, and creeks.

The Battle of the Wilderness was chaotic, bloody, and up close. It was the first stage of a major Union offensive toward the Confederate capital of Richmond, Virginia, and newly appointed Union General-in-Chief Ulysses S. Grant commanded the forces. When the Army of the Potomac crossed the Rapidan River on May 4, General Robert E. Lee of the Confederacy decided to confront the enemy deep in the midst of the woods of the Wilderness. The rebels' familiarity with the density of the woodland negated the Union's superior troop numbers, a lopsided 65,000 Confederate soldiers to 115,000 Union men.

When the two-day clash was over, the Union suffered 2,246 killed; 12,037 wounded; and 3,383 captured or missing. The Confederates listed 1,495 killed; 7,928 wounded; and 1,702 captured or missing. Ewell lay among the severely wounded. Never again would he see his little girls Elizabeth and Hannah. In the camp hospital he lingered, sick and injured with one leg amputated, until at last he died on June 17, 1864. Ewell was buried in the Confederate Section of the Old City Cemetery at Lynchburg, Virginia, a year before his Confederate brothers laid down arms and surrendered.[13]

❦ ❦ ❦

Ewell Chamberlain died of wounds suffered in the Battle of the Wilderness 1864. *Lithograph by Kurz and Allison.*

Healing the country's cavernous wounds after the Civil War presented a vast challenge. Life had been shattered or devastatingly altered for countless families. Yet, in the gloomy midst of hatred, political distrust, and cynicism, Herb Bassett of the Union Army and Elizabeth Chamberlain of a Confederate family found each other.

When Elizabeth and Herb spoke their wedding vows on September 21, 1871, Elizabeth, beautiful with silken blonde hair, was just fourteen years old; exactly the age her mother had been on the day she married. During that same time, Elizabeth had surely been heartbroken when her grandfather, George Crawford Miller, died. In Herb, she found comfort and stability. Thirty-seven at the time and a prestigious Clerk of Court, Herb was kind, dignified, and a learned gentleman.

Elizabeth was a charismatic daredevil and an irresistible chatterbox. Although the Civil War decimated Arkansas, Elizabeth was still raised with a southern graciousness. While her family's prosperity and much innocence was lost into the deep well of the past, her grandfather Miller did the best he could for the family. While he may or may not have truly recognized the heinous truth of owning slaves, he swore a loyalty oath stating that he would henceforth obey the United States Constitution and abide by new federal laws that ended slavery. Because of that oath, he was able to hold on to all of his land. Likely he created a sharecropping or tenant relationship with his or other freed slaves, as many landowners did.[14]

Forty percent of livestock in the south was annihilated by the war, but Elizabeth was fortunate that her grandfather provided her fine horses from the time she was a little girl. Elizabeth loved being on the back of a horse, riding sidesaddle across the countryside on thoroughbreds that gleamed in the southern sun.

Because of Elizabeth, Herb suddenly discovered that his life sang with possibilities. The couple gave each other love and loyalty and on January 17, 1874, baby Josephine "Josie" arrived. Then on October 30, 1875, little Samuel Clark "Sam," named after Herb's father and brother, was born.

All the while, the Arkansas climate was doing harm to Herb's worsening asthmatic condition and, in spite of the benefits he found in the hot springs, he suffered in the damp cold of winter and summertime's sultry heat. Herb and Elizabeth decided to make a change, not only for Herb's health but because Herb had suddenly lost his job and prospects weren't at all good. Arkansas continued a bitter struggle with the aftermath of the war. After reading the encouraging letters from Herb's younger brother, Samuel Clark Bassett, they began to plan their departure from Arkansas, even though Elizabeth was expecting her third child.

Herb's brother, Sam, had several years previously found a special place in the mountain west; a sheltered valley originally called Brown's Hole where the air was semi-arid and the winters typically mild. He probably discussed with Herb and Elizabeth the Homestead Act, which gave them an opportunity to acquire 160 acres of land in that valley, now known as Brown's Park, and to build a future for themselves and their children.

Elizabeth's sister, Hannah, was now settled into a life of her own in Hot Springs, making it easier for Elizabeth to leave her behind, although they kept in touch through letters. Hannah was eventually blessed with sixteen children and a long life of eighty years. She named her second child and first-born daughter Mary Eliza after Elizabeth.[15]

In March the Bassetts left behind their lives in Arkansas. Elizabeth was seven months pregnant. One can only imagine her thoughts, enthusiasm, and uncertainties as she, Herb, and their children, Josie and Sam, climbed aboard a train bound northwest. They were all about to enter into a new existence that would ultimately secure their place on the pages of books.

A changing scene of vegetation, mountains, and plains drifted past the windows as hours and days scattered along the tracks behind them. The train rumbled and sighed to a final stop for the Bassetts, when it reached Green River City, Wyoming Territory. Buildings had been sprinkled across the young railroad town set in the midst of an open shrub and high desert landscape framed by high hills and rock formations. The Green River flowed through the middle of it all.

Herb's brother Samuel waited with his team and wagon. Samuel was accompanied by his Brown's Park neighbor, Dr. John D. Parsons. Dr. Parsons drove a second wagon pulled by two enormous oxen to assist in transporting the family. Dr. Parsons, a medical doctor, and his wife, Daphne, had lived in Brown's Park the last four years. Undoubtedly, knowing that a doctor would not only be present during this last part of the journey but that he would be one of their neighbors once they reached their new home, must have been an enormous comfort for Elizabeth. Her time was quickly approaching.

When the wagons were loaded with travelers, bedding, food, and important household essentials, the horses and oxen began the first steps of the one hundred-mile trek southeast. Although the season of spring at the end of March was responding to a strengthening in the sun, the day breezes could be very chilly and the nights frosty. Travelers kept coats and lap robes handy.[16]

Only a vague road led the travelers as the wagons climbed up and down slopes. The weighty wagons bumped over brush and rock; across gullies, creeks, ridges, and flats; and across basins and down draws. Samuel and Dr. Parsons knew the best route when they followed Little Bitter Creek down a long valley and then over a flank of Mellor Mountain before descending into the Red Creek Badlands. It was not a journey of ease or haste.

Elizabeth learned early in life what it took to be brave. She must have smiled while observing her four-year-old daughter. Every morning after breakfast, Josie watched with big eyes from a safe distance while the men harnessed the oxen, then she hurried to jump up on the wagon and settle alongside Dr. Parsons. The little girl was frightened of the mammoth

Dr. John Parsons, a physician, served the residents of Brown's Park and was a steadfast friend of the Bassett family. *Author's Collection.*

oxen yet utterly infatuated with them and insisted on riding every mile in the wagon they pulled. The gentle, lumbering beasts etched the trip forevermore in Josie's young memories.[17]

Finally, after several days of travel, the wagons followed a military road established fifteen years earlier. Then they came to the top of Red Creek Canyon and started down what was an entryway to Brown's Park. With the exception of the east end of Brown's Park, access into the valley passed through one of a series of beautiful canyons. Shimmering creeks adorned each one, sparkling in tune with their wildness as they made their journey downward, to the heart of the valley which held the supple flow of the Green River.

Red Creek Canyon was a roughhewn entry. The wagons had to cross the rocky creek numerous times as it snaked its way back and forth before them. At last as the air grew soft and noticeably warmer, the long-awaited valley began to reveal itself and soon the wagons passed through the mouth of the canyon and into Brown's Park.

As the travelers moved onward, the river flowed and the mountains rose above them in a creation of palpable intimacy steeped in ancient history. The stirring aromas of spiced willow and sage, grass blades greening up from winter's beige, and cedar and pine surging with the nectar of spring formed an intoxicating fragrance. The valley spoke to Elizabeth, telling her that her dreams for Josie, little Sam, and her unborn child belonged here. Elizabeth said aloud that the valley should never be called a "hole" and that "park fit it perfectly."[18]

One hopes Elizabeth was prepared for a bachelor's rustic log house that was, for at least the foreseeable future, her family's home. After Josie gave it the once over she looked up at her mother and said, "This is a funny little cabin, isn't it?" It had two rooms with a dirt floor, dirt roof, and no windows. But it did have a good fireplace for warmth and cooking. The cabin sat on a natural meadow beneath some tall cottonwoods and next to a pretty creek. There was a stunning view of high hills, ledge-streaked mountain peaks, and of the grassy meadow as it sloped to the river that was fringed with willows and cottonwood trees. The closest neighbors were Utes, unknown to the Bassetts but very old friends with the valley, living in an encampment of tepees scattered about the meadow and along the creek all the way to the river.[19]

If Elizabeth was afraid, had any regrets, or felt overwhelmed in this new and unfamiliar environment, she never showed any of it to her children. Instead she went to work turning a bachelor's cabin into a family home. It is likely, though, that when she gave birth just a few weeks later she was still fatigued, not only from the difficult trip from Arkansas but also the physical demands of taking the lead in settling her family into a life of meager circumstances. Now in a weakened condition from bringing Ann into the world, she must have been distressed and frightened to discover that she had no milk to give.

A Brown's Park character named Buffalo Jack soon arrived at the cabin door, however. He knew precisely the solution to Elizabeth and Herb's anxiety. The answer was right next door, in a long-treasured shelter made of tall and slender poles of sweet-smelling lodgepole pine, covered with animal hides tanned white and creamy soft.

NOTES TO CHAPTER ONE

1. J.S. Hoy letter to Esther Johnson, Catherine Sevenau, and Gordon Clemens. "Lore, Libel, & Lies: A Family History," 106, The Museum of NW Colorado–Craig.

2. Ann (Bassett) Willis letter to Duward and Esther Campbell, 10 Dec 1952. The Museum of the West through the Museum of NW Colorado–Craig.

3. According to notes written by Crawford MacKnight, Ann's given name is Anna Marie Bassett as recorded in Herb Bassett's bible. The Museum of NW Colorado–Craig.

4. Richard Nelson, *Lincoln's Loyalists: Union Soldiers from the Confederacy* (Northeastern University Press, 1992).

5. "Army Bands," www.goarmy.com/band/about-army-bands/history.html. Accessed 12 Jan 2015.

6. Adjutant General of the State of Illinois (1900), *Report of the Adjutant General of the State of Illinois*, Vol VI, containing reports for the years 1861-1866. (Springfield, Ill: Journal Company, Printers and Binders).

7. "10 Surprising Civil War Facts," www.history.com/news/10-surprising-civil-war-facts. Accessed 15 Jun 2017.

8. "Rockport, Second Oldest Post Office In Arkansas," in *The Heritage,* (Hot Springs County Historical Society, Jul 1974). The Rockport post office was located near the Quachita River.

9. "Marriage Age," True West Historical Society, https://truewest.ning.com/forum/topics/marriage-age. Accessed 15 Jul 2017.

10. The group of volunteers named the Hot Spring Hornets was organized in Newport, Arkansas, by Daniel Newman, sheriff of Hot Spring County.

11. "Ewell Chamberlain," *Ancestry.com*, https://www.ancestry.com. Accessed 28 Jun 2017.

12. James B. Parker, "Wm Pulaski Chamberlain Family Facts Part 1," *Ancestry.com,* http://www.ancestry.com. Accessed 12 Feb 2014.

13. "Battle of the Wilderness," www.history.com/topics/american-civil-war/battle-of-the-wilderness. Accessed 2 May 2015; "The Battle," http://totallyhistory.com/battle-of-the-wilderness/. Accessed 5 Jun 2015.

14. "Reconstruction Plans Under Lincoln," www.education.com/study-help/article/us-history-reconstruction-civil-war-lincoln-johnson. Accessed 15 Sep 2014.

15. David Rennow Rutherford, *Ancestry.com.* Accessed 28 Jun 2017.

16. Josie Bassett Morris interview with Murl Messersmith, 18 Jul 1960; Morris Interview with Untermann, Mortensen, and Cooley, 25 Sep 1959. The Museum of NW Colorado–Craig.

17. Morris interview with Messersmith.

18. Ann Willis, "Queen Ann of Brown's Park," in *The Colorado Magazine*, Apr 1952, p. 85.

19. Morris interview with Messersmith.

CHAPTER TWO

SINCE TIMES PRIMEVAL

Ann Bassett, a baby born with wisps of red-tinged hair in the spring of 1878 in a barely settled country, provided an instant source of curiosity to the mountaineers, trappers, prospectors, and cowboys. Many visitors came to the Bassett cabin to catch a glimpse of her. One of the first to see baby Ann was a young man in his mid-twenties named John "Jack" Rife. As soon as he heard of the dilemma the Bassetts were in, Jack went about making sure this little girl got fed.

Jack Rife was born in Illinois in 1855 and arrived in Brown's Park as a teenager. While spending time among the Utes, he made a study of their language and learned it well. He was a jovial sort and a bit eccentric. He liked spending time in the mountains, had a fondness for animals, and found work as a ranch hand. His friends had begun calling him "Buffalo Jack" because he had two pet buffalo that he named Samson and Delilah.

After he consulted with Dr. Parsons and Herb and Elizabeth, Jack left the cabin to confer with the neighbors. Before long, the big man returned for tiny Ann. During those same moments, a young Ute mother named See-a-baka put her own little boy, Sunrise, down to nap. Minutes later, See-a-baka gently saw to the needs of a white child brought to her through the storm from the nearby cabin and into the cedar-toasted warmth of her tepee. Both Chief Marcisco and the family unit's poo-wagudt (or shaman) had agreed for See-a-baka to become Ann's wet nurse and allow the baby girl to be foster sister to Sunrise.

Jack had assured the survival of Herb and Elizabeth's babe. To Herb and Elizabeth's relief and delight, Anna quickly began to flourish. However, Uncle Samuel explained that it wouldn't be long before See-a-baka and her band would be leaving their winter campsites along the creek and river bottoms to spend the summer on the mountain at the head of Willow Creek. As Herb did his best to work the ground in his brother's garden plot, Samuel Clark Bassett packed up provisions and tools and made his way up the mountain to construct a double cabin. Elizabeth and the children would accompany See-a-baka to the mountains for the summer.

Most of the Ute people then lived on reservations. Many, with government leniency common, returned to their traditional life at Brown's Park and its surrounding country to hunt and, no doubt, once again feel the solace of the way of life they knew so well. Memories, dreams, and countless scattered artifacts left behind by them and their long-gone ancestors likely haunted the thoughts of those trying to recapture the life that disappeared into the rumble of change.

Since times primeval, a conglomeration of geological events and the rising and falling of the ages cleaved and forged the valley. Thousands of years before the arrival of the Bassett family, different factions of native hunters and gatherers came and went as nature, tradition, beliefs, and survival dictated. By 1200 A.D. the most ancient cultures of this mountainous region had either vanished or been assimilated into tribes to the south as the Ute culture rose to dominance.[1] Speaking in a Shoshone dialect the Ute people called themselves different variations of the word Nuciu. It simply yet profoundly means "The People."

In the mid-1600s a group of Utes journeyed to the Rio Grande valley to visit the Spanish colonists and first saw the stunning image of the horse. Soon after trading the Spaniards buckskins for horses, the Utes began their enduring enchantment with the spirit-like creatures. The acquisition of the horse brought swift and powerful changes to the Utes. Once a nomadic and rather impoverished people, they found themselves almost instantly lifted into an expansive and exciting domain filled with possibilities. Their prospects grew in tandem with their skills in horsemanship.[2] By the time the Bassetts made their acquaintance with them, the Utes had long lived a life of political autonomy and military might.

The territorial bands which populated the valley of Brown's Park and its mountains used the abundant natural resources with efficiency. The valley usually watched over these Northern Ute people with tenderness, offering them a yearly supply of pine nuts and a variety of wild game for food and fine furs and skins. The rich valley contributed plentiful fish, berries, seeds, blossoms, roots, tubers, and bark. It proffered a winter sanctuary protected by mountains along with the air currents that kept the weather a good bit milder there than in the surrounding country. During the evenings of winter, for longer than anyone could remember, much time was spent around the flames and ember-filled glow of fires listening to the elders narrate accounts of the people's creation and history. Winter allowed time for large gatherings, festivities, socializing, and contracting marriages. Dance and song were central in Ute religious and social structure.

In late spring the Utes split up and went separate directions to designated territories that sustained the individual family units throughout the warm months without overstressing nature's resources.[3] Without fail, though, as winter stepped in front of the withering amber of autumn, the people came together within the valley again. All the while, through countless winters, they must surely have believed that their drumbeats and songs at winter's end would carry on and be eternally drifting into the valley's reddening gold of sunset swirls. However, destiny for the Utes began to twist. All was fated to change no matter what the Utes did to try to hold back the current that trickled and then rushed like a river through a canyon. The mountain men, fur trappers, and settlers were finding their way to the shining mountains; from the first tracks of these curious strangers, the Utes were being pushed toward cataclysmic change.

In 1830 with the passage of the Indian Removal Act, the president of the United States gained the authority to designate specific lands for Native Americans. The purpose of the Act was to relocate all Indian people living east of the Mississippi to territory west of the Mississippi. The westward movement of settlers, however, caused designated Indian lands to steadily shrink, right along with the well-being of the Native Americans.[4]

In 1861 President Abraham Lincoln signed an Executive Order that continued the policy of separating the Indian people from the rest of the population by creating the Uintah Indian Reservation southwest of Brown's Park in the Uinta (Duchesne) Valley.[5] After the passage of the Homestead Act of 1862, thousands of settlers surged into the mountainous West, many desiring lands already promised to the Indian people. Congress dissolved the "broken" treaty system in 1871, did away with the designation of sovereign nations, and declared the Indian people wards of the government. So far, though, even as the Bassett family arrived, the Utes of Brown's Park were free to retain segments of their old life.[6]

❧ ❧ ❧

While Ann Bassett was the first white baby born in Brown's Park, it was fifty-three years earlier when the first recorded white men visited there and began adding new and fetching charms to the necklace of the valley's memoir. Floating the Green River in two bull boats, William Henry Ashley and six members of his Missouri-based fur company, explored new waterways that might furnish a direct route to Saint Louis to transport furs. Also, they hoped to discover fresh trapping opportunities.

On May 5, 1825, the Ashley party looked upon the nameless valley that would soon become known as Brown's Hole. They made camp about six miles into the valley on a grassy river bottom interspersed with clusters of willows. Ashley wrote about his exploration of the valley and described signs left there by its indigenous inhabitants:

> We remained at our encampment of this day until the morning of the 7th, when we descended ten miles lower down and encamped where several thousand Indians had encamped during the last winter. Their camp had been judiciously selected for defense, and remains of their work around it accorded with the judgment exercised in the selection—many of their lodges remained as perfect as when occupied. They were made of poles two or three inches in diameter set up in a circular form, and covered with cedar bark.[7]

Time and legend shrouds exactly who lent his name to Ann Bassett's valley. One possibility is French-Canadian fur trapper Baptiste Brown who arrived in the valley two years after Ashley's voyage. Another is the trapper's apprentice, "Bibleback" Brown. He was said to have recommended the valley as a good place to "hole up" during the winter.[8] But other early-day mountaineers expounded that the valley was named after a man who once had a cabin in Brown's Hole and was murdered there. Still another explorer, Rufus B. Sage, wrote:

> This locality has received the soubriquet of Brown's-hole from the following circumstance: Some six or seven years since, a trapper, by the name of Brown, came to it in the fall season for the purpose of hunting in its vicinity. During his stay a fall snow closed the passes so effectually, he was forced to remain till the succeeding spring before he could escape from his lonely prison.
>
> It was formerly a favorite resort for the Snake Indians, on account of its exhaustless stores of game and wild fruits, as well as its security from the approach of enemies.[9]

Around 1826 Brown's Hole first watched the mountain men and fur trappers come through its canyons and passes, crossing its river and creeks. Some of the newcomers rode horses and mules, others stepped from dugout canoes, which had been made from hollowed-out trunks of cottonwood trees, while still others simply followed the trails on foot. Each man had his individual interests and desires and together made Brown's Hole a significant fur trading center and a renowned rendezvous site as well as a favored wintering place. Some of these trailblazers kept journals and wrote letters and books as they created word portraits of their time in the valley.

In 1836 William Craig, Philip Thompson, and Previtt Sinclair built a fort in the valley, named Fort Davy Crockett in honor of frontiersman David "Davy" Crockett who was killed that same year at the Alamo. The fort in Brown's Hole was not a military fortress but rather a headquarters for the fur trade of the area.[10] Christopher "Kit" Carson, Uncle Jack Robinson, Joseph "Joe" LaFayette Meek, and Robert "Doc" Newell all first arrived in the valley in 1829. Kit Carson was later employed as a hunter for Fort Davy Crockett. During the winter months of 1838, he spent his days keeping twenty men at the fort supplied with meat.[11]

The following August in 1839, a tired and hungry Thomas Jefferson Farnham made it to the fort. He was disappointed that most of his men deserted him along the way. Brown's Hole and Fort Davy Crockett were a most welcome sight to Farnham and he left his impression of the place in his notes:

> The dark mountains rose around it sublimely, and the green fields swept away into the deep precipitous gorges more beautifully than I can describe.
>
> There is in this valley a fruit called bulberry…of these berries I obtained a small quantity, had a dog butchered, took a pound or two of dried buffalo meat which Mr. St. Clair [Sinclair] kindly gave and on the morning left the hospitality of Fort David Crockett.[12]

One of the last rendezvous Brown's Hole saw was in November 1842. William T. Hamilton reported it as a success despite the dwindling demand for beaver pelts. He wrote:

> Besides the trappers, there were at the rendezvous many Indians— Shoshones, Utes, and a few lodges of Navajos—who came to exchange their pelts for whatever they stood in need of. Taken all in all, it was just such a crowd as would delight the student were he studying the characteristics of the mountaineer and the Indian. The days were given to horse racing, foot racing, shooting matches; and in the evening were heard the

music of voice and drum and the sound of dancing. There was also an abundance of reading matter for those inclined in that direction.[13]

That same year, 1842, apparently adventurer/explorer Rufus B. Sage of Independence, Missouri, was captivated in the identical way that Elizabeth and Ann Bassett would come to be enamored. They each, in their own time, came to drink deeply from the valley's mesmeric depth. They all listened with their hearts as the tranquil valley spoke to them in poetic phrases. Sage wrote:

> Few localities in the mountains are equal to this, in point of beautiful and romantic scenery. Every thing embraced in its confines tends to inspire the beholder with comingled feelings of awe and admiration.
>
> Its long, narrow gate-way, walled in by huge impending rocks, for hundreds of feet in altitude,—the lofty peaks that surround it, clothed in eternal snow—the bold stream traversing it, whose heaving bosom pours sweet music into the ears of listening solitude,—the verdant lawn, spreading far and wide, garnished with blushing wild-flowers and arrayed in the habiliments of perennial spring,—all, all combine to invest it with an enchantment as soul-expanding in its sublimity as it is fascinating in its loveliness.
>
> Spring wedded to summer seems to have chosen this sequestered spot for her fixed habitation, where, when dying autumn woos the sere frost and snow of winter, she may withdraw to her flower-garnished retreat and smile and bloom forever.[14]

Brown's Hole's time with the mountain men was as brief as it was intense. Their voices along with their fort had all crumbled to silence by the time young Ann Bassett came dashing over the skyline while chasing cattle across the rubble of their era. Her uncle, Samuel Clark Bassett, arrived in Brown's Hole just ten years after the last major rendezvous. He was an explorer of trails and regions and witnessed the same pristine valley as the trappers. Words Ann would discover decades later in her uncle's journal weave a depiction of not only Brown's Hole and its inhabitants but of Uncle Samuel's character as well:

> Brown's Hole. November, the month of Thanksgiving, 1852. Louie and I down in. Packs off. Mules in lush meadows. Spanish Joe's trail for travel could not be likened to an "up state" high lane, suitable for coach and four.
>
> Mountains to the right of us, not in formation but highly mineralized. To the south a range of uncontested beauty of contour. Its great stone mouth drinking a river.

> Called on our neighbors, lest we jeopardize our social standing.
> "Chief Catump" and his tribe of Utes. "Male and Female created He
> them" and Solomon in all his glory was not arrayed so fine. Heads,
> bones, quills and feathers of artistic design. Buckskin tanned in exquisite
> coloring of amazing hues, resembling velvet of finest texture. Bows
> and arrows. "Let there be no strife between thee and me."
>
> Samuel Clark Bassett [15]

Although Ann came to believe that it was her mother who so tenderly softened the name of their valley from Brown's Hole to Brown's Park, the credit does not lie with Elizabeth. Nine years before Elizabeth gazed upon the beauty of the valley, Major John Wesley Powell on an expedition with a nine member crew wrote of arriving in Brown's Park on the Green River in June 1869. After navigating the river through the valley, Powell stood at the eastern edge of Brown's Park, facing the opening of a towering canyon where the flowing riffles of the Green River beckoned through. It was the very canyon Uncle Samuel Bassett described as "a great stone mouth drinking a river."

In the bright warmth of the day, the doorway out of Brown's Park offered a promise of adventure hidden within for Powell and his men. Powell wrote:

> June 7, 1869—When I came down at noon, the sun shone in splendor on its vermillion walls shaded into green and gray when the rocks are lichened over. The river fills the channel from wall to wall. The canyon opened like a beautiful portal to a region of glory. . . .[16]

Andrew Hall, one of the crew, quoted some of the last lines of "The Cataract of Lodore" by the famous poet, Robert Southey. The last five lines read:

> And dashing and flashing and splashing and lashing,
> And so never ending, but always descending,
> Sounds and motion for ever and ever are blending,
> All at once and all o'er, with a mighty uproar,
> And this way the water comes down at Lodore.

Just as Andrew Hall desired, the mouth of the canyon became known as the Gates of Lodore and the canyon beyond was named Lodore Canyon. The Utes believed that the mouth of Lodore Canyon was the entrance to their Happy Hunting Grounds and that the Indian gods controlled the gate and passage into Paradise.[17] The stunning view of the Gates of Lodore was one of the soothing constants of Ann Bassett's lifetime.

❧ ❧ ❧

During the summer of 1878 Ann thrived as the foster child of See-a-baka. Elizabeth stayed busy caring for her children in the mountain retreat shared with Utes. Food supplied by Herb and Uncle Samuel was meager but as the peas, carrots, and potatoes from the garden grew, the selection of food became more adequate. Elizabeth grew evermore acquainted with her Ute neighbors. She and the children learned a few Ute words including "maiku" which is a friendly greeting and "tog'oiak," meaning thank you. Elizabeth chattered to the Utes and the children so much that the Ute families began calling her "Magpie."

Sometime during the fall, Judge Asbury Bateman Conaway, an attorney visiting the lower end of the valley, showed up walking behind a slow-moving gift brought to the family, especially for the baby Ann. Sauntering along in front of Judge Conaway strode a milk cow, gently nodding her head with every step. At last, Ann was weaned from her wet nurse.

While Herb did what work he could as he regained his health damaged by his war years, Elizabeth learned important skills from both Uncle Samuel and her Ute neighbors, including how to stitch rawhide into clothing, make deer and antelope jerky, and harvest and prepare dandelions, watercress, and a variety of edible berries and roots. Josie and Sam sometimes took Ann along when they played with the Ute children. The youngsters had already discovered that it made little difference if they didn't speak each other's language because they made gestures and signs and drew pictures in the dirt to converse. Giggles were the same in both languages.[18]

In the coming years, Ann held a deep affection for the Indian people and came to believe that hers was an uncommon connection with them.[19] However, as her family spent the winter of 1878-1879 in Brown's Park alongside their Ute neighbors, they could not know that southeast of Brown's Park on the White River Reservation, events were leading to a fierce unrest among the Utes. That turbulence fumed and gathered into a violent episode that exiled the Bassett family.

NOTES TO CHAPTER TWO

1. "What is a Ute?" University of Utah, www.utefans.net/home/ancientute/ utetribe.html. Accessed 29 Jul 2016.

2. "What is a Ute?" Accessed 29 Jul 2016.

3. "What is a Ute?" Accessed 29 Jul 2016.

4. "Indian Territory," in *The Columbia Electronic Encyclopedia*. Columbia University Press. www.infoplease.com/encyclopedia. Accessed 17 Jun 2016.

5. "What is a Ute?" Accessed 29 Jul 2016.

6. "Uinta vs. Uintah," *The Edge Magazine*. Neola, Utah. www.theedgemagazine. gldgspot.com/2010/uinta-vs-uintah.html. Accessed 25 Mar 2018. The federal government's effort to standardize a naming system resulted in the different spellings of Uinta and Uintah. When spelling natural geographical features, such as the Uinta Mountains, no "h" is used. The "h" is added to the end of the word when spelling something that has been created by man, such as the Uintah Indian Reservation. Variations to this system exist.

7. William Henry Ashley letter to General Atkinson, Dec 1825, 28- 29, C1939, Folder1. The State Historical Society of Missouri: St. Louis, MO.

8. Ann Willis, "Queen Ann of Brown's Park" in *The Colorado Magazine,* Apr 1952, p. 84.

9. Rufus B. Sage, *Rocky Mountain Life* (University of Nebraska, 1982), 255.

10. Thomas J. Farnham, *Travels in the Great Western Prairies: The Anahuac and Rocky Mountains, and in the Oregon Territory* (London: R. Bentley, 1843), 57.

11. Kit Carson, *Kit Carson's Autobiography*, ed. Milo Martin Quaife, reprint edition (University of Nebraska, 1966) 54.

12. Farnham, *Travels in the Great Western Prairies,* p. 57.

13. William T. Hamilton, *My Sixty Years on the Plains: Trapping, Trading, and Indian Fighting* (Forest and Stream Publishing, New York, 1905) 84-85.

14. Sage, *Rocky Mountain Life*, 256.

15. Willis,"Queen Ann of Brown's Park," 84.

16. Wallace Stegner, *Beyond the Hundredth Meridian: John Wesley Powell and the Second Opening of the West*, (Penguin Books, NY., 1953) p. 62.

17. J.S. Hoy as told to him by Pah-in-rats, Hoy Manuscript, (unpublished).

18. Josie Bassett Morris, interview with Untermann, Mortensen, and Cooley, Sep 1959, The Museum of NW Colorado–Craig.

19. Willis, "Queen Ann of Brown's Park," 82.

CHAPTER THREE

A FRIGHTFUL FATE

Ute Uprising! Attack! During the days following September 29, 1879, these and similar exclamations shivered across the country from the Ute Reservation at White River in Colorado, traveling in all directions, including northward into nearby Brown's Park. While Ann Bassett was too young to understand the cause of it, the toddler must have sensed the anxiety that churned in the Bassett cabin. Her father was frightened. "We must leave here immediately!" Herb repeated. Ann's mother, Elizabeth, however, insisted she was not afraid. Elizabeth made some strong arguments to Herb while reasoning that his own brother, Samuel, agreed with her that most of the Utes in the area were kindly. Certainly, some of them were their friends. Samuel had no intention of leaving, although he had begun siding with Herb about the family's safety.[1]

Elizabeth didn't want to leave behind their herd of twenty newly purchased and branded heifers. The heifers could mean their future. The cattle had been a large expense and branding them had been no small task, even with Samuel's help. Herb did not relish this type of work; however, Elizabeth loved it and took to the chore naturally. She likely still wore some bruises from the endeavor and could remember the branding's distinct smells and sounds.

Elizabeth was fascinated by the process as Samuel roped one of the heifers and showed Elizabeth and Herb how to restrain and position it for branding. Elizabeth made sure the intense fire was fed as it devoured its fuel of spicy-sweet sagebrush and cedar. It hissed and crackled its melody of heat as flames thrashed around the curved ends of long-handled branding irons. When those ends began a flushing glow of orange and red, Samuel taught Herb and Elizabeth how to quickly sear the brand they had chosen as their own, across the ribs of the bellowing cattle. Now all twenty wore a large and impressive U with a P connected.

Never mind that she and Herb didn't yet know much about raising cattle. The pretty heifers signaled the beginning of their entry into an industry that flourished in many places around them. The thought of leaving behind not only the herd but Brown's Park, with no idea of when or even if they would ever return, made Elizabeth miserable.

Nonetheless, Herb made it clear this was not the time for further discussion, bolstered by the fact that this was happening on the heels of other uprisings such as the Great Sioux War of 1876–1877, which included Custer's Battle of the Little Big Horn. The uprising of a band of Northern Cheyenne exactly a year ago had left seventeen Kansas settlers dead. Herb was not alone in his distress. The White River Agency, by the most direct path, was only about sixty-five miles from Brown's Park. Dr. Parsons and his family were already packing up to leave Brown's Park for Ashley Valley, Utah. Most of the whites in Brown's Park had left or were considering leaving. Alarm was sweeping across the territory along with echoing accounts that soldiers from Fort Steele were pinned down by Ute warriors at Milk Creek. Reinforcements were on the way but the battle was far from over. A great dread hung in the air about what may have happened to Nathan Meeker and the others at the White River Agency because that agency sat just twenty-five miles south of the bloody battleground.

At last, Elizabeth could no longer deny the stark reports and descriptions of brutality when confirmation arrived that a horrible massacre at the White River Agency had indeed been carried out the previous week. Indian Agent Nathan Meeker and all the agency employees had been killed. Three white women and two little children had been whisked away as captives of the Utes. Families near and far were fleeing their homes for the security of populated areas. Elizabeth knew Herb was right, that they should hurry to the safety of Green River City, Wyoming. Elizabeth must have looked at her small children and felt heartsick for the women and children of the agency now being held against their will somewhere in the wilderness. One of those captives was Elizabeth's own age of twenty-two and that young woman shared the name of Elizabeth's eldest daughter, Josephine.

The next day, accompanied by nearby neighbors, Charles B. and Molly (Mary) Sears, the family of seventeen-month-old Ann Bassett left their little home behind. The travelers made their way out of Red Creek Canyon following in the tracks of Edward H. and Jennie Rife toward

Tittsworth Gap about forty miles away. Before long they met up with James "Jimmie" Goodson and his Native American wife, Margaret. Surprisingly, the couple was headed toward Brown's Park. Jimmie, an experienced frontiersman, was adamant that he was not in the least fearful. The Bassetts wished the couple well and soon the distance took Jimmie and Margaret out of sight.

When the Bassetts reached Tittsworth Gap, the ranch home of William G. "Billy" Tittsworth, they and Charles and Molly Sears rendezvoused with several others who had fled the Brown's Park area. Jimmie and Margaret Goodson soon arrived. Jimmie had lost his courage and defiant attitude when, upon arriving in Brown's Park, he and Margaret saw a half-dozen Indians creeping through a thicket of willows along the river.[2] Jimmie immediately turned the wagon around and ignored a Ute calling out a friendly greeting: "Uike! Uike!" Instead, he urged his team into a trot and headed for Red Creek Canyon and Tittsworth Gap.

After a few days of rest Herb, Elizabeth, and the children said their goodbyes to their neighbors. The others had all decided to remain at Tittsworth Gap after Billy offered to share the $800 worth of fresh provisions he'd recently laid in for the winter.[3] The group, including Billy, eventually traveled to Ashley Valley to wait out the uprising. The Bassetts drove northwest, alone, toward an uncertain future.

At that very moment in time, riding southward, captive Josephine Meeker was astride an Indian pony heading into the depths of her own indefinite fate. Her father lay murdered and her world broken, beyond any thoughts of grace.

The uprising of a small group of Utes at the White River Agency grew into an act of vengeance which came to be known as the Meeker Massacre. Intricate and passionate in its causes, it was nonetheless blunt in its inevitability.

❧ ❧ ❧

The roots of the Meeker Massacre reached all the way from that remote Indian Agency near the banks of the White River on the Western Slope of Colorado, across the United States to Washington, D.C. It found its reasons in many forms, not the least of which was a Federal Government with the enduring tactic of making promises to and agreements with Native Americans in order to gain not only their submission and cooperation but also control of their homelands. Washington had a pitiful record of holding to the promises made. Some very good and thoughtful officials worked with Indian affairs, but different agencies often had contradictory agendas. Squabbles and problematical communications erupted between Washington, its army, and the states' governors as each contended with ongoing challenges of dealing with Indian conflict amid the advancing mining frontier and unstoppable rush of white expansion into the West. The government had, in general, a policy it wished to be carried out: The Indians should be kept upon the reservations, civilized, taught the art of peace, and made to behave themselves in their relationship with the whites.[4] However, most prominently entangled within the reasons for the Meeker Massacre was a mandate given to a totally inexperienced and overeager agent—to "civilize" a complex people of an ancient society.

Just sixteen months earlier, during the very month of May that Ann Bassett was born, idealistic Nathan C. Meeker's duties as Indian Agent to the White River Agency had begun. Unfortunately the Indian Department veered from its established policy in selecting Indian agents and allowed political favor and old friendships to sway its decision to appoint Meeker.[5] The appointment proved to be a grim error with terrible and widespread repercussions. In the aftermath of those repercussions Clinton Fisk, a member of the Board of Indian Commissioners, testified that "The Indian Office decided to do it themselves and nominated Meeker, a most excellent gentleman, who I had known for a great many years, but [who was] about as unfit for the position as a man could possibly be to go into that country, take hold of the White River Utes and manage them; destitute of that particular tract of knowledge of the Indian character which is required by an agent; a man of too many years, unhappily constituted in his mental organization for any such place."[6] Nevertheless, in the beginning, the appointment of Nathan Meeker came with positive expectations for both the Utes and the Meeker family.

Naturally gracious and spirited in manner, Josephine, "Josie", the youngest daughter of Nathan and Arvilla Meeker, had her father's blue eyes and tall and slender form. Dark blonde hair fell to her waist.[7] Josie Meeker recognized that her father was a failed business owner but also that he was a first-rate war correspondent during the Civil War and then a diligent agricultural editor for the famed Horace Greeley at the *New York Tribune*. Her father had connections to New York City and Washington and was known as a man of principle but also unyielding idealism.

In 1870, when Josie Meeker was thirteen, with Horace Greeley's blessings and financial support her father moved the family from New York City to Colorado and founded Union Colony, soon to be named Greeley, after its benefactor. Union Colony was a social experiment in search of creating a utopian society. After Horace Greeley's death, Josie's father sought out the Indian agent job west of Greeley at White River in order to earn enough money to pay back a debt he owed Greeley's estate. Josie knew her parents worried that the colony might end in failure. Attaining the agency appointment gave sixty-one-year-old Nathan Meeker new vigor and a reason to sharpen his staunch ideals.

Josie had lived in Greeley for nine years and at twenty-one was likely excited to join her parents at the agency to do the cooking and be the schoolteacher for the Ute children. Although Josie had no medical training, she would be employed under the title of teacher/physician and receive the housing benefits and salary that accompanied that position. In reality, her mother, Arvilla, dispensed medicine and tended to wounds and illness using the knowledge she gained from life experience combined with the guidance of a large medical book.[8]

Josie Meeker's much loved and admired older brother, Ralph, was living abroad in London working as a correspondent for the *New York Herald*. Her two older sisters, Rozene and Mary, stayed behind in Greeley. Josie arrived at the agency on July 17, 1878, a couple of months after her father took over there. In addition to her mother, whom the Utes called "Piatz" (Ute's mama), the only other white woman there was a young mother who was just a year older than Josie Meeker named Flora Ellen Price, the wife of a blacksmith and master farmer named Shadrach Price. Shadrach and Flora Ellen and their two-year-old daughter, May, and baby son, Johnny, made the journey along with several other Greeley men hired as employees of the agency. And so, the fateful tenure began for them all at the remote White River Agency.

Despite Ute protests, the agency was moved about twelve miles downriver to Powell Valley (Park), named for explorer John Wesley Powell, where Ute horses had long grazed and many of the Utes spent their winters. Josie's father told the last of the Ute holdouts that if they didn't move to the new agency, he had the assistance of soldiers to oblige them to move.[9]

The newly built agency provided Josie Meeker with a nice area for cooking and serving meals. A conveniently located milk house sat just off the kitchen. She had her own bedroom in the south wing of the main house while the Price family had the bedroom in the north wing. Nearby were the quarters for her father and mother where, being an avid reader and inexhaustible writer, Josie's father spent much of his time in his office.

As a matter of practicality and comfort, Josie changed her appearance. She cut her long hair into a bobbed style and replaced her shoes with moccasins.[10] She had inherited much of the vigor and enthusiasm of her father and formed relationships with some of the Utes so that they would allow the children to attend school.[11] She was not deterred when she was laughed at by the Utes for suggesting such a thing. She conversed with Jane, wife of Powvitz. Jane had once lived with a white family and spoke English. Jane and others warned Josie that she must stop asking parents to send their children to school, as it would make enemies. She was told that the Utes feared giving up their own ways and especially their horses. If they had to give up their horses, they exclaimed, the Utes might as well be civilized and be done with it.[12]

Josie Meeker learned that there were several groups of White River Utes who were part of the Numpartca band.[13] Each group had its own leader who held influence over the daily lives of his followers. The leaders included: Piah, Sowawick, Washington, Colorow, Johnson, Jack, and Douglas. Although the head of each group was commonly given the title of chief, only Chief Douglas (Quinkent) officially held that rank, while the others were sub-chiefs or captains. Chief Douglas was about thirty-five-years-old, muscular, about five feet nine inches tall and 160 pounds with deep-set piercing eyes.[14] Captain Jack (Nicaagat) was younger, and had, by far, the largest following, numbering over two hundred. Jack was intelligent, strong, and fearless. He had a reputation for robbing the camps of other tribes, taking women, and stealing horses to sell to the whites.[15]

Several Ute men offered Josie marriage proposals.[16] Her charm, along with her father's assistance and pressure, resulted in getting three Ute children to attend her lessons. One of those children, Frederick, was the son of Chief Douglas.

Josie made friends with Susan (Shawsheen)[17] who was thirty-three, friendly, and could speak English. Besides being the oldest wife of Johnson (Canalla), she was also a sister to the powerful and wise Chief Ouray, leader of the Uncompahgre Utes and considered by Washington D.C. to

Arvilla Meeker tended to wounds and illnesses at White River Agency. *The Museum of NW Colorado–Craig.*

be Chief of the Ute Nation. Ouray lived near the Los Piños Agency about two hundred miles south of the White River Agency.[18]

Although her father was rigid, Josie also saw him as a man of intelligence and integrity. Following government directives—ones that Josie's father took most seriously—along with his own intense socialistic idealism, Nathan Meeker daydreamed about transforming his Utes into prosperous farmers and stockmen. This and more would be accomplished by continuing to strip the Utes of almost everything their history had sculpted them to be.

Most of the White River Utes were often away from the reservation hunting, as they had always done; a fact that thoroughly irritated Agent

Susan (Shawsheen) was the sister of Chief Ouray and the oldest wife of Johnson. *Ronzio Collection, #ZZR710030460.tif, History Colorado.*

Meeker. He tried to induce the Utes to work at clearing land and building fences. Only a few of the younger ones who didn't yet own horses and therefore didn't have wealth, could be persuaded to grub brush and dig ditches and postholes.[19] The Ute men identified themselves as hunters, so farm work was demeaning. The older men sometimes ridiculed and threatened violence to those who did work. Josie's father didn't understand any of it, and handed out government rations along with more aggressive demands that they work and stay on the reservation.

Josie witnessed her father's early successes and good cheer fade as the atmosphere around the agency deteriorated. She probably didn't realize, though, that paramount to her father's failings in the job was his portentous misconception about Ute culture. In his desperate efforts to succeed, Meeker threatened the Utes that the U.S. Government and its army might put them in chains and take them off to Indian Territory or to the prison at Fort Steele if they didn't do as they were told.[20] Of course, these threats did nothing to help, but instead planted and nurtured fears, distrust, and resentment.

Agency employees cultivated and planted eighty acres of grassland into potatoes, corn, and wheat. When Agent Meeker decided fifty additional acres should be plowed, he upset several Utes when he told them they would have to move their belongings and horses from their chosen home sites. Sowawick, Powvitz, and others were told that the blankets, shoes, flour, and such things provided to the Indians by the government were equivalent to its purchasing the land.[21] He reiterated to Chief Douglas that Washington had all the say.[22] Powvitz's wife, Jane, who had once been friendly, was vehemently vocal in ongoing objections to Agent Meeker's directives.

Captain Jack traveled to Denver to ask Governor Pitkin to influence Washington to replace Meeker. The governor knew the agent could be peevish but never planned to intervene.[23] Governor Pitkin was more concerned with complaints coming in from settlers and miners, that some Utes were off the reservation and trying to run the whites out of the area by being threatening, setting fire to grass and timber, and killing antelope by the herd. [24]

Meeker lashed out at Captain Jack for criticizing him to the Governor, "Is it your business to go around finding out what I have written?"[25] Meeker further retorted, "Anyhow, your tongue does not amount to anything. You don't know how to write and I do; what you say amounts to nothing. The words you say don't go very far; my papers and what I say travels far and wide." Captain Jack replied, "I suppose you think you have beaten me now with those words that you have spoken."[26]

Nathan Meeker then made a monumental error when he expressed the ultimate injustice to Douglas, telling the chief that too many horses were eating up the grass and that the Utes needed to kill most of them and only keep a few.[27] Agent Meeker didn't see what lurked behind Chief Douglas's immobile expression.

Plowing was halted after threats were made to the plowman, Shadrach Price. On September 8, Meeker wrote to E.A. Hayt, Commissioner of Indian Affairs. The last line of the letter read: "This is a bad lot of Indians; they have had free rations so long, and have been flattered and petted so much, that they think themselves lords of all."[28]

Shadrach Price resumed plowing around Susan and Johnson's newly built house, but stopped when a bullet zinged over his head. Johnson confronted Meeker in his office. During an angry back and forth, Meeker told Johnson that he had always been a troublesome man and that it was likely he might come to the calaboose! Johnson replied that it would be better for another agent to come, who would be a good man and not talk such things![29] A tussle ensued and the chief grabbed Meeker by the shoulders and pushed him around the office before shoving him out the door and over a pole hitching rail. Agency employees hurried to Meeker's rescue as Johnson stormed off. Already somewhat debilitated and bruised by a recent accident when a wagon tipped over on him, the sixty-two-year-old man was badly shaken.

Propped in his chair with pillows, Meeker was disheartened when he received a visit from Colonel John W. Steele, owner of the Rawlins, Wyoming, to White River mail contract. Meeker said, "I came to this agency in the full belief that I could civilize these Utes; that I could teach them to work and become self-supporting. I thought that I could establish schools and interest both Indians and their children in learning. I have given my best efforts to this end, always treating them kindly, but firmly." Describing the assault he suffered from Johnson he was indignant that the Indians stood by and laughed. He said, "They are an unreliable and treacherous race." Colonel Steele spoke up and told Agent Meeker that he feared an uprising was imminent and that he should abandon the agency at once.[30]

That night the Utes held a boisterous war dance around Meeker's quarters. Fragile remnants of goodwill had now frozen into hatred. Behaviors and misunderstandings from the preceding sixteen months continued to drive events toward a deadly place of no return.

The next morning Nathan Meeker called for troops in telegrams he sent with Colonel Steele to be forwarded from Rawlins. This action was a fatal error. Josie's father should have gathered his family and employees together and left, as he briefly considered. The Utes had often been threatened with troops, and they held fear and anger that the arrival of soldiers meant shackles, prison, or nooses, so they prepared for such an event.[31]

By September 19, Meeker knew that troops would be coming. He apparently felt less blue about his situation and more defiant when he wrote to Governor Pitkin: "I think it is high time these Indians should be taught to behave themselves equally with white people, and I might as well try them on as anybody else. Things are quiet because we have stopped plowing and fencing."[32]

Josephine Meeker, little May Price, baby Johnny Price, and Flora Ellen Price shown after the Meeker incident. *AI3192, City of Greeley Museums, Permanent Collection.*

Although it had taken about two weeks to get organized, on September 22, Major Thomas T. Thornburgh from Fort Steele in Wyoming led a detachment of just over 150 troopers when he left Rawlins, Wyoming, for the White River in Colorado. Unbeknownst to him, he marched along the edge of his life and toward an event that would come to be known as the Battle of Milk Creek. On Monday, September 29, a week after Thornburgh and his troops left Rawlins and about twenty-five miles from the White River Agency, the soldiers crossed onto the White River Reservation. This intrusion was the final ignition in the flaming of old furies. Thornburgh and his men were soon ensnared and under attack by Ute leader Captain Jack and sixty or seventy warriors.

The agency had no knowledge of what had befallen the troops. Josie Meeker watched for the soldiers and hoped their arrival would assist her father and quiet things down. The previous night she and the others had listened to the unsettling chants and drums of another war dance. The sounds had permeated the night until daylight when wafts of Chief Douglas's blustery words could be heard. There were other signs that an uprising was in the making. Two days before on Saturday, Chief Douglas had removed his son from school. On Sunday the Ute women and children either left the agency or moved their lodges a distance away. Only Captain Jack's empty wickiup used for talks remained.[33]

The agency stayed calm throughout the morning until eleven o'clock when Flora Ellen Price and Meeker's wife, Arvilla, saw a Ute messenger ride his horse at a dead run up the wagon road from the east. He galloped past the agency and on to Douglas's camp. "Just see that Indian run," Flora Ellen said. "It must be he has news."[34] They couldn't know that the rider brought word to the chief that soldiers had crossed onto the reservation and Captain Jack and his warriors had attacked. Major Thornburgh and a number of white soldiers were dead. Several Ute warriors had also fallen.

Douglas came to council with Agent Meeker one last time. Afterward, Meeker told Arvilla and Josie that Douglas said he didn't want to talk about plowing and he didn't want the soldiers to come. Meeker said he answered with "Let them come if they want to; they will not harm a hair of your head; no fight." He told Douglas that when the soldiers came they all would sit down and have a good long talk over the matter and set it right.[35]

Just after the noon meal finished up and the agency men all went back to work, Chief Douglas, in the company of a couple of his men, stopped by the dining room to ask for food. Josie gave them some bread and butter and other victuals. It wasn't unusual to have the Utes in and out of the kitchen and dining area.

Looking at Douglas, Josie asked, "When are you bringing Freddy back to school?"

Douglas smiled and said, "This afternoon."

Josie laughed. "You'd better!"

"I will," he said. Then she and the chief laughed together as he turned and left.[36]

Moments later, her father stopped by asking Josie about the keys to lock up the employees' room where the guns were stored. As he left with the keys, Josie went back to clearing the table. About fifteen minutes later, Josie was washing dishes and her mother was wiping them dry as Flora Ellen did laundry just outside the door. A teenage Ute stopped by to ask for matches. After Josie handed them to him he made an odd-sounding giggle and said, "Me now going to smoke." With her suspicions pricked, Josie turned to her mother and said, "I'll warrant he will set something on fire."[37]

A bloodbath would soon be upon them. Although the Meeker Massacre was done by men to men, it would cause certain women, white and Native American, to arise from their ordinary lives and stand in the light of their individual valor.

At approximately 1:30 p.m., Flora Ellen looked up from her washboard just in time to see Douglas meet up with over twenty armed Utes. One handed Douglas a rifle, then they all walked together toward the agency. The young mother dropped the washing and hurried to get her little daughter. The Utes weren't more than ten feet away from her when they all raised their guns and began shooting at the agency employees. She saw one shoot Frank Dresser, who was working with Flora Ellen's husband in a wagon pitching dirt to Arthur Thompson on the roof of a new building. As she ran for the door she saw Thompson topple from the roof, but never saw what happened to her husband, Shadrach.[38]

Josie ran to the window and glimpsed several Utes firing and the employees running in all directions, trying to escape.[39] Flora Ellen flew into the house with May, grabbed up her sixteen-month-old boy, and ran into her bedroom. There she spotted Shadrach's rifle lying on their bed. Suddenly Frank Dresser, wounded in one leg, staggered into the house asking for a gun. Flora Ellen grabbed the firearm to pass to him and, just as she reached the door between her bedroom and dining room, half a dozen shots smashed through the windows. Frank quickly aimed out one of them and hit Johnson's brother in the shoulder. Ducking back, Frank told the women he had already been to the room where the government guns were stored but discovered they had all disappeared.

"It is not safe here," Josie said. "Let's go to the milk house."[40]

Hidden from view of the fighting, the group hurried to the small building, slipped inside, and locked the door. The milk house had only one small window which Frank quickly covered by stacking a crockery bread jar, some cans, and others items in front of it. Then, in horrid suspense, they all huddled together beneath a large shelf. For the next several hours they listened to intervals of gunshots. After long periods of stillness several guns would boom at once only to be followed by another lull.[41] A much feared hint of the smell of smoke was their first inkling that the agency would burn. Still, they remained, crouching in their hideout until they felt they would choke to death on the ever thickening smoke snaking its way into the milk house. It was just a bit before sundown when they were forced to make a move.

Josie's bedroom had been set on fire first and its roof crashed in as flames licked the smoldering air. Josie carried three-year-old May Price as she and the others ran into her father's quarters. It was painfully, beautifully peaceful there; completely undisturbed. A copy of *Pepys' Diary* lay open on a table.[42] Out a window they saw reality. Several Utes, mostly men but also a few women, were taking away all the annuity goods they could carry from the store rooms. Some of the men drank from pint bottles of whiskey. Where those came from, none of them knew. For a brief moment they considered secreting themselves under the bed, but they all agreed that everything would soon be burning.

Flora Ellen said, "Let's try and escape to the north, in the sagebrush; it will not do to stay here; they will be in here in a minute."

Frank said, "Let's go while they are so busy."[43]

Although they quickly slid through the fence and ran for their lives across a field of plowed earth, none could move with great speed. Josie carried May; her mother, at age sixty-four, was frail in health and lame from not having fully recovered from a broken femur two years previous; Flora Ellen had Johnny in her arms; and although Frank was quickly outpacing them, he had a bullet wound in his thigh.

The women made it only about a hundred yards when a dreaded terror sprang up from behind. Several Utes came in rapid pursuit and began firing as they ran. Bullets whizzed past and spat upon the earth all around them, kicking up cruel puffs of dirt. A ball hit Arvilla just above the knee of her crippled leg, leaving a three-inch flesh wound. She threw herself onto the ground, thinking she might somehow hide. However, a Ute was quickly upon her.

"I am heap sorry; I am heap much sorry," he said. He asked Arvilla if she would get up and go with him.

"Yes sir," she answered.

Then the Ute gently and most politely gave her his arm and escorted her toward Chief Douglas's headquarters.[44]

Persune (pronounced Pah-sone) called to Josie, "Come to me; no shoot you."

Josie stopped and turned. "Going to shoot?"

"No," the Ute answered.

Putting May down Josie said, "Better not."

"Come to me!" he repeated.[45]

She saw that her mother and Flora Ellen were already in hand but the last Josie saw of Frank Dresser was him running in the distance and disappearing into some four- to five-foot tall sagebrush, giving her the hope that he would escape. Persune took one of her arms and another Ute seized the other and ushered her in the direction of the river. The smell of whiskey was on their breath and the men continued to drink from their flat shaped pint bottles. When they came to a wide irrigation canal Josie balked saying that she couldn't cross it in her moccasins as the water and mud were deep. They answered her by pushing her through it. Little May followed behind and waded across. Both May and Josie came out of the water soaked to the skin and shaking in the chill.[46]

A few moments later, Chief Douglas tried to push Persune aside and take Josie away. Persune became aggressive in his determination to keep her and was prepared to fight. Angry words passed between them before Douglas turned and left. Persune then took Josie and May to the river where his saddled ponies stood. There he had Josie and May sit on a pile of blankets while he went to get more to pack on the backs of two government mules he'd secured. The Utes were on all sides of the captives, leaving no chance of escape.[47]

Flora Ellen had been captured by an Uncompahgre Ute; a small man in his late twenties. She didn't know him, but was immediately struck by the meanness of his expression. As he and others started marching her to the river, she was in tears as she told them she had read about how the

Indians treated captives and was afraid they would want to torture her.

"No kill white squaw; heap like them," he said.

"You are going to burn me!" she cried.

"No burn white squaw," he answered and guided her through the brush.[48]

As Arvilla Meeker and her captor walked near the burning agency, the Ute asked, "Any money?"

"Very little."

"Go in and get money."

Looking at the partially burning building Arvilla said, "You go in and get it!"

The Ute nudged her through the door. All the while she was in the building he kept saying, "Hurry up, hurry up; got to go a great ways tonight."[49]

The sun was down by the time Arvilla reached Douglas's tepee. The Ute handed the chief the money Arvilla had retrieved, including twenty-six dollars in greenbacks and about four dollars in silver. Referring to herself, Arvilla said to Douglas, "Piatz, no blanket." Douglas agreed to let Arvilla go back for her blanket and Spirit book. Douglas told another Ute to go with her and directed him to get the medicine chest. [50]

Arvilla Meeker was walking a few steps behind when she glimpsed the body of a man. She barely breathed as she made her way closer to it. There he was, her darling, shot in the forehead and entirely undressed except for his shirt. He lay posed in the flickering light of dusk and fire, perfectly straight with his arms at his sides and blood trickling from his mouth. Silence caressed them, husband and wife, amid the rampaged ruins of their agency. As she stooped to kiss his face, her Ute companion turned and looked at her. She instantly knew that would not be acceptable, so she stood up, lifted her chin, and continued onward.[51]

Still, only parts of the house were burning, allowing Arvilla and her chaperone to make their way inside. Arvilla hurriedly got her cherished book, *Pilgrim's Progress,* and handed the Ute the medical book, which he laid down and left. Finding the chest filled with medicine too heavy he also left it behind. Arvilla then handed the man some blankets, towels, and other items before grabbing her shawl and hat. And then, with resolve, delicate Arvilla Meeker, described as being the gentlest and most motherly of women with a kindly disposition, gentle manner, and heart large enough to embrace all humanity,[52] stepped through the doorway of the life she had known and left the remnants in the care of the flames.

When they rode into the darkness and away from the agency, Arvilla was mounted bareback behind Chief Douglas; her crippled and wounded leg hanging limp without the aid of a stirrup for support. As the horse broke into a trot, the chief asked Arvilla where the agent was, and then laughed with liquored breath.[53] In a separate group, following a different route, Flora Ellen Price rode a saddled horse alongside her Uncompahgre captor. The Uncompahgre had made a gift to her of head clerk William Post's watch.[54] She clutched her young son close and rode toward an indefinite dread.

Persune, in a show of bewildering gallantry, got down on his hands and knees so that Josie, the daughter of his slain agent, could mount her horse from his back. May was then tied on behind her. Josie had a saddle but her horse didn't wear a bridle. Instead he wore just a simple halter with a too-short strap for a rein that was hard for Josie to hold. Heading south among a party of about twenty men, Persune and his assistant rode beside Josie, always staying very close on either side of her horse as they drove the two Interior Department pack mules ahead, into the darkening wilderness. [55]

They all stayed on a steady trot traveling upriver for some distance before crossing at the White River Ford. At that point Persune filled his hat with water for Josie and May to drink. They hurried on, mile after mile until close to 9:30 that night when they halted for a half-hour break.[56] The Utes spread some blankets on the ground and then searched Josie and Arvilla, even looking in their shoes. They took away Arvilla's sewing needle book but gave back her pocket handkerchief.[57]

Not being allowed to get very near her mother, Josie lay down to rest a small distance from where Arvilla rested. Chief Douglas angrily walked up to Josie with a gun in his hand and went into a rant. Animated and angry he made large gestures saying that Captain Jack met with Major Thornburgh before the fight at Milk Creek and that Thornburgh said he was coming to arrest the head chiefs, calling them each by name. Thornburgh said the Indians were a bad lot who had beaten Agent Meeker terribly and left him in his sick bed; that his soldiers would take the Indians in manacles to Fort Steele to put them in the calaboose and maybe hang them.

Douglas paced back and forth in front of Josie raging to her that her father was responsible for all the hostility going on against the Utes; that the agent had written many letters about the Indians to the Denver newspapers which then circulated the wild reports. He said her father had always been writing to Washington; that whenever Douglas went to the office, he always saw him writing. "It was write, write, write all day!" Then Douglas swore a fearful oath in English and said if the soldiers had not come and threatened the Indians with Fort Steele and the calaboose and threatened to kill the other Indians at White River, her father wouldn't have been killed.[58]

Continuing his tirade, the chief told Josie that papers with drawings were found on Thornburgh's body depicting the fate of the agent and the white women and children of the agency. Josie's father must have made the drawings, Douglas said, and sent them to Washington to stir up sentiments against the Indians and urge the troops to come fast. Douglas described the drawings as showing knife cuts and blood all over the bodies with throats cut. He told Josie that in the drawings she had been shot through the breast and Meeker in the head.[59] The messenger that Arvilla and Flora Ellen had seen coming on the run just before noon had not only brought news about the battle but had also informed Douglas about the slanderous drawings.

Douglas then shouldered his gun as he imitated the employees at the agency and sneered before singing some songs in English including a rendition of "Swing Low, Sweet Chariot."[60] After walking off a few steps he suddenly turned and pointed the gun muzzle to Josie's forehead and asked if she was scared and if she was going to run away. Three times he did this and received the same response from his unflinching captive that she was not afraid and would not run away.[61] Just then, Josie didn't much care if he killed her.[62] When the others saw that Douglas wasn't able to frighten the young woman, they laughed at him. Douglas left Josie and went to Arvilla. Lying down, she didn't spot the gun until it flashed in the moonlight very near her face. She hiked up on one elbow and screamed, "Oh!" Josie called out to her telling her she need not be afraid, that he was only playing soldier and just trying to frighten her. Standing in a row around Josie's bed, the Utes looked at each other, took a drink, and went to saddle the horses.[63] As he would always do, Persune got on his hands and knees to assist Josie in mounting her horse.

On they rode, beneath massive silhouettes of mountains. None of the white women were accustomed to hour upon hour on horseback. Their muscles ached terribly. The discomfort for Arvilla was immeasurable. May whimpered and cried a couple of times that she was cold and hungry and wanted her mother. Mostly, though, the little girl rode the jogging horse bravely quiet as she sat the many uncomfortable miles strapped behind Josie.[64]

It was the middle of the night by the time they reached Douglas's camp. The encampment consisted of about eighty lodges pitched in a high-walled canyon where the women and some others of the band had been sent before the uprising. Douglas took Arvilla a half mile further into the canyon to his lodge. Once inside the lodge, she was, not kindly, prepared for Douglas by members of his family. There was no mistaking what was coming. The chief himself made her bed and told her where to sleep before he called a council in his lodge with several men. All were sober now and the Utes spoke in low tones. Arvilla knew what was inevitable when the meeting ended and the men left her alone with Douglas. She must survive it, for there was no argument she could make when the Chief came to her bed and took her.[65] It was the same for Flora Ellen six miles away in Jack's camp where she lay beneath Ahutupuwit, the Uncompahgre.[66] *Endure; sweetest souls; endure…*

In his lodge, Persune spread some of his new government blankets upon a place where the ground had been softened, and rolled another for Josie's pillow. After Josie lay down, two Ute women, one older and one young came up to her. At her feet they began to sing. Soon they were both singing and dancing with great joy before suddenly breaking into laughter. Persune gave them each a blanket which they took and went away.[67]

Although Josie understood that she dared not resist Persune to any great extent, when the time came she struggled and pushed him off her, even though there was probably never doubt in either of their minds what the outcome would be. After the rape was over, Josie lay awake until dawn when she fell into a dazed and exhausted slumber[68] and, blessedly, had no more thought of the last twenty-four hours until she was awakened by the golden sunlight upon the mountains.[69]

During that day men spent much of their time cleaning their guns and loading up on ammunition. The next day, they rode out, heading back to fight the soldiers. Persune left Josie in the care of his two wives and three children. The women were friendly and felt sorry for Josie.

Johnson's wife, Susan, immediately went to work persuading him to go to Jack's camp and bring back Flora Ellen and Johnny. That evening when Johnson returned with them, one of the Ute women picked Johnny up and wept the entire time she cradled him saying she was sorry for the captives. One of Supanzisquait's three wives put her hand on Josie's shoulder and began to cry, "Poor little girl, I feel so sorry you have no father and you are away off from home with the Utes." She told Josie her own little papoose had just died, and her heart was sore.[70] But when Josie saw Powvitz's wife, Jane, who had once been a friend, it was not with kindness but disdain and bitterness that Jane responded: "We will give you enough to eat and you won't starve while you are with us. If he wants to protect you, I cannot help it!"[71]

Before Chief Douglas left, he told Arvilla to remain living at his lodge where she felt protection from the other men. Several did ask her to come and sit in their lodges, but each quickly cleared out when she said she was Douglas's squaw. Powvitz came three different times and asked her if she was not afraid.

"You no scared?"

Arvilla answered, "No."

"No afraid?"

"No. No one hurt me; Great Spirit protect us. If Powvitz like Great Spirit nobody hurt him."

Powvitz looked at her and said, "Good woman."[72]

However, Douglas's children were cross and his two wives jealous and filled with hate for Arvilla Meeker. During the five days Douglas was gone, his family found many ways to torment her frailty. A son-in-law to Douglas jumped at her, pretending to stick knives in her. The women pushed her around, ran into her, and made the motions of building a fire and burning her. It was made clear to Arvilla, that she wouldn't be allowed to live with Josie or Flora Ellen, so she stiffened her posture as best she could and faced them all, determined not to be driven out.[73]

On Wednesday, October 1, the entire camp moved twelve miles south to a beautiful valley. By Saturday Persune, Douglas, and most of the others of the camp had returned. Persune wore soldiers clothing and offered them to Josie for a pillow. The next day the Utes held a war dance.

They stacked sagebrush into a pile then covered it with soldiers' clothing. Dressed in their best clothes accented with ornaments of eagle feathers, some Utes donned caps made from the fur of skunk or grizzly bear. Men and women, each carrying a knife, sang and danced around the pile, occasionally rushing in and stabbing at the garments.[74]

❧ ❧ ❧

Governor Pitkin telegraphed to all frontier points with instructions to send out couriers to warn settlers and miners.[75] On October 2, a Ute messenger arrived at Chief Ouray's farm with details of the massacre and the ongoing battle at Milk Creek. The chief of the Ute nation hurried to the Los Piños Agency. That same afternoon Joseph W. Brady, a miller at the Los Piños Agency, accompanied by an Uncompahgre Ute named Sapovonari, headed north to deliver urgent messages meant to elicit an end to the conflict. The Los Piños Indian Agent Wilson Stanley had written to the officer in command of the troops, and Chief Ouray had written to the White River Utes. Stanley explained that he was writing at the request of Chief Ouray; that the head chief of the Utes deplored the trouble and was anxious that no further fighting or bloodshed take place. Chief Ouray's message commanded the Utes to stop all hostilities. When Brady arrived at the battle site, Captain Jack read the message and said, "That is all right; we will not fight anymore." The Ute warriors rode past Brady in single file. Each stopped to shake hands with him.[76]

A couple of days before Brady arrived at Milk Creek, Captain Francis Dodge in command of Company D, Ninth Calvary and thirty-four of his black (buffalo) soldiers rode past the Utes and into the military corral without a shot fired, bringing with them some relief of food and ammunition. A large number of military reinforcements led by Colonel Merritt arrived the same day as Joseph Brady. Therefore, the messages from Agent Stanley and Chief Ouray were delivered on that Sunday, October 5. This was the same day the Utes displayed their grand war dance to the white captives. That night, when Captain Jack arrived with Johnson to report the arrival of the reinforcements at Milk Creek, the camp went into a flurry trying to decide whether to go or stay.

The Utes waited until Tuesday before they started for the Grand River (the Colorado River) in a procession that stretched for over two miles, and it stirred the soil and sage into heavy shrouds of dust.[77] Arvilla Meeker still had no saddle, but Josie had managed to convince Henry

Jim, the Ute interpreter, to give her mother one of his good horses to ride. Although Arvilla had nothing but a couple of pieces of canvas strapped onto the gelding on which to sit, she loved and was so grateful for the horse, for he was gentle and sure-footed and took good care of her on the journey. When a sickening weakness swept over her suffering body causing her to collapse onto the horse's neck, the horse never flinched. Douglas, however, cursed Arvilla furiously until she forced herself upright.[78] When they finally halted on the bank of the Grand River to make camp in the sagebrush, Arvilla couldn't dismount without the assistance of someone first lifting her injured leg. She sat waiting for someone to help her when one of Douglas's wives rushed up and grabbed hold of her and wrenched her from the back of the horse. Douglas saw, but offered no response. On the other hand, he worried that she didn't eat and broke a piece of bread in two and told her to put it in her pocket.[79] The day had been brutal: the Utes had fasted and all went without food or water until that night.[80]

The next day they rode five more miles downriver. Because they had part of the agency's cattle with them, they usually cooked fresh beef. Josie spent time helping Persune's wives with the cooking, often making the bread. When Persune and Jack returned after being away for four days, they had several fine horses, a sack of gunpowder, and lead for bullets.

Josie continued to be raped beyond the first night. It happened often. One night she asked Persune if he wanted to kill her. "Yes," he answered. Josie turned her face toward him and said, "Get up and shoot me then and leave me alone!" Persune turned over and said no more.[81]

❧ ❧ ❧

All three of the captive women felt great relief when Douglas agreed to let Johnson take Arvilla to his lodge to live. Johnson treated Arvilla gently as he brought her to his lodge to reunite with Flora Ellen and the children. The reason behind his actions, though, was Susan. She was faithful in her defense of and affection for the captives. She wept for what had happened at the agency.[82] She treated the white women with endearment and watched out for them all she could. She even entered councils, forbidden for women, and spoke with what authority was bestowed to her because she was the sister of Chief Ouray. The white women were deeply grateful to Susan. They didn't know, though, that Susan had a dramatic and gripping past and had, herself, been an innocent captive and in great fear for her life.

The Ute Delegation in Washington, D.C., 1880. Standing: Woretsiz, General Charles Adams. Seated (l. to r): Chief Ignatio of the Southern Utes, Secretary of Interior Carl Schurz, Chief Ouray, and his wife Chipeta. *Ronzio Collection, 20009564.tif, History Colorado.*

In 1862 when Susan (Shawsheen) was seventeen, she was taken prisoner during a raid on her camp by Arapaho warriors. A year later a battle broke out in North Park, Colorado, between Shawsheen's Arapaho captors and a band of Ute fighters. The Arapahos were badly beaten.

Settlers got word that the Arapahos were about to take vengeance against the Ute captive, Shawsheen, and burn her at the stake. The settlers rushed word to Camp Collins. Sergeant William C. Carrol and a squad of twelve men rode at a quick pace for more than ten miles to the

Arapaho village on the Platte River near the mouth of the Cache La Poudre River. At the center of the camp, the soldiers saw an erected post surrounded by tinder. They found Shawsheen hidden beneath some buffalo robes. Her hair had been closely shaven in preparation for sacrificial cremation. Amidst a swelling of protests the sergeant quickly lifted the girl onto his horse and the soldiers rode for Camp Collins.

Sergeant Carrol took Shawsheen home to live with him and his wife. Mrs. Carrol made dresses for her, taught her English words, and gave her the name of Susan. The Carrols returned home from attending a dance to discover Susan had left. She had taken her new clothes, a butcher knife, and a piece of meat for her journey home.[83] Sixteen years later, Susan retained the name Mrs. Carrol gave her and did what she could to soften the suffering and distress of the white captives of the Meeker Massacre.

❧ ❧ ❧

When the Ute scouts stationed on different mountain peaks with binoculars spotted the troops advancing, the encampment erupted, causing the horses to spook. Johnson went into a rage and pulled the hair of his youngest wife and flayed her with a whip. A young man rushed up to Josie and Flora Ellen and threatened to shoot them. Josie looked him in the eye and said, "Shoot away!" Flora Ellen pointed to her forehead and said to shoot her there. The young man frowned and told them they were not good squaws because they weren't afraid.[84]

Josie was again separated from her mother and Flora Ellen, as tepees were quickly brought down. Soon on the move the cavalcade continued traveling until dark. The next day they pushed hard as they hurried south for another twenty-five miles. Rain set in and continued for two full days and nights drenching them with misery. After another full day's ride they stopped at Plateau Creek. The Utes would make their stand to fight if the soldiers came.

In a few days around fifteen lodges moved to take the white women several miles away to camp near a small tributary of Plateau Creek. A messenger dispatched by General Charles Adams rode in and informed the Utes that Adams and his party would arrive at the camp the next day from Los Piños. Adams was in the company of four white men and an escort of thirteen Uncompahgre Utes sent by Chief Ouray. Chief Douglas knew and respected General Adams. Adams had served as the Indian agent at both the Los Piños and White River Agencies.[85] The Utes openly shared with Josie that white men were coming. While she was hopeful that it was true, she had heard similar things before, but no one had come. Persune asked her what she was going to tell about the Utes. He said, "You go back and tell them that they are no good." She answered, "No, I should not."[86]

The next morning, October 21, Josie sewed while she and May waited inside Persune's lodge with his wives. Persune's twelve-year-old son arrived, handed Josie a buffalo robe, and told her to go to bed. Josie refused. Then as they heard horses approach, one of Persune's wives suddenly tried to hide Josie with the robe while the other wife held a blanket over the tepee entrance.[87]

The Adams party heard the commotion and halted. Just then Josie pushed the women aside and peered out. Then, on their twenty-second day of captivity, Josie and May stepped into the sunlight and the stunning visual of General Adams and his party. Adams dismounted his horse and Josie put her hand out to his. Tears coated her words as she said, "I'm so glad to see you."[88] She responded to his question and pointed out where her mother and Flora Ellen were, along the creek about a half mile away.

General Adams asked, "Do you know who of these Indians killed your father and the other employees?"

"No, I could not tell," Josie answered.

"How have the Indians treated you?"

"Oh, well, better than I expected."

"Have they offered you any indignity to your person?"

"Oh, no, Mr. Adams. Nothing of that kind." [89]

Before mounting his horse, Adams told Josie to get prepared to go. When he and his group approached the tepees Josie had pointed out, they could hear a council in session including thirty or forty men. The Ute escorts immediately got off their horses and joined the fiery discussion inside the lodge. "They have hid the women," Adams said to his companions.

Adams went inside and was greeted with hostility. Although he knew all those present, none of the Utes would speak with him except to ask him to wait for the arrival of Chief Douglas. After about an hour's delay Douglas arrived and said to Adams, "Come, let us go inside."[90] Five hours later General Adams stepped from the lodge and said, "They have sent for the women."[91]

From a brushy thicket of willows along the creek Flora Ellen appeared being trailed by Susan with Johnny on her back in a blanket sling. Following behind, Arvilla walked with the aid of a cane. Arvilla appeared dazed and bewildered at the thought of release, leaving her rescuers to fear that her mind had been affected. A tear escaped General Adams' tightly wound emotions and slid down his cheek. He spoke softly, "Poor woman, how much she has suffered."[92]

Every movement and conversation was closely observed by the Utes, so the captives and their rescuers spoke few words. Adams, finding a moment alone with Flora Ellen, took the chance to ask if she had been offered any indignity to her person. It must have been with immeasurable relief that Adams then quickly wrote a dispatch to Secretary of the Interior Department, Carl Schurz, that the women had been given up and no indignities offered to them. Adams immediately sent it out with an Uncompahgre runner to Chief Ouray about 120 miles away, then on to the Los Piños Agency, before taking it to Lake City to be telegraphed from there.[93] He made arrangements for the women to be brought together for the night and arranged for horses and saddles for them to ride. The next morning the women would be escorted to Los Piños by three of Adams's companions. Chief Ouray was to have pickets all along the way so the women would never be without protection. General Adams rode away in the company of Chief Douglas to council with the Utes at the main camp. Adams would then ride to try to halt Colonel Merritt's pursuit of the Utes.

Flora Ellen walked to Persune's tepee to get Josie. Josie then spent an anxious night in Johnson and Susan's lodge with her mother, Flora Ellen, and the children while the white men, without General Adams, spent a very nervous night in the company of the Utes. But morning came at last and Susan had breakfast ready for them all by eight o'clock. Persune was nowhere to be seen as farewells were said and Josie mounted a saddled pony given to her by Susan. Her little companion, May, took her familiar place behind Josie's saddle. Flora Ellen, "seeming fit and filled with Saxon pluck," sat atop a mule with Johnny.[94] Before getting on her horse, Arvilla turned and walked to Susan. She put her arms around Susan's neck and lovingly embraced her. Then Arvilla kissed her Ute champion on the forehead before turning back to her horse provided by one of her rescuers, who helped her into the saddle. "God Bless Susan," she said. "She has been as kind as a mother."[95]

Chief Johnson, benevolent Susan's husband, pointed to Flora Ellen and said, "Heap fine squaw. Me like her stay."

Flora Ellen smiled, but only because she knew she was free. Behind the smile that hid her scorn was a secret that she bore. The previous morning, knowing General Adams would soon arrive, Johnson chose his moment when Susan was busy and Arvilla lay taking a nap in his lodge. Hidden among the undergrowth and willows along the creek, he raped her. Still, Arvilla, Josie, and Flora Ellen meant to share their shameful secrets only with each other.[96]

As the group rode out, the men intended to hold the horses at a walk, out of care and consideration for the perceived fragility of the women, especially the pitiful and elderly Mrs. Meeker. The three men were amazed when Arvilla, brightening by the moment, broke her horse into a trot and insisted on keeping up the pace for nearly all of the forty miles of the first day of the journey.[97] All three women rode with toughened ease and their heads up. Hundreds of miles lay before them, though, on the long road home.

❦ ❦ ❦

October 22, 1879, the day the captives rode away from the Ute encampment into freedom, was only about a week after the Bassett family arrived in Green River City. The Bassetts moved into a boarding house where the activity of the railroad town hammered and clanked around them. Herb found work as a laborer, and Elizabeth suspected she was once again pregnant.

The fate of the women and children captives was still unknown to most, but news of their rescue by General Adams would soon blaze across the headlines. The uprising in Colorado was an event that held the Bassetts and the entire nation, spellbound.

For all of the White River and Uncompahgre Utes, life in their age-old domain among regal mountain peaks and the treasured sustenance of grassy valleys was shattering and falling into the past. The skill and dedication of a few honorable men including General Charles Adams, Secretary of the Interior Carl Schurz, and the ailing Chief Ouray held firm against a fevered cry to drive the "red devils" not just out of Colorado but into annihilation.

NOTES TO CHAPTER THREE

1. Josie (Bassett) Morris interview with Messersmith, 18 Jul 1960, The Museum of NW Colorado–Craig.

2. Hoy, J.S., "Hoy Manuscript," 200.

3. Hoy, 200.

4. *Testimony in Relation to the Ute Indian Outbreak, House of Representatives,* 46th Congress, 2d Session, No. 38, May 1, 1880, 134, Taken By The Committee On Indian Affairs Of The House Of Representatives, Mr. Haskell.

5. *Testimony Ute Outbreak, House of Representatives,* 45, Clinton B. Fisk.

6. *Testimony Ute Outbreak, House of Representatives,* 45, Clinton B. Fisk.

7. Josephine Meeker's Obituary, Smithsonian Institution.

8. *Testimony Ute Indian Outbreak, House of Representatives,* 71, Josephine Meeker.

9. *Copy Of Evidence Taken Before White River Ute Commission, House of Representatives,* 46th Congress, 2d Session, No.83, May14, 1880, 66, Letter from the Secretary of the Interior, Captain Jack.

10. *Carbon County Journal,* "The Meeker Captives," Nov 8, 1879.

11. *Testimony Ute Indian Outbreak, House of Representatives,* 111, Col. John W. Steele.

12. *Testimony Ute Outbreak, House of Representatives,* 75, Josephine Meeker.

13. *Copy Of Evidence White River Ute Commission,* 2, Letter, Chief Douglas.

14. Hoy, 204.

15. Hoy, 153, 154.

16. "Brave Josephine!—Miss Meeker's Thrilling Story of Her Captivity," *New York Herald*, Oct 29, 1879 (By telegraph from Alamosa, Colo.).

17. The Smithsonian Museum determined this to be the proper spelling for Shawsheen.

18. Chief Ouray was well-known and respected not only among the Utes but by the Colorado governor and officials in Washington, D.C. The treaty in 1868 that created the reservation and consolidated approximately the western third of Colorado required the Utes to combine the seven bands which made up the three major groups of the tribe, the White River (Northern), Uncompahgre, and Southern Utes, to form one entity. Ouray was designated Chief of the Ute Nation.

19. *Testimony Ute Indian Outbreak, House of Representatives,* 73, Josephine Meeker.

20. "Brave Josephine!...." *New York Herald.*

21. *Copy Of Evidence White River Ute Commission*, 9, Letter, Chief Sowawick.

22. *Copy Of Evidence White River Ute Commission*, 3, Letter, Chief Douglas.

23. *Testimony Ute Outbreak, House of Representatives,* 110, Frederick W. Pitkin.

24. *Testimony Ute Outbreak, House of Representatives,* 77, Josephine Meeker. Chinaman and Bennett were accused of burning buildings and hay belonging to A.H. Smart and James Thompson at the settlement of Hayden about fifty miles northeast of the White River Agency.

25. *Copy Of Evidence White River Ute Commission*, 69, Letter, Captain Jack.

26. *Copy Of Evidence White River Ute Commission*, 70, Letter, Captain Jack.

27. *Copy Of Evidence White River Ute Commission*, 3, Letter. Chief Douglas.

28. *Copy Of Evidence White River Ute Commission*, 54, Letter. Nathan Meeker message to E.A. Hayt.

29. *Copy Of Evidence White River Ute Commission*, 7, Letter, Captain Johnson.

30. *Testimony Ute Outbreak, House of Representatives,* 111, Col. John W. Steele.

31. "Brave Josephine!..." *New York Herald.*

32. *Testimony Ute Outbreak, House of Representatives,* 109, Letter to Governor Pitkin from Nathan Meeker, Sep 19, 1879.

33. *Copy Of Evidence White River Ute Commission*, 7, Letter, Josephine Meeker.

34. *Copy Of Evidence White River Ute Commission*, 22, Letter, Arvilla Meeker.

35. *Copy Of Evidence White River Ute Commission*, 21, Letter, Arvilla Meeker.

36. *Copy Of Evidence White River Ute Commission*, 21, Letter, Josephine Meeker.

37. *Copy Of Evidence White River Ute Commission*, 41-42, Letter, Josephine Meeker.

38. *Copy Of Evidence White River Ute Commission*, 13–14, Letter, Flora Ellen Price.

39. *Testimony Ute Outbreak, House of Representatives,* 81, Josephine Meeker.

40. *Copy Of Evidence White River Ute Commission*, 15, Letter, Flora Ellen Price.

41. *Copy Of Evidence White River Ute Commission*, 15, Letter, Flora Ellen Price.

42. "Brave Josephine!..." *New York Herald.*

43. *Copy Of Evidence White River Ute Commission*, 16, Letter, Flora Ellen Price.

44. *Copy Of Evidence White River Ute Commission*, 24, Letter, Arvilla Meeker.

45. *Copy Of Evidence White River Ute Commission*, 42, Letter, Josephine Meeker.

46. "Brave Josephine!..." *New York Herald.*

47. "Brave Josephine!..." *New York Herald.*

48. *Copy Of Evidence White River Ute Commission*, 17, Letter, Flora Ellen Price.

49. *Copy Of Evidence White River Ute Commission*, 24, Letter, Arvilla Meeker.

50. *Copy Of Evidence White River Ute Commission*, 24, Letter, Arvilla Meeker.

51. *Copy Of Evidence White River Ute Commission*, 25, Letter, Arvilla Meeker.

52. *Testimony Ute Outbreak, House of Representatives,* 111-112, Col. John W. Steele.

53. *Copy Of Evidence White River Ute Commission*, 25, Letter, Arvilla Meeker.

54. *Copy Of Evidence White River Ute Commission*, 18, Letter, Flora Ellen Price.

55. "Brave Josephine!..." *New York Herald.*

56. "Brave Josephine!..." *New York Herald.*

57. *Copy Of Evidence White River Ute Commission*, 25, Letter, Arvilla Meeker.

58. "Brave Josephine!..." *New York Herald.*

59. *Copy Of Evidence White River Ute Commission*, 46, Letter, Josephine Meeker.

60. "Brave Josephine!..." *New York Herald.*

61. *Colorado Daily Chieftain*, "Miss Meeker's Story," 31 Oct 1879.

62. *Copy Of Evidence White River Ute Commission*, 25, Letter, Arvilla Meeker.

63. *Copy Of Evidence White River Ute Commission*, 25, Letter, Arvilla Meeker.

64. "Brave Josephine!..." *New York Herald.*

65. *Copy Of Evidence White River Ute Commission*, 26, Letter, Arvilla Meeker.

66. *Copy Of Evidence White River Ute Commission*, 17-18, Letter, Flora Ellen Price.

67. "Brave Josephine!..." *New York Herald.*

68. *Copy Of Evidence White River Ute Commission*, 44, Letter, Josephine Meeker.

69. "Brave Josephine!..." *New York Herald.*

70. "Brave Josephine!..." *New York Herald.*

71. *Copy Of Evidence White River Ute Commission*, 44, Letter, Josephine Meeker.

72. *Copy Of Evidence White River Ute Commission*, 21, Letter, Arvilla Meeker.

73. *Copy Of Evidence White River Ute Commission*, 26, Letter, Arvilla Meeker.

74. "Brave Josephine!..." *New York Herald.*

75. *Testimony Ute Outbreak, House of Representatives,* 114, Frederick Pitkin.

76. *Testimony Ute Outbreak, House of Representatives,* 30, James W. Brady.

77. "Brave Josephine!..." *New York Herald.*

78. *Carbon County Journal*, "The Meeker Captives," 8 Nov 1879.

79. *Copy Of Evidence White River Ute Commission*, 26, Letter, Arvilla Meeker.

80. "Brave Josephine!..." *New York Herald.*

81. *Copy Of Evidence White River Ute Commission*, 44, Letter, Josephine Meeker.

82. *Copy Of Evidence White River Ute Commission*, 18, Letter, Flora Ellen Price.

83. "Squaw Susan's Send-Off," *Colorado Transcript*, Denver, 17 Dec 1879.

84. "Brave Josephine!..." *New York Herald.*

85. *Testimony Ute Outbreak, House of Representatives,* 1, Charles Adams. Adams had been serving as a special agent for the Postal Department but, for the delicate task of securing the release of the captives, had been named Special Agent for the Interior Department. His four companions were Captain M.W. Cline; two Los Piños Agency employees, George Sherman and W.F. Saunders; and an acquaintance of Major Adams, Count August Donhoff, Secretary of the German legation in Washington.

86. *Copy Of Evidence White River Ute Commission*, 44, Letter, Josephine Meeker.

87. "Brave Josephine!..." *New York Herald.*

88. "Douglass' Camp," *Solid Muldoon Weekly*, Ouray, Colorado, 7 Nov 1879.

89. *Copy Of Evidence White River Ute Commission*, 3, Letter, Charles Adams.

90. "Douglass' Camp," 7.

91. "Douglass' Camp," 7.

92. "Douglass' Camp," 7.

93. *Testimony Ute Outbreak, House of Representatives,* 3, Charles Adams.

94. "Douglass' Camp," 7.

95. "Douglass' Camp," 7.

96. *Copy Of Evidence White River Ute Commission*, 44, Letter, Flora Ellen Price.

97. "Douglass' Camp," 7.

CHAPTER FOUR

THE AFTERMATH

During the decade before the Bassetts arrived there on the train from Arkansas, Green River City had gone from a new and growing population of over two thousand in 1868 to a near ghost town shortly after.[1] By 1872 it had grown into an attractive town filled with life and 330 people when the Bassetts moved there from Brown's Park in the fall of 1879.[2] It was all about the Union Pacific Railroad.

In the beginning, the only manmade structures visible near what would become Green River City were the adobe-covered stone buildings and pole corrals of an Overland Stage Station. The coming of the Union Pacific Railroad changed everything. Land speculators and incisive businessmen recognized the location's potential because here the railroad would cross the Green River. The river offered an eternal supply of water for the steam-powered locomotives and other railroad operations. The entrepreneurs came just ahead of the laying of the tracks and acquired the land on which to establish a town from the Overland Mail Company.[3] Everyone anticipated the Union Pacific would make Green River City the division point for the railroad.

Adding to the activity surrounding Green River City was the timber industry that had developed in Wyoming because of the building of the railroad. In 1867 at the age of twenty-one Charles DeLoney, a Civil War veteran from Michigan, came to Wyoming and contracted with the Union Pacific to supply it railroad ties from timber harvested in the Wind River Mountains near the head of the Green River.[4]

Green River City was thriving by the time the railroad arrived. However, the Union Pacific was greatly displeased that the town did not sit on railroad land. The town was devastated when the railroad moved onward for another twelve miles to establish the division point. Soon, barely one hundred people remained in Green River City. However, it took only four years for the railroad to recognize that it had made a mistake when its main water source dried up. The division point was moved to Green River City and the town blossomed from there.

In December 1875, Green River City was chosen as the permanent location for the county seat of Sweetwater County. The legislature required a courthouse be constructed, resulting in an impressive two-story building that brought a refined style to the budding town. Judge Ashbury Conaway, the man who delivered the milk cow to the Bassett family in Brown's Park, lived there, successfully practicing law. He helped Herb and Elizabeth and the children settle in and then introduced them to the townspeople. Herb and Judge Conaway found they had many things in common including Brown's Park, the Civil War, and a penchant for knowledge.

Elizabeth, Herb, and Judge Conaway talked at length about the happenings still unfolding around the Meeker Massacre. They rifled through and read the many newspaper articles about the uprising at White River. Among the articles were ones reporting that when Colonel Merritt and his men rode into the White River Agency twelve days after the massacre on October 11, 1879, they found all the buildings burnt to rubble with the exception of the storehouse which stood ransacked but otherwise unscathed. Among the evidence of rage and rampage strewn about the agency were the naked bodies of Meeker and six of the employees.[5]

Flora Ellen's husband, Shadrach, had two bullet holes in his left breast. The clerk and postmaster W. H. Post was lying near the storehouse doorway and had been shot twice in the head. Frank Dresser's brother, Harry, was lying nearby. Frank Dresser must have initially escaped the Utes the night of the massacre. He had apparently returned to the agency after the Utes and captives rode out and retrieved his brother's coat. When Frank's body was found by the soldiers as they passed through Coal Creek Canyon on their way to the agency, Frank had Harry's coat folded beneath his head. His death had been a lingering one. In addition to the wound in his thigh Frank had later sustained a gunshot to his right breast. Gripped in his hands was a cocked rifle.[6]

At the agency as each body was discovered by the soldiers it was soon revealed that the crescendo of the Ute's fury was saved for the agent. Nathan Meeker was found about one hundred yards from where his house once stood with not only the bullet hole in his forehead that Arvilla witnessed but with the left side of his head mashed by blunt force.[7] One arm and hand was badly burned, a charred wooden stave from a barrel had been driven into his mouth and a heavy, four-foot logging chain was still around his neck. His body appeared to have been dragged all about.[8]

People speculated that the chain and dragging simulated Meeker's threats of putting the Utes in chains. Colonel Merritt's soldiers hastily buried Meeker and the employees as they waited for orders. Although they removed the barrel stave from Meeker's mouth, they left the chain that was about his neck.[9] Newspapers reported that Merritt hoped to soon be chasing down the Utes whom he believed were continuing to assemble for war. The Colonel wrongly surmised that in addition to the White River Utes, a large number of Uintah Utes from Utah and possibly the Southern Utes had joined the battle against Major Thornburgh. Although the force of Utes engaged in the fight never totaled more than 125, it must have sent chills through Herb and Elizabeth and countless others to read that Colonel Merritt guessed the number of warriors at Milk Creek at seven hundred.[10] Reading such things made it obvious to Judge Conaway, Herb, and Elizabeth that they were going to have to remain in town for the foreseeable future.

The early aftermath of the Meeker Massacre produced lengthy hours of hearings, councils, and exhaustive testimony. Under oath Arvilla, Josie, and Flora Ellen admitted that they had each been "outraged." All three women asked and were assured by General Adams that their testimony would be protected and not made public. Toward the end of her testimony, Flora Ellen said, "I want to have those Utes taken and killed, and I want to have the privilege of killing Johnson and that Uncompahgre Ute myself."

Government authorities argued, searching for answers that would bring not only justice but also workable solutions without triggering the annihilation of the Colorado Utes. The country, still unaware that the captives had been raped, was spectacularly divided about where the blame of the uprising should lie and that was reflected in the nation's newspapers:

> *New York Tribune:* "It would not be a violent exaggeration to say that the United States has been engaged for years in systemic lying, cheating, thieving and homicide."[11]

> *Washington Post:* "We cannot go on forever keeping up the illusion that these people are independent nations, fit subjects for solemn treaties. The lands they occupy must be opened up to civilization.

They must take up farms, divide into families, and adopt the ways of the whites."12

Catholic Mirror: "The bureau at Washington has failed to keep the stipulations of its compact with the Utes. It has not paid them money due them for lands ceded for settlement. It has not kept the reservation free from the inroads of prospecting adventurers."13

New York Herald: "The centre of the continent has begun to feel the effect of a vast tidal wave of emigration. The rapid building of railroads and the discovery of great mineral wealth have drawn and are drawing to that hitherto waste region, a great population of whites. These cannot be kept out, and they ought not be excluded, even if it were possible. They develop the country; their steady labor increases our wealth and prosperity. …it ought to welcome the opportunity which such an incident as this uncalled-for Ute war gives it to remove the wild Indians out of the way of the whites."14

Raleigh (N.C.) News: "The cause of all the trouble is this: Treaties have been made with the Indians in which they have been grievously cheated, and cheated knowingly, by the treaty-making officials, and after stipulations have been agreed to, they have been set aside by the government, as conveniences demanded."15

Laramie Sentinel: "The Indian is no more entitled to immunity from labor than the white man; nor ethically, is his claim to the land any more perfect than that of the white man. The bestowal of the Government of immense tracts of the richest mineral, and best agricultural and grazing lands in her possession upon a lazy, filthy, treacherous savage race, which never occupies one-hundredth part of them, except to exclude intelligent whites and annually terrorize the country by un-provoked and fiendish massacres of the families of sturdy pioneers who may settle upon their borders, is as imbecile, unjust and impolitic as it has proved futile in pacifying the Indians innate warlike disposition. The torch of war is the Indian's guiding star; the tomahawk his plow share polished, and blood his favorite harvest."16

No one was more poisonous in their hatred for the Utes than the oldest Meeker daughter, Rozene (Rose) Meeker, who had stayed behind in Greeley when the family moved to the White River Agency. Against all wishes expressed by her siblings Josie and Ralph, Rose would not be denied giving her lectures as she walked a celebrity's path stirring emotions while reciting the virtues of her father and the savagery of the Utes.17

Ralph and Josie failed in tempering Rose and her toxic influence over Arvilla. Just after a contentious Thanksgiving, Ralph and Josie left Colorado for jobs offered them in Washington D.C.[18]

At last Rose could convince her susceptible mother to confirm whispered suspicions and reveal all, so that the government would be forced to act against the Utes. At her home in Greeley, Colorado, on December 30, 1879, Arvilla wrote to the editor of the *Colorado Chieftain*:[19]

> Dear Sir:
>
> I arise from a sick-bed to state a few facts which you and the people of Colorado demand. We three captives of the Utes—Mrs. Price, myself and daughter—were all interviewed separately, being put under oath by the officers of the government to tell the whole truth of our treatment by the Indians, and if they outraged our persons, and each one of us gave in our testimony an answer in the affirmative against the Indians.
>
> I gave in my testimony for the use of the Government to do with it just as they should see fit. There was nothing said about its being suppressed on either side. I just simply gave my testimony to the Government officers innocently supposing that they knew their duty and would do it. I also thought I had done all that belonged to me to do by telling these officers the sickening and most humiliating misfortune that can befall a woman, and if they and the Interior Department have not done their duty by the people of Colorado, it is they who are to blame, and not me.
>
> On arriving home in Greeley, I have found myself completely broken down in mind and body, and have had a long spell of severe sickness from which I am just recovering.
>
> Yours truly,
> Mrs. N. C. Meeker

Arvilla's letter was quickly printed and reprinted across the country. Josie and Ralph understood the enormity of the firestorm Rose had ignited against all the Colorado Utes for what a handful of them had done. Citizens raised fists and voices with growing ferocity demanding that the government solve the Indian conundrum. While a good share of the public wanted a just solution for all, many screamed for vengeance:

> *Colorado Weekly Chieftain:* "Has it come to this that a great nation of forty millions of people must treat with a band of lousy, roving red devil cut throats, and wink at crimes that would make a demon blush? Out upon all such tomfoolery and temporizing. If the government at

Washington is too pusillanimous to send the army to punish the devils in human form, let it withdraw for ninety days and turn the fiends over to the men of Colorado to settle the question. It will not require any pay if the government will only turn the miners and frontiersmen loose and let them deal with the red-handed loathsome fiends. Vengeance should be the watchword from this time on till the last footprints of the fiendish Utes are obliterated from the soil of Colorado."[20]

Saguache Chronicle: "The facts of the case are…that the Indians killed the men and took the women captives, and that before the bodies of their dead had become cold, they were forcibly obliged to submit to the embraces of the fiends, whose hands were yet wet with the blood of their murdered relatives. To think of those women, the elderly lady and her daughter, and Mrs. Price, three helpless creatures in the hands of those infuriated demons, subject to their worse than beastly instincts whenever they demanded submission, is enough to sicken the heart and curdle the blood in the veins of every American citizen."[21]

Saguache Chronicle: "*The Denver Republican* says, the Utes will not go, if Congress is to supply the motive power. That is settled. But before the first of October next, captain Jack and Co., will wish they had not disturbed Father Meeker. Take the word of three thousand sturdy prospectors for that."[22]

During this same time in Green River City on June 21, 1880, Elizabeth Bassett gave birth to Elbert, increasing the family to two boys and two girls. Not long after, Herb was promoted from laborer to bridge inspector for the Union Pacific.[23] Several months after that, Herb was offered a job with the Union Pacific Coal Company. The Bassetts moved fifteen miles northeast to a Company house in the busy coal mining town of Rock Springs where Herb went to work as a boss for the No. 1 coal mine.[24]

Rock Springs had not been planned to be anything more than a coal camp where only the mine bosses were provided houses while miners lived in shanties or dugouts along Bitter Creek. However, by the time the Bassetts moved there, the place was showing real signs of becoming a community. The population had grown from forty people in 1870 to 763 residents in 1880.[25] Scottish immigrants John Jarvie and his partner George L. Young, Sr., started one of the first general merchandise stores in Rock Springs. In 1871 they took ownership of the Will Wale Saloon located on the north side of the tracks.[26] The first school in Rock Springs was held on the second floor of the saloon building until a schoolhouse was built in 1874.[27] As mine boss, Herb acted principally as a logistical coordinator; still the coal dust must have been an ongoing irritant to his weakened lungs.

An eternal friendship quickly developed between the Bassetts and newlyweds John and Nellie Jarvie. They spent much of their time together talking about the valley known as Brown's Park. Surely they were all relieved and encouraged that things seemed to be getting resolved with the Utes and therefore the danger was passing.

The government concluded that the Utes had been involved in a fair fight with the Army; no charges were called for against Captain Jack or his warriors. However, twelve Utes, including Chief Douglas, Johnson, and Persune, were asked to surrender to be tried in Washington D.C., for crimes surrounding the massacre. The accused Utes melted away into the countryside and obscurity, it was only Chief Douglas who, on February 25, 1880, was delivered to the military prison at Fort Leavenworth in Missouri, to await charges.

Although he was extremely ill, Chief Ouray endured until the Ute agreement he worked on so hard with Interior Secretary Schurz was ratified. The chief was valiant and pragmatic in the negotiations for his people. In August, Chief Ouray died from Bright's disease, a historical classification of diverse kidney disorders.

The White River Utes were already moved out of Colorado and into Utah where they settled on the southern portion of the Uintah Reservation. Although the reservation for the Southern Utes would be squeezed over toward Utah, it remained in Colorado. A new reservation was soon laid out in Utah for the Uncompahgre Utes.

During a Joint Committee meeting, Secretary Schurz was asked if the people of Utah and New Mexico were satisfied to have the Utes live there. Schurz replied, "A voice of the people of these Territories would probably favor having no Indians there. But the Indians must live somewhere. In justice to them we cannot always be governed by the wishes of people who do not want any Indians in their neighborhood. Indians have rights just as well as other men."[28] Schurz requested a military presence to be stationed between the rush of whites and a nine mile stretch near Ouray's farm that was covered with Uncompahgre Ute tepees. The soldiers remained there until the last of Chief Ouray's people departed in the fall of 1881.

Flora Ellen Price and her two children moved to Yakima County, Washington, to be with family. Chief Douglas's daughter and other Utes persistently inquired about Douglas saying they had lived during the winter on meat from their ponies and were very hungry and peaceable now.[29] In the early part of February, 1881, after 384 days in Fort Leavenworth without a trial or even charges, officials quietly removed Chief Douglas from prison and ordered him escorted to the Los Piños Agency to be set free to join his family.

Josie Meeker was working in Washington, D.C., for Secretary Schurz in the offices of the Interior Department. During the coming summer of 1882, she was promoted to assistant private secretary to Henry M. Teller, the man who replaced Carl Schurz as Interior Secretary. The following December she fell ill and spent Christmas in bed with a high fever. By December 30, her illness had progressed into pneumonia.[30] Her brother Ralph was at her bedside, clutching her hand as his sister, a woman whose name and story was known throughout the nation, died a sorrowful death. Heartbroken, Ralph escorted her home to their mother in Colorado.[31]

Ann Bassett and her family, just over a year and a half after the massacre, prepared to returned to Brown's Park in the late spring of 1881. Uncle Samuel arrived with his wagon to assist them. Their Rock Springs friends, John and Nellie Jarvie, also moved to Brown's Park to build and operate a store there. In doing so, they secured their place, along with the Bassetts, in the history of Brown's Park.

After leaving Rock Springs the Bassetts followed the wagon route that took them back to Gap Creek and through Tittsworth Gap where they stopped to visit Billy Tittsworth and his wife, Jean, and rest a bit at their ranch. They learned that they had made the wisest of decisions to go to Green River City and not Ashley Valley to wait out the uprising. The winter of 1879-1880 had turned out to be an unbearably hard one with deep snow and severe cold. Of course, there was no way the residents of Ashley Valley could have anticipated the Meeker Massacre, nor the large influx of people their valley would receive because of it. Those fleeing families brought little with them so when the weather grew worse, things like sugar and grain became scarce. Families ran out of fruits and vegetables. As the biting winter progressed, livestock suffered and perished by the herd, and the deer became so thin that they provided the people with little meat. Finally in March the weather broke and some brave men drove wagons out of Ashley Valley on a very tough journey over Diamond Mountain to Brown's Park and on to Green River City for supplies, which undoubtedly saved people from starvation.[32]

The Bassetts said their goodbyes to the Tittsworths and headed onward to Brown's Park. Because conditions were satisfactory, instead of taking the route that would lead them to Red Creek Canyon, the Bassetts made their way toward Willow Creek to enter Brown's Park through the beauty of Willow Creek Canyon.[33]

As the travelers bumped along the ill-defined wagon road following the creek, they passed through shimmering quaking aspens. Furry catkins on pussy willow clung to the creek banks among the green glimmer of narrowleaf cottonwood trees. Because wildlife was abundant in that area, the Bassetts had the opportunity to observe all kinds, a few of which included beaver, mule deer, antelope, elk, pheasants, mountain bluebirds, sage grouse and blue grouse. Varied shrubs of gooseberry, chokecherry, currant, and serviceberries displayed green beads of baby fruit.[34] The wagon followed the riffles and dimples of the trout-filled creek right to the dooryard of the little windowless cabin in the meadow.

The Utes still were a presence in the valley. Although restrictions would tighten, the events surrounding the Meeker Massacre had so far had minimal effect on the local Ute families traveling back and forth from the reservation to Brown's Park. They continued their usual hunting and gathering practices.

Almost immediately Samuel and Herb left Elizabeth and the children so she and the youngsters could rest a little before setting about the task of cleaning out the cabin in preparation for a move to the other end of Brown's Park. Samuel had already moved his things from the cabin after having squatted on some acreage on Beaver Creek where he built a cabin. Herb and Samuel were off to explore Herb and Elizabeth's newly acquired land and prepare a building site for a new home.

Herb and Elizabeth not only had a dream for their family, they had a plan. Judge Asbury Conaway had turned over to them his claim on a piece of land at the eastern end of the Park. Herb and Elizabeth had never seen that portion of the valley, and they were no doubt anxious.

There was no road to follow, only faint trails, as the Bassett family bumped and pitched during the eighteen-mile wagon ride toward providence.[35] Elizabeth was undaunted by the challenge. Not even when the kids came down with measles along the way did Elizabeth falter. Nor did hearing that Samuel had somehow lost their little cattle herd cause Elizabeth to waver. She was resolute in taking her family home, home to the place Judge Conaway had described to her in detail, telling of the land's fertile soil, its spring water of ice cold sweetness and the splendid views of unmatched beauty. Had it not been for the fearsome events of the Meeker Massacre which encouraged the opportunity for a close friendship between the Bassett family and Judge Conaway in Green River City, it is unlikely this land in Brown's Park would have ever become theirs. But, it had, and now was not the time for their resolve to fade for there was much exciting work to do if they were going to build a cow outfit.

In this, the sunrise of her life, doubt no longer existed about what three-year-old Ann Bassett's childhood would be. She was going to have the privilege of growing up in the mystical valley of her birth and be given the freedom to thrive, untamed, within the realm of a cattle ranch.

NOTES TO CHAPTER FOUR

1. *The Frontier Index*, traveling "end of tracks" newspaper, near Bitter Creek, Wyoming Territory, 11 Sep 1868.

2. 1880 U.S. Census population was 327.

3. The Overland Mail Company had been granted the property by Congress so it was excluded from being part of the government land grants given to the railroad in the Pacific Railway Act of 1862.

4. Laurence Parent, *Insiders' Guide, Scenic Driving Wyoming*, p. 81.

5. "Frightful Fate," *Cheyenne Daily Leader*, 14 Oct 1879.

6. "The Ute War–The Silent Witness," *Laramie Sentinel*, 18 Oct 1879.

7. "The Ute War–The Silent Witness," *Laramie Sentinel*.

8. "Frightful Fate," *Cheyenne Daily Leader*.

9. *Bangor Daily Whig and Courier*, Bangor, Maine, 20 Jul 1880.

10. "Frightful Fate," *Cheyenne Daily Leader*.

11. "Leading Journals Arraign the Rotten Indian System–What the Nation Calls for," *Carbon County Journal*, Rawlins, WY, 8 Nov 1879.

12. "Rotten Indian System," *Carbon County Journal*.

13. "Rotten Indian System," *Carbon County Journal.*

14. "Rotten Indian System," *Carbon County Journal.*

15. "Rotten Indian System," *Carbon County Journal.*

16. "The Ute War–Give Each a Farm," *Laramie Sentinel,* 18 Oct 1879.

17. "Rose Meeker's Lecture," *Colorado Miner,* Georgetown, Colo, 15 Nov 1879.

18. Marshall Sprague, *Massacre: The Tragedy at White River*, Reprint edition, (University of Nebraska, 1980) 302.

19. "Mrs. Meeker's Letter," *Saguache Chronicle,* Saguache, Colo. 10 Jan 1880.

20. *Colorado Daily Chieftain*, "Mrs. Meeker Explains," 8 Jan 1880.

21. "Mrs. Meeker's Letter," *Saguache Chronicle,* Saguache, Colo. 10 Jan 1880.

22. *Saguache Chronicle*, 8 May 1880.

23. Josie Bassett Morris, interview with Messersmith, 18 Jul 1960, The Museum of NW Colorado–Craig.

24. Morris interview with Messersmith, The Museum of NW Colorado–Craig.

25. 1870 and 1880 United States Census.

26. William L.Tennent, *John Jarvie of Brown's Park*, Cultural Resource Series No. 7, 1981.

27. Robert B. Rhode, *Booms and Busts on Bitter Creek* (Boulder: Pruett, 1987) 38.

28. Sprague, *Massacre*, 312.

29. "The Dead Buried," *Cheyenne Daily Leader*, 18 Jul 1880.

30. *New York Daily Tribune*, 31 Dec 1882, 2.

31. Sprague, *Massacre,* 321.

32. "Settlement of Ashley Valley, The Hard Winter," *Utah Genealogy Trails.* Delta County, Colorado, Genealogy and History. Genealogytrails.com/colo/delta. Accessed 15 Jan 2015.

33. This route took the Bassett family through present day Telephone Canyon, across Red Creek, over Willow Creek Butte and Bender Mountain before dropping into a cut where Willow Creek flowed.

34. Lizzie Delaney Bechdolt, letter written 21 Jul 1886, describing Willow Creek Canyon. Courtesy of Mary Bastian.

35. Josie Bassett Morris, interview with Untermann, Mortensen, Cooley, Sep 1959, The Museum of NW Colorado–Craig.

CHAPTER FIVE

ANN'S MENTORS ARRIVE

At age six, Ann was a pretty girl, fully capable of all day rides on horseback to help with the cattle. She was lightly freckled with long, reddish brown hair with loose strands of sun-bleached auburn framing the fairness of her face. Her father called to her using her given name of Anna or by her nickname, Annie. Most everyone else began simply calling her Ann. Ann's mother addressed her as Anna when she tried to convince the young firecracker to be more ladylike. Ann's big sister, Josie, the responsible one who was accustomed to helping with the children and the cooking and washing, needed no convincing to be ladylike and wear dresses. As for Ann, Elizabeth probably shook her head before giving in to Ann's protests against frilly clothes, then watched her young daughter shimmy into the buckskin britches Ann preferred.

Shortly after the Bassett family's return to Brown's Park from Rock Springs, Ann's mother underwent a transformation. Uncle Samuel had startled Herb and Elizabeth when he told them that he lost sight of their twenty heifers that were now grown into cows. Several herds of cattle, huge and small, had been in and out of Brown's Park, and Samuel feared the cows had been swept away in a cattle drive trailing out of the valley. The cows were fundamental to Herb and Elizabeth's plans and livelihood. Losing them would be a serious blow.

Just when it looked as though their search wasn't going to locate a single one of the cows, Herb and Elizabeth spotted a bunch of cattle branded across the ribs with a large 7UP. They immediately grew suspicious. Soon the Bassetts were convinced that thirty-nine-year-old Henry H. Metcalf had simply added a 7 to the Bassett's UP brand to claim ownership of the Bassett cattle. Metcalf, a cattleman who had once been a lieutenant in the Civil War,[1] had his home base in Elbert, Colorado, and was in Brown's Park seeking to build on his herd and land holdings.

Herb could not envision any recourse for proving ownership of the rebranded cows, even if there had been a law presence in the valley. He was demoralized and unnerved that the highly valued cattle were lost to them. He turned in circles and threw up his hands exclaiming, "We're stranded! We're just stranded!" Elizabeth, however, had other ideas and emphatically stated, "I know some of those cows and I'm taking them!"[2]

At that moment Elizabeth must have realized that she'd been naïve about how things worked in the ranching business in this remote country where the law resided a far distance away. All indications are that she decided a new kind of toughness was called for, and that was just fine with her. Soon she marched straight up to Henry Metcalf, looked fire into his eyes, and told him how things were going to be concerning the Bassett cattle. Wisely, Metcalf backed away and made no protest when Elizabeth directed a couple of local cowhands to cut twenty head of cows and calves from the Metcalf herd and rebrand them with a new Bassett brand, the Z bar K. The UP brand went by the wayside along with Elizabeth's blind faith in what it was going to take to succeed within the competitive cattle industry.[3]

Ann learned to love very few things as much as horses. She began riding as soon as she was old enough to keep her balance. Often shadowing her older brother, Ann likely let out a squeal as Sam dashed away on his horse, leading his little sister on a chase through the cedars and pinion pine, over stone ledges, and down a steep, sage-covered hill leading to the ranch house. This was home, the Bassett Ranch, with its endless places to seek out vignettes of perfect freedom.

The log ranch house Ann's father built for the family had become a low and rambling building. More than one of the rooms had hearth-warming fireplaces. They were each constructed with stacked and mortared native rock gathered off the mountainside nearby. The house had a dirt roof and, at first, dirt floors which Elizabeth covered with rugs and tanned animal hides. Before long, though, Herb went to work putting in wood flooring. Using his broad axe, he shaved and shaped freshly harvested cottonwood logs and laid them side by side to create a beautiful puncheon floor.[4] Elizabeth planted poplar and cottonwood trees around the house, and an orchard soon filled the spring air with the fragrance of apple blossoms. Herb piped the water of Joe Spring and diverted it here and there, to the benefit of all.[5]

Herb and Elizabeth sent for some of their stored belongings along with Grandfather Chamberlain's spool beds, feathered mattresses, and other furnishings. The items were shipped by rail from Arkansas to Rock Springs where they were loaded in wagons for the hundred mile journey to their new home. With Elizabeth's loving efforts of hand polishing, the wood on the spool beds beamed with family history. Some of the other furniture decorating the log house was pioneer-like, rustic and handmade.

Herb was a builder and used birch saplings to create frames for small tables and various sized chairs. The family wove rawhide strips across the chair seats and backs and then constructed pillowy cushions of stitched buckskin pouches stuffed with milkweed floss and placed them upon seats for comfort. Elizabeth traded ten pounds of sugar to a neighboring Ute woman named Mary for a bale of fringed buckskin smoked to a soft shade of tan. Elizabeth made the buckskin into curtains, and attached them to birch rods on rings made from the leg bones of deer.[6] Immediately after getting the house livable, Elizabeth convinced Herb to build a set of corrals and a bunkhouse. Soon, a sturdy corral awaited livestock and a one-room structure matching the house stood sixteen feet by eighteen feet with a fireplace at one end. The bunkhouse was furnished with four beds, a round table, and several chairs.[7]

On March 29, 1884, Elizabeth gave birth for the fifth and final time when their third son, George, arrived, joining ten-year-old Josie, eight-year-old Sam, six-year-old Ann, and four-year-old Elbert. That same year the government conducted a major survey, and the Bassetts discovered they had first lived in Utah Territory when on Willow Creek and that Uncle Samuel's place along Beaver Creek was in Colorado and so was the new Bassett Ranch. On September 22, Herb went to the county seat at Hahn's Peak over one hundred miles away and had the ranch properly recorded.

Also in 1884 Herb's organ filled the house with melodic notes swelling and receding. Because of that organ, Herb made a rare display of issuing a concrete pronouncement. He told Elizabeth he was putting his foot down—there would be no more transporting of large, bulky furniture over the hazardous route from Rock Springs. He'd had enough of agonizing when he made that last harrowing trip to bring his organ to the ranch. Several times the organ nearly toppled headfirst to a dreadful end.[8] Music would always be a constant in the Bassett household, with each of the children gaining a musical education from their father. Ann developed an exquisitely beautiful voice.[9]

A large cook stove fueled by wood was the centerpiece of the kitchen. Elizabeth acquired brass kettles and iron pots with which to cook for the family, hired men, and a steady stream of visitors. Located, as they were, on the eastern edge of the valley, just about everyone whether coming or leaving, stopped by the always hospitable Bassett Ranch. Neighbors, who were growing in number, visited often and the home gained a reputation for good conversation, plentiful food, and an extensive library of Herb's books. The reading material included *Shakespeare's Complete Works*, poetry by Longfellow, Keats, and Shelley alongside a variety of general literature. Some of Herb's newer additions to the library were gifts from Judge Asbury Conaway. Although Conaway continued to practice law in Green River City, he periodically journeyed to Brown's Park to visit the valley to which he was deeply attached.[10]

Ann Bassett's childhood home looked upon meadows sloping away southward while being bordered by the silvery growth of sagebrush and the varied green of greasewood. The grasses in the meadows were sustained by the water of Joe Spring gushing from the side of Cold Spring Mountain. The mountain, named for its many springs chilled within the earth before breaking free, formed the backdrop for the Bassett ranch house. The southern sky sat atop the crinkled folds and peaks of Diamond Mountain. Down that mountain to the southeast, the towering mouth of the Gates of Lodore drank in the Green River as canyon walls ushered the river out of the valley.

Brown's Park quickly became a social community where the miles between homes were of little consequence. Some rider would spread the word of a dance, party, or celebration, and the people would gather from both inside and outside of the valley. While food and drink was provided by the hostess and host, all the women contributed with some element of cookery. Some of the guests reached the host ranch a couple of days early to visit, rest, and help out before the festivities began. It wasn't unusual for the gaiety to last several days and nights with folks coming and going in buckboards and on horseback.[11]

Dances lasted from dusk to sunrise with a pause in the dancing coming at midnight for supper. All the children took part in the fun and as they grew sleepy were bedded down side-by-side in beds or were placed

John Jarvie was a talented musician. *The Museum of NW Colorado–Craig.*

in out-of-the-way corners on soft pallets on the floor. Several of the Brown's Parkers played the fiddle, John Jarvie was marvelous on the organ having nearly a hundred pieces memorized, George Law, Jr. played the accordion, and just about everyone played the harmonica. The rowdiest fun was had during the quadrilles when George Law's accordion pumped out spirited music and his deep voice resonated with rhyming words that led to twirls, howls, and stomps. One such verse was:

> *Allemande left and a do-si-do*
> *Birdie in a cage and round you go*
> *Promenade right when you get straight*
> *Take your own lady, and don't be late!*[12]

❦ ❦ ❦

Many of the Brown's Park settlers made their way to the valley and surrounding area by way of Rock Springs and Green River City, first drawn to those places by the mining and railroad work or the livestock industry. Many of them were immigrants. The different brogues, drawls, and inflections created a bouquet of expressions among the Brown's Parkers.

Ann loved being surrounded by the women who were, to her, all so very interesting and capable.

❧ ❧ ❧

The standard for the Brown's Park women had been set long ago by a trailblazer known as "Snapping Annie," the first recorded white woman to enter the valley. Loretta Ann Parsons and her husband Warren D. Parsons originally traveled from Quincey, Illinois, before making their home at Denver City. When they ventured to Brown's Park, Loretta Ann's arrival was a shifting event for the mountaineers, and that included Herb's brother. Samuel Clark Bassett enjoyed telling about his first glimpse of Loretta Ann on a dewy morning about a year and a half after he arrived in Brown's Hole. Out from the valley's stillness came an echoing, cracking report of a bullwhip. A wagon rocked and bumped across the brush as a woman called out commands before again letting fly with the whip. A white woman, with her man at her side, sat upon the rigid wagon seat, leather lines in her hands, and easily handled the oxen team. Samuel, a man who would remain a bachelor throughout his life, described the memorable day in his journal:

> "Brown's Hole," June 22, 1854.
> Warren D. Parsons and his wife Annie have arrived. And our first white squaw, "Snapping Annie," is expertly driving her slick oxen, Turk and Lion. "Whoa, Turk!" and "Gee, Lion!" Commanded by a female bullwhacker. "Houri" tells me that "Man's freedom in this Paradise is doomed."
> Samuel Clark Bassett.[13]

Snapping Annie and her husband stayed in the valley for some time before returning to Denver. Although Annie was never able to come back to Brown's Park, her husband returned to their cabin on Dummie Bottom in 1876. When he died three years later, he was considered to be the first white man to die a natural death in Brown's Park.[14] It was Snapping Annie's son, Dr. John D. Parsons, who attended the birth of Ann Bassett.

❧ ❧ ❧

One of Ann Bassett's favorites of the Brown's Park women was so stunning that she stood out like a single rose in a garden of other flowers. Known as "pretty little Nell" to the Brown's Parkers, Nellie Jarvie had an enchanting singing voice that filled eyes and hearts with emotion. She was born Nellie Barr in 1856 in Scotland and her future husband, John Jarvie, was born in 1844, also in Scotland. The couple's paths first crossed in Rock Springs in 1880. John was operating his store and saloon, and Nellie was passing through with her immigrating family. They married on June 17, 1880.[15] The Jarvies lived at the upper end of Brown's Park beside the flow of the river. The couple settled on the old military road on the north side of the river in a cove sheltered by hill and mountain, at first living in a dugout they'd hired built. It was a two-room shelter with squared sides and log supports. Hefty cedar posts split down the center supported the ceiling. A shaved cottonwood tree trunk was fitted to the entrance for a door.

The Jarvie dugout became a cellar when the couple moved into a newly constructed home. Their place eventually consisted of a general store, corral, shed, stables, blacksmith shop, and a stone building for storage. A large waterwheel built along the bank of the river lapped up and poured out water into a ditch that was used for irrigation. In 1881, after Dr. John D. Parsons died, his ferry and post office were moved up-river and across to Jarvie's ranch and John became the postmaster. The store sat on the stage route that came from Rock Springs and down Red Creek Canyon before crossing the river and traveling over Diamond Mountain to Ashley Valley. Nell Jarvie's life in the frontier was full and demanding and busier still, as four baby boys arrived, one by one. First to be born was John Jarvie, Jr., followed by Tom, Archie, and Jimmy.

❧ ❧ ❧

When Connecticut-born Elizabeth "Lizzie" Ann Wilkerson Smith Good-man met her English husband, Frank, she must have been fascinated that he participated in John Wesley Powell's famous expedition down the Green River in 1869. He had since spent many of his winters trapping in Brown's Park and exploring that entire part of the country. After Lizzie's mother married a man named Charlie Smith, Elizabeth took Smith for her own last name until she married Frank around 1879.[16] The couple and their growing family settled on a place in Brown's Park purchased from Molly Sears and began raising sheep. Their flock of sheep eventually caused the Goodman family's traumatic departure from Brown's Park.[17]

❧ ❧ ❧

Margaret Reed was a very pretty Shoshone girl. She was short and round with cropped black hair.[18] Margaret didn't speak English but that didn't prevent her from making friendships with the other women. Margaret had endured much when she was a young girl. During the early morning hours of January 29, 1863, Margaret's family was caught up in the Bear River Massacre near present day Preston, Idaho. The slaughter, led by Colonel Patrick Edward Connor, killed 450 and devastated the Northwestern Shoshone. Although Margaret was one of the few survivors, she suffered a severe foot wound that left her with a pronounced limp. A few years after the massacre, Margaret met her Jimmie. Jimmie Reed was an old friend of Jim Bridger, and Margaret and Jimmie wed at Fort Bridger. The couple settled on a picturesque piece of Brown's Park in Utah Territory near the mouth of what would later be named Crouse Canyon. There they began raising cattle and kids.[19]

❧ ❧ ❧

Before arriving in Rock Springs, the attractive Law sisters, Elizabeth, Jean, and Mary, traveled the Overland Trail with their other siblings and Mormon convert parents, George and Elizabeth Law. The Law family left their home in Scotland and sailed to America in 1868. In Rock Springs, George Law found work in the coal mines. At the young age of fourteen, Jean married rancher Billy Tittsworth and went to live with him at Tittsworth Gap. When the railroad was under construction, Billy worked as a game hunter to supply meat for the crews. Because of that work, he learned the country so well that he then acted as a guide for Texas cattle drives on their way through the area. Billy was able to acquire several head of cattle that had become sore-footed from constant trailing. Those cattle became the start of the Tittsworth herd.[20]

When George and Elizabeth Law left Rock Springs and moved to the Mormon community of Paradise, Utah, Elizabeth and Mary went to visit their married sister at her ranch. Before a year had passed, cheerful Elizabeth "Lizzie" had married prim and proper Charles Allen. They located on Green River Meadows (Allen Bottom) in Brown's Park.

On May 15, 1879, the month after her seventeenth birthday, Mary Law married Tittsworth's good friend and partner, Charles "Charlie" Crouse. After Jimmie and Margaret Reed lost most of their cattle herd to the elements, they sold their ranch to Charlie and Mary, and the legendary Brown's Park Livestock Ranch was born. Here, as Mary raised Minnie,

Stanley, and Clarence, Mary's husband raised cattle and horses, planted grain fields as well as an apple orchard on the large flat, or bench, on the hill above the house, and saw to it his children were educated. All the while, though, he took part in the seedier underbelly that persisted in Brown's Park including drinking whiskey to excess, gambling, killings, and providing sanctuary and fresh horses to his outlaw friends.[21] Mary's life with Charlie was not an easy one, but she persisted with a notable graciousness and love of life, family, and the Brown's Park community.

The first schoolteacher in Brown's Park was Jennie Jaynes who taught school in Lawton, Missouri, before coming west with her husband, Henry Whitcomb Jaynes. Jennie was defined as intelligent and good-natured and her ambitious husband, Henry, was labeled a working fool with a shovel.[22] In 1882 Herb Bassett became instrumental in forming the Brown's Park School District. In the beginning, Ann was too young to attend, but Josie and Sam Bassett boarded with their teacher and her husband in the Jaynes dugout during the school week. The Bassett children were taught their lessons along with the Jaynes children, Joseph and Levi. Before long, though, twelve students had been rounded up from throughout the valley, including Jimmie and Margaret Reed's children. By then the school had moved to a large barn at the horse ranch that Dr. John D. Parsons' son Warren Parsons and his Swedish wife Annie built on what was later called the Tommy White river bottom.[23] Herb hung tarpaulins to partition off a section of the barn. He put in a window for fresh air and light. Because the school session of three months would be January, February, and March, he built a fireplace for warmth. Benches and a table completed the school.[24]

When Mary Jane "Molly" Goodson married the first time and gave birth to a son, she was still living in her homeland of Wales. She later married warm-hearted James "Jimmie" Goodson. Jimmie, born in 1824 in South Carolina, was a hunter, trapper, and prospector and had for a time been involved in the Indian Wars. The family of three moved to Willow Creek and worked at raising enough vegetables, hay, and hogs to sell. The Goodson hogs eventually inhabited a lake area along the river about ten miles from home. Those pigs turned wild. Their sounds

Alice Davenport (left) and Nellie Jarvie (right) were two of the community favorites. Alice was inclined to mother anyone in need, and Nellie had a lovely singing voice. *The Museum of NW Colorado – Craig.*

emanated outward from within the tall, thick grasses and willows to create spooky tales of the place being haunted.

❧ ❧ ❧

Jennie E. Rife of New Hampshire was the wife of Buffalo Jack's brother, Edmund "Ed" H. Rife who was born in Virginia. Jennie and Ed arrived in the Brown's Park area around 1876, coming from Denver in the company of Charles and Molly Sears. The Rifes settled on Pot Creek on Diamond Mountain and were partners with A. J. Crittenden with holdings in Utah, Colorado, and Wyoming in an operation called the Pot Creek Horse Company.[25]

❧ ❧ ❧

Alice Davenport, a petite Englishwoman whose dresses billowed and swayed as she gathered up children to hug, lived on Willow Creek with her husband, Thomas, who described his wife as his guiding star and comfort.[26] Both were born in England in 1845 and were married in Lancashire, England. Shortly after suffering the sadness of burying both of their children they decided to go to America. Their next child, Joseph, was born in Pennsylvania in 1870 and then Thomas, Jr., William, and Esther were all born in Wyoming Territory where their father worked as a miner. Alice gave birth to Adam, her last child, in Brown's Park. Alice was inclined to mother anyone who seemed in need. She surely loved listening to her Tom when he joined with Nell Jarvie and Lizzie Allen in entertaining the settlers. All three were gifted with lovely singing voices. [27] Among their repertoire was *Last Rose of Summer, Believe Me If All Those Endearing Young Charms, Kathleen Mavourneen, and Annie Laurie*.[28]

❧ ❧ ❧

Mary Prestopitz was born in England and her husband, Antone, hailed from Austria. Although Mary, who was called "Red Mary," and Antone had two young sons, Frank and Phillip, they didn't seem to get along very well. No one was surprised when rumors of a divorce began to circulate.

❧ ❧ ❧

Although there was a twenty-four year difference in the ages between Catherine "Kate" and James Warren, it was a true love match. Tall and slender, Kate Delaney was born in Canada in 1859 to Irish Catholic parents whose families had immigrated within the fishing industry to the Canadian Province of Newfoundland. Both Kate and her sister Lizzie received good educations. In 1877 when she was eighteen, Kate married James "Jim" L. Warren in Carbon, Wyoming Territory. Jim was born in Mississippi in 1835 but his parents were from Ireland.[29] Although he had a trim physique, Jim was such a large man that all the horses he rode appeared small. He wore a full beard and was handsome. When he first came to the area, he had a small herd of cattle and built a sizable horse herd by capturing and gentling horses that were running wild on Diamond Mountain, where he had a squatters claim in Warren Draw. He and Kate relinquished most of that claim, except for some river bottom land on the south side of the river, and built up a cattle ranch in Brown's Park on Beaver Creek. Their homestead extended up Beaver Creek Canyon, over a mountain saddle, and into beautiful Little Beaver Meadows.[30] The Warrens almost always employed a few of the local cowboys, but Kate and her younger sister, Elizabeth "Lizzie" Delaney, picked up the slack whenever they were needed.

Lizzie Delaney was enthralled with the entire way of life in this "far away, half civilized country"[31] where the January snow fell in big soft flakes and the magpies chattered in the willows near the front door as if it were May.[32] Born in 1867 in Canada, she finished her schooling at Rocks Station (Point of Rocks), Sweetwater, Wyoming, before joining with her sister and family in Brown's Park.[33] Once she arrived at the ranch her delicate frame blossomed. Writing to her friend Hattie Reals in Laramie she stated, "I am getting splendid health and I weigh one hundred and fifteen pounds; that is just a gain of eleven pounds since I came down, and my cheeks are so red that I am almost ashamed of them."[34] Lizzie adored her young bay mare, Betsy, and loved taking rides with the young hired men who often teased her, until she blushed. She explained to Hattie that all the men were called "boys" in the phraseology of the cowhands.

❧ ❧ ❧

Elizabeth Bassett was instrumental in getting together the Brown's Park women, whose husbands were Colorado voters, to form a strategy that would enable them to vote in the 1884 election. If they became Wyoming property owners, the women would be eligible to cast their ballots in that state. Colorado was still nine years away from granting women voting privileges. So, Elizabeth acquired holdings in Rock Springs and several other Brown's Park women did the same. When election time came, the women left their children in the care of their fathers, climbed aboard a three-seated buckboard and drove away on an adventure of sisterhood.[35]

When Elizabeth and the others returned to the valley, they found most of the kids on their own. Elizabeth asked her brood, "Where is your father?" Young Sam took a pause in practicing jumping his horse over a hurdle of stacked kitchen chairs to ride up to his mother and answer, "Gone to hunt the ballot box."

The women learned that the men had ridden off in search of the wayward box that contained the newly cast votes of the men who had voted in the Colorado election. The box had been reported seen on the back of a wandering mule that was supposed to be in the care of Longhorn Thompson and on its way to the county seat at Hahn's peak.

When the Brown's Park men finally got home they said that all was well with Longhorn and the ballot box. The interlude in his trip happened when Longhorn found himself in view of a dandy herd of wild horses and the siren song of the chase couldn't be resisted.[36] The women didn't let the negligence of childcare suppress their excitement over their trip to Rock Springs to cast their own ballots. It was a precious right they had exercised together; a gift to the heart and spirit that bound them and would not be undone.

Ann Bassett adored these ranch women who filled her young life with examples of hardiness and grace. None, however, could match her mother. There seemed to be no end to Elizabeth's capacity to love her husband and children, run a demanding ranch, and still remain connected to the world. She adored having visitors and thrived on the grit of ranch life. Ann saw no difficulty that slowed Elizabeth's pace or ever caused her mother to shy away.

Because Dr. Parsons died in 1881, the Brown's Parkers looked to themselves to attend injuries and illness. When a young bronc rider named Harry Shannon had his leg severely torn open when his horse bucked into a fence, Elizabeth, along with the aid of Mary Crouse, attended the ghastly wound and saved Harry's life. After using Indian herbs to stop the bleeding and table salt as an antiseptic, Elizabeth stitched the gash. Tender nursing followed and soon Harry Shannon was back riding wild horses and turning them into working stock. Harry always credited Elizabeth and Mary for pulling him through. In the coming years he returned to Brown's Park to visit and give thanks, even after he joined Buffalo Bill's Wild West Show and traveled with the show across the ocean to perform for the royals in England.[37]

Daily, Ann watched her mother Elizabeth being the unstoppable force behind the building of the ranch. Elizabeth's charisma, natural ability, striking appearance riding sidesaddle across the western landscape, and her faithful inclusiveness sparked admiration in Ann and a fierce loyalty in the hired men. In the beginning Elizabeth could offer her cowboys little more than room and board but within that offer she gave them a home where they could feel they belonged, clean clothes in which to work, and plentiful, good food often shared with the family. This lifestyle was inspirational for the men and a form of tutoring for young Ann.

During that year when Ann was seven years old, an incident involving one of her mother's hired men deeply impacted the youngster. It was the first tremor of tragedy that she ever experienced. When the misfortune erupted, Ann watched her intrepid mother react, just as Ann had come to expect.[38]

Jack Rollas was a pleasant mannered young man, originally from Texas, who in the fall of 1884 rode in to the Bassett Ranch from Wyoming,

Charles Allen and his wife Elizabeth. *The Museum of NW Colorado–Craig.*

Left: Charles and Mary Crouse. Below: Mary Crouse. *The Museum of NW Colorado–Craig.*

Charlie and Molly (Mary) Sears. *The Museum of NW Colorado–Craig.*

looking for work. Because he had an excellent manner when gentling and training horses, he quickly became a real asset to Elizabeth. Not only did she need good horses for working cattle and pulling wagons, she was interested in breeding and raising team horses to be sold to the eastern market.

On a mild day in February, 1885, the adults' work and children's play at the ranch portrayed a peaceful scene. Two fellows, an Englishman in his mid-forties, Harry Hindle, and Perry Carmichael, who hailed from Missouri and was ten years younger than Harry, were helping Herb Bassett whipsaw lumber. Elizabeth was in the barnyard doing some chores. Hired as the ranch cook, Jennie Jaynes was inside the house preparing the noon meal. Her two sons, Levi and Joseph, were among the Bassett kids, scattered outside.

Jennie looked out the window and saw three strange men riding toward the house. After opening the door to greet the visitors, Jennie told them that they were just in time because dinner would soon be ready and they were welcome to eat. They thanked Jennie for her offer and then inquired about a man they were looking for by the name of Jack Rollas.

"Yes, that is Jack saddling a horse at the corral," Jennie replied.[39]

The three men, whose names were Jim Smith, Ira Hamilton, and Kelly, ate with the family and hired men, then went to the bunkhouse with Jack to have a talk. The four men sat around the fireplace for several minutes where, no doubt, the talk turned into an inquiry. A while later, Jack said he needed to get back to his work with a horse. With his back turned to the bunkhouse, Jack was reaching for a bridle when gunfire exploded. Jack lurched forward and then hobbled behind the barn. There he fell to the ground, mortally wounded.

In a startled flurry the ranch house filled with activity. Jennie dashed from the house and gathered Ann and the other children and swept them into the house just as Elizabeth, Herb and his helpers, all armed, rushed past. In an instant, the three strangers were looking up the barrels of rifles and a sawed-off shotgun while hearing the stark command that they drop their weapons. Expressing no resistance, the men placed their rifles on the ground.

Elizabeth had the strength of mind to carry on in the face of disaster and danger. Being well-experienced with her shotgun, she had no problem leveling it at the three shooters who had so recently shared the hospitality of her table. As she and Harry Hindle held the men at bay, Herb and

Perry Carmichael rushed to Jack's aid. They picked up the bleeding man and carried him into the bunkhouse where they gently placed him on one of the beds. They found three wounds: one bullet had entered Jack's back, another had found the side of his breast, and the third tore into the young cowhand's ankle. Furious, Elizabeth herded the three captives into the bunkhouse and ordered them to line up against the wall. Then she demanded they explain why they had so cowardly ambushed Jack. Jim Smith spoke up and said Jack had murdered his brother, and he had come with friends to avenge the killing. Jack weakly confirmed that he had killed Smith's brother, in self-defense, after the man attacked Jack for defending an older woman whom Smith's brother was abusing.

Elizabeth, while trying to put her shotgun in Jack's hands, told him to kill Smith or all three of them if he wanted. However, Jack was quickly failing and was far too weak to hold the gun. While Elizabeth and Jennie nursed the dying cowboy as best they could, Herb and Carmichael guarded the prisoners a distance away from the bunkhouse, and Hindle rode out to inform the Park people of the shooting. Most importantly, Harry Hindle needed to get word to Charles Allen, who'd recently been elected Justice of the Peace.

As the minutes and hours ticked away toward nightfall, Herb's apprehension grew. He was becoming dreadfully afraid that a lynching might be in the making. He needed to make a decision. At last, Herb spoke to the three prisoners and told them to go to the barn and feed their horses. Then he whispered instructions that they were to ride for the county seat at Hahn's Peak and surrender to the authorities. Elizabeth was stunned to look out the bunkhouse window and see the killers galloping away.

When the neighbors later rode in to the Bassett Ranch they discovered that the prisoners had somehow escaped. Although many were suspicious that Herb had purposely turned the murderers loose, Elizabeth and others who knew Herb understood his motive was to prevent further violence.[40] Of course Smith, Hamilton, nor Kelly ever went near Hahn's Peak. A $1,000 reward was soon offered in Wyoming for the capture of Ira Hamilton, where Hamilton was well known.[41] Nevertheless, not one of the three men was ever brought to justice.

It is unknown whether the Bassetts ever learned the full story of what led up to the shooting of Jack Rollas. The flame had been ignited when two wagons traveling together from Montana on their way to the new town of Meeker, Colorado, came to a halt at Meeteetse, Wyoming. A Mr. and Mrs. Baker traveled in one wagon and their daughter and son-in-law, Mr. and Mrs. Smith, rode in the other wagon with their small daughter. Jack Rollas was standing nearby when a quarrel ensued amongst the travelers. Smith, who had been tipping the bottle, became abusive to his wife. Mrs. Baker came to the defense of her daughter, remonstrating against such behavior. She then demanded that her drunken son-in-law drive his wagon out of the hot sun and into the shade for the benefit of her little granddaughter. Mrs. Baker cried out that she feared the child was so ill that she might not survive.

By way of an answer Smith sputtered the words, "If you was my wife I'd lick you, and I will anyway!"

Jack Rollas, a bystander, could hold his tongue no longer and exclaimed, "What a brute!"

Smith instantly went at Jack, kicking, slapping, and spitting on him. Then Smith attacked Mrs. Baker and viciously kicked and cuffed the older woman. Jack turned to Mrs. Baker's husband and said, "I wouldn't see my wife abused like that!"

Smith turned to go after Jack again. Jack quickly drew his pistol and fired, dropping the drunken thug in his tracks. Moments later Jack mounted his horse and rode away.

In time the Bakers, their granddaughter, and widowed daughter left Meeteetse and traveled to Rawlins, Wyoming, and then started for Meeker. Along the way they met up with W.B. Kinnear, who guided them to a ranch near Cross Mountain. There they talked to a sheepherder who had recently traded for Jack Rollas's gun, a very distinctive pistol with a steer's head engraved on an ivory handle. The sheepherder said Jack mentioned that he was headed to Brown's Park. So, when the dead man's brother, Jim Smith, came to visit the Bakers, they told him of the deadly events and the whereabouts of his brother's killer.[42]

Jack had tried to do the right thing in the face of witnessing a contemptible offense against a woman, but his gallantry cost him his life. In his last days, though, he had found a genuine home in Brown's Park at the Bassett Ranch. Young Ann was glad for that, as she stood on the sidelines and watched Jack's burial. She was still dazed with the abrupt shock that such a terrible thing could happen in her world. Lizzie Allen conducted the funeral service, Tom Davenport led the singing, and C.B.

Sears offered an invocation.[43] It was with sadness and prayer that Jack was buried at a chosen spot that would become a cemetery, located on a sagebrush hill that looked toward Lodore Canyon, and the forever beyond. As the last of the sun's light settled upon the mound of Jack's grave, tranquility began returning to the Bassett Ranch. The serenity would settle and soothe, but just for a while.

❖

NOTES TO CHAPTER FIVE

1. "Henry H Metcalf," *Find A Grave Index,* 1600-Current, https://www.finda-grave.com/memorial/26583258

2. Josie Bassett Morris, interview with Untermann, Colley, Mortensen, Sep 1959, The Museum of NW Colorado–Craig.

3. Morris, interview Untermann etc.

4. Morris, interview with Messersmith, 18 Jul 1960, The Museum of NW Colorado–Craig.

5. Morris, interview with Messersmith, 6 Aug 1960.

6. Ann Bassett Willis, "Queen Ann of Brown's Park," *The Colorado Magazine,* Apr 1952, 88.

7. Morris, interview with Messersmith, 6 Aug 1960.

8. Willis, "Queen Ann of Brown's Park," 88.

9. Enola Chew letter to her niece, Kristy Wall, 17 Feb 1972, The Museum of NW Colorado–Craig.

10. Willis, "Queen Ann of Brown's Park," 88.

11. Willis, "Queen Ann of Brown's Park," 89.

12. Willis, "Queen Ann of Brown's Park," 89.

13. Willis, "Queen Ann of Brown's Park," 84.

14. J.S. Hoy, Hoy Manuscript, 103.

15. Western States Marriage Record Index, ID No. 267157; *Ancestry.com.*

16. 1885 Colorado Census.

17. "Frank Goodman," biography by Mary Goodman Bennion, daughter of Frank and Elizabeth Goodman, The Museum of NW Colorado–Craig.

18. Morris, interview with Messersmith, 6 Aug 1960.

19. Hoy, 110.

20. William Daniel Tittsworth, son of Billy Tittsworth, transcribed from taped interview with C.A. Stoddard Jr., The Museum of NW Colorado–Craig.

21. Minnie Crouse Rasmussen, interview by Marie Taylor Allen, Author's Collection.

22. Jesse Taylor, interviews with author, 1981-1982.

23. Thomas White homesteaded the property in 1890.

24. Morris, interview with Messersmith, 18 Jul 1960.

25. Dick and Daun DeJournette, *One Hundred Years of Brown's Park and Diamond Mountain* (Vernal: DeJournette Enterprises, 1996), 186-187. Deed in Uinta County Courthouse recorded in the Recorder's Office.

26. Dick and Daun DeJournette, *One Hundred Years*, 35

27. Willis, "Queen Ann of Brown's Park," 89.

28. Willis, "Queen Ann of Brown's Park," 90.

29. 1880 United States Federal Census for Utah, Uintah, Ashley.

30. Patent Details, U.S. Department of the Interior, Bureau of Land Management, *General Land Office Records,* https://glorecords.blm.gov: Accessed 20 Jan 2016.

31. Lizzie Delaney, letter to Hattie Reals, 11 Jan 1886, courtesy of Mary Bastian.

32. Delaney, letter to Reals, 11 Jan 1886.

33. 1880 United States Federal Census.

34. Delany, letter to Reals, 2 Apr 1885.

35. Willis, "Queen Ann of Brown's Park," 231.

36. Willis, "Queen Ann of Brown's Park," 231-232.

37. Willis, "Queen Ann of Brown's Park," 91.

38. Willis, "Queen Ann of Brown's Park," 92.

39. Willis, "Queen Ann of Brown's Park," 91, 92.

40. Willis, "Queen Ann of Brown's Park," 92.

41. "A Mean Murder: A Brute Who Abused His Wife Meets a Deserved Death," *Aspen Weekly Times*, Aspen, 28 Feb 1885. Apparently the newspaper mistakenly gave Jack Rollas the name of McWallace. Although Ann Bassett's account in *The Colorado Magazine* proves only partially correct, it is probable that she remembered Jack Rollas's name correctly.

42. "A Mean Murder."

43. Willis, "Queen Ann of Brown's Park," 91.

CHAPTER SIX

BUCKSKIN AND THE JUDGE

Ann Bassett was of a new generation born into the bronco west and growing up among cowhands, dust, mud, and steers. She cared little about customary rules that bridled females. She wanted to obey her mother and please her tender-hearted father, but she couldn't overcome that wildness swirling within her thoughts that often spilled into her behavior. Ann felt empowered after she learned that she was nourished in infancy by a Ute mother. She believed that more than ordinary milk had been imparted into her through her wet nurse See-a-baka.[1] She felt the spirit of the Ute Nation in her blood. The ruggedness of Brown's Park and the rough-and-tumble family business of the Bassett Ranch fed the young girl's hunger for independence and adventurous escapades.

No matter how intense her mother's lectures became about the proper conduct of little ladies, Ann was determined to continue wearing her buckskin breeches, usually reserved for boys. In addition to her unwillingness to give up that puritanical taboo, she steadfastly refused to ride sidesaddle. It was illogical and she was quite sure that it was uncomfortable to the horses, causing back sores and galled withers. Ann couldn't relate to the grownups' certitude that a girl's legs were to be kept hush-hush, hidden beneath lengthy skirts. Riding through cedar and pinion and down rock-strewn slopes on a skittish horse while bound to the lopsided contraption called a sidesaddle, and doing so swathed in elongated riding togs, was not her idea of frolic.[2]

Ann did love the sight of her mother, Elizabeth, riding sidesaddle, especially when Elizabeth was on her favorite horse, Calky, riding to some special event. Elizabeth had a beautifully fitted riding habit of plush dark blue that she wore for special occasions. The long-skirted outfit draped and folded perfectly. A number of brass buttons stitched along the trim gleamed in the sunlight. The sumptuous blue accentuated Elizabeth's blonde hair and her straight posture enhanced the garment. Ann would remember and cherish that picture her entire life.[3] However, none of that convinced Ann to change her mind. Listening to Lizzie Delaney tell about falling from her horse while riding sidesaddle made Ann all the more determined to sit astride her own horses.

Ann's mother loved company, anytime, but especially during Christmas. In 1885, as they usually did just after cutting a pine tree from the mountainside and placing it in a corner of the living room, Ann, Josie, and Elizabeth gathered some trinkets of fall; the round, red and orange rose hips from wild rosebushes. Mother and daughters sat together for hours stringing the orbs for the tree. As the day of celebration drew near, the kitchen grew busy with baking, roasting, and candy making. By the time Christmas day arrived, so had wagonloads of neighbors.

Amid carols, food, and chatter, seventeen-year-old Lizzie Delaney told the other women and girls about the Christmas gifts she'd received. She described the pressed flannel dress she got from her brother-in-law, Jim Warren. From her sister Kate she received a pair of French kid shoes and five pairs of cashmere stockings. And, she said, "Two of the young gentlemen gave me a lovely pair of bridle reins and a horse hair riata."[4] Talk then turned to Lizzie's horse, Betsy, and the scary affair Lizzie and "Betts" had been through together when Lizzie nearly "cashed in her chips."

> It was in the month of August. A horrible old bull got into the pasture with the cows and as Jim was down in the Park (this was up at the summer ranch on the mountain) and Kate was doing the milking we resolved that out he must go so we armed ourselves with sticks and sailed in but he turned on us and we were glad to climb the fence. Well we got no milk that morning and in the afternoon I saw my mare Betts up in a little draw. So I went up and caught her and saddled and bridled her but she blew herself up and I could not cinch the saddle very tight but I thought it would stay for a while.
>
> Well, I went into the pasture, hopped on my horse and loped up to the other end of the pasture and there I saw the old snooper with the cows. He put down his head and bellowed and ran at my horse and she would not face him. So I went to a little bunch of quaking aspens, got a big stick, came back and told him to go and he came for my horse again but I made her stand and when he got close I wheeled my horse so as to dodge him and gave him a crack across the nose. Then I got him started down the hills and just as I was going after him to turn

him – I was going very fast and had to turn very quick and short. My saddle turned and I lit on my shoulder but my foot caught in the stirrup and the horse dragged me a few steps and then when I got my foot loose, I was almost under the bull's horns! And, there was no young gallant there to save me as there is in novels, either! I did not wait to see if I was hurt but ran and was over the fence in a jiff while Betts kicked my sidesaddle to pieces and then stood trembling when I came to unsaddle her and take her bridle off.

The saddle has been fixed again, but it took the two men a while afterward to fix it. I got some bruises and scratches but that was all, but the bull stayed until Jim came home and then they had lots of fun at my expense![5]

The Bassett Christmas celebration of 1885 continued on. As teakettles sang on the wood stove, women scrubbed and dried stacks of dishes. Some men played chess while others discussed books and livestock. Bundled up kids ran the hills pretending to be wild horses. Ann took it all in, including the full details of Lizzie Delaney's sidesaddle wreck. She heard details about riders being paralyzed or killed when their horses fell and instead of being thrown free ended up crushed beneath the horse. Ann treasured freedom in all its forms. Sitting awkwardly on a sidesaddle was never going happen for her.

Through trial and error Ann became an expert at evading her mother's authority. She giggled when with speed and concealment she raced to the bunkhouse and rushed into a world flavored with the aroma of leather, white muslin bags of smoking tobacco, and half-open foil packets of chewing tobacco smelling of licorice and molasses. Ann made herself at home hopping up on a chair or the edge of a bed and listening to the men talk of cattle, horses, storms, and memories. Sometimes men squeaked doleful tunes out of a fiddle and sang ballads of the range. In a corner of the bunkhouse, other men sometimes gathered for a poker game. The forbidden copies of National Police Gazette proved an irresistible lure. Elizabeth had caused her daughter's ears to perk when she emphatically denounced the magazine of true-crime, gossip, and buxom women as "awful."[6] One day when Jennie Jaynes was cleaning the bunkhouse, she gathered up the magazines, tore them apart, turned the pages upside down, and plastered them to the bunkhouse walls. The result was a bit startling to the eye but the walls sported fresh topsy-turvy wallpaper, and the exotic articles became exceedingly difficult to read.[7]

A perfect challenge for Ann came along when the adults conceived a ranch game for the kids to play at get-togethers. The rambunctious fun included cowboys acting as the bucking horses and kids trying their best to ride or rope the wild and wooly pretend broncs. Adults assumed that the youngsters would learn valuable balancing, riding, and roping skills. The fun usually began in the cool of a summer evening after work had been completed.[8]

Rocks, hardened clumps of cow and horse manure, sticks, and any other debris were all raked from the corral. Next, men and kids spread a thick layer of fresh hay out evenly to act as a cushion for knees, elbows, and hips. Following the precedent of actual rodeos, they charged a modest admission which they used for the prizes awarded to the best performers as decided by judges perched on the top rail of the corral. Spectators sat on benches and parked wagons.

At last a cowboy, down on all fours, bounded out of a constructed bucking chute with a courageous little rider on his back. Hanging on with one hand, the youngster clung to a bandana tied around the "front legs" of the human horse. The wild critter reared and fishtailed and bucked across the corral. So it went, as one performance after another played out with the bronco busters making thrilling rides on wild-eyed horses. Some of the tykes flew this way or that, tumbling across the piles of hay, while other stayed put until the cowboy's strength gave out and the bronc was broke to ride.

After participating in such rodeo gatherings, Ann became quite good at making her rides. The judges decided to have her try to best a big stout cowboy originally from Prescott, Arizona, who could really kick up a dust. As Ann waited her turn, one of the neighbors took Ann aside and on-the-sly handed her a small pair of English spurs. Ann was all for it, when her self-appointed sponsor encouraged her to secretly buckle the spurs onto her moccasin-clad feet.

Keeping her feet hidden in the hay, Ann knew she was going to get into trouble, but it was in her unruly nature to play the exciting conspiracy to its end. Ann shuffled to her ride and alighted on the cowboy's back.

The unsuspecting man from Arizona had no more than come out of the chute when Ann let fly with the spurs with all force and strength, jabbing the cowboy hard in the shoulders and ribs. The cowboy yelled and jumped to his feet, detaching Ann and sending her flying backward, into the hay. The cowboy quickly grabbed the young brat by the arm, knelt down, and took her across his knee. Amidst hilarious cheers and jeers from the onlookers, the cowboy gave Ann a spanking. In the process the cowboy made sure that, for at least a day or two, Ann would need a pillow if she tried to ride any other horses, whether pretend or real.[9] While she didn't blame the Arizona cowhand for his reaction, neither did she muster much remorse for the effect of the spur rowels. Although dejected that she was disqualified from the competition, it didn't stop her from cheering for her younger brother, George, who became champion at roping the cowboy steeds.

In addition to her mother and father two others were heroic influences in Ann's preteen life, her brother Sam and the portly Judge Asbury Conaway. Asbury Bateman (A.B.) Conaway was born in 1837 on a farm in McLean County, Illinois. Asbury's father was staunch in seeing his children well-educated. After moving the family to Mount Pleasant, Iowa, he enrolled the children in private school. Highly intelligent, Asbury completed the four-year liberal arts program at Wesleyan University in three years. In 1860 he received his LLB degree with honors from the university law school. He acquired the title of Judge when he was elected Justice of the Peace in Mount Pleasant. After moving with his parents to Chariton, Iowa, he found employment as a schoolteacher. Then, just as it had for Herbert Bassett, Asbury's life took an abrupt turn when he answered President Lincoln's call and volunteered to join the fighting in the Civil War.[10]

In 1862 Asbury Conaway mustered into the Eighteenth Regiment Iowa Volunteer Infantry and quickly rose to the rank of lieutenant. On January 8, 1863, the rebel forces, thirty-five hundred strong, attacked Springfield, Missouri, which was then being held by Asbury's regiment with the aid of a few hundred militia soldiers. Although the Union soldiers were outnumbered three to one during the engagement that lasted the entire day, the Eighteenth Iowa stood its ground. At last, the enemy retreated and Springfield and its valuable stores were saved, but Lieutenant Asbury Conaway was counted among the wounded.[11] In time he recovered and was promoted to captain. At the conclusion of the war, Captain Conaway was honored with the rank of Brevet Major for meritorious conduct. He was admitted to the bar at Mount Pleasant and reentered civilian life as a practicing attorney. He served a term in the Iowa State Legislature. Judge Conaway was a depiction of a man destined for success.

The life of Judge Asbury Bateman Conaway held remarkable transformations. *Emmett D. Chisum Special Collections, University of Wyoming Libraries, Laramie.*

Shortly thereafter, the sturdy, good-looking bachelor was nearly broke, drinking too much, and living alone clear out in Wyoming Territory at the gold mining town of South Pass City.[12] In the summer of 1867 he, along with the rest of the country, had learned that a party of Mormon prospectors had spent the winter in hostile Indian country in the Wind River Mountains on a tributary of the Sweetwater River. The group had returned to Fort Bridger with fifteen-thousand dollars in gold from the Carissa Lode causing two hundred citizens, Gentiles and Mormons alike, to rush to South Pass.[13] The following year in 1868 the Treaty of Fort Bridger gave a large piece of land in central Wyoming to the Shoshone Indians for a reservation and friendly relations were established between Chief Washakie and the white men. That same year along the southern tip of the Wind River Mountains a few thousand people swamped three South Pass mining towns, South Pass City, Atlantic City, and Hamilton City (Miner's Delight). Included in the populace were Judge Asbury Conaway and Asbury's recent acquaintance and drinking partner from New Mexico, Juan Jose "Joe" Herrera who was often referred to as "Mexican Joe."

In 1870 both Joe Herrera and Asbury Conaway were thirty-two years old. Joe, whose first language was Spanish, had held the rank of lieutenant during the Civil War while serving in the Third Regiment, New Mexico Mounted Infantry,[14] and went on to reach the rank of captain in the Fourth Regiment, New Mexico Infantry.[15] A handsome and intelligent young man, he had a temper. Men he wished to intimidate stepped away with caution or paid the price. At South Pass, Joe made a living with his younger brothers Pablo, Nicanor, and Catarino[16] hauling freight between South Pass and the Union Pacific Railroad. After Joe ran into trouble for fatally shooting a black man, Asbury Conaway successfully defended him but Joe knew it was past time for him to get out of the area.[17]

Joe Herrera knew about the cattle raising advantages of the Brown's Park country. The valley called to the Herrera brothers and they left gold fever behind and moved to the east end of Brown's Park near the Green River. There they built a cabin with a dirt floor and roof and developed a small cattle ranch. During that same time Asbury Conaway moved to Green River City and spent much of his time in Brown's Park living with the Herrera brothers and other Mexicans.

During Asbury's time with the Herreras, the valley's breezes sighed with the drifting melodies from Asbury's violin as he performed songs he had learned to play by ear. After listening to the neighboring Utes celebrate life and legend with their own form of music, Asbury reproduced the sounds of their vocal art on his violin. That pleased the Utes; some of the youngsters danced about as the white man played. Chief Dana, one of the best known and admired of the Brown's Park Utes, and his little son loved it when Asbury played "Rye Straw." Many a night the little boy amused everyone as he danced, either naked or in a short shirt and moccasins, around the wickiups and tepees. It was heartrending when the little boy grew ill and died. Asbury watched Chief Dana, who was grief-stricken, release his son's body to the river through a hole cut in the ice.[18]

Asbury's educators had described him as having an unusually active brain combined with a love for study, and they said he read mathematics as others read books.[19] However, during this early period in his life in Brown's Park he was veering awkwardly from his customary manner of achievement. Perhaps it was the horrors of the war that drove him to alcohol abuse, or maybe some unrelated but painful circumstance came in waves to haunt his mind. James Smith "J.S." Hoy lived on a place in

Brown's Park that was not far from Mexican Joe's cabin. As J.S. became acquainted with both men, he came to fear Joe and despise both Joe and Asbury. In the fall of 1874 J.S. went to Joe's searching for a missing steer. Joe was furious when J.S. asked to examine the brands on cattle hides thrown over the corral poles and strewn about on the ground. J.S. Hoy described the incident as follows:

> Joe drew from his pocket a long-bladed knife sharpened to a razor edge, using it to point out brands for me to inspect. The sight of this weapon in the hand of Joe, who was known to be ugly, sly, treacherous, venomous, deep and deadly, had a tendency to make cold chills run up and down one's back and goose flesh crawl all over him. At the sight of this knife and the gathering of the clan, the man with me left, having, I thought, an abhorrence of the shedding of human blood.
>
> Just at the most critical moment Conaway's huge bulk appeared upon the scene. Joe was war-chief, but Conaway was Big Medicine. He said nothing; his presence alone was sufficient—was like pouring oil on the troubled waters. Such is the power of Justice! Justice made manifest by two hundred and twenty-five pounds of an abandoned, degraded semblance of his kind, with a face as big, flat, fat and round as a full moon, partly masked with straight, stiff, unwashed, unkempt hair. One would think that out from the cavernous depth of such a ponderous mass would precede a voice compared to which a lion's roar would be as the cooing of a dove. But no, when he did speak it was in tones sotto voce and sub rosa, smooth and soothing, acquired by art and practice, in courts and in making love.
>
> I thought then and since if it had not been for Conaway the enraged Mexicans would have killed me. Joe hated me ever after; nor was there any affinity between Conaway and me, then or thereafter. Conaway was the dirtiest and laziest man in the Hole—white, red or yellow.[20]

The contrast of J.S. Hoy's description with the distinguished man who came into Ann Bassett's life four years later could not have been greater. Judge Conaway had regained his footing and was becoming a man of great and positive influence. As time went by, Conaway continued to practice law and serve as County and Prosecuting Attorney in Green River City. He became Territorial Judge of the Third Judicial District and then Chairman of the Constitutional Convention Judiciary Committee helping to write the Wyoming Constitution. On September 11, 1890, he was elected one of the three first Justices of the Supreme Court of the new State of Wyoming and became Chief Justice in 1897.[21] Judge Conaway

Juan Jose Herrera, "Mexican Joe," went from leader of a group of masked riders to a respected lawyer. *The Museum of NW Colorado – Craig.*

was described in glowing terms: "…of stalwart build, large stature and dignified appearance, and possessed a kind of unassuming character, approachable by all men, and liked by all for his genial and kindly disposition. He possessed the highest integrity and an unsullied character."[22] This dignified public figure was the man Ann Bassett knew and loved and who came often to the ranch to visit. Both Judge Conaway and Joe Herrera made remarkable transformations after their time together ended.

Joe and his brothers left Brown's Park in 1881 and returned to Las Vegas, New Mexico, where at age forty-four Joe married seventeen-year-old Juanita Baca. While his wife bore his many children, Joe and his brothers saw the encroachment of American Anglos into the prime northwestern grasslands of New Mexico. They watched land speculators, settlers, commercial ranchers, and the Atchison, Topeka, and Santa Fe Railroad work in tandem to displace the native, Spanish-speaking families. In 1889, this perceived injustice caused the brothers to organize a clandestine group of masked night riders called Las Gorras Blancas (The White Caps).[23] Joe, called El Capitan by his followers, and Pablo became famous for their vigilante activities, attempts to organize labor, and political activism.[24] In 1891, Pablo resigned in disgust from the legislature because he saw it as a failed vehicle for radical political and economic changes. Shortly thereafter, Pablo was killed by a deputy sheriff as he walked, unarmed, past the San Miguel County courthouse. It was rumored that he was gunned down because the law feared Pablo would reorganize Las Gorras Blancas. After his brother's death, Joe went on to become a lawyer[25] and fathered at least eight children. He died in New Mexico leaving Juanita to apply for his Civil War veteran's benefits on November 2, 1902.[26]

Ann never met the Herrera brothers before they left Brown's Park, but the two springs which gave life to the Bassett Ranch were named for Joe and Pablo, either by Judge Conaway or the brothers themselves. One day, when Ann and her brother Sam were old enough to make the climb, Judge Conaway took them on a remarkable adventure that taught the children the meaning of being in the presence of something sacred. Their journey began with a trek along the base of Cold Spring Mountain to Pablo spring and a place where a number of huge boulders had long ago tumbled off the side of the mountain to the meadow. Judge Conaway showed the children tiny moccasin tracks that had been chipped into the surface of slanting boulders and pointed to a twisted cedar growing from a rock crevice about a hundred feet up. The trio climbed up the mountainside, slowly making their way to the cedar. Once there, they observed a small but sturdy scaffold that had been constructed in the top branches of the tree. The structure was made from willow switches bound firmly with sinew. The top of the platform was covered by a pelt made from shredded cedar bark interwoven with downy rabbit fur. Wrapped closely within these folds was the skeleton of a baby that Judge Conaway explained was most likely Ute.[27]

Being in the presence of the burial cradle brought a feeling of reverence to the children causing them to step carefully upon the ground and to only talk in whispers. They could not have imagined causing a disturbance of any kind. Here was a mysterious and godly place, a location that they vowed to keep secret forever. On that summer day, a man who would never marry or have children of his own, gave young Ann and Sam a special moment in time that bonded them closer as brother and sister. The peppery side of Ann needed that connection with Sam, along with the stability of his guiding hand.

Sam, already a serious young cowhand, witnessed his little sister's desire and potential to be a top hand. He apparently knew that he needed to be unyielding in his expectations of her as he vigorously "rode herd" on her. He espoused a philosophy to Ann, "If you are going to be a full-fledged cow puncher you must play the game square, take it on the button, and never shy at rope burn or pistol smoke."[28] This guidance came to form the bedrock of Ann Bassett.

<hr />

NOTES TO CHAPTER SIX

1 Ann Bassett Willis, "Queen Ann of Brown's Park," *The Colorado Magazine*, Apr 1952, 82.

2. Willis, "Queen Ann of Brown's Park," 94

3. Willis, "Queen Ann of Brown's Park," 95

4. Lizzie Delaney, letter to Hattie Reals, 2 Apr 1885.

5. Lizzie Delaney, letter to Hattie Reals, 18 Sep 1885. The two who repaired Lizzie's saddle worked for Jim and Kate Warren. Their names were Angus McDougal and Andy Bechdolt and both were handsome young men who delighted Lizzie by accompanying her on horseback rides and taking turns among other suiters in twirling her around the dance floor. Less than three months passed after the 1885 Christmas get-together when at age eighteen she married Andy on March 19, 1886. They stayed in Brown's Park trying to build a ranch of their own for just a couple of years before moving on and ultimately spending long lives together in California.

6. Willis, "Queen Ann of Brown's Park," 95

7. Willis, "Queen Ann of Brown's Park,"96

8. Willis, "Queen Ann of Brown's Park,"94

9. Willis, "Queen Ann of Brown's Park," 93

10. "Chief Justice Dead," *Cheyenne Daily Sun-Leader*, 8 Dec 1897.

11. Iowa, Adjutant General Office. *Roster and Record of Iowa Soldiers in the War of the Rebellion, Together with Historical Sketches of Volunteer Organizations, 1861-1866* (Des Moines: E.H. English, State Printer, E.D. Chassell, State Binder)

12. American Bar Association, (1898), *Report of the Twenty-First Annual Meeting of the American Bar Association, Volume 21, Part 1898,* (Philadelphia: Dando

Printing and Publishing Company, Philadelphia, 1898), Pages 715-717.

13. T.A. Larson, *History of Wyoming* (University of Nebraska Press, 1965), 112.

14. National Park Service, "U.S. Civil War Soldiers, 1861-1865," *Ancestry.com,* 2007.

15. National Park Service, *The Civil War Soldiers and Sailors System: Soldiers Database*, 11 Nov 2015. https://www.nps.gov/civilwar/search-soldiers-detail.htm?soldierId=AA2EEFA7-DC7A-DF11-BF36-B8AC6F5D926A

16. 1870 U.S. Census, South Pass City, Sweetwater, Wyoming Territory, Roll: M593 1748; Page: 499B; Image: 293; Family History Library Film: 553247.

17. J.S. Hoy, Hoy Manuscript,172-173.

18. J.S. Hoy, letter published in the *Routt County Courier*, Volume 11, Number 1, 20 Jul 1905; Hoy, J.S., Hoy Manuscript, 147, 148.

19. T.A. Larson, "Wyoming Statehood," *Annals of Wyoming*, Vol. 12, No. 4, 1940, 286.

20. Hoy, Manuscript, 174.

21. Larson, "Wyoming Statehood,*"* 286-287.

22. American Bar Association, *Report of the Twenty-First Annual Meeting of the American Bar Association, Volume 21, Part 1898,* (1898), 715-717.

23. David Correia, "Retribution Will Be Their Reward: New Mexico's Las Gorras Blancas and the Fight for the Las Vegas Land Grant Commons," *Radical History Review Issue 108*, Fall 2010.

24. John Nieto-Philips "Herrera, Juan Jose, (ca. 1840s–1902)," *Encyclopedia of the Great Plains*, http://plainshumanities.unl.edu/encyclopedia/doc egp.ha.019. Accessed 11 Nov 2015.

25. Twelfth Census of the United States., Schedule No. 1–Population, State of New Mexico, County: San Miguel, Precinct: Las Vegas Precinct No. 26, 30 Jun 1900.

26. National Archives and Records Administration, "Civil War Pension Index: General Index to Pension Files, 1861-1934," *Ancestry.com,* Accessed 11 Nov 2015.

27. Willis, "Queen Ann of Brown's Park," 97-98.

28. Willis, "Queen Ann of Brown's Park," 95.

CHAPTER SEVEN

THE ORPHAN

The rush of the American cattle boom brought about the creation of cattle industry giants backed by wealthy investors. They grew accustomed to high returns while having their way with the western range, running massive herds on public lands. These types of ventures meant clashes, sometimes deadly, with newcomers who desperately wanted herds of their own and the respectability of being cattle ranchers, with an opportunity to make a profitable living for their families. Such were the dreams of the Bassetts and most of the other Brown's Parkers who were trying to build good lives on their own small ranches.

The Middlesex Live Stock Company was a voracious corporate giant that was formed in about 1877. Although its corporate headquarters was based in Boston, one of its operating headquarters was located on Currant Creek not far north and west of Brown's Park. The Middlesex employed what seemed to the Bassets to be, an army of cowboys. The big outfit turned out thousands of cattle on Middlesex range which took up a great deal of southern Wyoming. It claimed that its range also went beyond the Wyoming border and into Brown's Park and along Vermillion Creek.[1] The Middlesex sent agents into the Brown's Park country, riding in with the threat that Middlesex would buy out or drive out anyone in the way. Only a couple of outfits located just outside of Brown's Park agreed to sell.

Ann was just about to turn eight in the spring of 1886 when about a mile from the house she came upon a lone, scruffy-looking calf of the long-horned Texas breed. A bunch of cattle had recently passed nearby as herds were driven from the lower winter range to the grasses of the high country. The calf had apparently been left behind and for some reason, its mother had not returned to find it. The orphan calf, called a dogie by cowboys, sheltered itself by a clump of willows and tried to

110

nibble on the tender shoots of grass. Ann was charmed by the little heifer and knew in order for it to survive she was going to have to get it back to the house where it could be fed with milk from the milk cows.

Just because the calf was tiny, emaciated, and covered in burrs didn't mean it wasn't a wild little brute. Ann worked all day to coax and outrun the orphan, back and forth, before finally getting it to the corral. When Elizabeth saw the pitiful, pot-bellied creature that had, too young, been left on its own, she gave her approval for Ann to rescue the calf. However, it had been branded with the Two-Bar on the shoulder, two horizontal bars with one directly below the other.[2] This was the main mark of several belonging to the Middlesex.[3] Elizabeth sought to make it clear to Ann that she could keep and care for the calf only until it was old and strong enough to rustle its living without milk. "Then, you must turn it on the range, for you know very well that it belongs to Mr. Fisher." Fred C. Fisher was general foreman for the Middlesex. That fact of ownership caused Ann much worry and secret planning because she knew that she could never give up the precious little thing that she named Dixie Burr.[4]

The challenge of force-feeding Dixie Burr soon turned into a routine as the calf learned to drink fresh milk from a bucket. Eventually the dogie began to resemble a real calf instead of a motherless stray. By then, Ann had come up with a plan. She'd heard that Mr. Fisher had an office in Green River City. So when her father made ready to take a trip there for supplies Ann begged to go along. Both Elizabeth and Herb were surprised that she was willing to leave Dixie Burr because for six weeks the two hadn't been separated for more than a few hours at a time.

Ann was peeved at Josie and Sam because they had agreed that her wonderful calf was an ugly little runt. Ann refused to rely on their help with Dixie Burr. Instead she enlisted Jim, one of the ranch hands, who expressed to Ann that he thought highly of her little longhorn treasure saying, "This will be a big herd of cattle someday, good uns too, the kind that have sense and can find their own feed, not like them old Durhams."[5] Durham cattle, also known as Shorthorn, was the breed that Elizabeth and Herb raised because of the cattle's desirable dual-purpose as both beef and dairy cattle.

The trip to Green River City and back left Ann excited and happy. Fred Fisher, when approached by the eight-year-old, had given her Dixie Burr. She was joyful that Dixie Burr was safe, and proud that she was the new owner of an extremely valuable, according to Jim, bit of livestock. All of Ann's affection focused on Dixie Burr. The young girl was entirely convinced that the little tangle of hair loved her back.

Jim was Ann's assistant with the calf and helped her build a small corral with a shed just for Dixie Burr. The calf's accommodations adjoined Ann and Josie's bedroom, which soon became Ann's quarters alone. When Josie moved to another room, Ann couldn't imagine why. To her, there was no more peaceful or pleasant place in the world.

When the time came for Dixie Burr to be turned out to graze with the other cattle, Ann remained vigilant. Although the calf now wore the Z-K brand, it also retained the Middlesex brand so Ann was ever watchful when trail drives went by or cowboys rode through, looking for stragglers. Ann followed her routine one evening and rode away from the house in search of Dixie Burr to bring her to the corral for the night. The eight-year-old looked everywhere but the calf was nowhere to be found. Ann searched for signs at the pasture gate and found the very tracks she dreaded seeing; horse tracks following the tracks of a calf. Ann was desperate to follow the trail but because it was nearing nightfall she knew she couldn't.

Ann hurried home, found Jim, and told him about her fear for Dixie Burr. Jim's face showed the little cowgirl that he might be as hurt by the news as she. Jim was tall and lean with sandy-colored hair and a no-non-sense expression. His upper lip sprouted a thin mustache beneath a hooked nose. He was a Civil War veteran who rarely smiled but he was loyal to the Bassett family. Jim was serious about his responsibilities on the ranch.[6] His advice to Ann about Dixie Burr was to "git out and find that herd and stay on the job 'til you ride it from end to end. Yore dogie is there, so wash the tear tracks ofe'n yore face, git to bed, and be ridin' at the crack o' day."[7]

It's likely that Ann's sleep was not restful but rather filled with fantasies of the day that lay ahead. At first light she was up, dressed, and hurrying out the door to catch and saddle her horse. It wasn't hard to follow the course the herd had taken as the ground was pulverized by so many hooves trampling through the brush. She saw the dust hanging in the air long before she saw the herd. Staying on a trot, she finally saw the cattle, moving like a flood slowly engulfing the countryside.

As the youngster drew closer to the herd she saw that one of the men riding drag was hitting a calf with the end of his rawhide rope in order to stop it from turning back. When Ann realized that the little waif being abused was her beloved Dixie Burr, her temper fired. She grabbed her quirt from around the saddle horn as she rode up beside the unsuspecting cowhand. Ann screamed as she began whipping him over the head and across the face. Shocked and angered, the man yanked the quirt out of Ann's hand and roared with exasperation.

No matter how forceful or desperate Ann's explanations were, nothing worked. The cowboy was steadfast against giving her the calf. Ann's emotions turned to a cold fear that she might very well lose Dixie Burr.

The spirited ruckus drew a few other cowboys including a man named Joe Martin Blansit. He was a cowboy originally from Texas representing himself and some of his neighbors in gathering any cattle that had strayed from their range along Bear River.

Joe shifted position in his saddle and said, "Roark, why not just let the kid take the calf and settle the ownership later. It's evident the calf and the girl know each other."[8]

Roark whirled around and answered, "You son of a bitch, who asked for your advice?" Then Roark, already pushed as far as he was going to allow, fumbled for his gun. Joe beat him to the draw and in a moment took Roark's gun away. The two men got off their horses and Joe calmly put both pistols aside. They would hash things out on the ground, with their fists.

In the end, Joe came on strong and leveled Roark with a punch that sent him sprawling. When Roark hit the dirt, he was more or less knocked out. Ann instinctively jumped from her horse, ran to where the bloodied man was lying, and started kicking him.

Joe quickly grabbed her by the arm and exclaimed, "Shame on you, that's cowardly. Don't you know you should never jump on a man when he's down?" The words brought her up straight. She felt ashamed. Joe's words settled into her young foundation in a way that she would never forget. After Ann retrieved her quirt out of the dirt and climbed back on her horse, she cut Dixie Burr away from the herd. The calf left the other cattle without a fuss, eager to return home.

Ann later gave Jim her account of the incident. He mumbled that something should be done about that Two-Bar brand on Dixie Burr. The idea stuck in Ann's thoughts. She decided to add some marks to the Middlesex brand and make it look different enough that her worries would be over. She'd heard enough about the altering of brands to know that it was a risky move. She understood that such an act was outside of range ethics.

Nevertheless a few days later Ann took her calf to an isolated spot and tied her tight to a stout limb on a cedar. Then she pulled some matches from her pocket and built a fire and heated a branding ring. It was quite an operation with Dixie Burr jumping around and kicking to avoid the hot iron and Ann dodging and maneuvering. Somehow Ann managed to get a couple of marks scorched onto the old brand, changing its appearance from two bars to a rectangle.

After leaving Dixie Burr in a grassy place near a spring, Ann was nearly breathless with thoughts of her lawbreaking when she spotted her brother Sam. She confided in him about what she had done. Ann had heard the adults talk of horse and cattle rustling in Brown's Park. She knew that altering a brand was a crime and had little doubt that her mother would be very angry with her. On occasion, she had seen her mother's temper. Ann was relieved that Sam, now eleven, was not only sympathetic about the calf but also willing to become a fellow conspirator in keeping Dixie Burr safe.

During the first year that the Bassetts lived on their ranch, Buffalo Jack Rife took Herb on a twelve- or fifteen-mile ride southeast to show him Douglas Mountain. Herb was immediately taken with the loveliness of Zenobia Peak and its far-reaching views of Brown's Park.[9] Zenobia Basin became part of the Bassett cattle operation as the family's prime summer range. As Ann and Sam pondered where to take Dixie Burr, they knew their father was staying at Zenobia Peak while building a three room cabin. Herb rarely paid much attention to the livestock, leaving that to his wife and her hired men, but he enjoyed construction.

Elizabeth was happy to hear that Ann and Sam wanted to go visit their father overnight and readily gave her consent for them to ride their horses to Zenobia Peak. The children were in their saddles before daylight the next morning. Soon they were trying to get Dixie Burr pointed toward Douglas Mountain. Even though the calf was accustomed to being driven back and forth from pastures to the corral, she balked at leaving her familiar surroundings. By sundown, they were all three worn out with a few miles yet to go. Ann and Sam knew they couldn't stay out all night so they tied Dixie Burr to a tree and built a fire that would, at least for several hours, repel coyotes, wolves, or mountain lions. At a trot brother and sister headed for their father's camp.

Herb was happy to see them when they rode in and he never suspected that they had a secret purpose. After breakfast the next morning, the young cowhands left camp to find Dixie Burr. Although the heifer was hungry and thirsty, she remained tied to the tree and safe. The big cattle drive finally ended a few hours later when Sam and Ann got Dixie Burr to a far corner of Zenobia Basin where the calf very contentedly found other Bassett cattle with which to graze. Satisfied, the youngsters rode home.[10]

Roark, the man who worked for the Middlesex as one of the overseers, was suspicious of most of the Brown's Park people. He spent a lot of his time riding through the settler's cattle checking brands. He made it clear he wasn't interested in getting to know the residents or talking to them over matters of ownership.

In Ann's version of what happened next, Roark rode to Zenobia Basin soon after Herb left the area. There Roark found Dixie Burr wearing the childlike job of brand altering. According to Ann, Roark went to Hahn's Peak to lay out his complaints to the law which resulted in the sheriff delivering warrants to most of the adults in Brown's Park, including Elizabeth and several other women. Ann was convinced that it was her childish efforts to protect Dixie Burr that caused her valley to be branded a place of rustlers and wrongdoers.[11] In reality, the warrants issued to the Brown's Park people had nothing to do with Ann or Dixie Burr.[12] There were plenty of other things among the hidden deeds of Brown's Park that fed into a reputation that the valley was a hideaway for the notorious.

Notes to Chapter Seven

1. Wyoming Stock Growers Association, *Wyoming Brand Book*, (Cheyenne : The Northwestern Live Stock Journal, 1887) American Heritage Center Digital Collections, University of Wyoming. Retrieved from http://digital-collections.uwyo.edu/

2. J.S. Hoy, Hoy Manuscript, 216.

3. Wyoming Stock Growers Association. *Wyoming Brand Book*.

4. Ann Bassett Willis, "Queen Ann of Brown's Park," *The Colorado Magazine*, Jul 1952, 219.

5. Willis, "Queen Ann of Brown's Park," 220. In her memoir, Ann refers to Jim as "Slippery" Jim. However, Josie disagreed with Ann and said Slippery was a man who lived in Rock Springs.

6. Willis, "Queen Ann of Brown's Park," 287.

7. Willis, "Queen Ann of Brown's Park," 222.

8. Willis, "Queen Ann of Brown's Park," 222.

9. Douglas Mountain was likely named for Chief Douglas of the White River Utes who often hunted deer there. John Wesley Powell named Zenobia Peak and Basin after the warrior queen of the Palmyrene Empire in present-day Syria. During her reign in the third century she challenged the Roman Empire.

10. Willis, "Queen Ann of Brown's Park," 223-224.

11. Willis, "Queen Ann of Brown's Park," 224-225.

12. Valentine Hoy was the main instigator behind the warrants. The event is fully explained in Chapter 9.

CHAPTER EIGHT

IN THE COMPANY OF OUTLAWS

Within the rhythm of the valley's silver winds of winter and fragrant notes of spring, wolves on the hunt, and children learning to be cowhands, there also came wrongdoers. An element of lawlessness infused itself into the framework of Brown's Park, coming right up to the settlers' doors but not quite intruding into their world of dances and celebrations. Some men, often those who had been involved in the brutality of the Civil War and Indian Wars, interpreted daily life struggles as ruled by the law of survival of the fittest, or the most cagey and callous. Whether their personal hauntings raged or whimpered, sometimes with the aid of the fire in a liquor bottle, these men could snuff life away as though it was worthless.

Ann was charmed by Charlie Crouse's thoroughbreds, admiring their arched necks and beautiful bodies that gleamed muscle and speed. The young girl knew Charlie Crouse as just another hard working neighbor, building a ranch to better his family. His wife, Mary, was dear to all. In truth, Charlie was excellent in many ways but he was also the possessor of deadly traits. He was the epitome of the contrast of good and evil reputed to reside within the underbelly of Brown's Park.

Charles "Charlie" Crouse was born in 1851 in North Carolina. On October 10, 1853, James Franklin "Frank" Tolliver married Mary Jane Moxley in North Carolina, eleven days after she gave birth to a daughter, Clarinda. Just one month after that, on November 10, 1853, Frank also married Sarah Rebecca Crouse, Charlie's mother. Some descendants believe Frank, an apparent "slick talker," was actually two-year-old Charlie Crouse's biological father; the same was almost certainly true with Clarinda.[1] One can deduce that Frank Tolliver was abusive to Charlie. At age nine, Charlie ran away from home, taking little more than his mother's maiden name of Crouse with him. The young boy made his way alone across the miles of an unstable country shaking with the tension of the impending Civil War.

In his early teens, Charlie Crouse took the place of an older boy and wound up in the Civil War serving as a general's orderly. At war's end, the teenager had undoubtedly lost any semblance of youth along with the thumb on his left hand. He'd accidentally chopped it off with a hatchet as he was making a brake block for a wagon.[2] Charlie went on from there to haul freight across the Laramie Plains. He learned enough of the language of the Native Americans so he could readily converse. However, he could also shoot them without any apparent remorse if he saw the need or was hired to do so.[3]

The place Charlie and Mary Crouse took over from Jimmie and Margaret Reed was described by fellow rancher J.S. Hoy as the most romantic place in Brown's Park and an ideal Robber's Roost for Charlie Crouse.[4] Unlike the Bassett Ranch sitting at the eastern gateway to Brown's Park and highly visible to all, Crouse's Park Live Stock Ranch (later named the Brown's Park Livestock Ranch) was secluded. How many men came to the end of their lives there because of Charlie is unknown. There is proof of a few.[5]

Outlaws and Ann Bassett's valley were companions. Most often, the arrival and departure of men on the run happened in secrecy and without fanfare. The valley's privacy, close proximity of three state and territorial boundaries, secluded cabins, and relationships built with some residents gave outlaws a destination that offered refuge and fresh horses. It lay midway between Wyoming's Hole-in-the-Wall and Utah's Robbers' Roost and not far from Powder Springs, Wyoming, another congregation spot. Whether the coming and going happened on a large scale, Ann did not know. What she did know was that outlaws both in the making and hardened, rode the trails of her place and time. Some were her friends.

❧ ❧ ❧

Willard Erastus Christiansen, alias Matt Warner, was born in 1864 in Ephraim, Utah Territory, where at age five he was witness to the killing of a man and woman during a Ute uprising. His Swedish father and German mother were poor but good people who were Mormon converts. They raised Willard in the faith on a small farm in a two-room cabin in Levan, Utah. Willard didn't like farming or his job of tending the town's milk cow herd, but he liked horses and life on the range. By age eight he was spending most of his time on the back of a horse and relished taking part in the cooperative cattle roundups that occurred twice a year.[6]

Mary Crouse, an unidentified man, and Charlie Crouse pose at the Park Live Stock Ranch. *Used with permission, Uintah County Library Regional History Center. All Rights Reserved.*

Willard Christiansen was in his mid-teens when he got into a fight with another teenager, Andrew "Andy" Hendrickson, who was provoking Willard over a girl both boys had fallen for named Alice Sabey. One evening after dark Andy goaded Willard into a rage by gestures and name-calling in front of Alice. Willard first knocked Andy Hendrickson down with a large rock and then grabbed a scantling from a fence and used it to beat Andy's head bloody.

Wrongly believing that he had killed Andy, Willard ran for home. Once there, he hollered his goodbyes to his parents who had gone to bed, grabbed a few belongings and a loaf of bread, mounted his best horse, and fled. After traveling through storms and Ute territory, the fifteen-year-old made his way to the cattle country of Brown's Park and Diamond Mountain. Along the way, he decided to adopt the name Matt Warner. In a draw that led to Brown's Park, Matt rode into a place that had several log cabins and corrals. It was Jim Warren's cattle and horse ranch. Jim Warren had not yet met his love Kate. A single man who had once studied for the priesthood, he had been seduced by the call of the western rangeland. His ranching operation employed several cowboys, including George Law, Jr., Charley Ward, Jimmy Ryan, and Buffalo Jack Rife. The men took Matt Warner in and nicknamed him "Mormon Kid." Matt

Ellsworth "Elzy" Lay. *Bob McCubbin Collection.*

Willard Erastus Christiansen, alias Matt Warner. *Author's Collection.*

Warner described the situation: "I could see right off that Jim Warren's outfit was too free with the brand. In fact I could see that their main business was hunting horses and cattle that didn't happen to be branded, and they was crowding the Warren brand as close to sucking calves and colts as they could get away with."[7]

Jim Warren wanted his cowhands to have an opportunity to improve their status in life so he encouraged all the young men to lay out plans for their own herds and ranches. Matt Warner recognized that just about everyone accepted small-scale rustling from the huge herds on Diamond Mountain. Matt soon did the natural thing. Within three years, Matt Warner had a place including over a hundred head of horses he'd acquired by trading, breeding, and rustling. Matt's ranch often housed men who enjoyed hard drinking and poker playing at night and range riding by day. Matt Warner and the others often rode into Rock Springs to get supplies and carouse at the saloons. Only rarely did a lawman come near. Reality was that it wasn't uncommon for disputes to be settled with guns.[8] This mentality defined Matt Warner's close friendship with Charlie Crouse and their partnership in disposing of certain individuals, such as Buckskin Ed.

Charlie Crouse shot a man named Travis over a debt Travis intended to collect. Charlie admitted the killing but said that after an argument between the two, Travis shot at him and missed him but killed his horse. Charlie claimed he used the downed animal as a breastwork and then shot Travis dead. The only witness to the killing was Edward Rowley who was called Buckskin Ed. Before long, Buckskin Ed disappeared. Word circulated that Charlie Crouse shot Ed, knocking him out of the saddle as he was riding his horse across the frozen river on the Crouse ranch.[9] A cowboy named Joe Rose said that Charlie Crouse, with the help of Matt Warner whom he called a young outlaw in the making, chopped a hole in the ice and slid Buckskin Ed's body into the flowing water beneath.[10]

❧ ❧ ❧

During the summer of 1884, William Ellsworth "Elzy" Lay arrived at the Bassett Ranch along with some other young people from Rock Springs whom Herb hired to put up hay.[11] Elzy Lay was ten years older than Ann, born on November 25, 1868, in Mount Pleasant, Ohio. At a young age he traveled west with his best friend, William H. "Bill" McGinnis, and the two ended up together in Denver. After spending some time there, Bill McGinnis decided to head back home to his family. Elzy stayed behind and before long traveled to Rock Springs looking for work. When a wagon from the Bassett Ranch arrived in town with the mission of recruiting a haying crew for Brown's Park, Elzy climbed aboard.

Elzy had sandy colored hair and light brown eyes.[12] The teenager impressed young Ann with his good looks and well-bred manners. He was strong and energetic with a gentle, good-natured character that appealed to most. He wasn't a cowpuncher, nor did he show any interest in being a cowboy, but when haying season ended and the rest of the crew went back to Rock Springs, Elzy stayed. He worked at a variety of ranch jobs but his most prominent value to the ranch was the way he gentled and trained horses. After a year or so, when the time came for him to move on, Ann had no idea that the charming young man would tie up with others who had worked on Brown's Park ranches and ride with them into a bullet-riddled life as an outlaw.

About a year after Elzy went back to Rock Springs, Robert Leroy "Roy" Parker arrived in Brown's Park. Roy Parker, a couple of years older than Elzy, was born in Beaver, Utah, on April 13, 1866. Calling himself Ed Cassidy, the slender brown-haired young man of nineteen or twenty years of age went to work for Charlie Crouse. Cassidy was fascinated by Charlie's thoroughbreds, and Charlie quickly came to admire Cassidy's skill at handling and riding the racehorses. When a large celebration and horse race was held on an old Indian racetrack in lower Brown's Park, Cassidy was the jockey for the Crouse horse.

The much anticipated race was between a swift black mare owned by Ken Hatch of Vernal and a sorrel gelding from Charlie Crouse's herd. Ann Bassett and her family were all there amongst a large crowd and watched and cheered as the Brown's Park sorrel flashed past the mare and won the race.

During the socializing and dancing afterward at Charles and Lizzie Allen's ranch, Ed Cassidy appeared to Ann to be modest and undersized for his age. Although he joined the Brown's Parkers for supper, when he finished eating, he left quietly and went to bed without ever really taking part in the festivities that continued throughout the night. That young man Ann knew as Ed stayed in Brown's Park working for Charlie Crouse for about a year before leaving.[13] When next he returned to Brown's Park in 1889, he was on the run from the law and looking for sanctuary at the ranch of his good friend, Charlie Crouse. He returned to Brown's Park several times in the years to come as he rode the Owl Hoot Trail, later called the Outlaw Trail. He became one of the most famous outlaws of all time, Butch Cassidy.

❧ ❧ ❧

As for Elzy Lay, his first recorded participation in thievery came after he left the Bassett ranch and returned to Rock Springs. In 1887 a freighter named Bill Sparks told Elzy that a local dry goods store was going bust and that lenders had attached the store's goods. The Jewish storeowner had hired Bill to thwart the creditors.

After most of the store's inventory was packed into Bill's covered wagon, the unimposing storekeeper went to the sheriff and reported that his store had been robbed. The covered wagon soon drove away from Rock Springs with the store owner believing Bill Sparks was taking him and his ill-gotten merchandise to Uintah Basin where the goods could be sold.[14]

Nineteen-year-old Elzy Lay arrived at Matt Warner's ranch on Diamond Mountain where he found his friend, Matt, and Matt's thirteen-year-old nephew, Louis "Lew" McCarty. Elzy wanted Matt to help Bill Sparks double-cross the storeowner. Bill and his passenger were camped nearby, spending the night at Jim Warren's ranch. Elzy told Matt that Bill Sparks said that if someone helped themselves to the goods, the storeowner couldn't do anything about it since he was already guilty of stealing the stuff himself. Elzy added that it would be, "like taking gumdrops from a child."[15]

View of Crouse ranch in Brown's Park, originally named the Park Live Stock Ranch. *Author's Collection.*

Elzy Lay made it clear, though, that he didn't want to be actively involved in the hold-up. He hadn't yet strayed very far down the wrong path. He did, however, hope to share in the spoils as payment for the information he was supplying.

The next morning Matt and Lew sat on their horses, hidden in a growth of timber with four packhorses tied nearby. Before long, just as the conspirators had planned, the covered wagon came jangling around the bend with Bill Sparks driving the team of horses at a trot. The unsuspecting storekeeper, a smallish man with rounded shoulders and scraggly whiskers, sat on the spring seat beside his driver. Matt and Lew drew their guns and spurred their saddle horses to jump in front of the horses pulling the wagon and yelled, "Stick 'em up!"[16]

The shopkeeper's mouth flew open as the startled team skidded to a stop. Ordered to get down from the wagon, the man was limp as he slid over the front wheel and awkwardly landed on his feet. Bill pleaded for his life which further terrorized his passenger. The storekeeper was tied to a tree and Bill to a wagon wheel.

It wasn't until all the loot was loaded on the packhorses that Bill and the storeowner were released. When Matt told the two to get going and not look back, Bill clapped the reins across the rumps of his team, urging

Site of the outlaw's cabin on the Crouse ranch. *Author's Collection.*

them into a fast trot. After the wagon had traveled about a mile and a half down the road, the freighter pulled on the reins to stop the horses. As if the idea suddenly occurred to him, he began charging the horrified storekeeper with being in on the robbery and ordered him out of the wagon. After the stupefied man loped out of sight heading toward Vernal, Bill turned the wagon around and headed to Matt Warner's cabin to divvy up the goods.[17]

Elzy Lay, Bill Sparks, Lew McCarty, and Matt Warner had a grand time sorting through the items of their first holdup and taking all that they wanted from the haul. They all agreed, though, that it wasn't much of a challenge to deceive the helpless fellow, and they didn't take a whole lot of pride in it. Regardless, it was really fun, and the easy con ended up being lucrative.

When the dispersal was completed, the men were left with piles of items for which they had no use. Someone mentioned that the struggling ranchers and nesters in Brown's Park might want the stuff. All four brightened and agreed that it would be a manly thing to do. They nearly got emotional when discussing how noble it was to be generous, and it would undoubtedly make them instantly popular with the unattached young ladies of Brown's Park.[18]

When Elzy, Matt, Lew, and Bill got to Brown's Park with the goods, they learned that come Friday night there would be a dance at the schoolhouse. A plan had formed by the time they lugged all the stuff into John and Nellie Jarvie's store. The Jarvies agreed to distribute the items with instructions that everyone, young and old, attend the dance dressed up in them.

Word spread throughout the valley along with the merchandise. The conspirators hyped up the story so that no one had any sympathy for the corrupt store owner. Instead, the Brown's Parkers took it as an occasion to have fun. Friday evening arrived at the school and so did the foot stomping, dancing, and laughter. Everyone, including the entire Bassett family, was comically dressed in the rather cheaply made and ill-fitting clothes. Matt Warner described the event:

> It was the funniest sight I ever saw in my life. That trading post man done the best misfitting job I ever saw. It wouldn't have been so bad at that but most of the people persisted in hanging on to parts of their old cowboy and rancher outfits and mixing up clothes dreadfully. The way store clothes and cowboy clothes, celluloid collars and red bandanna handkerchiefs, old busted ten-gallon range hats and cheap derbies, high-heel boots and brogans, Prince Albert coats and chaps, and spurs and guns was mixed up would give you the willies. One old weather-beaten rancher was dressed like a minister, except he had his gun belt and gun on the outside of his long black coat. A cowboy was dressed like a gambler with a bright green vest and high hat, but persisted in wearing his leather chaps, high-heel boots, and spurs. A weather-beaten ranch woman, with a tanned face, and hands like a ditch digger, had on a bridal veil and dress with a long train. A big cowgirl come with a hat on that looked like a flower garden, a cheap gingham dress, and brogans.[19]

Daylight signaled it was time for everyone to head home. Ann and Josie agreed that Elzy Lay was charming and handsome as always. They sized Matt Warner up as being nice enough and pretty good looking, but a bit of a braggart, which was not in the least appealing. They were probably not surprised when a couple of years later Matt Warner had a posse chasing him.

If that first armed robbery hadn't been such an easy game to pull off; if there had been any sort of repercussions rather than the reinforced notion that robbery was exhilarating and could make a hero out of a chump, perhaps Elzy Lay, Matt Warner, Butch Cassidy, and the others who rode beside them wouldn't have been as inclined to continue down a murky road. Regardless, the seduction that pulled them into such a life found them to be eager students.

❧ ❧ ❧

Tom McCarty was married to Matt Warner's sister, Marie Christina "Tinny," and he was the father of Lew McCarty. In 1889 Tom McCarty, Matt Warner, and Roy Parker (Butch Cassidy) partnered up. While all three were lawbreakers and had, by now, done enough outside the law to brag about it, none had made the push to be full-fledged outlaws. That changed on June 24, 1889, when together they held up the San Miguel Valley Bank in Telluride, Colorado.

Days of harrowing and brutal travel while eluding the law in both the cold of darkness and days of high summer heat exhausted the men and their horses. The outlaws' heavily packed money belts rubbed raw rings around their bodies by the time the bank robbers arrived at the secluded Crouse ranch in Brown's Park. They were welcomed inside the log ranch house and given hot water and soap in order to clean up before being fed. Along the way they'd traded their fatigued getaway horses for some White River Ute horses. Charlie had them turn loose the spent horses and replaced them with three of the Crouse thoroughbreds.

Charlie Crouse gathered some supplies for his friends and had them follow him on horseback up along the hill's ridge to a cabin about a mile and a half southwest. The cabin sat sheltered by pinions and cedars not far from the mouth of a roadless canyon.[20] Charlie Crouse had constructed the cabin near a vigorous spring as a home for his parents when they came to Brown's Park to live. Just recently the Tollivers had moved to a place across the river, leaving the cabin unoccupied. The fugitives and Charlie Crouse had an understanding, an arrangement that would be repeated in the future.[21] The cabin was an ideal temporary hideout where the outlaws could return, whenever they found the need for shelter and fresh horses.[22] Swift horses and hideouts were going to be invaluable in the years to come.

The trio of outlaws enjoyed relaxing and playing poker as they rested from their grueling flight from Telluride. Three or four days later one of Charlie Crouse's hired men galloped up to the cabin door with news that a posse was down at the ranch house. The rider told the fugitives that they needed to saddle up and "hit the high places."[23]

Continuously looking over their shoulders, the outlaws hid by day and rode by night as they made their way to the relative security of the Robbers' Roost country in Utah. Their flight ended for a while when at last they found a place with plenty of grass, water, and shade on top of a high mesa at the end of a steep and crooked trail.[24] Of course, because of the life they'd chosen, there would be no lasting place of safety.

❧ ❧ ❧

In time Butch Cassidy and Elzy Lay became the closest of friends and began riding, planning, and stealing together. Ann Bassett described Brown's Park's relationship with the outlaws:

> Elza[25] and Butch returned to Brown's Park at times, but we did not pry into affairs concerning their private lives, for we were not the instigators of the short cut to riches Elza was taking and we did not channel the course he had set.
>
> Friendly relations between the Brown's Parkers and the bank robbers caused a great deal of comment. The question has frequently been asked "How could a people permit themselves to harbor committers of crime without becoming involved in the deals." The answer is simple. We were in a constant struggle to protect our own interest on the range where our living was at stake. Bank robbers were not a menace to personal interests, and we had no reason to carry the ball for the banks and trains. We had a fair sized job to do in itself. Law officers were elected and paid by the taxpayers to assume jurisdiction over legal matters of the country.
>
> We had accepted Elza Lay as our friend. And friendship among those youthful pioneers was no light bond. Because he had with youthful foolhardiness stepped into the limelight of crime, seemed insufficient reason to desert him. That breaking of the law could not contaminate us, unless we permitted it to do so. And we believed that possibly, given time, true friendship might become a substitute for the excitement of robbery. This was not a futile gesture. In the end, the purpose was accomplished.
>
> The older men and women among our neighbors, wiser in experience, were not so confident of the ultimate reformation of Elza Lay. They quite justifiably feared the structure of illegal acts he was building around himself would forever cut him off from reliable contacts, or a settled life. But youth ignored the protesting of the venerables, and "fanned" on for Elza whenever he appeared.[26]

A group of young people, male and female, from Ashley Valley were hired by the Hoy brothers to come to Brown's Park and put up hay on the meadows along the river. A dance at the Harry Hoy ranch was being planned when Elzy Lay, in his early to mid-twenties, rode in to the Bassett ranch to say hello. Ann and Josie were so happy to see their handsome friend that they decided he should be the guest of honor at the dance.

The splendor of young romance dominated the night after Elzy Lay took hold of the hand and heart of the princess of the evening, Maude Davis. Maude, the much loved daughter of Albert Davis from Ashley Valley, was a beautiful and graceful girl to whom Elzy had some time earlier been briefly introduced when he was putting up hay alongside Maude's brother.[27] On this night, Maude and Elzy were inseparable from first touch.

When Ann and Josie later rushed into the house, they chattered to their father all about Elzy and Maude. The girls were suddenly taken aback when Herb looked at them with the shadow of sadness in his eyes. Then, without a word he turned, walked slowly to his bedroom, and softly closed the door.

Although Ann would one day come to understand her father's reaction, at the time she was too young and happily excited for Elzy and Maude to be reflective about their feelings for each other. She and Josie knew that their plans to give Elzy lodging wouldn't do, so instead they sheltered him at the schoolhouse which sat over the hill and out of sight from the Bassett ranch house.

The next day Ann rode to the Hoy ranch where Maude and the haying crew were staying. Under the guise that she was taking Maude back to the Bassett house, Ann instead took Maude to meet with Elzy. When Elzy confided to his new love about his tarnished way of life, Maude was not dissuaded in her affections for the gallant Elzy Lay, not by his revelations nor by the weight of the standards by which she'd been raised.

When the haying was nearly finished and the crew of young people, including Maude, about to return home to Ashley Valley, Maude asked Ann to take her for a last visit to see Elzy. Elzy was by then staying at a hideout southeast of Brown's Park in Yampa Canyon. Ann would later tell that she was present there when Elzy Lay and Maude Davis were united in marriage in front of a preacher Maude had persuaded to secretly accompany her. Ann said that immediately after the ceremony she left the young couple to their destiny and rode for home.

Between robberies in the years to come, Butch Cassidy and Elzy Lay took jobs on a number of ranches and blended into the different communities as they meticulously planned and executed their hold-ups. The pair occasionally returned to Brown's Park where they had loyal friendships, if not approval, for the destructive lifestyle that saddened Herb Bassett. The charismatic but criminal pair rode together on an infamous journey leading an evolving gang of men. During its heyday, the band was called the Hole-in-the-Wall Gang, the Robbers' Roost Gang, the Powder Springs Gang, the Train Robbers' Syndicate, Butch Cassidy's Gang, and Kid Curry's Gang. However the name that carried the furthest and became synonymous with Butch Cassidy is one that wasn't attached to him at all, until newspapers picked it up from a Pinkerton memorandum in 1902, after the gang had disbanded. The term that was used to describe a band of wild horses or a group cowboys on a spree became the celebrated name of the gang led by Butch Cassidy—"The Wild Bunch."[28]

Notes to Chapter Eight

1. Toliver Family Members, *Descendants of John Toliver*, a privately published family genealogy provided by Frank Hall, the great-great grandson of James Franklin Tolliver (also spelled Toliver and Taliafero).

2. Minnie Crouse Rasmussen, recorded interview with Marie Taylor Allen, Brown's Park, circa 1970.

3. Jesse "Jess" Taylor, recorded interview with author, 10 Oct 1981. Jesse Taylor's father, C.M. Taylor, relayed to Jess conversations C.M. had with Charlie Crouse in 1906 and 1907 about Crouse's involvement in the Indian Wars and of Crouse killing Indians for their horses.

4. J.S. Hoy, Hoy Manuscript, 216.

5. William "Bill" Allen, recorded interview with author (his daughter), Brown's Park, 6 Jun 1981. When ailing and not long before his death, Charlie Crouse's son, Stanley Crouse, asked Bill to drive him from Rock Springs to Brown's Park to visit the Allen ranch where Stanley grew up. This ranch, originally named the Park Live Stock Ranch, was founded by Charlie Crouse. Sitting at the kitchen table at the ranch, Stanley unburdened himself to Bill and talked about his dad, including accounts of his father's involvement with killing men.

6. Matt Warner and Murray King, *Last of the Bandit Riders*, (New York: Bonanza Books, 1940), 23.

7. Warner and King, 38.

8. Warner and King, 38.

9. Hoy, 218.

10. Hoy, 217, 221.

11. Willis, "Queen Ann of Brown's Park," *The Colorado Magazine,* 225.

12. Harvey Lay Murdock, *The Educated Outlaw: The Story of Elzy Lay of the Wild Bunch*, (Bloomington, AuthorHouse, 2009), 51.

13. Willis, "Queen Ann of Brown's Park," 229.

14. Warner and King, 54-59.

15. Warner and King, 55.

16. Warner and King, 56.

17. Warner and King, 57.

18. Warner and King, 57.

19. Warner and King, 58.

20. Warner and King, 136.

21. Minnie Crouse Rasmussen, interview with Marie Taylor Allen, circa 1970.

22. Rasmussen, interview with Allen.

23. Warner and King, 136.

24. Warner and King, 136.

25. The correct spelling is Elzy.

26. Willis, "Queen Ann of Brown's Park," 225-226.

27. Murdock, 8.

28. Dan Buck and Anne Meadows, "Who are those Guys?" *True West Magazine*, Nov/Dec 2002.

CHAPTER NINE

OF BRANDING IRONS

Ann Bassett was of branding irons, grizzlies, and drifting trail dust. Together, the girl and her valley were romanced by wild horses, cattle herds, chaps, and big hats. Throughout her childhood, Ann Bassett watched Brown's Park perform as a magnet to men of all sorts; many of whom left lasting impacts on the portrait of both the land and girl. Most held a gut desire to make a living out of cowboying and ranching. Included foremost in that group were the very handsome Mat Rash, with whom Ann Bassett would one day fall in love, and Isam Dart, the tall and talented black cowboy. Isam and Mat became noted figures in Brown's Park. The two cowboys made their way to the Bassetts while looking for a home base from which to build something of their own. They rode in a tumultuous time; a tumult that built and swelled and, in the end, consumed them both.

Since before the coming of the railroad across Wyoming, accounts lingered in the air about Brown's Park being a haven for rustlers. Tales circulated that anonymous men smuggled stolen cattle and horses from wagon trains, into the upper end of Brown's Park. Once within the protection of the valley, the animals were said to have been rested, fattened, and branded before being driven over Diamond Mountain and onward to buyers in the settlements.

Some of Brown's Park's ever-expanding bad reputation was justified; much wasn't. Amplifiers, such as the highly intelligent but eccentric Hoy brothers, played a part in both Brown's Park's positive image but also in a narrative that became linked with assassination. James S. Hoy, especially, colored his valley home with dark strokes of a pen to newspapers and others, selling Brown's Park as "a den of unclean beasts, and a roost for unclean birds."[1]

After the Civil War, many cowmen got their start by rounding up and claiming unbranded or "slick" cattle from the open range. The common term for unbranded calves or yearlings was "mavericks" after Samuel Augustus Maverick of Texas. For many years, the practice of gathering and claiming mavericks was perfectly legal, though perhaps not neighborly, as indeed it was hard to determine to whom they belonged. However, as more cattle were pushed in, it became more likely the mavericks were the offspring of the massive herds of the big cow outfits and the branding of slicks came to be looked upon as cattle rustling.

While never on a large scale, there is little doubt that Elizabeth Bassett accumulated slicks from the thousands of encroaching and trailing "through" cattle, especially in the beginning, to help build the Bassett herd.

A story that would pass down in the Bassett family tells of one event in the very early days of the ranch: Herb spent a lot of his time indoors doing paperwork and reading; Elizabeth took the lead in working the ranch. One mid-afternoon Herb looked up from his reading to notice activity around the corral. Curiosity took him out the door and across the barnyard. He was shocked to see Elizabeth inside the corral with several large calves; each one appearing old enough to be weaned. A fire blazed nearby. It became obvious what was occurring. Herb couldn't abide it. His deeply religious convictions were wounded. Yet, this was his wife's domain, and she had the responsibility of competing on the range while building a ranching operation for her family. Herb said not a word. Although, as he sometimes did to express his disapproval, he clicked his heels together before he turned around and went back to the house.

Branding a few slicks or butchering and serving up the meat of a stray beef most certainly occurred. Yet, for the Bassetts and their loyal cowboys, including Isam Dart and Mat Rash, rustling never dominated their business of building respectable and productive lives. However, the description made by Matt Warner of what he observed goes a long way in explaining a common mindset held by small ranchers as they battled for a place among the politically and financially powerful cattle owners. His words also explain the inevitable anger, frustration, and deadly actions that came to pass on the side of the owners of the huge herds:

> Cattle ranged far and wide. The owners couldn't keep the growing stock all branded. If one finder didn't brand an unbranded critter, the next one would. This kind of condition always led to competition in branding that pushed most of the cattlemen and cowboys over the line in the direction of plain cattle stealing and led to all kinds of trouble.[2]

Isham "Isam" Dart,[3] was born about 1858 in Guadalupe, Texas. Whether Isam was born into slavery is not certain because a population of free blacks existed in Texas. However, Texas was admitted into the Union in 1845 as a slave state and did not officially end slavery until June 19, 1865. During the 1870 census, Isam was recorded as twelve years old. His father Cyrus, born in South Carolina, is listed as a farmer. Isam's mother, Indianna, originally from Mississippi, was only twenty-five with her eldest child Joseph listed as thirteen. Indianna was notated in the census to be "keeping house." Besides his older brother Joseph, Isam had two younger siblings at the time, Cyrus and Elizabeth.[4]

During the 1850s, Brown's Park was on a route for Texas cattle being driven to California to supply the influx of people involved in the gold rush. Herds often wintered in the valley before moving on in the spring. During the Civil War, most of the cattle industry in Texas stagnated, leading to an over-abundance of wild longhorns in Texas after the war ended. When Isam spoke about his childhood, he told that the white boys his age all had ponies and horses to ride, but Isam had none. When those boys went riding through the brush, Isam ran along with them on foot, always carrying his rope. Sometimes the boys would round up a longhorn for Isam to rope and then gentle well enough to ride. No doubt Isam was in training to be the top notch cowhand he soon became. It's not known how it came about, but in his youth, one of Isam's ears was partially cut off.[5]

Isam Dart grew up in the presence of a wide-ranging community including blacks, Anglos, Spaniards, Mexicans, and Native Americans. Although English was his first language, he was fluent in Spanish. During his teens, Isam was hired by the Blocker brothers to help round up wild cattle, a job that no doubt provided Isam good horses to ride. Isam's employers, John Rufus Blocker and his brother Bill, were ranchers and trail drivers. They made their first drive in 1873 and for many years after that the Blockers delivered Texas longhorn cattle to buyers in the northern states. Each Blocker longhorn was marked with a trail brand consisting of a simple reverse number seven. According to cowboy Tap Duncan, who knew Isam in Texas, in 1881 the Blockers, if their separate drives were counted together, had around one hundred thousand head of cattle on the trail between Texas and Wyoming. Isam Dart was one of the drovers among them.[6]

Perhaps this wasn't Isam's first big cattle drive for the Blockers, but it was his last. After the Blocker cattle were delivered, Isam found himself in the Sandhills area of north central Nebraska.[7] Not long after, Isam worked in Wyoming as a horse wrangler for the giant Middlesex outfit. In time Isam made his way into Brown's Park where he was enticed to stay by the appeal of the Bassett family and Brown's Park's aura. Elizabeth hired him, and he was welcomed into the circle of her cowboys. Isam was not only an expert with horses, but he was also a fantastic cook and played both the fiddle and harmonica.[8] But, his long journey from his Texas upbringing to the Bassett Ranch in Colorado had placed him on a path of clashing notoriety.

Madison Matthew "Mat" Rash was born about seven years after Isam Dart, on January 4, 1865. His family home was in Acton, Texas. His parents, Samuel and Mary Ann Rash, came to Texas from Jackson, Alabama. By 1880 Mat was the sixth child growing up amongst nine brothers and sisters.

Mat Rash went north driving Texas longhorns, the same as Isam Dart and countless other young men. His particular trail drive for the Turkey Tracks Ranch took him into Wyoming in 1882 to the Middlesex Ranch. Mat stayed in Wyoming and went to work for the "G" outfit, south of Bitter Creek, one of the Middlesex outfits. Mat discovered he didn't like the way the corporation did business. To him it seemed greedy, always hungry for more land, and bent on pushing against the small ranchers to swallow up whatever it could. Mat Rash left the throng of cowboys working for the Middlesex and went to work as range manager for Tim Kinney's Circle K Cattle Ranch northeast of Brown's Park. He watched the Brown's Park ranchers join forces to hold on and stand against the Middlesex and its deluge of cattle.

After the Middlesex overran Tim Kinney's range and forced him out of the cattle business, Mat Rash took the small bunch of cattle he'd accumulated and some financial backing from Tim Kinney and drove the herd into Brown's Park. There he, too, ended up at the Bassett Ranch. In the meantime, after Tim Kinney gave in and sold his land to the Middlesex, Tim bought sheep. Along with two early-day Brown's Park cattlemen, Griff and Jack Edwards, he put large flocks of sheep on the surrounding range.

More and more people were filing for land claims on the western rangeland putting further pressure against the free-range era of operations such as the Middlesex. The competition from sheep for grass on land that the Middlesex was already overgrazing, a drop in cattle prices that hit hard in the mid-1880s, and the deadly-fierce winter of 1886-1887 all worked together to greatly diminish the Middlesex Live Stock Company. The corporation ultimately failed. This, of course, was a great relief to the Brown's Park cattle ranchers who were dealing with their own struggles against the elements and cattle prices. J.S. Hoy, who had a love/hate relationship with Brown's Park and life in general, was the one Brown's Parker who stated that he regretted not selling out to the Middlesex when he had the chance.

James Smith "J.S." Hoy, in 1872 and at the age of twenty-five, was employed by the Crawford-Thompson Company near Evanston, Wyoming. J.S. was directed to help take a herd of cattle to Brown's Park and stay there through the winter. He agreed to go but was uneasy after he heard talk that the valley was a haven for lawless men and blood-drinking Utes.[9] The cattle drive was a brutal one with frigid cold and a blizzard that ushered the cattle into the mysterious valley. When J.S., the other cowboys, and their weary horses and cattle came out of the mouth of Red Creek Canyon, the relief to their bodies must have been extraordinary. J.S. Hoy later noted:

> While winter storms raged on the mountains around about, and snow fell deep and lay until warm spring rains and summer came, down in Brown's Hole all was calm with bright sunshine, although cold enough to freeze Green River over except where it ran rapidly. When we emerged into the Hole the ground was bare of snow, while the mountains all around showed white except where the ground was hidden by cedars and pinions. This difference was one of the mysteries of this unknown, wonderful and dread country. Nothing here was like things elsewhere.[10]

Four years later, J.S. Hoy and his brother, Valentine, had a flourishing partnership, Hoy Brothers, Inc., with holdings and livestock in Brown's Park, Evanston, and Fremont, Nebraska. Their brother, Adea, taught school in Evanston. Adea wrote their only sister, Emily, that Valentine and J.S. had one of the finest cattle herds in the country and that Valentine stayed in the mountains with the cattle, though he was a scholar on any subject.[11] J.S. wrote Emily that Valentine "is as big and as rough as a grizzly bear, but a more whole souled and better hearted fellow never lived."[12]

Valentine Shade Hoy was born in 1849 in Pennsylvania. The third of six children, his siblings oldest to youngest were Frank, J.S., Emily, Adea, and Henry "Harry." All the brothers at one time or another lived and ranched in Brown's Park. Their properties lined the north side of the river and took in all the natural meadows along the river that became known as Hoy Bottoms.

Valentine was the star of the brothers in personality and ambition. Good looking with grey eyes and brown hair, he dreamed big, sometimes to the detriment of others. Herb and Elizabeth Bassett were distressed to learn that their neighbor and friend tried to snatch the Bassett Ranch right out from under them.

In 1884, J.S. Hoy was away in France purchasing draft horses when Deputy U.S. Land Surveyor Major D.C. Oakes arrived in Brown's Park.[13] Valentine hired on with the surveying crew as cook. That gave Valentine inside access to where and when the area's boundaries were designated. Up until the survey, residents could claim squatters' rights on their places. Once the boundaries were formed, legal title could be filed. Herb went to the county seat at Hahn's Peak as soon as his ranch's boundaries were designated and filed the proper paperwork. He and Elizabeth were stunned when they heard Valentine Hoy had arrived at Hahn's Peak shortly after Herb and tried to file on the Bassett Ranch.

Herb and Elizabeth continued to be neighborly and share a social life with the Hoys. They cordially welcomed Valentine's new wife, Julia Blair Hoy, when she arrived from Nebraska. Nonetheless, Herb and Elizabeth never again trusted the Hoys nor forgave Valentine for his treachery. [14]

In early July 1888, Valentine had taken part in the big Brown's Park roundup and branding that was just concluding. The roundup had involved fifty cowhands from throughout the valley, including Elizabeth Bassett. Frank Hoy had recently passed away but Adea, J.S., Valentine, and Harry were all in the Park and living in close proximity. That didn't work out so well.

A court case between Adea and Hoy Brothers was ongoing from 1887 to 1890. In August 1888, J.S. went to Green River City and filed papers to sue his brother Adea for $4,184 for a debt he claimed was owed to Hoy Brothers. Adea countered with his own bill of between $6,000 and $7,000. The whole affair took the heart out of the horse and cattle business for Adea, and he began making plans to leave. He described

Brown's Park as having as many outlaws and thieves to the square inch as could be found anywhere in Texas and said that although Valentine took an active part in helping a sheriff with a wholesale roundup of thieves, a grand jury in Hahn's Peak failed to indict anyone. Adea went on to say that when Valentine returned to the ranch, he found some of his fences cut and downed and a herd of twenty of his horses missing.[15]

The event described by Adea Hoy about Valentine assisting a sheriff in the wholesale rounding up of thieves was in 1888 and was perpetuated by Valentine Hoy against his neighbors. Over a dozen arrest warrants were sworn out against mostly Brown's Park people, some of whom were wives and mothers, including Elizabeth Bassett. The Hoy brothers were experiencing hard times in the livestock business and believed that everyone was against them. Valentine complained that those who weren't stealing his cattle were in league to protect those who did. There was not yet a courthouse or jail at Hahn's Peak. Court was held in a log cabin. The prisoners, including Herb and Elizabeth Bassett, were guarded by Sheriff Robert "Buck" Buchanan and his deputies. Some of the accused were housed in a washroom, others in a mining cabin. Elizabeth was locked in a hotel room. In the end, no indictments were made and all of the Brown's Parkers were released for lack of evidence.[16]

Valentine wrote to his sister Emily and expressed to her that their youngest brother Harry was turning into a bad man and getting one of the worst names of any man around for stealing cattle and that none of the other brothers was on speaking terms with Harry.[17] In March 1889, Harry sued Valentine and J.S. for selling four head of his steers and several tons of his hay. Harry won in district court and his two brothers were ordered to pay him $280.[18]

Harry wasn't getting along with Elizabeth Bassett and her cowhands, either. Apparently Harry was making plenty of enemies. During different times when Harry was away from home, intruders went inside the house and stole provisions and other things. It appeared to be more about pestering and animosity than thievery. Regardless, having had enough of the interlopers, one of Harry's brothers helped a hired man rig up a spring gun to fire if Harry's door was opened while Harry was away bringing some of his cattle off Diamond Mountain for the winter.[19]

On November 5, 1889, ranch hand Charles Colan was the unfortunate fellow who felt the deafening blast from the spring gun rip through his leg. Colan was accompanied by some of Elizabeth Bassett's men including Isam Dart, Angus McDougal, Fred Reynolds, and Jack Fitch. The group was at first stunned, but moments later tempers roared and Harry's home, barns, corrals, and haystack were soon burning in a tantrum of flames. The chilling declaration was made that if Colan died, there wouldn't be a Hoy living by morning.[20]

Because Charles Colan was one of Elizabeth's men, she may have been the one who tended the wound. The injury wasn't life-threatening and before long he was able to ride away and disappear before the law got involved. On January 21, 1890, Elizabeth Bassett, the missing Charles Colan, Isam Dart, Fred Reynolds, C.W. Carrington, J.C. Allen, Willis Rouff, and George Law were named in a complaint of arson and grand larceny stemming from events at Harry Hoy's place. Isam Dart, Jack Fitch, and Angus McDougal eventually had charges filed and warrants issued against them.

The arson case was ongoing when the following May, Elizabeth found out that Harry Hoy had possession of one of her calves, a distinctive several-month-old blue roan heifer. The following morning Elizabeth sent Mat Rash, Joe Redford, and Sam Bassett, now fourteen, to retrieve the calf. After arriving at Harry Hoy's place, which was in the process of being rebuilt, they asked if there were any Z-K cattle in his pasture. Harry boldly answered that he had a calf wearing a Z-K but was adamant that it belonged to him. Harry wouldn't let the men see the heifer.

That same afternoon, Elizabeth Bassett was fuming when she mounted her horse and positioned herself in the sidesaddle. Ann desperately wanted to go along but her mother told her that this was not the time. Instead, it was Mat Rash and Sam who rode beside the poised and assertive cattlewoman as the three riders made for Harry's Hoy's place.

In the meantime, Harry was making sure that he and the roan calf were nowhere in sight in anticipation of a confrontation with Elizabeth Bassett. He knew Elizabeth's temper; it could scald a man. Harry and others were certain Elizabeth's men were behind the damage at his place. He couldn't be sure how this new conflict between the Bassetts and the Hoys would play out. He quickly packed some supplies, climbed on his horse, and gathered up several head of cattle including the blue roan calf that was now wearing not only the Z-K brand but also his own A6 brand on not one, but both, sides, proving his determination to claim the calf. Harry pushed the heifer and other cattle across the river and headed them up country, trailing them to Sears Canyon and on to his summer range on Diamond Mountain.

When Elizabeth, Sam, and Mat reached Harry's place they were met by Valentine Hoy's father-in-law, William Blair, and a hired man named John Martin. Although the two admitted to having possession of such a calf, they said they had been instructed to say they would release it only after Elizabeth provided a writ of replevin, a legal claim to get back stolen property, from J.C. Allen, who was still the local Justice of the Peace. And so, a legal battle ignited with Elizabeth as plaintiff and Harry the defendant. The wrangling went on for months with fees, witnesses, and paperwork mounting, all of it over a ten-dollar calf. Elizabeth never saw the heifer again but by the end of the year, Harry was ordered to pay Elizabeth ten dollars for the calf but also $212 in court costs.

Back in September during the term of court in Routt County at Hahn's Peak, Isam Dart, Angus McDougal and Jack Fitch had been arrested and not only charged with the arson and larceny of Harry Hoy's property, but Isam and Angus had also been charged with stealing a grey two-year-old colt valued at $25 that was branded HOY, a three-year-old colt worth $100, and a $60 bay mare also branded HOY. The evening before the trial got started Isam simply walked away and absconded. Apparently the law had little incentive to go after him for he was little pursued. Angus and Jack were found guilty and both did a stint in prison.[21]

This wasn't Isam's first go round with the law since coming to Brown's Park. On September 1888, he had been indicted on three counts of branding "neat" cattle, filed in Sweetwater County, Wyoming Territory. *The Rock Springs Miner* reported the eventful arrest:

> When Deputy Sheriff E.P. Philbrick, accompanied by Robert Franklin, was bringing in under arrest Isam Dart, the horses became frightened and there was a lively run away down Quaken [Quaking] Aspen Mountain. Jim was thrown out, also Isam Dart, and both received severe injuries. Jim was cut about the head, while Isam's principal mishap was a sprained leg. Both were confined to their bed for several days, but we are glad to state that Jim is able to be around again, and Isam after giving $2,500 bail has returned to his ranch. Isam Dart is the colored gentleman who was indicted during last term of court for misbranding cattle. He had no difficulty in finding good bondsmen. His case will probably be tried at the spring term of the district court.[22]

Isam never did go to trial. Instead, on April 30, 1889, each of the charges was dropped by the prosecuting attorney in and for Sweetwater County, who happened to be Brown's Park's old friend, Asbury B. Conaway, Esquire. No doubt Isam was relieved and grateful to Judge Conaway but he was very angry at the deputy sheriff who arrested him. Isam hired a lawyer and filed suit against Philbrick accusing the deputy of not having the authority to arrest him and take him to Wyoming which caused him to be falsely imprisoned for five days. Isam asked for $5000 in damages. In this case, though, Asbury Conaway represented the deputy, and on October 4, 1889, Philbrick was found not guilty.[23]

Just a month later, Isam found himself entangled in the Harry Hoy incident. After slipping away from the jail guard at Hahn's Peak, Isam stayed away from Brown's Park for an extended period. In time, he openly returned and continued his loyalty to Elizabeth and the Bassett family.

In May 1890, the Bassetts were terribly saddened when they received word that the exquisite and much loved wife of John Jarvie, pretty little Nell, was dead. Her passing on May 9 was shocking and horrific. The sweet mother of four boys had been stricken at home with a pulmonary hemorrhage: acute bleeding from the lungs, upper respiratory tract, and trachea. It was an unimaginable ending for one still so young and radiant. Nellie was just thirty-two years old.

John Jarvie and the children accompanied Nell's body for burial to Ogden, Utah, where her sister Giesy Spango and Giesy's husband, James, resided. Giesy had very recently given birth so word of Nell's death was withheld from her until she got stronger, for fear she would be unnerved by the shock.[24]

Ann Bassett lived, rode, and matured among both the prickles and roses of her notorious valley. As she entered her teens, she was still as carefree as the daubs of orange and mint lichen that wove upon the rocks that were her stepping stones. Harsh realities tipped things this way and that, but, still, at thirteen Ann could be counted among the young innocents capable of sleeping and dreaming of tomorrow without fear, for she knew her mother to be fearless and strong enough for them all to lean against. Sadly, though, as the Jarvie family had just experienced, nothing remains the same.

NOTES TO CHAPTER NINE

1. Frank Willis, *Confidentially Told,* unpublished manuscript, The Museum of NW Colorado–Craig.

2. Matt Warner and Murray King, *The Last of the Bandit Riders*, (New York: Bonanza Books, 1940), 39.

3. It is almost certain that Isam Dart's given name was spelled Isham. In the 1870 U.S. Federal census and in almost all legal papers concerning him, Isham is the spelling used, including when his attorney signed for him. However, when he signed his own name, he used the spelling Isam as shown in the document dated October 4, 1889, testimony by Isham Dart, plaintiff v. Elroy P. Philbrick, defendant. Others, including Ann Bassett, spelled his name Isom.

4. 1870 United States Federal Census, Precinct 1, Guadalupe, Texas. The 1900 census done in Routt County, Colorado, lists his birth date as 1855 in Texas.

5. Nellie Snyder Yost, segment of manuscript, 41, The Museum of NW Colorado–Craig; Tap Duncan letter to Ann Bassett Willis, 25 Mar 1941, The Museum of NW Colorado–Craig.

6. Duncan, letter to Ann Bassett Willis.

7. H. Ry Baker, *Denver Post,* 5 Mar 1961, The Museum of NW Colorado–Craig.

8. Crawford MacKnight, letter to Cary Stiff, 12 Nov 1968, The Museum of NW Colorado–Craig.

9. J.S. Hoy, Hoy Manuscript, 124.

10. Hoy, 124.

11. Catherine Sevenau and Gordon Clemens, "Lore, Libel, & Lies: A Family History," 29, The Museum of NW Colorado–Craig.

12. Sevenau and Clemens, 29.

13. Sevenau and Clemens, 40.

14. Josie (Bassett) Morris, interview with Messersmith, 7 Jul1961, The Museum of NW Colorado–Craig.

15. Sevenau and Clemens, 44- 45, letter from Adea Hoy to his sister, Emily, 3 Dec 1888, The Museum of NW Colorado–Craig.

16. "Tales of Early Days," *Moffat County Bell,* 5 Dec 1919. In her memoir, Ann incorrectly states that the arrest warrants were issued because she altered the Two-Bar brand on Dixie Burr and hid the heifer in Zenobia Basin.

17. Sevenau and Clemens, 44.

18. Sevenau and Clemens, 46.

19. "Court Proceedings in Routt County," Aspen *Evening Chronicle*, 30 Sep 1890.

20. "Court Proceedings in Routt County," 30 Sep 1890.

21. Court records supplied by The Museum of NW Colorado–Craig.

22. *Carbon County Journal*, "Wyoming Newsy Items Plucked from Our Exchanges," 17 Nov 1888.

23. Sweetwater County Court records, The Museum of NW Colorado–Craig.

24. "The City In Brief," *Salt Lake Herald*, 13 May 1890; "Died At Brown's Park," *Ogden Standard*, 13 May 1890.

Chapter Ten

The Grizzly

Ann Bassett was not unkind, but she continued to have a stout side-trait of self-interested orneriness, which Sam and Elizabeth were usually able to keep in check. Nonetheless, on certain occasions when no one had her in hand, Ann could still make imprudent and sometimes perilous decisions.

A mellow summer afternoon in 1891 bathed the pines and sage of Zenobia Basin on Douglas Mountain in a warm fragrance of serenity. Teenagers Ann and Sam rode on a section of the Bassett summer range with a couple of other Bassett cowboys who had gone off in a different direction, looking for cattle. Ann and Sam were lethargic as they listened to the sleepy repetition of their horses' hooves clopping and grinding in the dirt of the cattle trail they followed along the Green River slope. Ann rode a fine young gelding that had turned out to be an excellent cow horse for her. She called him Milo.[1]

All at once the dreaminess fragmented as both horses came to an abrupt stop. The horses held their heads high with ears perked and nostrils flaring. Plainly, they had caught the scent of something startling. Ann's eyes were wide and searching. Suddenly she glimpsed movement in the near distance.

Ann had wanted one from the very first time she ever saw a bear cub. Now, right in front of her, there were two. The furry balls were adorable and playful, wrestling and tumbling and peeking under rocks for insects.

Before Sam could get a word out, Ann spurred her horse into a dead run with her rope dangling at the ready. In two swift motions the loop of the lariat caught one of the cubs around its middle and Ann wound the other end of the rope around her saddle horn. The snared cub squalled and fought against the rope as its twin bolted. Almost simultaneously, far above on the timbered hillside, the silhouette of something huge erupted with shattering velocity. Still shadowed within the tall pines, an enormous silvertip mother with ears pinned back stormed down the steep mountain slope. The grizzly burst onto the scene of horse, girl, and cub.

Ann spurred her panicking horse to get him to lunge away while frantically trying to undo the rope that was tied hard and fast to her saddle. In a flash, Sam was there, desperately trying to get his horse alongside the frenzied Milo to hand Ann his pocketknife, but in the melee he couldn't get close enough.

The two Bassett cowboys came into sight and although their horses were running wide open, the men were still quite a distance away and well out of range for their revolvers. The men shouted repeatedly as they tore across the sagebrush flat and fired their guns into the air in an effort to distract the mother grizzly, but she was fixated on the arena in front of her. Milo was berserk with terror, twisting and jumping sideways, dragging the cub all the while. When the gelding reared and then plunged downward, the forcefulness of the lurch tore Ann loose from the saddle and flung her into the brush. The bear ignored her as she scrambled into a scrubby pinion pine.

The thirteen-year-old turned her head just in time to see the grizzly rise to an unbelievable height and strike Milo in the head with a fierce blow. The gelding was dead before he hit the ground. Just a moment later, the cowboys peppered the mighty sow with Colt .45 bullets, and she fell, bleeding and lifeless.

Mack, one of the cowhands, rode over to the roughed up and shivering cub to cut it loose and watched as it scuttled away into the timber. Neither of the men said a word to Ann and both were stern as they removed her bridle and scarred up saddle from the dead gelding. Then Mack walked over to Ann, who, like the cub, was scared and trembling.

Mack reached up, pulled the young girl from her cramped perch in the pine, and said, "Come out of there you little hellion. I am going to give you the lickin' your father has been puttin' off years too long." Then he jerked her around to face Milo's body. "See that poor dead horse over yonder? Well, that's what I'm lickin' you for." Mack gave Ann a few forceful whacks with his fringed gauntlets and then gave her a shaking to punctuate his anger with her.[2]

Minutes later Ann found herself behind Mack's saddle holding on to him with all her strength as his rough-gaited horse stayed on a steady trot. Ann bounced up and down all three of the miles back to the cabin at the summer ranch. As they got into camp they rode by two ranch hands digging postholes for a new corral. When those men spotted Ann's battered saddle and Ann sitting behind Mack, it was obvious there had been some sort of wreck. "What's up?" one of them asked. Only Sam spoke back and simply said, "Ask Ann."[3]

When the riders reached the saddle shed, Ann was relieved to slide off Mack's horse and be done with the silent and miserable trip. Mack hung her saddle by one stirrup on a wooden peg in the shed. The cowboys, including her brother, didn't even look her way as they mounted their horses and rode back to complete their workday.

As soon as the cowboys went out of sight, Ann made her way over to the curious ranch hands working on the corral and poured out a full account of what happened. She made a plea: "Please go bury my horse, and the bear, too. And maybe you might just take along a hunk of fresh meat for the cubs." Ann went along to show the men the spot of the calamity and was glad when Milo received a burial. However, the mother bear was too large for such an additional effort.

Later that evening, a thunderstorm arrived, bringing blackened, low-hanging clouds. Rain was steadily pouring by the time Sam and the other worn-out cowhands returned. Ann sheepishly made her way through the puddles to meet them at the saddle shed. By now Mack's anger had mostly run its course but his distress about what she'd caused to happen to both Milo and the mother bear had not.

"Ann," Mack said, "we'll fix your saddle, but you're goin' back to the home ranch. If we ever see you carryin' a rope again, you'll get another lickin'. You can tell your father or not, just as you like. We'd rather not talk about it anymore."

Ann wasn't equipped to absorb reprimands of length. While Mack was speaking, her thoughts drifted. Instead of hearing Mack's words she found herself fixed on watching the rain drizzle brilliantly in a string of droplets from the slouch of his big hat.[4] Mack, like others before and after him, tried his best to get through to Ann. Apparently his admonishment had some impact because his words did implant themselves in her thoughts and memories as she recounted the story as an adult.

Sam accompanied his sister on the fourteen-mile ride back to the ranch in Brown's Park. He still hadn't spoken to her about what happened.

Ann moved uncomfortably in the saddle and then timidly broke the quiet. "You tell the folks, Sam. I'll keep quiet this time."

Sam looked at her and asked, "What do you want me to tell them?"

"Oh, I donno, maybe we better not tell about the horse getting killed."

Sam nodded. He had probably been more traumatized for Ann than angry with her. He, as usual, wanted to shield his little sister. "You got plenty of saddle horses," he said. "Milo won't be missed for a long time."

Ann was feeling the discomfort of gloom and regret as Sam practiced what he was going to say to their parents. When the well-rehearsed account was at last laid out to Herb and Elizabeth, Ann felt a prick of shame when her upset father exclaimed, "Thank God, Ann was saved!"[5] Within the disquiet of her contemplation Ann was pretty certain that Mack would have preferred that the young gelding had been spared instead.

NOTES TO CHAPTER TEN

1. Ann Bassett Willis, "Queen Ann of Brown's Park," *The Colorado Magazine,* Jul 1952, 233-235.
2. Ann Bassett Willis, "Queen Ann of Brown's Park," 234.
3. Ann Bassett Willis, "Queen Ann of Brown's Park,*"* 234.
4. Ann Bassett Willis, "Queen Ann of Brown's Park," 235.
5. Ann Bassett Willis, "Queen Ann of Brown's Park,"235.

CHAPTER ELEVEN

FAREWELL, SPLENDID MATRIARCH

Life in Brown's Park continued in a paradox, revealing moments of grace and others of deadly darkness. Every part of that contradiction twisted its way toward Ann Bassett's family. On Christmas morning, 1891, when the Bassett house was filled with the smell of sap-laden evergreen mixing with sugared and spiced baking, an agitated rider arrived from Charlie Crouse's ranch with news that there had been a stabbing. The rider was sent to the Bassett Ranch to get Herb with the hope that he would know what to do to save the young cowboy, Charlie Seger.

A celebration of the season featuring a poker game lured several men together in the Crouse ranch house on Christmas Eve. Charlie Crouse, Mary, and the children, Clarence, Stanley, and Minnie, had gone to Vernal providing the opportunity for these men to celebrate without restraint. Well into the night Charlie Crouse's brother, Joseph "Joe" Tolliver began harassing Charlie Seger. Charlie was a kindhearted young man with whom the Bassetts were well acquainted. Josie Bassett was especially fond of Charlie Seger, and had on more than one occasion enjoyed dancing with the slender, small-built cowboy. He didn't drink alcohol and Josie considered him a gentleman in every way.[1] He and his brother Albert came into Brown's Park with the Hoys and both were well-liked by the Brown's Parkers.

Although Joe Tolliver had a wife and three young children, he had left them alone on Christmas Eve to go carousing. During the night, he fatally wounded Charlie Seger with a knife. Two accounts of the incident later emerged.

According to Josie Bassett, Charlie Seger took a break from the ongoing poker game at the kitchen table and went into the living room to sit down by the fireplace. Joe Tolliver was very drunk by then and made the crass decision to force this amateur, Charlie Seger, to take a drink. Joe

147

made his way over to Charlie and stuck his whiskey in front of Charlie's face. Charlie turned his head back and forth and said, "I'd rather not. I don't touch that. I don't care to drink. Let's wait until tomorrow."

Irritated, Joe grabbed hold of Charlie and jerked him out of the chair and shoved him around. Charlie, not understanding the danger he was in, continued to refuse and said, "I will not drink—I'm not going to!" The two continued to scuffle. Charlie overpowered his drunken opponent but instead of Joe backing down, he pulled out his white-handled pocket knife, snapped the knife open, and stabbed Charlie in the heart.

When Herb returned home from tending Charlie Seger, he was somber. Shaking his head he said, "I couldn't save him. Charlie was scared to death, and he really hurt. His back was as black as black before he died. He bled inward. I couldn't do anything for him."[2]

Joe Tolliver immediately left for Vernal and once there was accompanied by Charlie Crouse when he turned himself in to the authorities. *The Salt Lake Herald* and *The Cheyenne Daily Sun* both reported that the incident started when cowboy John "Jack" Martin was sparring with Joe Tolliver and Tolliver was thrown down. Charlie Seger and others laughed that Tolliver was being bested and that was the cause of the stabbing.[3] *The Salt Lake Herald* said that the greatest contention for the grand jury was whether or not the men were so drunk on strychnine whiskey that they were not responsible for what was done. Apparently that argument won out because charges were dismissed against Joe Tolliver.[4] All accounts agreed that the young cowboy's stabbing and death were over nothing more than a trivial matter.

Although it was wintertime, great effort was made on Charlie Seger's behalf to bury him on a sagebrush rise between the Crouse ranch house and the river. Slabs of red sandstone were carried to the site and then stacked to create a sturdy, three- or four-foot tall border around the grave. Charlie's body was placed in the center of the burial plot and the grave was filled with dirt to the top of the border. Charlie's younger brother, Albert, was grief-stricken. He rode to Salt Lake City and by packhorse brought back both a granite headstone and matching footstone to mark his brother's grave. The inscription on the headstone reads: *To the Memory of Charles W. Seger–Born Jan. 20, 1867–Died Dec. 27, 1891.* Albert placed the beautiful markers and left his brother to rest in a place where serenity and blue-grey, yellow-belled racer snakes interweave with time and stone.[5]

As for the Bassetts, Herb was apparently more content than ever. His friend John Jarvie served as postmaster for the Utah end of Brown's Park from February 14, 1881, until he resigned in June 8, 1887. On January 8, 1890, Herb was appointed postmaster for what was named the Ladore Post Office, and he loved it.[6] He was very pleased with the new sixteen-by-eighteen foot log building that he helped construct among the other ranch outbuildings to serve as his post office.[7] Having mail delivery was, of course, a real boost to the community. Herb thoroughly enjoyed his work tending to the post office because it suited his constitution. As a bonus with the mail came plenty of interesting reading material to devour, along with a flow of visitors stopping by to pick up or send mail. That, in turn, led to discussions on current events and a variety of other stimulating subjects. This was Herb's place of comfort.

Besides her children, Elizabeth's source of fulfillment at her Brown's Park home was in building the cattle herd, raising fine horses, and extending the Bassett influence and land holdings. Being a woman at the head of a cattle operation brought challenges from many directions, including preventing the ranch from being swallowed up by the big outfits and their ongoing quest for domination of the range. She cautiously watched events unfolding in Wyoming, for such things had a way of spilling Brown's Park's way.

Wyoming was the hub of the cattle industry which was ruled by the powerful Wyoming Stock Growers Association. Small ranchers persisted in growing in numbers and crowding the cattle barons while elbowing their way onto the range to run a few head of cattle and provide for their families. Utilizing the public lands was as much their right as it was the right of the big outfits. However, the dominance long enjoyed by the barons of at-will grazing on federal land was not easily conceded. The theft of mavericks, pockets of rustling, and infuriating confrontations over control of water sources and grass, kept tempers and conversations raw. Each side dealt with complex truths and falsehoods that blended to a toxic brew on the range and in the courts. In April 1892 the mixture ignited into the Johnson County War, an armed conflict that shook the region. Unfortunately, trouble on the range was far from over and no one knew that more clearly than Elizabeth Bassett.

When the fall of 1892 arrived in Brown's Park, things seemed as they should be. Elizabeth was constantly busy seeing to it that the ranch and

Pages from an autograph book which belonged to Daisy Dowden, signed by Josie Bassett and Anna Bassett. *The Museum of NW Colorado–Craig.*

her children were flourishing and ever-growing. The Bassett family and cattle ranch were on the upswing with a future being carved by Elizabeth. She commanded her crew of ranch hands and cowboys (called the Bassett Gang by J.S. Hoy) with unquestioned authority, stood up to and outma-neuvered the Hoys and others who would be her enemies, and made highly respected handshake agreements about grazing with other ranchers such as Griff Edwards, all to the benefit of the Bassett Ranch. She was grooming her oldest son Sam while his little brothers Eb and George were following Sam's lead. Although Josie was then attending school in Craig, Colorado, she had spent time at St. Mary's Academy in Salt Lake City.[8] Elizabeth kept a close eye on her willful and rambunctious cowgirl daughter, Ann. Sam, who was then seventeen, and Ann, fourteen, were also enrolled in school in Craig, and Eb and George were taught at home by a rudimentary teacher who boarded with the Bassetts.

Young ladies commonly exchanged autograph books at school in which they signed their names to poetic phrases for each other. On November 14, 1892, both Ann and Josie, while attending school in Craig, wrote in an autograph book belonging to Daisy Dowden:[9]

> Craig Colo. Nov 14, '92
>
> Dear Daisy
> May a happy future
> And a present wisely spent
> Loving deeds of truth and duty,
> Lead you through a life of beauty,
> Into paths of sweet content
>   Your loving Deskmate
>   Josie Bassett

On a different page, Ann wrote her message to Daisy:

> Dear friend Daisy
> May all on Earth can give be given
> And what is wanted be found
>   In heaven
>   Your friend
>   Anna Bassett
>   Craig Colo
>   Nov 14-92

That fall Elizabeth was often in the saddle, but, lately, each time she rode, she mentioned a real discomfort in her abdomen. She said the pain came and went and usually felt better once she was off her horse. She was not accustomed to being ill and continued to demand much of herself. Because she loved the celebration of Christmas she was no doubt looking forward to its arrival in a couple of weeks. All her children would be home and the ranch house would once again be twirling with crowded merriment.

A hard day of riding all the way to Zenobia Basin and back had exhausted Elizabeth and left her dealing with the nagging soreness in her

This is the only known photo of the Ladore Post Office at the Bassett Ranch. *The Museum of NW Colorado–Craig.*

belly. Nevertheless she was able to eat a good supper. Herb was away but Elizabeth went to bed that night following her regular routine.

At four in the morning pain struck throughout Elizabeth's midsection. She doubled over in agony when she tried to stand. The household, including Eb, George, and their schoolteacher, awakened to the sounds of Elizabeth's anguish. Without Herb, no one knew what to do. Eb was twelve and George just eight. They ran to the bunkhouse for help, and the cowboys, including ranch foreman James "Jim" McKnight, Mat Rash, and Isam Dart, were soon at Elizabeth's bedside. The only thing anyone could think to do was apply warm compresses. That did seem to ease the sharpness of the pain just a bit. What they did, though, wasn't of consequence. Apparently Elizabeth's appendix had ruptured and oozed bacteria into her body. In disbelief, her men and her children watched Elizabeth suffer terribly before she perished.[10]

Elizabeth's death swooped like a bird of prey and tore at the Bassett family. Herb shattered into a void of loss as a wagon was sent to retrieve Ann, Sam, and Josie from Craig. At eighteen, Josie was facing insurmountable stress and grief. Not only had she just been told of her mother's death, she could no longer deny to herself that she was pregnant with the ranch foreman's child. How in the world could she tell her father?

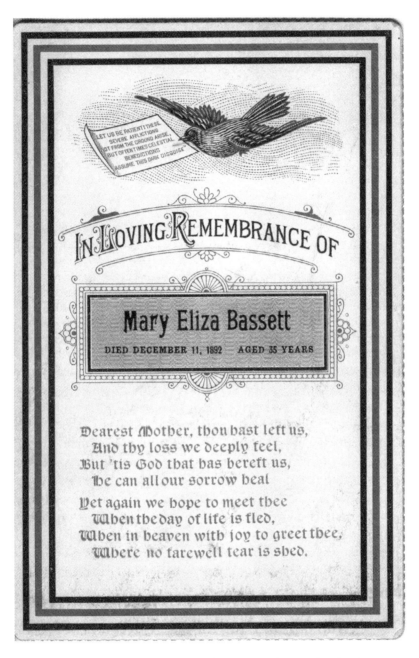

Elizabeth Bassett's funeral card. *The Museum of NW Colorado–Craig.*

Elizabeth's death occurred at five in the morning, on December 11, 1892. Five days later, a newspaper article further announced the news of Elizabeth's death:

A Sad Event.

A messenger from Brown's Park arrived Monday bringing the sad intelligence of the death of Mrs. E. Bassett. Her children, Sam, Josie and Anna who have been attending our school, immediately started for home, accompanied with Mrs. William Morgan. Mrs. Bassett's death occurred on Sunday after an illness of two weeks, while her husband was absent. The deceased is one of the best known women in the county where she has lived since the earliest settlement. She was a natural pioneer, possessing the most remarkable courage and energy. She was highly esteemed by those who knew her and commanded the respect of those who, from conflicting business interests, were her enemies. The most conspicuous and admirable trait in Mrs. Bassett's character was her unwavering loyalty and devotion to her friends. She was only 35 years of age and apparently in the meridian of health and vigor. The sympathy of the community is extended to the motherless children.[11]

The valley residents told and retold the detailed account of a ruptured appendix (inflammation of the bowels) which had been the diagnosis at the time by the family doctor.[12] However, there was another scenario that, much later, was told by Ann that possibly the harrowing loss of Elizabeth was the fatal result of a miscarriage.[13] If that is true, tender-hearted Herb would likely have been all the more wrecked in his anguish.

The finality of the death of the center of not only the family but also of the ranch must have been stunningly surreal for all those involved. As for Ann, never again would she have the luxury of an unblemished belief, which her mother always exuded, that no matter what happened all would be well.

The end of Ann Bassett's mother's life coincided with the pinnacle reached by the Bassett Ranch and the Bassett family. They tried. They all tried. But, reality ruled. It was the beginning of the long decline.

NOTES TO CHAPTER ELEVEN

1. Josie Bassett Morris, interview with G.E. Untermann, A.R. Mortensen, and E.L. Cooley, Sep 1959, The Museum of NW Colorado–Craig.

2. Morris, interview with Untermann, etc.

3. "Knifed to Death," *The Cheyenne Daily Sun*, 10 Jan 1892.

4. "First District Court: Application for Bail Refused," *Salt Lake Herald*, 13 May 1892.

5. The environment of the grave was witnessed many times by the author in her youth. Information about Albert Seger and the gravestones is courtesy of Seger family descendant Linda Marie (Stehr) Farnsworth.

6. The spellings of Lodore and Ladore were interchangeable in Brown's Park for several years.

7. Morris, interview by Messersmith, 7 Jul 1961, The Museum of NW Colorado–Craig.

8. Morris, interview by Messersmith, 18 Jul 1960, The Museum of NW Colorado–Craig. Although Josie stated she was attending St. Mary's when her mother died, she was actually in school in Craig.

9. Daisy Dowden autograph booklet, The Museum of NW Colorado–Craig.

10. Morris, interview by Untermann, etc. Sep 1959.

11. "A Sad Event," *Craig Courier*, 16 Dec 1892.

12. Josie Bassett Morris, interview with Messersmith, 7 Jul 1961, The Museum of NW Colorado. Josie stated the family doctor was Dr. Arborgast from Juniper Springs. However, Dr. Arborgast didn't move to the area until 1905.

13. Grace McClure, *The Bassett Women*, (Athens: Ohio University Press, 1985), 44.

CHAPTER TWELVE

A REBELLIOUS NATURE

At the moment of Elizabeth's death, Ann's foundation of gravity was undone. The fourteen-year-old girl was untethered from all things untroubled and familiar. The mirror reflecting her mother's force was blurred and confused in a world where hardly anyone spoke about any part of it. The intensity of Ann's rebellious nature, which had always had a tendency to flicker, was now unchecked and on the rise.

While Ann and her sister Josie loved each other without question, they usually found it difficult to be close in proximity. Because Josie was the oldest child she took the lead with household chores and child care. Ann, five years younger, never did. Instead, her privileged spirit ran free when she was turned loose on the ranch. Although both girls had independent personalities, Josie, heavily freckled with light copper hair, was more serious; Ann, who was lightly freckled and had darker hair, was tenacious and at times dreamily poetic. The sisters often clashed. Now, when they likely needed each other most in dealing with their mother's death, their lives were still on different courses. Josie was fully occupied in her struggles regarding her pregnancy. On her own, Ann sought out proof that she would recover, by reinforcing that she was tough and fearless.

Once Herb could manage, he put together a plan for Sam, Ann, Eb, and George. He hired a woman in her late twenties, Armida Thompson, to take over the household chores and help with the children. Armida and her husband, Elijah B. "Longhorn" Thompson, left their ranch east of Brown's Park and moved to the Bassett Ranch. The Bassett children called Armida "Aunty" and the couple proved to be tremendous help and comfort to the Bassetts.

Armida Boomer was born in Wisconsin and had also lived in Kansas before coming west as a teenager. She came to Colorado with her mother after the Meeker Massacre in 1879. Armida's half-brother, who was a scout for Major Thornburgh, was wounded during the conflict. The young man's mother and sister came to nurse him back to health. Armida stayed in Colorado and ten years later on May 13, 1889, in Lay, Colorado, Armida married Longhorn Thompson.[1]

Elijah Thompson's parents were Virginia farmers who moved to California during the gold rush where in Tuolumne County in 1856 Elijah was born. As soon as he was old enough, he became a range rider in the cattle industry and drove cattle north while working for Texas ranches including the huge Pitchfork Land and Cattle Company in central West Texas. That occupation earned him the nickname "Longhorn." After serving as foreman a few years for the Pitchfork, Longhorn settled in Colorado.[2] He married Armida in 1889 and in 1890 they purchased their ranch on Little Snake River.

Both Ann's father and Aunty Thompson found Ann to be unmanageable. She was defiant at every turn. Looking back at those days many years later Ann wrote: "With all her common sense and abilities, Aunty Thompson could exert no restraint to my turbulent nature." About her father she said, "An eastern college man, although wise in many ways, he was too tender and kindhearted to control a girl of my temperament. Even the faintest suggestion of a big stick wielded at the proper time, hurt his gentle soul. Nevertheless, it would have been a helpful initiation to an inflammable thunderbolt, dictatorially charging over all obstructions. I was a child possessing the energy of young wild things in the open, developing as a nature-child, and occupied chiefly with outdoor work and play on a cattle ranch in a primitive west. I was about as responsive to father's idea of 'rule by love alone' as a fragment of granite on a winter morning."[3]

Rancher Tim Kinney suggested to Herb that he send Ann to St. Mary's Academy in Salt Lake City for the spring term. Ann was in dire need of structure. As it turned out, she wasn't hard to convince. Rather, she was glad to leave the painful aftermath of her mother's death behind to have a new adventure on her own. After the hundred-mile wagon ride to Rock Springs, Ann boarded the westbound train.

Herb and Aunty Thompson were explicit in their instructions. They told her how to act during the trip and what to expect upon her arrival in Salt Lake. Aunty gave detailed instructions on how to properly conduct herself at St. Mary's. The often unfettered girl apparently took comfort in having parameters, for she took the guidance to heart. As the train chugged toward its destination and the countryside coasted past the windows, Ann Bassett sat primly with a straight back and lips pressed firmly together.

Ann was met at the Salt Lake train station by nuns who regularly performed such duty. Pat, the gardener and driver, helped bundle the nuns and Ann into a carriage and then drove them through the awesome streets. Buildings towered, humans walking and traffic of horse-pulled freight crisscrossed each other, and store windows showed off wondrous displays.[4]

At St. Mary's, Ann traded the rustic grace of Brown's Park and the confusion of dealing with grief, for a welcoming brick building surrounded by lawn, shapely trees, and ivy. All would eventually be shading the school in green surroundings. After being ushered into a large waiting room she met Sister Superior, whom Ann later described as "a dignified woman from whom radiated the authority and responsibility given into her hands for the guidance and sheltering of just such little girls as I."[5]

Ann found herself dressed in a smartly pressed uniform among four hundred girls where it seemed that her every wish and need was attended. Watched over by a young, soft-spoken nun, Ann loved and looked forward to the chiming of the bells, meals in the dining hall accompanied by soothing strains of music, Benediction, Mass, and even the classroom instruction. The school, conducted by the Sisters of the Holy Cross, provided a course of study that embraced all branches of a thorough and accomplished education, including language and music.[6] Ann found everything orderly and planned right down to the moments of play where rackets and mallets were laid out in a row to be used at the tennis courts and croquet plot. During this hiatus from broncs and bruises and the learned art of dodging flying hooves, Ann floated in a maze of comfort and fun.

While Ann was living in Salt Lake, eighteen-year-old Josie wed James Fielding McKnight on March 21, 1893, in Green River City. Uncle Samuel Clark Bassett turned over his squatter's rights to his place on Beaver Creek to Jim and Josie before leaving Brown's Park to spend some time living in Montana. Jim immediately filed the paperwork to homestead the place, giving the newlyweds a place of their own. Uncle Samuel had a small cabin there where the couple stayed for a little over two months until they moved into a newly constructed cabin. Then work began on a new barn, sheds, and corrals.[7]

The spring term ended at St. Mary's and Ann, looking and acting like a modest young lady, returned to her valley and the ranch. Her mother had been buried on the crest of a sage-covered hill that overlooked the ranch house, the same hill Ann had so many times delighted in dashing down, whether loping off its steepness on foot or on one of her cow horses. Now, it was transformed. A lovely steel fence with corner braces of rock set in concrete stood there, encircling her mother's grave in the new Bassett cemetery. Her father had called upon his abilities as a crafts-man to create this resting place for his wife. Because Ann's father and sister had adorned the steel with a pretty coat of white, it shone brightly in the spring sun.[8]

Once she was home Ann exchanged her dresses for overalls and buck-skin before somersaulting right back into her role on the ranch. Once again she felt rebellious and saw herself as "a cross between a Texas cow-puncher and a Ute Indian."[9] The latter was on full display when, just be-fore her fifteenth birthday, her father hosted not only their loved family friend Judge Asbury Conaway but also a couple other men of distinction.

Judge Conaway was now living with his sister in Cheyenne and had, three years earlier in 1890, been appointed by President Harrison as As-sociate Justice of the Supreme Court for the Territory of Wyoming. He had many acquaintances in high places. This planned visit to the ranch caused a flurry in the Bassett household in preparation, because the judge was to be accompanied by Dr. Nicholas Senn and Major Harrison Otis. The two men were famous in their fields but were no doubt glad for an interlude from the stresses of dealing with a financial alarm that was be-ginning to absorb the nation. They must have been intrigued to be visiting a cattle ranch in the wilds of Colorado in a valley where cowhands rode and roped and desperados came and went.[10]

Civil War veteran Major Harrison Otis was sole owner, president, edi-tor-in-chief, and general manager of the *Los Angeles Times*. He had a bois-terous, take-charge nature and his large size and thick mustache gave him the appearance of a walrus.[11] His traveling companion, Dr. Nicholas Senn, had a brilliant career in medicine and was highly influential and prolific.[12] Herb Bassett respected his distinguished guests and naturally wanted their visit to the Bassett Ranch to be dignified and enjoyable. Herb, Dr. Senn, Major Otis, and Judge Conaway had much to discuss about the Civil War and world affairs as they relaxed in the living room of the ranch house.

Although nearing seven months pregnant, Josie was there, at the Bassett Ranch, to help with the preparations for her father's guests. Also there was Sam's pretty girlfriend, Wilda Mack, along with a close family friend, Lizzie Brown from Rock Springs. Ann, however, was squarely in her own world and although she knew company was coming she wasn't much interested. She was oblivious to the arrival. Instead, she picked that day to decide she was going become a full-blooded Ute.[13]

When Ann strode into the living room in full view of the guests, she had her hair in long braids and was dressed in an Indian headdress, beaded moccasins, and a form of her own war paint. The sudden sight of the guests surprised her. She stood frozen as she realized she was the center of fascination. Then she caught sight of her father's face as it went from the pallor of despair to angry red.

Judge Conaway broke the silence when he introduced her. "This is Miss Ann. She will conduct our horse-back trips to places we will want to visit while you are here." Ann thought for sure the expressions on the men's faces meant they were ready to fly if any more primitives like her showed up. Feeling an unpleasantness in the pit of her stomach, Ann was all the more embarrassed and wanted to dash away when, dressed primly in starched gingham and ruffles, Josie appeared and announced the meal was ready.[14]

Instead of allowing her to escape, Judge Conaway gave the painted up Ann a bit of a shove toward the dining room. After everyone was seated the girl felt herself shrink as she sat near the towering Major Otis. She endured the endless meal, all the while trying to look dignified in the manner she imagined an Indian chief would be.

Judge Conaway suggested the visitors take a short rest before Ann took them on a ride to view Lodore Canyon at sunset. Ann's shame was not long-lasting. As the judge kept an eye on her and then suggested she ride bareback like an Indian, Ann decided Judge Conaway wished to use her embarrassment as a lesson against her. Her mutinous stripe began to search for some dire deed to perform.

The feathers of the headdress draped and dangled and fluttered as Ann rode her horse in the lead. The riders took their time as they traveled over hills and through the brush and gullies. Ann appreciated that Dr. Senn was deeply engrossed in the landscape of her beloved Brown's Park. However she quickly grew annoyed at the gruff union-busting newspaperman Major Otis and his bragging and complimenting himself on his splendid way with horses.

Ann Bassett on left and her friend Lizzie Brown. *The Museum of NW Colorado—Craig.*

While watching the glorious tints and towering shadows wash over the walls of the canyon, the city men gawked and talked about Ann's world as she formed a plan. When it came time to mount up for the homeward ride, she kept an eye on the bulky Major Otis and maneuvered her horse next to his. As Ann rode up on the opposite side of his horse, the unsuspecting fellow put his foot in the stirrup and with great effort began pulling himself upward to mount. Before he made it all the way into the saddle, Ann used as much force as she could gather without revealing herself and jabbed her toe into the flank of Otis's horse. The normally gentle gelding with the sweet name of Gussie literally detonated. An all-out rodeo bucked and kicked across the grass and sand of the river bottom meadow. Major Otis went airborne and long before Gussie gave up his bucking fit the newspaperman was sprawled out flat, atop a sandy patch of ground.

Ann rode her horse in a lope to catch Gussie. The gelding eyed Ann and acted like he knew she was behind the poke to his flank as she reached for his bridle reins.

Back at the rising heap that was Major Otis, Dr. Senn administered a thorough check-up before announcing the roughed up patient had not sustained any serious injuries. Otis was brave and remounted Gussie, though he wondered aloud on the journey home about the cause of Gussie's homicidal tendencies.

As the riders returned to the ranch, Sam met them at the corral to take care of the horses. The minute he learned of Gussie's misdeed, he was pretty sure he knew where the fault lay. He squinted and gave Ann a critical look. In a whisper he said to her, "Get out of the way and forget to show up while we have company."[15]

It wasn't Sam or her father who had her worried. She figured she'd be in for the worst of it from Jim, the hired man from Kentucky who continued to be Ann's self-appointed custodian. She knew Jim would be appalled at the way she had embarrassed her father. Years later Ann wrote about this incident in her memoir.

Ann wrote that she stayed to herself throughout the evening and night. At daylight, she made her way to the kitchen for something to eat; Jim was already there. After he left the house to do his morning chores she followed behind as he scolded her. He told her that wanting to be an Indian and dressing like one was okay when she was little. Now he wished she'd act like she did after first returning from St. Mary's. He blamed himself for discouraging her mother from giving her the lickings she deserved and made it clear that the fact that he had helped raise her was nothing for him to brag about.

After sighing he continued, "I ain't forgot the time you got that bunch of kids down sick with the grip by havin' them take their shoes off and stand in the mud and water for hours at a time makin' them believe they had heel flies. You had them poor kids snifflin' and snufflin' and as red as beets, an you, all dirtied up and as husky as a young mule! Heel-flies, nawthin,' it was only one of your streaks of meanness, scarin' them with that stuff."

The lecture went on for quite some time as Ann stayed silent, with an air of indifference. Jim wasn't nearly finished. He said, "I was so ashamed of you yesterday in that terrible riggin'. And I know you was in a mood to do somethin' awful mean. I says to Miz. Thompson, that young'un can't behave herself one minnit. Just look at Beth [Lizzie] Brown and Wilda Mac, all dressed up and smellin' as sweet as posies. Them is the gals that is goin' to get the pick of the fellers, an' you'll be one of them old maids, goin' round as sour as a pickle. I was set on you gettin' one of the good men around here, an' marry. But taint no use, all you can see is cattle an' hosses!" Jim lifted a thin hand and wiped his brow. "Fetch me my tobacker. It's in my coat pocket, hangin' on that limb there. I'm a-goin' to set again this cedar and do some whittlin'. My old bones is tired."

Rather than being subdued, Ann sensed her old friend was weakening and piped, "Jim, you should say 'please' when you ask for something."

That ignited him again. "See here, Ann Bassett, don't give me any of your back talk, I won't have no smart alecks in our family. Now get on your horse an' go to the Pablo place and stay there while your Pa's big friends are here. An' say, while you're about it, don't forget to wire the bull pasture gate,[16] and drive the cows away from the bog holes, an' run in the saddle horses. A body can't depend on the boys no more, with all them pretty gals around the ranch. Come to think of it, I always did get you to do such things." Leniency crept into the ranch hand's eyes.

Looking for sympathy Ann replied, "There is no food at the Pablo, and you know it."

He responded that she could catch frogs from the pond and fry their legs to eat. "I'll tell Sam and Wilda to take you some biscuits." The thought of that young couple caused Jim's mind to wander. "Them two is sure going to be a match. Sam is tall an' good lookin', and so is Wilda with her yellow-bird hair, and them pretty slim laigs. She walks like a deer, an' sings, too. Yes'sir-ee, that girl sings like a meadowlark."

Ann interrupted to ask if that's what he called being in love. She said she'd seen them both acting droopy and thought about asking her father to give them each a pill of asafetida gum to perk them up. Chirping with disdain she went on, "This thing you call 'love' is too complicated for me to want to tackle. And where do you get the idea that I want a husband? Being side-hobbled to any man doesn't seem a bit exciting to me! Of course, men are sometimes fun, and they are handy to have around, but I like them better grazing in herds. I don't intend to cut one out to put my brand on. I have a purpose in life, and it hasn't got anything to do with falling in love and getting married. And now, just where did you get the idea that I don't intend to go on and be an Indian? I'm on my way this minute, to Pablo Springs to carry out your orders. G'bye."

Exasperated, Jim replied that was a "helluva idea" and told her he was giving up on her. She knew he wouldn't, and he didn't. As a matter of fact, Ann wrote, she heard him brag more than once, "I cut that young'un's teeth on porcupine quills, and she ain't never been sick a day in her life."[17]

Dr. Senn and Major Otis survived Brown's Park and Ann Bassett and returned to their proficient lives. First the men needed to work their way through the challenges of the financial panic that was quickly growing in intensity across the country. Nonetheless, both men went on to further high accomplishment including serving in the Spanish American War.

❧ ❧ ❧

The economic depression of 1893 did not bypass Brown's Park. The earliest sign of the country's financial trouble was in February when the over-extended Philadelphia and Reading Railroad went into bankruptcy followed by President Grover Cleveland's repeal of the Sherman Silver Purchase Act of 1890. In reality, the underpinnings of the financial system were already beginning to snap. A run on banks even as the banks were failing and a credit crunch was rippling throughout the economy.[18]

At this same time, there was a financial panic in the United Kingdom and a drop in trade in Europe. Foreign investors sold American stocks in order to get American funds while they were backed by gold. On and on it went as the dominos fell. In total seventy-four railroads and over five hundred banks and fifteen thousand companies failed. Rampant unemployment joined with the widespread loss of life savings. Huge damages were realized in the agricultural and livestock businesses. In Brown's Park, everyone was hurting in one way or another. John Jarvie put an ad in the newspaper saying: "For each and every five hundred pounds of oats delivered at the J. Jarvie Store one hundred pounds of sugar will be given."[19] The successful and heavily invested brothers, Valentine and J.S. Hoy, seemed to fare the worst and went broke. To hold on to the Red Creek Ranch, Valentine signed a warranty deed over to his wife, Julia.[20] The holidays brought a time of relief and friendship.

Brown's Park's 1893 Thanksgiving celebration must have been a delightful festivity for all who attended. Ann said the dinner was given by a group of friends including Butch Cassidy, Elzy Lay, Dick Bender, Les Megs, and Harry Longabaugh. Although it would come soon enough, these young men hadn't yet earned the reputation of being outlaws. Ann, who was fifteen-years-old[21] when the dinner took place, later wrote a detailed description of the event which she titled "Wild Bunch Dinner."[22] This account is a direct transcription with Ann's spelling and style left intact. It offers a glimpse through the window into what she described as "a high class affair" that came to be known as "Brown's Park's Outlaw Thanksgiving":

Wild Bunch Dinner
Where party was given

The cabin was located on east side of Willow Creek near the canyon,[23] it belonged to Tom Davenport and the ranch was leased by Billie [Dick] Bender and Les Megs, by the year. There was about 100 acres of hay land and pasture in that part of the Davenport ranch. Bender and Megs did not stay there in summer. They hired the work done by a native and had the hay stacked for winter use when they returned in late fall.

Brown's Hole was a rest retreat for the men we called the "Bender gang." Billie [Dick] Bender and Les Megs were men of education and refinement. None of them ever gave the people of Brown's Hole any trouble. They were quiet peaceful citizens while there. Their profession or business was rather a mystery to the settlers but it was not our business to question that since they were well behaved and kept their boys in line.

Butch and Lay were on friendly terms with Bender and Megs and their boys, so they gave the Thanksgiving party for the Brown's Hole[24] families together and did not spare expenses in putting over a grand spread of the best delicasies Rock Springs could supply.

Tom Davenport raised the turkeys and the "gang" bought them. The dishes, linens, and silver was furnished by the women of the Hole.

The Menue

Blue point cocktails, roast turkeys with chestnut dressing, giblet gravey, cranberrys, mashed potatoes, candid sweet potatoes, creamed peas, celery, olives, pickled walnuts, swee[t] pickles, fresh tomatoes on crisp lettuce, hot rolls and sweet butter, coffee, whipped cream. Roquefort cheese, pumpkin pie, plum pudding, brandy sauce, mints, salted nuts.

…Isam [Dart] cooked the dinner dressed in snowy white from cap to shoes. Mother's beautiful silver candelabra graced the table. Choice fruit and dainties came from Rock Springs.[25]

How the people dressed

Men wore dark suits (vests were always worn) white shirts stiff starched colars, patent low cuts. No man would be seen minus a coat and a bow tie at the party—if it killed them and it almost did I am sure. If a mustache existed that must be waxed and curled.

The women wore tight fitted long dress with leg-o-mutton sleeves and boned collars—hair done on top of the head either in a French twist or a bun and bangs curled into a frizz. Girls in their teens wore dresses about 3 inches below the knees—spring heeled slippers and their hair in curls or braids tucked up with a big bow of ribbons at nap of neck.

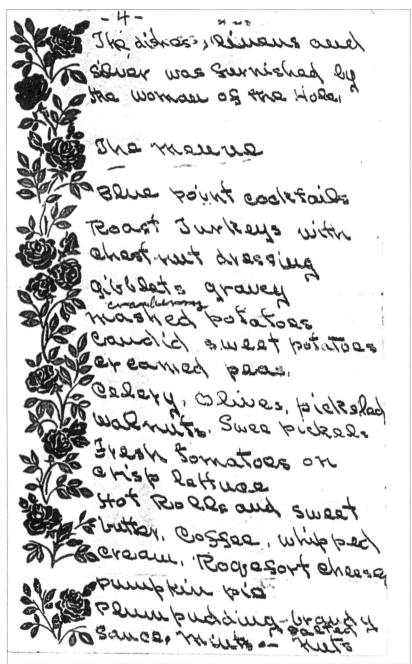

- 4 -

The dishes, linens and silver was furnished by the Woman of the Hole.

The menu

Blue point cocktails
Roast Turkeys with chestnut dressing
giblets gravey
cranberry
mashed potatoes
candid sweet potatoes
creamed peas.
Celery, Olives, pickeled walnuts. Swee pickels.
Fresh tomatoes on crisp lettuce
Hot Rolls and sweet butter, Coffee, whipped cream, Roqsort cheese
pumpkin pie
Plum pudding - brandy sauce, mints - salted Nuts

Sample page from Wild Bunch Dinner, also know as the Outlaw Thanksgiving, written by Ann Bassett. *The Museum of NW Colorado – Craig.*

Esther Davenport had the pretty dress for the party. A yellow silk mull over yellow taffeta she looked very pretty. Now I will tell you what Ann wore at the party—silk mull powder blue accordion pleated from top to bottom, camisole and petticoat of taffeta, peter pan collar, buttoned in the back puff sleeves to the elbows, belted by a wide sash with a big bow in back. The mull pleated well and how it swished over the taffeta undies. A narrow black velvet ribbon around the neck a gold locket fastened in the front.

Now for the stockings. Hold your hat on and smile. Lace made of silk and lisle thread black to match shoes. They were precious and worn only for parties. We had to be careful with them they cost 3.00 per pair and lasted a long time.

I wore my hair in three curls fastened at nap of neck held in place by large barrette beau catcher curl on forehead. Spring heeled shoes like the baby doll shoes shown in catalogues now.

The older women wore black taffeta with tucking at the neck and sleeves. High button shoes often with white tops and high curved French heels. (Always too tight as were their corsets.) Josies dress for the party was a sage green wool buntting. Many gored skirt, tight to the knees then flared to the floor to sweep up the dirt.

Josie was married, I was not and girls were not permitted to wear long dresses, put up their hair or wear high heels.

The party lasted about six hours. That evening we danced at the Davenport home, I say evening, I mean until sun up the next day. . . .[26] Program at the dinner was put on by the guests.

The hosts waited table, Megs-Bender, Butch [Cassidy], [Elzy] Lay and Harry Roudenbaugh [Longabaugh]. The other boys helped [Isam] Dart in the kitchen. All but the cook wore butcher aprons over their white shirts and suit trousers. Megs, Bender and Lay received their guests then slipped on aprons to help serve the crowd of 35 or more. Lots of work for the dinner was served in courses.

This was a joke, that is it was to some of us young rough necks just itching for an excuse to kick each other under the table and slightly grin. Butch was pouring coffee, poor Butch he could [later] perform such minor jobs as robbing banks and holding up pay trains without the flicker of an eyelash but serving coffee at a grand party, that was something else. The blood curdeling job almost floored him, he became panicky and showed that his nerve was completely shot to bits. He became frustrated and embarrassed over the blunder he had made when some of the other hosts better informed on the Emily Post slant had told him it was not good form to pour coffee from a big black coffee pot and reach from left to right across a guests plate, to grab a cup right under their noses. The boys went into a hudle in the kitchen and instructed Butch in the more formal art of filling coffee cups at the table. This just shows how etiquette can put fear into a brave mans heart.

The room was large: Tables placed [in a T shape]. Mr Jarvie a Scotch man with snow white curley hair and beard at the head of the long table. Mr and Mrs Blair on one side of him and Mr and Mrs Charley Crouse on the other, then Mr and Mrs Billie Rife and so on down the table—Buffalo Jack at the foot. Ten men and women on each side of the big table. The overflow sat at the other table. Esther, [others], and Ann Bassett [age] 14 or 15 sat there. Most of the crowd at this table were the younger ones. I remember Charlie Sparks was among us.[27]

The Entertainment

Mr Jarvie—Invocation

Ada Morgan and Tom Davenport a song—Mr Jarvie accompiment on the accordion. The song, "Then You'll Remember Me" and "Last Rose of Summer." Josie her zither with the boys backup [of] Joe Davenport on the guitar and Sam Bassett fiddle—"The Cattle Song."

Ann—a reading (She had been coached a week by John Jarvie.[28]) The origin of Thanksgiving and what it means—This was before we sat down to dinner— when we were seated Mr Jarvie asked the blessing briefly.

That nite we danced at Tom Davenports home.

Ann went back to St. Mary's for another term but then did not return to school there.[29] Instead, she was sent east to school, possibly to Miss Porter's School for Girls.[30] There, she felt stifled from the beginning. The atmosphere was strange to her and at times unbearably disagreeable. Unlike the nurturing environment at St. Mary's, play and exercise were replaced with a restrictive aura of quaint gentility. Although she did her school lessons and followed the written and spoken rules, it was just a matter of time until that reserve would break down because Ann's natural forces were clearly at odds with this place.

The predictable eruption happened when Ann was on horseback, the place where all her life she'd felt at ease and in control. However, the school's riding master made it clear that she rode incorrectly and must be taught proper horsemanship and posture and that she needed to learn how to post while being properly positioned in the saddle. Ann was mounted on a dun-colored horse that had one light blue eye. She lined her horse up with about a dozen other girls on horses and awaited directions for venturing onto a bridle path. When the snobby riding instructor stepped away, walking a few yards to converse with a stable boy, the ranch girl broke out of her restraints. Ann suddenly threw her right leg over the sidesaddle to sit astraddle, let out with a shrill yell, and kicked the startled gelding into action. The glass-eyed dun sent gravel flying from his hooves as he galloped, spun, and pranced about.

The master instructor dashed to catch up, hurling blistering ridicule at the girl. He made a grab for the bridle and ordered, "Dismount!" Ann never had more swagger than when she was on the back of a horse. She was the offspring of both Brown's Park and a magnificent cattlewoman, and she had been raised to ride and work beside top cowhands. Such a command was beneath her. Instead she neck reined the gelding to whirl away. Then the young renegade leaned from her saddle and spat out the words, "Go to Hell, you repulsive, little, monkey faced skunk!"[31]

When brought before the faculty, none of the girls who were present during Ann's glory ride admitted that they had heard Ann use any profanity. Ann was certain she would be expelled by the stony-faced people sitting in judgment of her. However, after her father's half-brother Louis La Monte Bassett of Cleveland arrived and spoke on her behalf she was allowed to finish out the term. The school officials and Ann's family decided that during the next term, she would go to Cleveland to live with her Aunt Jessie and Uncle Louis and attend a school for girls there. The allure of a warm family sanctuary was enticing to Ann. The place proved to be a welcoming home where her wounds of grief could heal.

⟡

NOTES TO CHAPTER TWELVE

1. State of Colorado Division of Vital Statistics Marriage Record Report, Film Number 001690141, *Ancestry.com*. Accessed 4 Feb 2017.

2. *Progressive Men of Western Colorado*. (Chicago: A.W. Bowen and Co., 1905), 794, 795.

3. Ann Bassett Willis, "Queen Ann of Brown's Park," *The Colorado Magazine*, Oct 1952, 285.

4. Willis, "Queen Ann of Brown's Park," 285.

5. Willis, "Queen Ann of Brown's Park," 285, 286.

6. *Rock Springs Miner*, No. 37, 14 Sep 1892, 4.

7. Homestead Proof–Testimony of Claimant, James F. McKnight; Homestead Proof–Testimony of Witness, E.A. Farnham, documents from The Museum of NW Colorado –Craig.

8. Josie Bassett Morris, interview with Untermann, Cooley and Mortensen, 1959.

9. Willis, "Queen Ann of Brown's Park," 285.

10. Although Ann described Senn and Otis as boyhood friends of her father, that is not likely.

11. Information about Major Harrison Otis gleaned from: "Meet General Otis and His Los Angeles Times," www.latimesbomb.com/2010/09/meet-general-otis-his-los-angeles-times, Accessed 25 Jan 2017; and "Californians and the Military, Major-General Harrison Gray Otis, U.S.V., Publisher of the Los Angeles Times," californiamilitaryhistory.org/Otis. Accessed 24 Jan 2017.

    Senator Harrison Gray Otis, uncle to Major Harrison Otis, was appointed attorney for the District of Massachusetts by President George Washington and U.S. District attorney for Massachusetts by President John Adams. He served five years as a U.S. Senator. During the Civil War he took part in the battles at Bull Run, Lynchburg, and numerous others. He was honorably discharged in 1865. In Washington, D.C., he served in the Government Printing Office, was correspondent for the *Ohio State Journal*, editor of the *Grand Army Journal*, and served in the U.S. Patent Office. In 1882 he bought a quarter-interest in the *Los Angeles Times* and was sole owner by 1886.

12. "Who was Nicholas Senn?" www.sennfriendsforever.org/Who-is-Nicholas-Senn-html. Accessed 30 Mar 2016. In 1884 Dr. Senn was living in Chicago where he was appointed professor of surgery at the College of Physicians and Surgeons. In 1890 he became professor of surgery and surgical pathology at Rush Medical College. The following year, in 1891, Dr. Senn became head of the department of surgery at that medical college.

13. Ann told the tale in her memoir, possibly with enhancements.

14. Willis, "Queen Ann of Brown's Park, "288.

15. Willis, "Queen Ann of Brown's Park," 289.

16. Willis, "Queen Ann of Brown's Park," 290.

17. Willis, "Queen Ann of Brown's Park," 291.

18. Gleaned from *Were Causes of Depression*, www.reference.com/history/were-causes-depression-1893-62d1353f9e7b10b1. Accessed 5 Feb 2017; Panic of 1893-Saylor Academy, https://www.saylor.org/site/wp-content/uloads/hist312-1a-2-panic-of-1893.pdf. Accessed 5 Feb 2017

19. "Reward! One Hundred Pounds Of Sugar," *Vernal Express,* 14 Sep 1893.

20. Red Creek Ranch abstracts.

21. Ann wrote that she was fourteen or fifteen when the celebration was held. Because Ann also states that her sister Josie was married, that sets the year at 1893 and Ann's age at fifteen.

22. Ann Bassett Willis, handwritten account of "Wild Bunch Dinner," Museum of the West through The Museum of NW Colorado–Craig.

23. The cabin located near the mouth of Willow Creek came to be known as the George Kelvington place.

24. Although Brown's Park was rarely referred to as Brown's Hole during this time period, perhaps Ann, as have other writers, felt it was more colorfully descriptive when telling stories about the valley's outlaws.

25. Ann Bassett Willis, letter written to Duward and Esther Campbell, 23 Apr 1950, Museum of the West through The Museum of NW Colorado–Craig.

26. The dance was held at the Davenport Ranch (known later as the Radosevich Ranch), located down the creek from where the dinner took place. This ranch was Tom and Alice Davenport's home and ranch headquarters.

27. Charles Louis "Charlie" Sparks came to the area in 1885 when he was eighteen to work for his uncle, Sam Spicer. Charlie Sparks greatly admired Isam Dart who not only gave the young man his first horse but also taught him to ride and rope. Charlie became a highly successful and influential rancher. *Craig-Moffat Golden Jubilee, Inc. 1908-1958 Historical Booklet,* The Museum of NW Colorado–Craig.

28. Ann Bassett Willis, letter to Duward and Esther Campbell.

29. Morris, interview with Messersmith, Jul 1960.

30. In her memoir, Ann states that she attended Miss Potter's [Porter's] School for Girls in the exclusive suburbs of Boston. While it is possible that she did attend Miss Porter's School for Girls, since 1843 the school has been located in Farmington, Connecticut, approximately one hundred miles from Boston.

31. Willis, "Queen Ann of Brown's Park," 292.

CHAPTER THIRTEEN

TO PREVENT TROUBLE

In 1896, eighteen-year-old Ann Bassett's life was occupied with school days, friends, and trips from Cleveland that brought her back to Brown's Park for holiday visits and summer break. Her valley home, on the surface, was still her sheltering place of pastoral beauty, social acquaintances, roundups, and the most common of life events. Yet also ever-present was the incursion of the cattle wars, sheep wars, horse thieves, cattle rustlers, killers, and bank robbers—Brown's Park had them all, in varying degrees.

Before Elizabeth Bassett died, Butch Cassidy stopped by the ranch saying it reminded him of home. According to Josie Bassett, Butch grabbed up and wrung the necks of two or three chickens, then laughed with an ever-present sense of fun while handing them over to the cook and asking, "What's for supper?" He and Elzy Lay were both well-liked by the Brown's Parkers who knew them both in their youth.

At this time, 1896, most of the Brown's Park people, including the Bassetts, didn't know much, if anything, about the unlawful deeds of Butch Cassidy, Elzy Lay, Matt Warner, the Dick Bender gang, or the McCarty boys who congregated in secluded and abandoned cabins such as Dr. Parsons' cabin or the one at the Park Live Stock Ranch. These men were well-behaved and their coming and going wasn't given much attention. That's not to say there weren't bona fide rustlers, horse thieves, and camp robbers skulking about causing depredation for the Brown's Park settlers. Three years earlier, so many horses had been stolen from the ranchers in the valley and surrounding country that Harry Hoy told the *Rock Springs Independent* newspaper that if the organized bunch of horse thieves weren't disbanded, ranchers would be compelled to leave.[1]

The horse stealing continued on into the following year and was reported in the August 16, 1894, edition of the Rock Springs Miner:

Butch Cassidy entered the Wyoming Territorial Penitentiary on July 15, 1894, where this mugshot was taken. He learned that it was not proper to serve coffee from a big black pot at a formal dinner when he helped wait tables at the Thanksgiving Dinner of 1893. *Wyoming State Archives.*

Horse Thieves
Raids Upon Ranch Horses in this Vicinity
Following the Trail.

Some time during the latter part of July a number of saddle horses belonging to the 4J ranch and [the] Valentine S. Hoy summer ranch, Brown's Park, Sweetwater County, Wyo.,—some thirty head altogether—disappeared. Notwithstanding that it seemed improbable thieves would take property that was substantially without commercial value, circumstances indicated that the animals had been stolen, and saddle horses are yet valuable in the estimation of ranchmen. When they want a horse they are like the fellow who wanted a revolver—they want it blank bad and blanked quick, too. So Henry [Harry] Hoy, shortly after the horses were missed started in search of them and followed the trail to Powder Springs where Hoy went to hunt them up.

On August 1, John Blair and Paul Walker, who were in search of cattle in the vicinity of Bitter Creek, were held up near La Clede Spring and shot at several times by two horse thieves who were driving a band of some twenty-six or more horses. The cattlemen thought by the dust in the distance that the men were driving a bunch of cattle, but upon approaching nearer were waived back, they state, by one of the men, while the other made them the target of his Winchester. Thereupon Blair and Walker repaired to Bitter Creek station and Walker took the first train for Green River and got a couple of guns from the sheriff's deputy. Returning they took up and followed the trail until, north of the Sweetwater, it was merged with those of other range horses.

One of the thieves is described as a tall man who wore a dark hat and shirt and carried a rifle. The other was a short and heavy man, who wore a light hat and shirt and carried a nickel-plated pistol.

Twelve of the horses stolen belonged to Valentine S. Hoy and he offers a reward of $100 for the arrest and conviction of the thieves.

Jim Peterson, also of Brown's Park had two horses stolen on Tuesday night, the 6th inst., and this leads to the belief that there are a number of thieves probably acting in concert, in different sections of the country, who gather the horses together to be driven either into Montana or Nebraska, and possibly farther east, where horses can be sold for cash.[2]

When Christmastime 1896 arrived in Brown's Park, the sheep wars came to call. During this time, a series of armed conflicts concerning grazing rights were occurring along the border region of Colorado and Wyoming between the sheepmen and cattlemen. When Wyoming sheep flocks and herders began spilling into Colorado, anger among Colorado cattlemen boiled over.

Brown's Park sheep and cattle ranchers had coexisted up until then. Griff Edwards had run, for several years, a nice sized sheep business on his private holdings just southeast of Brown's Park. The Bassetts sometimes ran a very small band of sheep along with their cattle as did others in the Park. Tom Davenport whose headquarters was on Willow Creek in the Utah end of Brown's Park had a relatively large flock. Bassett neighbor Frank Goodman had gone exclusively to raising sheep, and his operation had grown large enough to sustain his family. The common practice among the Brown's Park area stockmen was to have their sheep sheared on a corresponding schedule and sell their wool to the same buyer, as they did in 1892.[3] They were all simply trying to make a living on their individual places in an unpredictable livestock business.

Most assuredly, many things would have turned out differently if Elizabeth Bassett had been granted a longer life, not only for Ann and the Bassett family, but also for some of the other people of Brown's Park. Elizabeth had come to understand the power of diplomacy and loyalty along with playing from a hand of strength in order to become a successful cattlewoman. She might have been able to calm tempers and negotiate fairness for her sheep-raising neighbors. She almost certainly would have stood up for her old friend Griff Edwards for he had pioneered the settling of Brown's Park and had well-earned his place on the range, which included helping to act as a barrier for Brown's Park against the encroaching Middlesex outfit. She and Griff made a handshake agreement years ago about Zenobia Basin, which greatly benefitted the Bassett Ranch. Griff continued to honor the pact even after Elizabeth's death.

Griffith W. Edwards was born in 1849 in Wales.[4] His wife Annie was also Welsh. Griff was among the earliest cattlemen of the Brown's Park area, arriving there nine years before the Bassetts in 1869. Five years later, Griff and his then partner, Billy Tittsworth, bought several hundred head of cattle in Oregon. After the men drove the cattle hundreds of miles back home, a hard winter dropped feet of blowing snow on their range in Salt Wells Basin. Griff and Billy knew the only way they were going to save their cattle was to battle the terrible cold and snow and get the cattle to Brown's Park. The task was almost insurmountable, but they eventually found all the cattle and pushed them down into the valley. There, the ground was bare of snow. All Brown's Park's inhabitants survived the severe winter of 1874-1875 in excellent shape.[5]

Now, more than twenty years later Griff was being attacked because he had an impressive sheep operation in Northwestern Colorado, even though he grazed the sheep exclusively on his private holdings. Other sheepmen, most prominently Griff's brother, John "Jack" Edwards, were expanding their range and flocks from Wyoming and utilizing what they saw as their right to graze the public domain in Colorado. That was not the same circumstance with Griff Edwards, however, and he was distressed by the injustice of the warnings being leveled at him from not only a group that called itself The Craig Committeemen but also from some of his long-time friends who were his Brown's Park neighbors.

A chilling notice was received by Albert Seger[6] who was employed by Griff Edwards as ranch foreman:

Ann Bassett (tall with big hat) in New Mexico. *Courtesy of Jo Semotan.*

Craig, Colo., Nov. 3, 1896
Mr. Al Seger, Ladore, Colo.

Dear Sir:

As cattle growers of Routt county, we have investigated the situation in Brown's Park and the lower country and have decided the sheep men must go. That the state line shall be the boundary line. We hereby kindly request you as sheep raisers, to stop infringement on the ranchmen of the Park and take your sheep to other grounds.

We mean business, and should you fail to heed this request you will suffer the consequences.

Craig Committeemen[7]

The organized committeemen represented the Routt County Anti-Sheep Society and were on a mission to adopt a policy to get all the sheep and sheepmen out, and keep them out, of northwestern Colorado. The group advised the Brown's Park cattlemen to form their own organization in unison with theirs. The committeemen were persuasive in their arguments that no sheep grazers, regardless of circumstances, could be left in Routt County without risking everlasting damage to the land and cattle operations. Thus, the Brown's Park Ranchmen's Protective Association was formed with Mat Rash as president. A communication was composed and delivered to area sheepmen including Frank Goodman and Griff Edwards:

> To all sheep men now ranging sheep
> in Routt County, Colorado:
>
> We, a committee, appointed by the Brown's Park Ranchmen's Protective Association, a branch of the Routt County Anti-Sheep Society, to visit sheep owners or their representatives, now in Ladore Precinct, Routt County, Colorado, request them to remove their sheep now ranging in Routt County to a range outside the Colorado state line. They, the sheep men, if they grant our request, are to commence the removal of their sheep within six days from now, not later than the 17th of November 1896, otherwise we, the cattle men of Routt County, will understand that they do not intend to remove their flocks and we will govern our acts accordingly.
>
> Brown's Park Ranchmen's Protective Association
Ladore, Colorado, Nov. 11th, 1896[8]

Griff Edwards, highly respected and supported in the Rock Springs community where he owned a town residence, responded from Rock Springs with a poignant reply that must surely have touched, if not shamed, some of the cattlemen:

> Dear sir:
>
> Your letter enclosing a notice to me from the Brown's Park ranchmen's association has been received and fully noted, and in reply I will say to you, that they have overlooked some very important facts in relation to my ranging sheep in that part of Colorado. I have been a taxpayer in Routt county, Colorado, for twenty-two years, and I am the first settler to range stock and to settle south of the Vermillion, and to prove up on a homestead and pre-emption, which, in my opinion, entitles me to some consideration, possibly, more than may have been extended to others.
>
> I have never, to my knowledge, in any manner, interfered with the stock or property of any man in Routt county. I have repeatedly surrendered rights to the range in that country which law and justice

would have helped me to hold, and in particular do I remember to have surrendered all my rights to range in Zenobia basin to Mrs. Bassett. I promised to keep my stock out of there, and none of it, to my knowledge, has ever been in there since that time. I was the first settler at Douglas springs. I built a fence there and improved it. I was asked to give it up to the exclusive use of my neighbors, and I did. Matt Rash and Bassett, in particular, have had almost the exclusive use of it, and with my constant good will. I have a patent to my ranch at Ladore. I have had no use for it. I did not need it in particular, and it has been, of late years, used all the time by the cattle men, as a round up station and for pasturage and their general accommodation, against all of which I have not objected, for the reason that I have always felt that if the property belonging to me in that country was of little use to me it might as well be used by my neighbors, if they saw fit. . . .

Now, to prevent trouble. I am willing to draw a line from Hogback valley, inclusive of the valley, taking in all the mountains to Snake river, and all springs at their base, barring Douglas springs, and I will agree not to put a sheep within that line. It would be a line drawn which would give them range for years to come. I have always been in favor of some such arrangement between sheep and cattle men.

Now, I want you to say to these men that I have all of my property there. I have my hay, oats and all of my supplies there. There is no where I can go, if I wanted to. I have a right there by every argument known, and while I do not want trouble with men with whom I have always been friendly, yet I cannot move my outfit. I trust largely to the sober second thought of the cattle men to prevent any trouble in this matter.

Yours Truly,
Griff W. Edwards[9]

The cattlemen weren't much dissuaded. They truly were up against a major issue with what they saw as a literal invasion of sheep that was taking a serious toll on rangeland and cattle operations. Had the fundamentals for proper grazing management been understood and followed, the rangeland could have supported multispecies grazing. However, overgrazing was a matter of routine and that was devastating to cattle. Opposition to and the detestation of sheep and sheepmen was deadly serious. Some of the reasoning behind their determination to be rid of the animals and their human tenders was revealed in a public statement on behalf of the cattlemen that read in part:

> They have built dipping pens at springs poisoning the sources of water supply and leave the rotting carcasses of their dead sheep in springs and creeks polluting the water, rendering it unfit for human use, bedding their sheep on hill sides when after a rain most of our water courses are not unlike a city sewer carrying to the larger streams a mass of stench and rottenness. The sheep eat and trample out every vestige of grass, poison and destroy flowers, shrubs and bushes and trample the earth until water can not penetrate it but runs off as fast as it falls cutting the ground into gulches, thus drying up springs and lessening the water supply for irrigating purposes.
>
> After much work and great expense to ourselves and to the county to make the roads passable they drive their flocks over them leaving them in worse condition than before being repaired.
>
> The herders have cut our fences and drove in or allowed the sheep to run over our lands, not being satisfied after getting all the feed on the outside.
>
> To sum it all up their entire course has been and is unjust and tyrannical, and our organization today is our just and indignant protest against their ruinous sway over the land to the loss and ruin of our homes; be it resolved by the members of our organization that we will individually do all in our power to protect ourselves in our rights and rid the ranges of what we rightly consider a pest only equaled by a devastating pestilence, and resolved that we make the state line between Colorado and Wyoming on the north and the state line between Utah and Colorado on the west the dividing line between the cattle and sheep ranges.[10]

On Tuesday, December 22, cowmen began gathering at a camp on lower Little Snake River, representing various sections of northwestern Colorado. A newspaper described the scene:

> They came in companies, in two and three, until by evening there was an aggregation of armed men camped on Snake River that was formidable to look upon. The men were well mounted and thoroughly armed and their object was to wait on the sheep men and inaugurate the removal of sheep from Routt county. During the following day horsemen continued to arrive and that evening an organization was affected. The force was divided into companies, each with a captain and the entire command placed in the charge of a commander-in-chief.
>
> Thursday morning camp was broken and the command started for Brown's Park.[11]

On Friday, December 25, the Bassetts and others looked upon a fearsome scene arriving in Brown's Park. Supply wagons rolled in, one by one, to a count of seven, accompanied by forty-seven mounted and well-armed men.[12] The wagons pulled to a stop near the Green River where camp was established. Then, joined by Mat Rash and Isam Dart, the men rode in force up the Park to the ranch where Frank Goodman, his wife Lizzie, and their children lived on a homestead they had purchased from the widowed Molly (Mary) Sears.[13] The Goodman's had put together a pretty place at the foot of Cold Spring Mountain.

The Goodman home was filled with children, which meant plenty of activity doing laundry, raising food, and preparing meals, settling squabbles, and braiding hair. As part of the social circle of the valley, the family attended the dances and other celebrations. All the while they worked to build up a sheep herd after getting their start from gathering stragglers abandoned on the open range between Rock Springs and Brown's Park.[14] If any outlaws, known or suspected, rode up the trail Lizzie hushed her children and hurried them under the beds to hide with instructions to stay put until she came for them.[15]

By 1894 the Goodman sheep herd had grown to about 2,500 ewes plus lambs. As a common matter, Frank went out early one morning in May 1894, to tend the sheep. Lizzie, carrying a shovel, walked among the birds and scents of the young day to adjust the glistening pathway of the irrigation water. It was an ordinary routine, and common that she had left her oldest daughter Sarah who was fourteen, to build a fire in the stove and get breakfast started. It was also a normal thing that three-and-a-half-year-old Martha Rose "Rosie," fresh from a night of slumber and still wearing her nightdress, would want to help her big sister. Even so, there is no innocent moment which can't be shattered. In a sudden and horrific flash, the warped tongue of a flame snaked outward to savor the threads of little Rosie's gown.

Lizzie heard the screams of tragedy unfolding. She dropped the shovel and ran. After grasping hold of Rosie to pick her up, she rushed to the creek. Then Lizzie soaked her child in the crystal cold and drenched the viciousness that was going to kill her daughter, anyway. Rosie's lungs were injured beyond a mother's help. In the sorrowful aftershock, a grave was dug nearby, just east of Goodman Draw. A little mound of dirt appeared, surrounded both by sagebrush and a fence built of wood.

Then, on Christmas day two years later, Lizzie witnessed dozens of armed men, some of whom she knew well, surround her home and family. Lizzie and the children watched, in a stupor, as Frank's face turned white. Several men held him, while others hitched up the Goodman sheepwagon. They gathered some of the sheep and trailed them away from the Goodman place across the state line into Utah.[16] Confident that their performance had been well understood, the armed men rode off and returned to their camp near the river.

Although Frank wanted to stand his ground and hang on to what he and his family had built, it only took until the next morning for him to send a messenger notifying the cattlemen that he would take his sheep out of Colorado as soon as possible.[17] That same day the entire contingent departed Brown's Park, leaving behind their message of rank intimidation.

John Hennessy, a fellow who worked for Griff Edwards, arrived in Rock Springs and reported he had witnessed forty-seven mounted and well-armed cattlemen from Little Snake River ride up and instruct Mr. Edwards' foreman to move the sheep across the line and not return. He said that no further threats were made beyond that and the armed men hadn't been seen since, although the sheep were still on their wonted range.[18] However, on January 16, 1897, the following notice appeared in the Craig newspaper:

To the Stockgrowers of Routt County:

I write to inform you that Griff Edwards' sheep are on the move out of the State of Colorado to stay.

Yours truly,
Willis Rouff, Foreman for Griff Edwards[19]

Although he still had a home in Rock Springs, Griff Edwards died in Hooper, Nebraska, the following spring on April 20, 1897, leaving Annie a widow. All his years of work, pioneering an unsettled country and building a respected life and livestock operation, was readily reduced to probate forms. Five months after his death, Griff's sheep went to the massively large Warren Land and Livestock Company owned by Wyoming's former Governor and then U.S. Senator and President of the National Sheep Growers Association Francis E. Warren. Senator Warren traveled from Cheyenne to Rock Springs to oversee his new flock of sheep loaded onto the train.[20]

The Goodmans, no doubt sad and deeply stung by the turn of events in their lives, decided to move to Vernal. They sold their entire flock of sheep to Tim Kinney in Wyoming and their ranch to the man who headed up the Brown's Park Ranchmen's Protective Association, Mat Rash. Frank and Lizzie loaded up their belongings, children, and wounded sentiments and drove away from their home and the grave where their little daughter lay. Mat Rash was already in the process of transitioning the place into a cattle outfit.

While Ann Bassett's sister, Josie Bassett McKnight, was in Brown's Park raising two sons—Crawford born on July 12, 1893, and Amos Herbert "Chick" on April 14, 1895—the current of Ann's life took her gently to Ohio, to a place of family life and higher learning. Indications are that the stability there soothed her and added to the refinement her mother tried so hard to instill, although it hardly tamed her. She continued to study in Cleveland until September 1897 when she returned to reside in Brown's Park.[21] She had barely grown accustomed to spending long hours in the saddle when she found herself in a chilling circumstance.

NOTES TO CHAPTER THIRTEEN

1. *Vernal Express*, taken from the *Rock Springs Independent*, 23 Nov 1893.

2. "Horse Thieves," *Rock Springs Miner*, 18 Aug 1894.

3. *Rock Springs Miner*, 1 Jun 1892.

4. 1880 United States Federal Census.

5. J.S. Hoy, Hoy Manuscript, 109.

6. Albert Seger was the brother of Charlie Seger who was stabbed and killed by Joe Tolliver at Charlie Crouse's ranch.

7. "Threatening Letters," *Rock Springs Miner*, 10 Dec 1896

8. "Threatening Letters," *Rock Springs Miner*.

9. "Mr. Griff W. Edwards' Business-like and Cool Reply," *Rock Springs Miner*, 10 Dec 1896.

10. "Cattlemen vs. sheep," *Craig Courier*, 26 Dec 1896.

11. "Cattlemen vs. sheep," *Craig Courier*.

12. "Cattlemen vs. sheep," *Craig Courier*.

13. This location is now known as the Sterling place.

14. Dick and Daun DeJournette, *One Hundred Years of Brown's Park and Diamond Mountain*, (Vernal: DeJournette Enterprises, 1996), 38

15. Mary Goodman Bennion, "Frank Goodman," biography by a daughter of Frank and Elizabeth Goodman, The Museum of NW Colorado–Craig.

16. Mary Goodman Bennion, "Frank Goodman."

17. "Cattlemen vs. sheep," *Craig Courier*.

18. "The War Between Cattle And Sheep Men In Brown's Park," *Rock Springs Miner,* 31 Dec 1896.

19. *Craig Courier*, 16 Jan 1897.

20. "Personal," *Rock Springs Miner*, 16 Sep 1897.

21. "Personal," *Rock Spring Miner.*

CHAPTER FOURTEEN

HUNTING GROUNDS

Ann often had school friends visit the ranch. She enjoyed taking them riding and encouraged participation in her way of life as a cowhand. Her closest friend was a very pretty girl from Rock Springs named Lizzie Brown. Lizzie was a familiar face at the Bassett Ranch, spending most of her free time from school at the ranch. She was nine months younger than Ann, born in February 1879 in Park City, Utah. When she was three weeks old, her family moved to Rock Springs.[1] Lizzie especially was drawn to Brown's Park and loved helping out with the ranch work. Ann admired Lizzie's natural ability in handling livestock and considered her to be an excellent hand. The two teenagers spent a lot of time riding together.

In October 1897, the following month after Ann's return from Cleveland when she was nineteen, she and Lizzie Brown helped Sam deliver a bunch of cattle Herb sold to a man named Jim Norvell. The three drove the cattle about thirty-three miles to Longhorn and Aunty Armida Thompson's ranch on Little Snake River.[2] After their arrival, they found the Thompsons concerned about the number of White River and Uintah Utes from the Utah reservations coming to hunt in Colorado. Heavy gunfire echoed across the countryside. The Thompsons were certain that both wildlife and cattle were being killed.

J.S. Hoy in Brown's Park described the Ute game hunts as being a slaughter of deer. Settlers in the area, throughout the 1890s, voiced complaints that while residents had to abide by the law, the Utes continued to get away with ignoring it.

A posse made up of nine cowboys and ranchers being led by W.R. Wilcox, the newly appointed game warden of Routt County, arrived at the Thompson Ranch. Wilcox had been notified by the chief game warden of Colorado that Indians from Utah were probably violating

Lizzie Brown (left) and Ann Bassett were close friends and Lizzie often visited the Bassett ranch. *The Museum of NW Colorado–Craig.*

game laws and should be arrested unless they left the state. Wilcox mentioned that his plan was to arrest a couple of the Utes and take them before a justice of the peace. Perhaps if their agent had to come pay fines, the agent might be more inclined to keep the Utes on the reservation.[3]

Early the next morning on Sunday, October 24, 1897, as the posse prepared to ride to the nearest Ute camp, Sam left Ann and Lizzie behind telling them to take care of the extra saddle horses while he took the cattle on to a place called Big Gulch.[4] Throughout the morning and first part of the afternoon, Ann and Lizzie visited with Aunty Armida Thompson,

Armida's mother, Sarah Boomer, and the two Thompson children. Lyman was five and toddler Anna May was two years old.

At about 2:30 P.M. most of the posse rode in and hurried to the house. The men were unnerved and in a rush to get the women and children to safety. They had just had a shootout at the Ute camp while attempting to arrest Star and Shinaraff. They feared an outbreak.

The following is from a newspaper article containing an account relayed by Game Warden Wilcox about the tragic incident that happened just three miles from the Thompson ranch:[5]

From outside sources will probably come words of reproach regarding the conduct of Game Warden Wilcox in the recent Indian trouble in western Routt county. The dispatches from Ft. Duchesne states that Wilcox's deputies fired the first shot which lead [led] to the battle between the Indians and whites on Sunday Oct 24th; that the Utes were unarmed and that their guns were stacked in their tepees; that the whites numbered twenty-five and showed no quarter or mercy in their attack.

All of these statements are false. According to Game Warden Wilcox there were but eleven men in the party which undertook to arrest the Indians. Warden Wilcox and his men are to be commended rather than censured. He used every precaution to avoid trouble and repeatedly cautioned his men not to precipitate matters and refrain from using violence or shooting unless forced to do so in self defense. In an interview with THE COURIER Warden Wilcox stated as follows:

"My instructions were to arrest any Indians violating the game laws and to use the utmost precaution in the performance of my duty. These instructions I endeavored to carry out and I took no steps until I found abundant evidence of guilt. Fresh venison, beef, deer and beef hides were found concealed in Snake Pete's camp on Snake River.

"I urged the Indians to submit to arrest peaceably and they understood English perfectly, one of their number spoke English quite fluently, claiming that he was an educated Indian.

"For nearly four hours I parleyed with the Utes and exhausted every means to induce them to quietly submit to the law. The chief, whom we supposed to be Old Star, wanted to wait for Snake Pete and said that he would not go to Craig with me.

"All the while we were talking with the Indians the squaws continued to interfere and one or two bucks that had been disarmed were supplied with guns by them. Besides several squaws and papooses two bucks left the camp and struck out in the direction of other Ute camps lower down. I knew that there were a large number of Indians below us and

Longhorn and Armida Thompson with their children Anna May and Lyman. *The Museum of NW Colorado – Craig.*

it would have been folly to attempt to comply with Star's wishes and finally it became evident that the Indians expected reinforcements. As a last resort I ordered my men to place the bucks on their horses so that we could take them away. As fast as I put a buck on a horse he would slip off on the other side and the squaws and dogs would pull and tug at myself and men. All was confusion and when Al Shaw came to my assistance an Indian pulled his gun on him and just as it was discharged Tom Kimbley struck it aside, thereby saving Shaw's life, as the bullet found a lodging place in the body of a squaw. Shaw escaped the bullet only to be clubbed into insensibility by a buck who struck him on the head with a rifle. We thought that Shaw was killed and when he fell the fight became furious, bucks and squaws doing their best to annihilate my force. However with the exception of Shaw, none of my men received serious injuries, though several had narrow escapes.

"When the firing ceased we found that six Indians had fallen, four bucks and two squaws."

Henry Templeton, a rancher on Bear River who was acting as guide and go-between for the posse, later expressed that after first arriving at the Ute camp and while the rest of the posse waited at a distance, he and Warden Wilcox went to the camp and found it nearly deserted, although some Ute hunters soon arrived. In the distance he saw Chieftain Star (Ungutshoone) and Kent (Soonamunche),[6] riding towards camp but they grew startled and tried to flee when they spotted the posse. The posse rode quickly to cut them off. Although Kent got away, Star was captured and disarmed. Other hunters arrived in an excited state.

When Templeton and Wilcox saw the commotion concerning the posse, they rode back to the group. Soon the entire squad of eleven white men, with Star in tow, went to the Ute camp and faced down Shinaraff and Cooamunche. It was by then about 10 A.M. and for the next four hours Wilcox attempted to arrest Star and Shinaraff and convince them to go with him, back to Thompson's ranch.

Henry Templeton said, "Star, me your friend! We no hurt you. Just take you to justice of peace. Make agent pay your fine."

Star replied, "No! Me no go! Me fight!"

Templeton then said, "Well, Wilcox, that settles it."

"Surround the camp," ordered Wilcox. "You with short guns, come with me."[7]

One of the deputies with a pistol, Jack White, dismounted his horse and handed Templeton his horse's bridle reins. Just a moment before the shooting erupted, Templeton saw the wife of White River Chief Colorow holding a large pistol in both hands and aiming it at Wilcox. Templeton said he didn't see what happened next because everything was confusion punctuated with the snap of rifles and the boom of heavy pistols that caused his horse to take fright and start bucking. At the same time Jack White's horse went berserk trying desperately to pull away from Templeton, resulting in the added chaos of two frantic horses plunging through the brush and cedars on the steep hillside.

After the horses were under control, Templeton saw that Star was still a prisoner and being marched away between two horsemen. Suddenly the captive ducked under one of the horse's necks and ran down a steep slope through the cedars. Although several shots were fired at him, Star disappeared into the trees. Because of the bloody melee that had so unexpectedly happened, the posse did not give chase.[8] Instead, couriers were dispatched to Meeker and Craig calling for aid, a posse member named Charles McCormick rode to notify Sheriff Neiman in Egeria Park and the rest of the men went to Thompson's ranch to remove the women and children to safety.[9]

Not long after Wilcox and his men arrived at the ranch, Ann and Lizzie saddled their horses and prepared to leave. Aunty Thompson and the children were loaded into a wagon to be escorted to the Boyd Vaughn ranch on Bear River.

Throughout her nineteen years, Ann's partiality and affection continued to be with the Native Americans with whom she, in part, self-identified. However, this was no time to linger. She and Lizzie turned down the men's offer to go along with them and instead rode away from Thompson's ranch and hurried along the trail to home.

It was Ann's nature to be the contrast to Lizzie's jitters and instead act as the brave and experienced one, whose pinto horse, she decided, would be recognized by some of her Ute friends. She was certain they would not harm her. However she knew all too well the danger that could surface if this was an uprising. The fact that her only riding companion was another teenage girl made it scarier and they stayed alert to every sound and shadow. A lot of lonesome country stood between them and home.[10]

As they rode, Ann instructed Lizzie that if any Indians attempted to take them captive, Lizzie was to bolt into the cedars to find a hiding place. She was to remain silent and not come out until the afternoon of the next day. Then, she should not look for Ann but instead head for the Bassett Ranch, miles away. Such instructions probably did little to ease Lizzie's fright. But, at least there was a plan to follow.

With darkness descending the two girls were alarmed by the clapping and clattering of horses on the run and closing in. Lizzie immediately reacted and without a backward glance spurred her horse to run into the trees to disappear. Moments later, Ann was relieved to be surrounded by a band of wild horses stopping to look her over before shaking their heads, blowing wind through their nostrils, and loping away.[11]

Lizzie had taken Ann's emergency plan seriously and had disappeared. Ann made an exhaustive search but Lizzie was nowhere to be found. Not until Ann gave her pinto his head allowing him to sniff the ground and follow the scent of Lizzie's horse, was the well-hidden pair finally discovered. Before long they were back on the trail, although moving more slowly into the deepness of the night.

Seeing home finally come into view must have been a most welcome sight. Immediately upon hearing the news Ann and Lizzie shared, Mat Rash saddled up and rode to join Sam and assist the posse. Ann and Lizzie hadn't eaten since breakfast the morning before and were famished. Soon a couple of beef steaks sizzled in a skillet.[12]

Herb, Ann, and Lizzie were anxious for their neighbors and concerned for the safety of Mat Rash and Sam. There was much to learn about the whole affair.

When the posse was taking Armida Thompson and her children to safety, they met a traveling salesman from Kansas City named Coombs being driven to Craig by a Brown's Parker named Charles Gable.[13] They all spent that night in the Vaughn ranch house. The men slept on the floor, fifteen in a row.[14] The next morning Cy Baily and Charles McCormick rode out to warn the settlers on the White River and upper Bear River. Thomas Armstrong, Jack White, and Charles Gable headed west planning to go to Lily Park to bring out the families of John W. Lowell, Jr. and Henry Goodwin. Henry Templeton loaned Gable a saddle and a horse to ride named Little G. As Armstrong, White, and Gable passed the north end of Cross Mountain they were suddenly surprised by an ambush which broke into a fierce, running fight.

After the thunder of the first volley, Armstrong and White, galloping for the top of Cross Mountain, were immediately separated from Gable who disappeared over a hill towards Thompson's Ranch. Both White and Armstrong had bullets tearing at their clothing when Armstrong's horse fell and died.[15] At that instant, White had to abandon his horse in the steep terrain and the two men on foot hid and dodged and made their way together up the mountain. Exhausted, shaken, and footsore, they finally made it back to Boyd Vaughn's ranch about midnight.

The twenty-seven-year-old Charles Gable had a different outcome. Thinking both his partners had been killed, Gable rode Little G as fast as he could get the horse to run, taking a route up Little Snake River to Longhorn Thompson's place. By the time he reached the evacuated ranch, Gable was desperate to change mounts because it seemed to him that Little G did more jumping up and down than running. He was afraid the Utes weren't far behind. He was right.[16]

One of the horses in Thompson's field was from the Bassett Ranch. Bill Snort was his name and he had a reputation. The gelding was known as an outlaw because no one could ride him. He had white patches of hair here and there on his body that had, long ago, grown over healed sores he acquired after bucking off a rider and running wild for a week with the saddle still on his back.[17] Bill Snort was very gentle otherwise and easy to handle until someone tried to mount him so the Bassetts kept him in the cavvy as a bell horse. Sometimes they hung a bell around Bill Snort's neck so the herd could be left to graze the countryside overnight and be easily located in the morning. Bill Snort greeted Gable and Little G in a friendly manner.

Luck was with Gable that day as Bill Snort not only let the man saddle him, but also allowed him to mount up. Before Bill Snort could react, gunfire whizzed and then thumped through the cantle of Gable's saddle.[18] Although Bill Snort bucked a little, with more bullets flying around him and ripping into Gable's clothing, the savvy old horse jumped to a dead run heading in the direction of his original home in Brown's Park.[19]

Not long after Charles Gable and the gelding escaped, Charlie Marsh, Ed Brotherton, and F.O. Clark arrived on the scene to find a dozen Utes rounding up all the horses in the field and setting fire to the Thompson stables, corral, and haystacks. The three deputies shot in the direction of the Utes sending them scattering. The men then prevented the fire from spreading and were able to save Longhorn and Armida's ranch house.

The next morning, Tuesday, Sam Bassett and Mat Rash were with Warden Wilcox and five other men riding for Lily Park on a second mission to bring out the Lowell and Goodwin families. Without incident the entire group arrived back at Vaughn's ranch about eleven that night.[20]

Tempers against the Utes were running intensely hot in some of the surrounding communities including Rifle, Colorado, as revealed in the closing paragraph of an article from that town. It is ripe with contempt:[21]

> The trouble convened last week when the White River, Uncompahgre and Uintah Utes began pouring over the line from Utah on their annual fall hunt. The White River Utes are exceptionally ugly and apparently anxious to pick trouble with parties of whites with whom they have come in contact. These Utes were in the Meeker Massacre and have never been anything but ugly and waiting for an opportunity to do mischief. There are several hundred of them now in the state.

Over one hundred and twenty settlers came together in the tiny town of Lay for two weeks to wait out the trouble.[22] A range rider from Diamond Mountain rode into Vernal, Utah, to report that between Vernal and the mountain, he witnessed about fifty Utes holding a war dance. Also, a group of Utes forced some sheepherders away from their camp and drove their herd of sheep away five miles before leaving them.[23]

Nonetheless, the Utes launched no further revenge attack and things quieted down rather quickly. Soon after the incident the Utes had started returning to their reservation in Utah. Six days after the shooting, Dr. Reamer[24] from White Rocks, Utah, traveled to meet up with a group of Utes so he could attend the two wounded women. One was too badly injured to continue traveling.[25]

After returning to Fort Duchesne from Colorado with his troops, Captain H. H. Wright made a report of his expedition to the site of the event in Routt County. An Associated Press dispatch from Washington indicated that Captain Wright secured a statement of the trouble from the Indians. His empathy was clearly with the Utes. The *Craig Courier* printed the substance of Capt. Wright's findings:[26]

> "That a small party of them were camped on Snake Hill hunting deer, the majority of them in the hills, and but four bucks were in camp, when a party of armed white men came into camp. They remained there some time, the Indians not understanding them. Finally one opened his coat, showed a star saying they were buckskin police and the Indians must go with them; the Indians refused, upon which the whites covered them with their pistols, and several grasping the two bucks by the wrists, a struggle commenced; a squaw ran to their assistance, when the police literally riddled the two with bullets. A warden on the outside of the party shot the squaw in the back of her head and another in the arm. The two surviving bucks saw their chance to run for horses, which they had in the brush, did so, making their escape. The Indians insist that neither at that time nor since have they fired a shot at a white man."

Captain Wright went on to state that the citizens of the area referred to the affair as not an Indian outbreak but a white man's and that Warden Wilcox had been heard to say that if he could not arrest the Indians he would kill them. The Captain confirmed the torching of the corral and haystacks at Thompson's ranch and said that the Indians did acknowledge it to be true but that it was done in anger after the killings.

The *Courier* printed a rebuttal to Capt. Wright's findings. A portion of it reads:

> The statement that the Indians could not understand is entirely wrong, for they fully understood what was wanted and one of their number, a young buck, talked good English with one of the wardens and stated that he had attended the Teller Institute at Grand Junction. When the fight commenced this same young buck attempted to knife the young man with whom he was talking.

The report that Warden Wilcox stated that if he could not arrest the Indians he would kill them, is absolutely untrue. That the Indians did not fire a single shot at the white men is also false, as Thomas Armstrong's dead horse and the bullet holes in the saddles and clothes of Jack White and Gabel [Gable] will show.

As to the wardens depriving Boyd Vaughn of his hay and winter supplies, there is no misunderstanding in regard to that matter. Mr. Vaughn will no doubt be paid for everything furnished by him. His bill amounts to $175 and it has been approved by Warden Wilcox and Sheriff Neiman. Mr. Vaughn's bill will come up before the county commissioners at their next meeting.[27]

Although it was thought the Ute people had all gone back to the reservation, there must have been a final breath of dissent that caused Longhorn and Armida Thompson concern as they worked at rebuilding their corrals and stables. Although nothing came of it, the following appeared in the *Salt Lake Herald* on December 2:

E. B. Thompson, who lives in the western part of Routt county, near the scene of the recent fight between Utes and game wardens, arrived in town [Craig] yesterday and gave the startling information that the Indians were again invading that section. Mr. Thompson says that, although he has not seen any of the Indians, he has heard the shooting and has seen fresh moccasin tracks on Douglas Mountain and also the tracks of the ponies.

The mail carrier whose route lies between Maybell and Lily Park, reports having seen four Indians, who were some distance from the road. Mat Rash and Sam Bassett, residents of Brown's Park, also report having seen several Indians and say they are killing game, as they heard a great deal of shooting.

Mr. Thompson has notified Game Warden Wilcox of the matter and that official is expected in town tomorrow on his way to the Lower country to investigate. No anxiety is felt by the residents of the country over the report, but they are somewhat excited over the matter, they may be called on at any time to aid in the driving out the redskins.

E. B. Thompson is the man whose home was reported to have been burned by the Utes just after the late trouble, causing him a loss of about $4,000.[28]

Colorado governor Alva B. Adams appointed three Colorado men, Judge David C. Beaman of Pueblo, Senator C. E. Noble of Colorado Springs, and Joshua Walbridge of Steamboat Springs to investigate the incident. Elisha Reynolds from Crow Agency, Montana, was appointed Special Agent by the Federal Government to accompany the state committee and also take separate testimony.[29]

Testimony was taken on December 7 in Craig and the next day Agent Reynolds and the commissioners went with Warden Wilcox to the deserted camp where the incident happened. Settlers who were involved were asked to supply depositions. Herb assisted Ann and Lizzie and their statements were submitted. Ann Bassett was staunch in her defense of the Utes and disgust with the game wardens' actions that resulted in preventable violence. Many others voiced the same opinion.

The Commissioner of Indian Affairs reported the investigation showed that when the warden and his deputies were trying to make the arrests at the Ute camp, there were six Indian men there along with eight or ten women and a few children. All the Ute men were armed, and some of the women had arms in their tents. Found in the camp were a quantity of deer hair, two deer yet to be dressed, many deer hides, and some beef hides.

The report by Special Agent Reynolds reads, in part:

> In the final attempt to arrest the Indians; an Indian, unexpectedly to all, fired his gun at one of the wardens, Al Shaw, and as he was about to fire, a warden, Mr. Kimberly, standing near Shaw, struck the gun to one side, and the shot missed Shaw and hit a woman. At this moment the firing was commenced by the wardens and Indians, which was participated in by about only five or six of the wardens and lasted but a few minutes, and when it had ceased, it was found that some Indians had been killed and some wounded, and Shaw was lying on the ground in a senseless condition, having been stricken down by the Indian who had fired the first shot. The wardens then went away to Thompson's ranch.[30]

The Utes testified that those who either escaped the wardens or were away hunting during the killings came back to camp to bury the dead. That evening, all started for the agency in Utah, traveling all night to get out of Colorado.

The Commissioner of Indian Affairs wrote in his report:

> This was the old hunting ground of the Utes before they were removed from Colorado and they have always depended on game for no small part of their food and clothing. They can not understand why they should be shut out from it during certain seasons of the year by State laws, especially when the right to hunt game in this region was

guaranteed to them by a treaty with the Government, which provided that such right should be inviolable and continue so long as game existed there. However, the United States Supreme Court has held, in Ward v. Race Horse (163 U.S., 504), that the admission of a State into the Union annuls such treaty rights. Therefore the Utes could legally be held by the officials of the State of Colorado to be violating the game laws. The testimony shows that the Indians were aware that their hunting was liable to be objected to, and that they had been for some time rather apprehensively on the lookout for the "buckskin police," and had made inquiries as to what they would be likely to do to them.[31]

Special Agent Reynolds finished his investigation and reported he was inclined to acquit the posse of anything deliberate or malicious.[32] Captain Beck said the Utes had been told repeatedly about the law and warned not to go to Colorado to hunt. He said only one individual permit had been issued. That lone permit was for Star to visit Sam Bassett at the Bassett Ranch to hunt horses.[33]

❧ ❧ ❧

Charles Gable had been terrorized by the Ute bullets that had come so close to finding their mark. He made a wild ride to Brown's Park on the Bassett gelding Bill Snort at a sustained and fast pace. He rode desperately and alone, thinking that at any second he could be shot while trying to get home to his wife Cora and their new baby.

After making it safely to Brown's Park, Gable concluded his ride on Bill Snort when the pair arrived at the Bassett barnyard even though Gable's home was still miles away in the Utah end of the valley. He unsaddled the spent and lathered gelding. The horse known as an outlaw in his youth, had, on this day, served his rider superbly. After the bridle was removed from his proud head, Bill Snort walked across an alfalfa field to a creek, drank, and then fell to the ground, dead. Although it is hardly believable, Gable claimed that Bill Snort, the only time he was ever ridden, made the thirty mile run in a mere two hours' time.[34]

Ann was sad about Bill Snort's passing saying she had known him for a long time and had considerable respect for his cunning. The gelding once made an impressive spectacle, unseating bronc busters who took every advantage of him with their ropes, bits, and spurs.[35] Also, Ann was very sad for the Utes, feeling that the wardens and other government officials were arrogant and overbearing; that it was totally uncalled for to remove the Utes from their cherished hunting grounds.

The Utes, however, had long been on this course of collision. If only they had followed the game laws, or even harvested only reasonable amounts of wildlife, and, most certainly, if they had not been tempted by the easy mark of cattle, perhaps they could have continued with the hunts. Most likely, though, it was inevitable that it would end this way, for laws and their enforcements were growing in number in the West, and those laws would never favor the native people over the settlers and developers of the land.

All was set in motion. Although some of the Utes occasionally returned to hunt leaving the wardens frustrated about how to handle them, any real conflict with the Utes in northwest Colorado ended with the 1897 skirmish. The Colorado Utes living in Utah learned that they would have to accept the final closure of their hunting grounds. The annual hunts in the manner of their heritage, and the passing down of remembrances of such hunts would, forever, be no more.

NOTES TO CHAPTER FOURTEEN

1. "Death of Miss Lizzie Brown," *Rock Springs Miner*, 31 Mar 1904.

2. Anne (Bassett) Willis, "Queen Ann of Brown's Park," *The Colorado Magazine*, Oct 1952, 295-297.

3. "Tragedy Of Early Days, *The Steamboat Pilot,* " 13 Nov 1947, 8.

4. Anne (Bassett) Willis, "Queen Ann of Brown's Park," 295-298.

5. "Facts About The Utes—Wardens Used Every Precaution To Prevent Trouble—Indians Fired The First Shot, *Craig Courier,* " 6 Nov 1897.

6. "Killing of Utes in Colorado," Annual Reports of the Department of the Interior for the Fiscal Year Ended 30 Jun 1898, Indian Affairs. (Washington: Government Printing Office 1898.), 71.

7. "Tragedy Of Early Days," *The Steamboat Pilot*, 13 Nov 1947, p. 8.

8. "Tragedy Of Early Days, " *The Steamboat Pilot*, 8.

9. "Facts About The Utes," *Craig Courier*, 6 Nov 1897.

10. Willis, "Queen Ann of Brown's Park," 296.

11. Willis, "Queen Ann of Brown's Park," 296.

12. Willis, "Queen Ann of Brown's Park," 298.

13. 1900 United States Federal Census, Utah, Uintah, Vernal, Dist. 0152.

14. "Tragedy Of Early Days," *The Steamboat Pilot*, 8.

15. "Still Another Version," *Craig Courier*, 4 Dec 1897.

16. "Tragedy Of Early Days," *The Steamboat Pilot*, 8.

17. Willis, "Queen Ann of Brown's Park," 297.

18. "Tragedy Of Early Days," *The Steamboat Pilot*, 8.

19. "Game Warden Wilcox's Story of His Fight With the Indians," *Vernal Express*, 18 Nov 1897.

20. "Facts About The Utes," *Craig Courier*, 6 Nov 1897.

21. *Salt Lake Herald*, 27 Oct 1897.

22. Wilson Rockwell, *The Utes A Forgotten People* (Denver: Sage Books, 1956), 192.

23. "Trouble With The Utes," *Vernal Express*, "Trouble With The Utes," 28 Oct 1897.

24. "Killing of Utes in Colorado," 71.

25. "Killing The Utes," *Vernal Express*.

26. "Still Another Version," *Craig Courier*, 4 Dec 1897

27. "Still Another Version," *Craig Courier*.

28. *Salt Lake Herald*, 2 Dec 1897.

29. Wilson Rockwell, *The Utes A Forgotten People*, 192.

30. "Killing of Utes in Colorado," Annual Reports of the Department of the Interior for the Fiscal Year Ended 30 Jun 1898, Indian Affairs. 72.

31. "Killing of Utes in Colorado," Annual Reports of the Department of the Interior for the Fiscal Year Ended 30 Jun 1898, Indian Affairs. 73.

32. "Killing of Utes in Colorado," Annual Reports of the Department of the Interior for the Fiscal Year Ended 30 Jun 1898, Indian Affairs. 72.

33. C.A. Stoddard, *Tales of the Old West Retold*, (Montrose: Lifetime Chronicle Press, 2007), 159.

34. "Tragedy Of Early Days," *The Steamboat Pilot*, 8.

35. Willis, "Queen Ann of Brown's Park," 298.

CHAPTER FIFTEEN

THE LYNCHING

The vanilla musk of chilled cedar bark, sage, and fallen leaves filled the November air of the ranch. Perhaps Ann and Lizzie noticed as they breathed it in while walking to the wagon that was hitched to a team and waiting. Ann would spend the winter months in Rock Springs with Lizzie and Lizzie's mother, Annie Brown.[1]

Ann probably gave the ranch house a goodbye glance but likely didn't even take notice of the familiar crosspiece pole that topped the frame of the entry gate near the barn. She couldn't know that soon these peaceful surroundings would be violently afflicted. A man whom she didn't know well, but had seen once or twice at the Bassett dining table, would be held by a noose around his neck as he dangled from the cross pole. Ann's little brother Eb, at age seventeen, would play a part in the lynching and be plagued by it—the rest of his life.

Eb Bassett was a teenager of classic good looks. Close to reaching his final height of five feet, eight inches, Eb had his father's black hair and black eyebrows. The young cowboy's eyes were a captivating shade of grey.[2]

Just a year earlier, in the late fall of 1896, Herb directed Eb to ride to the summer range on Douglas Mountain, find the saddle horses still grazing in Zenobia Basin, and bring them home. Winter was coming on and, although the cattle had been trailed home for the winter, several head of horses were still out. Herb worried that the feed would become scarce as the snow cover increased.

After riding about twelve miles, Eb reached the little valley on the mountain where the long, three-room log cabin his father built sat surrounded by high peaks. The pinnacles and pines were swathed in snow and their shadows were growing long as Eb put his saddle in the open-faced middle room of the cabin and then hobbled his horse and turned him loose to graze. Inside, Eb built a fire and started fixing supper when he heard a distant howl.[3]

Eb had grown up with the sound, for the calls from packs of grey wolves trailed like tendrils across the Brown's Park and Douglas Mountain rangeland. Any time of day or night the howls could come, whether gliding through the spaces between snowflakes on the fly or chasing away tranquility on a summer night. Although the rendition was familiar to all creatures living there, it stirred angst, nonetheless.

As dusk arrived at the cabin on Douglas Mountain, the howling grew so close that Eb's horse startled. Bound by the hobbles, the frightened gelding started jumping in circles, frantic to flee the danger. Eb had left home without a gun but he knew he had to do something to protect his saddle horse. After going outside, Eb gathered some armloads of firewood and worked until he had several fires glowing against the darkness. Hoping that would keep the creatures at bay, the teenager hurried back to the security and warmth of the cabin.

The stillness along with the comfort of his bed and the nodding flames from the fireplace brought both the subsiding of fear and the rising of drowsiness. Nearly asleep Eb was suddenly scared awake by the sounds of a crackling snort blown through the nostrils of his horse, accompanied by a frightful snarling. Eb sprang out of bed and rushed to the window. Nothing; he could see nothing. Fearing for his horse, Eb dressed and hurried outside. When Eb caught hold of the gelding he removed the hobbles before leading the trembling animal through the door of the vacant room on the opposite end of the cabin. Then Eb closed the horse inside and barred the door from the outside.

Terribly frightened, the sixteen-year-old's steps crunched in the snow as he rushed back to the door. He agonized that the cabin door wasn't sturdier as he shut it behind him. Shortly after getting back inside, the howling became louder and drew nearer by the moment until the sounds were unbearably close. After stoking the fire in the fireplace, Eb got nerve enough to peek through the window. There, by the light of the dying bonfires, he saw countless dark shapes mingling and smelling at his and the horse's tracks. When the wolves began excitedly sniffing around the perimeter of the cabin the panic-stricken gelding erupted in clatters and thumps against the log walls.

The only thing Eb could think to do was to make noise. He grabbed a tin pan and started beating on it with the fireplace poker creating such a clanging that it reverberated off the logs and rafters. To his dismay, it had no effect on the hungry wolves for they were emboldened by their number and spurred by the smell of prey.

Driven as much by a need to release his fear as the hope of scaring the monsters away, Eb screamed and howled and yelled until he became utterly exhausted. He sat quietly then, waited, and longed for the coming of the light.

The pack had vanished when at last the gift of morning came. It arrived in a blush of raw winter pink that came spreading across the wildness. Young Eb, filled with relief, admired the exceptional beauty surrounding him. The gelding was alert and nervous when Eb led him out the cabin door. Soon, though, the horse lowered his head to lick the snow for water and then fed on tawny stems of grass. After finishing with breakfast and waiting until the sun was fully up, Eb rode away from the lonesome cabin.[4] The teenager went on to do his job. He tracked down the free-roaming saddle horses and took them on a trot to Brown's Park; where another form of predator dwelled.

The Brown's Park area was enduring ongoing petty thievery and the constant dribbling of livestock theft. Sheepherder camps and cow camps were easy targets from which to steal all sorts of supplies. Horses and range cattle were always vulnerable. Patrick Louis "P.L." or "Pat" Johnston[5] (often spelled Johnson) and John Bennett were two of the culprits. They were familiar faces not only in Brown's Park but also Powder Springs, an outlaw hangout twenty-five miles northeast of Brown's Park in Wyoming, near the Colorado line.

P.L. Johnston worked for Frank Goodman when the Goodmans were still sheep ranching in Brown's Park. The young man was badly injured and took several days to recover after being knocked out by a ewe ramming him in the side of his head.[6]

John Bennett, a heavy drinker, was about ten years older than P.L. Johnston and had a large scar which extended from above his right eye into his dark hair. Originally from Arkansas, he peddled liquor to the Native Americans while running the Bridge Saloon in Lander, Wyoming.[7] After making his way to Brown's Park, Bennett sometimes worked for John Jarvie and did a good job of constructing a stone building at the Jarvie ranch. He, like any other traveler coming or going, enjoyed the hospitality of the Bassett Ranch. Bassett neighbor, J.S. Hoy, saw Bennett as a gunman, cattle thief, and member of the Powder Springs gang.[8]

On February 16, 1898, P. L. Johnston was twenty-four when he rode along the Green River in Brown's Park, whistling and throwing loops with his lariat. He stopped by John Jarvie's store and began conversing with a teenager named Willie Strang.

Sixteen-year-old William "Willie" Strang's stepfather Albion Strang and mother, Sarah, had a place near Vernal. Albion was a former Indian scout for the army and now enjoyed prospecting. Willie often accompanied his stepfather on such excursions. Most everyone in the Park knew and liked Willie and he sometimes did odd jobs for them. Willie and Eb Bassett were good friends.

Willie didn't want to make the quick trip back to Vernal with his stepfather just to get fresh supplies and check on things at home before returning to Brown's Park. Albion made arrangements to leave his boy in the care of Albert Williams, a well-liked black man who was running the ferry for John Jarvie. When P. L. Johnston invited Willie to ride along with him to Valentine Hoy's Red Creek Ranch and maybe rope a few steers in the Red Creek badlands, Willie hurried to saddle his horse. Albert Williams voiced his strong objections, but there was no convincing Willie not to go.[9]

The pair rode out of Brown's Park through Red Creek Canyon and followed the creek across the Wyoming line and through the badlands, arriving at the Red Creek Ranch that evening. Living at the ranch in the two-story house was Valentine Hoy's in-laws William H. and Elizabeth Blair and their fifteen-year-old son, Carl. Valentine's wife, Julia, was in Chicago recovering from surgery. Valentine Hoy had been spending the winter at his town residence in Rock Springs but had left his and Julia's two children, Neva and Valentine Jr., there with Willis Rouff and wife when he got word he had cattle disappearing in Brown's Park. Once he reached Brown's Park, Valentine Hoy rode with his ranch foreman, Larry B. Curtin, and Charlie Crouse in search of the missing cattle.

Others staying in the Red Creek bunkhouse when P. L. Johnston and Willie Strang arrived were John Bennett, William "Bill" Pidgeon, and Charles "Charlie" Teters. Part Cherokee, Bill Pidgeon first arrived in Brown's Park in the early 1890s[10] and was now about thirty. Charlie Teters, aged twenty-three, was only thirteen years old when he ran away from his home in Missouri. About leaving he said, "My mother refused to cut my long blonde curls, and I didn't want to run around like that anymore. Besides, I wanted to be a cowboy, so I headed west." Teters hired on with different outfits as a horse wrangler and cook's helper.[11] When he was a little older he worked as a ranch hand and did a bit of drifting. He came to Brown's Park with P. L. Johnston about 1891. He got into a bit of trouble for being at Powder Springs and earned a short stay in jail by refusing to reveal the whereabouts of a gang of horse thieves.

In the ranch bunkhouse the customary poker game fortified with liquor ensued. Willie Strang must have thought he was having a splendid adventure in such grown up and rowdy company, staying up all night and being treated as another one of the boys.

During the early morning of February 17, the poker game ended and attentions turned from cards and whiskey to breakfast. A spur of the moment decision by Willie to perform a playful prank on Johnston was a fateful one. As Johnston started to sit down in a chair, Willie quickly pulled the chair out from under him causing Johnston to fall to the floor.[12] It was in the spirit of fun and Willie laughed at first, but then he grew frightened when he saw the foul look in Johnston's eyes.

When Johnston started for him, Willie ran out the door. The teenager dashed down the hill making for the blacksmith shop on the other side of the creek. Just before he stepped onto the footbridge, Johnston lifted his revolver and fired. Almost instantaneously Willie collapsed.

With a bullet lodged near his spine, Willie was carried into the house. Johnston said he only meant to scare the boy and stayed a couple hours at the ranch before riding away with Bill Pidgeon. Johnston rode for Powder Springs and Bill Pidgeon went to find Valentine Hoy. John Bennett stayed close by as he and the Blairs tried to ease Willie's agony throughout the night until he died at about 2 A.M. the following morning. Bennett then left to meet up with Johnston. Charlie Teeters rode through the winter cold to Rock Springs to inform the coroner.

Three days after Willie's death, Valentine Hoy penned a letter to Willie Strang's brother-in-law, William McCaslin, who was living in Vernal:

> Brown's Park, Utah
> February 20th 1898
> Mr. W. McCaslin
> Vernal, Utah
>
> Dear Sir,
>   I have just received word that Willie Strang was shot last Tuesday morning by one P. L. Johnston at my ranch on Red Creek, Wyoming.

The boy died Wednesday morning, 19 hours after the shooting. A man left my ranch Friday morning for the coroner at Rock Springs and he will probably get there today or tomorrow. The body has been prepared for burial, awaiting the coroner's inquest and the wishes of the boy's parents. I [will] go up to the ranch today and will keep the boy from being interred until I hear from you. I suppose that Willie's parents would like to see him before he is buried. It would be almost impossible to take the body to Ashley now, as the snow is too deep. The killing was a cold blooded affair and no expense should be spared to punish Johnston for the cowardly deed. The citizens of Utah here would like to have the officers here to assist in making arrest. Mr. Davenport and Mr. Crouse and everyone else want them to come. P.L. Johnston the party who killed him has gone north or started in that direction. One John Bennett is supposed to be in his company. He is a man that formerly was in the employ of John Jarvie. Let me know if you wish the body buried.

The people over here are aroused to immediate action to rid the country of these desperate characters, and we all will render all the assistance we can.

Yours truly,
Valentine S. Hoy

P.S. This John Bennett is wanted. He stole the boy's horse after they killed him.[13]

D.L. McNamara, the coroner for Sweetwater County, Wyoming, traveled to the Red Creek Ranch but found the witnesses reluctant to talk.[14] He did get Carl Blair to give some details: The teenager said that he was upstairs in bed when he heard the gun go off. At first he thought a log had fallen or, perhaps, a quarter of butchered beef fell. Then he heard Willie's cries, and when he looked out the window he saw the boy lying on the ground. Carl said his father hurried down the stairs and soon returned to say that Johnston had shot Willie.[15]

In a separate incident away from Brown's Park, Utah lawmen had been trying to recapture some prisoners who escaped from the Utah State penitentiary at Salt Lake City on October 8, 1897. Two of the escapees, young men in their early twenties, were Harry Tracy and Dave Lant. Those two convicts made their way to the Brown's Park area before heading to Powder Springs. Now they were about to play a fatal role in the unfolding events. At Powder Springs the two escapees joined forces with P. L. Johnston and John Bennett and made plans to ride south to Robbers Roost.

Harry Tracy's gun is displayed at the Museum of Northwest Colorado in Craig along with a photo of Tracy. *Courtesy Paul Knowles and the Museum of Northwest Colorado–Craig.*

In the meantime and with no knowledge of the murder of Willie Strang, Sheriff Charles W. Neiman at Hahn's Peak, Colorado, received notice that Justice of the Peace J.S. Hoy in Brown's Park had issued warrants for P.L. Johnston and John Bennett. While searching for his missing cattle, Valentine Hoy discovered evidence which led him to believe that Johnston and Bennett had been killing his cattle on the range and selling the meat to men operating the copper mine and smelter on Douglas Mountain. After Valentine went to his brother J.S. Hoy with his suspicions the warrants were issued.[16]

Sheriff Neiman went to Craig and picked up his undersheriff, Ethan Allen Farnham, and the two lawmen left Craig on February 24, 1898, traveling to Brown's Park with the warrants for P.L. Johnston and John Bennett who were charged with killing steers belonging to Valentine Hoy.[17] The lawmen traveled in a sleigh as far as Lay but because the snow was lessening as they went, they changed to an axle-sprung buckboard. The officers continued to the Boyd Vaughn ranch near Cross Mountain, where they spent the night.

David Lant was one of two outlaws who escaped from the Utah penitentiary and went to Brown's Park. *The Museum of Northwest Colorado – Craig.*

Boyd Vaughn had lost several of his horses the previous fall and he believed they had been stolen. Sheriff Neiman urged him to saddle a horse and come along to Brown's Park where he might very well find his horses. The three men headed out on the forty-mile trip to the Bassett Ranch where they knew they would be welcomed to headquarter their operation while they searched for the rustlers.

Traveling down a long gulch known as Boone's Draw, the officers caught glimpses of moving objects in the distance. When the lawmen quickened their pace it soon became clear that they were following three armed men leading packhorses. The strangers, acting fearful of being overtaken, left the road without slowing and quickly made their way across a high bluff toward Douglas Mountain and Lodore Canyon. As evening fell, the lawmen delayed their chase until morning and rode on several miles to the Bassett Ranch. They were convinced the three illusive riders were outlaws. They were, in fact, Tracy, Lant, and Johnston.[18]

It was almost dark when the law officers made it to the Bassett Ranch. Herb and Josie were there along with Willie Strang's older brother, John.

After getting the news about Willie's killing, John had traveled to Charlie Crouse's ranch, and Charlie sent him on to the Bassett Ranch to see what information John could gain. Sheriff Neiman and Farnham were given the details about Willie's murder.

By daylight, a local posse was already formed and riding. Led by Sheriff Neiman they followed the hunch he and his undersheriff had about the men with packhorses. Included in the posse were Valentine Hoy, Josie's husband Jim McKnight, Longhorn Thompson, Tom Davenport's son Joe Davenport, Isam Dart, Boyd Vaughn, Bill Pidgeon, John Strang, and seventeen-year-old Eb Bassett.

Following horse tracks the posse came upon the fugitives' hastily abandoned camp in a ravine at the foot of Douglas Mountain near Lodore Canyon. The outlaws had been cooking a meal when they caught a glimpse of the posse and had fled on foot up the side of the mountain, taking only their guns and a sack of flour. Left behind were their horses, packs, bedding, overshoes, camp utensils, and food. While having no supplies put the outlaws at a disadvantage they did, however, have the advantage of the mountainside which offered nearly impregnable places to set up a defense.

Isam Dart took charge of the outlaws' packhorses and three saddle horses along with the entire camp outfit and headed back to the ranch with them. John Strang stayed a distance away tending the posse horses while the rest of the posse tried to figure out an approach.[19] Late afternoon came, bringing frigid temperatures, so the posse rode back to the ranch for the night believing that the outlaws were in a desperate situation with no provisions or horses.

During the night the three outlaws skirted the mountain and descended into the gorge of Lodore Canyon. They headed down the frozen river trying to make their escape. After some miles they came to a place where the canyon narrowed and the river rapids tumbled with such force that no ice had formed. They found themselves in a trap with only one option and that was to go back to where they started and make their way higher up the side of the mountain to make their stand.

When the posse arrived early the next morning they followed the tracks leading down to the Green River. The lawmen made the trip to the end of the ice before realizing the outlaws had doubled back. The officers came to the rimrock which had been the hiding place of the fugitives and

Herb Bassett, shown after the amputation of his fingers, allowed prisoner John Bennett to be held in the post office building which was presumed safe. *The Museum of Northwest Colorado–Craig.*

followed the fresh trail upward. It was too steep a climb for the horses, so the animals were left under the guard of Isam Dart and John Strang. After splitting off from the other posse members, Boyd Vaughn, Longhorn Thompson, and Eb Bassett were stationed on a prominent point in order to keep watch over the lower hills and valleys.[20]

Sheriff Neiman, Undersheriff Farnham, Valentine Hoy, Jim McKnight, and Bill Pidgeon followed the fresh trail in single file. There were places where the men had to take hold of trees and shrubs to pull themselves up; handing their rifles back and forth as was necessary. They spoke only in whispers and remained watchful and at the ready.

After following a narrow gulch, the posse came upon a scattering of tracks around a smoldering fire that still held chunks of hardtack. Flour had been mixed with snow and baked in the coals. About twenty feet beyond stood a huge rock that would have blocked the way except that it had split apart, leaving a crevice just large enough for a man to squeeze through.[21]

Sheriff Neiman had been in the lead the entire way until that moment when he stopped to examine the fire. Valentine Hoy walked ahead to the crevice. The sheriff warned Hoy not to get too far ahead because there could be an ambush. However, Valentine was of the mind that the outlaws had made the summit and already gained the other side of the mountain.[22] Valentine had just stepped onto a boulder to get a better look through the cleft in the rock when his life ended with the shattering sound of two rifle shots in quick succession ripping the stillness. Smoke curled from behind the split rock as Valentine Hoy crumpled, with a bullet just above the heart. The second shot had been the reflexive action of Valentine pulling the trigger of his rifle. The snow beneath the handsome cattleman melted crimson.

The four remaining posse men threw themselves behind the cover of rocks and trees and faced off with the outlaws in a nerve quivering circumstance for over an hour. Just for an instant, the malignant face of Harry Tracy peered through the crevice, but before the sheriff's gun could point the mark Tracy darted back. Outlaw Tracy and lawman Neiman were so close, though, that they saw into each other's eyes.

At this point, entrenched behind the massive rock, the outlaws held every advantage. It was impossible to retrieve Valentine Hoy's body. Rather than further risk his men, the sheriff decided to retreat. One at a time the officers wriggled backward down the steepness while the others gave cover. Finally, the posse dropped over the edge of the rimrock and made it back to the horses. They rode for the Bassett Ranch with a grim determination that they would return in the morning's light, and they would keep coming, until they brought the killers to justice.[23]

The sheriff and his three remaining men soon met up with Boyd Vaughn coming in search of them. Boyd, Eb, and Longhorn had spotted a horseback rider whom Eb recognized as John Bennett. Bennett was leading a packhorse toward the foot of the mountain.

When Bennett reached a certain place that would later prove to hold a cache of stolen provisions, he had pulled his six-shooter and fired three quick shots to signal his arrival and whereabouts to Tracy, Johnston, and Lant. Bennett had separated from the three men at Powder Springs and went alone to Rock Springs to obtain additional supplies. He was to

Herb Bassett sometimes fed the chickens (with Josie in the background) at the Bassett ranch house. *Courtesy of Jo Semotan*

meet up with Johnston, Tracy, and Lant near the mouth of Lodore Canyon. The four planned to then escape to Robbers' Roost.

Boyd Vaughn reported that Bennett waited for quite some time after firing his revolver. When he received no reply, Bennett repeated the signal, this time using a rifle. Still getting no answer, Bennett built a fire and made camp. Successfully staying out of sight, Boyd went to find the posse as Eb and Longhorn rode back to the ranch.

Josie was busy in the kitchen when the agitated posse arrived. Surrounded by the homey smell of cookies baking in the oven of a wood burning stove, Valentine Hoy's death was described and a plan of deceit was formed; Eb Bassett would be its key.

John Bennett knew Eb. Because he was unaware of not only Valentine Hoy's death but the warrant sworn against him for killing cattle or the whereabouts of his fugitive friends, he was not alarmed when the teenager rode up to his camp. Eb told Bennett he'd been looking for some of the saddle horses. Eb said, "Why don't you come on back to the house for the night and we'll play some cards?"[24]

The sheriff and two men were stationed just inside the Bassett's kitchen door which was about thirty feet from the gate that led to the stable yard.

Doing as he was instructed, Eb remained at the barn until Bennett's horses had been put away. Eb then walked to the house beside Bennett and opened the yard gate to let Bennett pass. Seconds later Bennett was startled by three lawmen pointing the barrels of their rifles at him. Then they sharply commanded to Bennett: "Throw your hands up!"[25]

According to Josie, once Bennett was handcuffed Herb was asked by the sheriff, "Dad, where can we put this man for safekeeping?"

"I don't know any place better than the post office," Herb said. "I'll turn it over to you. There's a fire and lights, water bucket, and everything you'll need, so take him right in there." Bennett was taken at gunpoint to Herb's post office and shut inside along with Undersheriff Farnham to guard him. Eb was shaking; Josie was terrified.[26]

At this point, the sheriff was confident that the three men on the mountain were P.L. Johnston and the two escaped convicts from Utah. Bill Pidgeon volunteered to head out on a ninety-mile round-trip ride, which would take him over the mountain through deep snow, to Vernal to notify the sheriff of Uintah County.

Upon being informed of the killing of his brother, J.S. Hoy asked Joe Moore, a man who had just ridden in from Vernal, if he would be willing to make the ride back to deliver a letter to the residents of Vernal. As Moore went to rest for a couple of hours before leaving on his charge, J.S. wrote a grim plea for help:

> Hoy's Ranch
> Brown's Park, Colo.
> March 1st, 1898
>
> To the people of Ashley valley:
>   An awful murder has been committed here today. V.S. Hoy was shot dead by a party of outlaws and murderers in the rocks at Ladore canyon. He lies where he fell. The murderer of Willie Strang is one of the three who shot V.S. Hoy. We need help to capture the outlaws, and you will please come with all the men that can be gotten together and assist us. Don't delay, come at once. I think it best to guard the country along Green River above Island Park and above the mouth of Pot Creek. A part of you can go there and as many as possible come to Ladore and cooperate with us from this side. The men are afoot and desperate, and the utmost vigilance and caution will be necessary to capture the villains.
>   Dave Lant, an escaped convict from the Utah Penitentiary, is supposed to be one of the three, and P.L. Johnson [Johnston], the murderer

of Willie Strang, another. The third man is unknown here. Please
come, that justice may be done.

     Respectfully,
      J.S. Hoy[27]

Josie said the prisoner at the Bassett Ranch was at first content and
jovial, but then paced and yelled out obscenities and threats. She shuddered when she screamed vows of murder and mayhem to all the people
of Brown's Park.

Early the next morning the posse rode out as the manhunt was
renewed. Undersheriff Farnham was left behind to watch over Bennett.
It was mid-morning, Josie later said, when eight masked men rode in
and quietly made their way to the post office.

Josie was on her tiptoes looking out the window and exclaimed to
Herb, "Oh, Dad, they're going to turn him loose! They're going to take
him out and turn him loose!"

Herb hushed his daughter and said, "Now you stay in the house.
That's not for you to see."[28]

Farnham was propped in a chair against the wall near the door facing
the prisoner who was lying on a cot when the door opened. When Farnham glanced around he was covered with revolvers in the hands of two
masked men. He was told in a low voice that all that was required of him
was to be quiet. More men entered the building and without a word
seized Bennett and placed a sack over his head.

The prisoner began cursing as he was forced out the door. While he
was being guided toward the gate with the high pole crosspiece he yelled
out, "Herb Bassett is the only white man in Brown's Park!" Upon hearing
those words Josie said to herself in disgust, "Well, isn't that a pretty
thing…" During his final moments, Bennett begged for mercy but the
men didn't flinch and went about the business of a well-executed lynching.
When at last the deed was done, Josie felt such relief and cheer that she
believed it was the happiest hour she ever spent on the ranch. She said,
"We won't be killed by John Bennett, anyway!"[29]

According to Josie, it wasn't long afterward when the executioners began pulling off their masks. The eight were revealed to be well-known
residents of Brown's Park, and they were men who had seen enough of
John Bennett. J.S. Hoy explained, "The law of the frontier had been
meted out to him [Bennett]. During a residence of about six years in the

Park he had been engaged in stealing horses and cattle and the law-abiding citizens stood in fear of him, for it was known that he was quick on the trigger and had murder in his heart."

A different version of the lynching of John Bennett later emerged. It describes an event where there never were any masked men. Instead, it was the incensed posse and Charlie Crouse who did the lynching. Joe Davenport, after spending years as a lawman in Rock Springs, told the newspaper:

> It was planned to have Eb Bassett entice Bennett into his cabin that night where the armed posse awaited to capture him. It worked and Bennett guilelessly followed Bassett into the log house where he was immediately covered by a man named Pigeon. Bennett was a bad actor and a quick man at gun play. The wiley Bennett hesitated before throwing up his hands. Another second and he would have been shot. After slowly raising his hands, he was handcuffed by Charlie Neiman, sheriff from Hahn's Peak and locked in the bunkhouse for safety. The party who captured Bennett in the house were Neiman, his deputy Farnham, Jim McKnight, Charlie Krause [Crouse] and Pigeon. I happened along afterward and saw Bennett in the bunkhouse. He seemed cheerful and had no inkling of the fate that awaited him. I went away but Bill Pigeon told me all about the disposal of Bennett the next day. He was given a kind of mock drumhead court martial and the members of the posse decided to string him up. He was brought out and told to prepare for death. Instantly his bravado collapsed and he begged piteously for his life and wept like a child. But to no avail. There was no mercy in those stout hearts. With a rope around his neck he was yanked aloft over a tall gate and suspended until dead. Later they buried him in a shallow grave on the hillside. And that was the end of a puzzling outlaw. He was well educated and came from the east as an asylum from other crimes, it was thought.[30]

The Brown's Park men waited a while before releasing John Bennett's body from the hangman's noose. They then wrapped Bennett in a blanket and buried him a short distance up from the Bassett house. When the job was complete, everyone went to the house, sat down at the dining table, and ate the noontime meal together.[31] It was reported that when Sheriff Neiman returned that evening, he was met at the corral by Farnham. The sheriff asked, "Where's Bennett?" Undersheriff Farnham supposedly answered, "I buried him. Didn't want to see him, did you?"[32]

As soon as Joe Moore made it to Vernal on March 2 with the letter from J.S. Hoy, Joseph M. Tolliver, the very man who had killed Charlie

Seger at Charlie Crouse's ranch in Brown's Park in 1891 gathered a posse of about twenty-five men. Now a respected deputy sheriff for Uintah County, Tolliver led the posse as they rode for Brown's Park. Men arrived at the Bassett Ranch from all directions to join the search.

In the meantime, the Brown's Park posse found tracks that showed the killers had escaped Douglas Mountain and were making their way north toward Powder Springs. They discovered evidence where the killers had slaughtered a colt and cooked its meat in the coals of a small fire.

On March 3, two days after his death, a group worked to recover Valentine Hoy's body. They had found a route that could be accessed by horses just above where the frozen body lay. Using lariats they hoisted the body upward to where it could be retrieved and lashed to a packhorse.

Ann, now twenty years old, was among several Brown's Parkers who spent the winter in Rock Springs. Scared for family and friends, they all kept in touch and shared grief and shock as they awaited any nugget of detail about the events playing out in and around Brown's Park.

By March 4, a large contingent of over fifty armed lawmen took the field, including posses from Utah, Colorado, and Wyoming led by lawmen from each of those states. They included Sheriff Neiman and Deputy Sheriff Farnham of Colorado, Deputy U.S. Marshal William Laney and Deputy Sheriff Peter Swanson of Wyoming, and Sheriff William "Billy" Preece and Deputy Joe Tolliver from Utah. Officers were divided among the posses in such a manner that the crossing of state lines would not deter the pursuit because of any lack of jurisdiction.

The men rode hour after hour in the extreme cold through places of deep snow and against a bitter wind. Sheriff Neiman believed the outlaws would make their way to one of three sheep camps in the vicinity. He divided his men into three parties to scout the surrounding areas of each of those sheep camps. Members in one such group were Isam Dart, Jim McKnight, and Joe Davenport of Brown's Park led by Undersheriff Farnham and Sheriff Peter Swanson. This unit finally spotted the targets of the search about six miles south of Powder Springs. When the scruffy fugitives saw the posse was overtaking them, they took off running on foot. The officers opened fire while shouting demands for surrender.

As Tracy and Lant ran to the cover of a steep-sided arroyo, Johnston stopped and put up his hands. He gave up his Winchester and revolver. The posse then surrounded the gulch that held the other two convicts,

John Bennett's grave still marks the earth, circa 1995. *The Museum of Northwest Colorado–Craig.*

dismounted, and took up places of cover. A standoff ensued and although Lant tried to surrender, Tracy threatened to kill him and Lant retreated back into the drifted snow in the gulch. Sheriff Neiman and his men had heard the gunshots and arrived at the scene. However, the stalemate with the fugitives continued for some time.

When Lant and Tracy finally gave up, the lawmen found them to be raggedly exhausted, hungry, and cold. Their boots were worn through to the point that sometimes blood was left in the snow of their tracks.[33] Their feet were wrapped in cloth torn from their garments and their boots were covered in hide cut from the butchered colt. Still, Tracy remained defiant.

Harry Tracy stood about five feet, ten inches tall with a dark complexion and beard and eyes to match.[34] The man looked Sheriff Neiman in the eyes. Referring to the brief encounter they shared on the mountainside, Tracy smirked and said, "I've seen you before, sheriff."[35]

Nightfall was coming and the cold deepening. The lawmen and prisoners made it to one of Jack Edwards' sheep camps to spend the night. The weather-beaten men warmed by the fires and ate generously. The next morning, the herder's cavvy supplied fresh horses for the ride back to Brown's Park.[36]

The following morning as the posse and prisoners were on the trail back to the Bassett Ranch, they met the wagon transporting Valentine Hoy's body to Rock Springs. J.S. Hoy and Willis Rouff rode horses to escort the wagon. Sheriff Neiman told Justice of the Peace J.S. Hoy he would need to return to the Bassett Ranch to do the preliminary examination of the prisoners. After arriving at the Bassett Ranch, John Strang faced P.L. Johnston. Growing furious at the sight of him, John Strang lunged at his brother's killer but was restrained before he could reach the man.

J.S. Hoy was not a brave man, neither riding in any of the posses nor helping with the removal of the body from the mountain. Still, he deeply loved and was often dependent on his more vital younger brother Valentine. J.S. did his proper duty in his determination that there was sufficient evidence to bind the prisoners over to the district court without bail. Custody of P.L. Johnston was turned over to Deputy United States Marshal William Laney who claimed Johnston for the killing of Willie Strang. Tracy and Lant would remain in the custody of Sheriff Neiman to be taken to the county jail at Hahn's Peak, Colorado.

Tracy, Lant, and Johnston were placed in the Bassett bunkhouse under the watch of two guards. Over sixty men from Utah, Colorado, and Wyoming now gathered at the ranch. Aunty Armida Thompson arrived and helped Josie feed them all. The men built a large bonfire in the yard, and most spent the night dozing around its warmth. Sheriff Neiman stayed up all night, mingling among the men, urging them against the talk of swift justice and convincing them to allow the law to take its course.

Tracy and Lant were safely delivered to Hahn's Peak and locked up. However, the two prisoners soon broke jail. Lant overpowered Sheriff Neiman and severly beat him. The sheriff feigned unconsciousness and that likely saved his life. The lawman endured a final and vicious kick from Harry Tracy as the two escapees made their exit. Sheriff Neiman stayed resolute and tracked the pair down and recaptured them. This time, he chained Tracy and Lant together by their necks and fixed weights, known as Oregon boots, to their ankles.[37]

At last, on April 9, Sheriff Neiman turned Lant and Tracy over to authorities in Pitkin County where they were held at what was thought to be a more secure jail in Aspen, Colorado. Sheriff Neiman warned the authorities about who Tracy and Lant were, yet just a few weeks later the pair escaped again after nearly beating their jailer to death with a weapon fashioned from a wire clothesline they'd been allowed to have in their cell. Lant then disappeared but Harry Tracy left a trail of death and robbery through the northwestern United States before finally, in 1902, killing himself after being wounded and cornered. Including Valentine Hoy, Tracy was instrumental in killing at least six men.

Valentine Shade Hoy's body was transported to Nebraska by train for his funeral on March 9, 1898, at the Congregational church in Fremont, Nebraska. Hoy was praised as a courageous hero and martyr to the cause of civilizing the lawless sections of the country. His remains were buried in Ridge Cemetery in Fremont.[38]

P.L. Johnston was initially taken to jail in Rock Springs. Convicted of killing Willie Strang, he was sentenced to life in the Wyoming State Penitentiary. The Wyoming Supreme Court later granted him a new trial because the lower court erred in not allowing evidence that Willie Strang may have made a deathbed statement indicating that the shooting was an accident. Prosecutors decided they no longer had sufficient evidence to convict Johnston, and he was released from the charge. He then served time in the Colorado state penitentiary for his part in Valentine Hoy's murder though he claimed the shooting was done by Harry Tracy over his protest. He was paroled in 1904.

Willie Strang was buried among the cedars on a peaceful ridge above the Red Creek ranch house. The young teenager was long remembered and written about for being the innocent catalyst for the binding of so many interlacing consequences. The manhunt was the first time that lawmen from three states joined forces in such a manner. This cooperation became a potent resource against the proliferation of outlaws whose era in and around Brown's Park was coming to an end.

Charlie Teters, who rode to Rock Springs to fetch the coroner for Willie Strang, was arrested as an accomplice in Willie's murder. After ten days passed he was absolved of guilt and released. He soon returned to his life in the Brown's Park area. Years later when working for W.H. Gottsche as ranch foreman, Teeters lived at the Red Creek Ranch with his wife Amelia and their children. His five-year-old son Valentine, named after Valentine Hoy, died from spinal meningitis. Little Valentine Teters was buried on the hill above the Red Creek ranch house alongside Willie Strang.[39]

Sheriff Neiman highly praised Isam Dart along with Jim McKnight and Joe Davenport for the way they assisted him in the capture. He said they were "brave men who stood by him throughout the trying ordeal in a noble manner."[40] Yet, these three reliable men were very soon targeted by a stock detective on a hunt.

Eb Bassett struggled in the aftershock of the death of his friend Willie Strang. Eb lived, worked, ate, and, slept with the horridness of the hanging and the role he played in it, but no one noticed. The shaky ground beneath the motherless teenager would have been steadied had his mother Elizabeth been alive and the breaking apart inside might have been soothed. Instead, he was alone in his torment when on the very first night after the lynching, and the next one after that, and every night after, the face of John Bennett entered the din of his nightmares.[41]

❦ ❦ ❦

During the last year of the nineteenth century Ann Bassett spent time living in Omaha, Nebraska, where she briefly partnered with another woman, Mrs. Snyder, in a dressmaking shop, before deciding to go home to the ranch.[42] During either late December or early January her father, now endearingly referred to as "Fuzzy" because of his long greying beard, received a slight scratch on the hand from a wire bale on a bucket. The wound festered and Herb ended up in the Rock Springs hospital with what the newspaper referred to as "blood poison." This resulted in his thumb and third and fourth fingers being amputated.[43] It is likely both his daughters came to his side and helped with the adjustments now necessary for Herb's daily life. Josie's marriage was collapsing but by Ann's twenty-second birthday in May 1900, she likely felt that her life was settling, with Mat Rash the anchor of the future she longed for in the cattle business.

NOTES TO CHAPTER FIFTEEN

1. "Personal Remarks," *Rock Springs Miner*, 18 Nov 1897.

2. Avvon Hughel, *The Chew Bunch of Brown's Park*, (San Francisco: Scrimshaw Press, 1970), 75.

3. Edna Bassett, "Besieged," unpublished manuscript as told to Edna by her uncle Eb Bassett, The Museum of NW Colorado–Craig.

4. Edna Bassett, "Besieged."

5. P.L. Johnston was born in Australia just before his family immigrated to the United States and settled in Ohio.

6. Dick and Daun DeJournette, *One Hundred Years of Brown's Park and Diamond Mountain*, 321.

7. "Nearly a Killing," Fremont *Clipper*, 31 Dec 1887.

8. J.S. Hoy "Some Noted Outlaws of Brown's Park Region, "Steamboat *Pilot*, 23 Oct 1918.

9. Jesse Taylor, taped interviews with author, 1981-1982.

10. Dick and Daun DeJournette, *One Hundred Years,* 371.

11. Hazel Teters Overy, taped interview with author, 1981.

12. "Powder Springs," *The Steamboat Pilot*, 9 Mar 1898.

13. Letter written by Valentine Hoy, The Museum of NW Colorado–Craig.

14. "Coroners Verdict," *Vernal Express*, 3 Mar 1898.

15. Douglas W. Ellison, *David Lant: The Vanished Outlaw,* (Aberdeen, SD: Midstates Printing, Inc. 1988), Carl W. Blair, written account of sworn testimony, undated, 70-72.

16. Hoy, "Some Noted Outlaws of Brown's Park Region."

17. "Outlaws Run Down," *Rifle Reveille*, 18 Mar 1898.

18. Hoy, "Some Noted Outlaws of Brown's Park Region."

19. "Brown's Park Killing Told by Strang," Vernal *Express*, 9 Oct 1941.

20. "Outlaws Run Down," *Rifle Reveille*, 18 Mar 1898.

21. Hoy, "Some Noted Outlaws of Brown's Park Region."

22. "Outlaws Run Down—Story of the Recent Lynching," *Silver Cliff Rustler*, 16 Mar 1898.

23. Hoy, "Some Noted Outlaws of Brown's Park Region."

24. Jesse Taylor, taped interviews with author, 1981-1982, story told to him by Eb Bassett.

25. Hoy, "Some Noted Outlaws of Brown's Park Region."

26. Josie Bassett Morris, interview with Messersmith, 7 Jul 1961, The Museum of NW Colorado–Craig.

27. Douglas W. Ellison, *David Lant: The Vanished Outlaw*, 92.

28. Josie Bassett Morris, interview with Messersmith, 7 Jul 1961, The Museum of NW Colorado–Craig.

29. Morris, interview with Messersmith, 7 Jul 1961.

30. *Rock Springs Rocket*, interview with Joe Davenport, 4 Apr 1929.

31. Morris, interview with Messersmith.

32. Hoy, "Some Noted Outlaws of Brown's Park Region."

33. "Brown's Park Killing Told by Strang," *Vernal Express*, 9 Oct 1941.

34. Description of Harry Tracy released by Sheriff Richmond Fisher of Pitkin County.

35. Hoy, "Some Noted Outlaws of Brown's Park Region."

36. "Editorial," Craig *Courier*, 19 Mar 1898.

37. Hoy, "Some Noted Outlaws of Brown's Park Region."

38. Valentine Shade Hoy (1848-1898), *Find A Grave Memorial.* https://www.findagrave.com/memorial/13593155/valentine-shade-hoy#

39. Hazel Teters Overy, taped interviews with author, 1981.

40. "Editorial," Craig *Courier*, 19 Mar 1898.

41. Taylor, taped interviews, story told to him by Eb Bassett.

42. "Personal Remarks," *Rock Springs Miner*, 13 Jul 1899.

43. "Happenings at Home," *Craig Courier*, 20 Jan 1900.

CHAPTER SIXTEEN

BECOMING QUEEN ANN

Ann Bassett's maturity was unavoidably fastened to the many conflicts of the times, for they came seeping down the canyons, creeks, and trails of her valley to form layers of lasting sediment. Perhaps Ann had some premonition of the new evil set to move into her valley; plenty of signs foretold that Brown's Park had an epic storm fermenting. Indeed, events past and those yet to come continued gathering into a phenomenon described as a perfect storm: a particularly bad or critical state of affairs, arising from a number of negative and unpredictable factors.

On the other hand being back in her world of mountains and steers, it's possible that Ann noticed little more than the booming of nighthawks in flight and her flirting affection for Mat Rash. Mat and Ann often attended parties and dances together.[1] All eyes in the Park followed the compelling Ann Bassett, especially those of her suitor, Mat Rash, for she was now a twenty-one-year-old woman with beauty and poise. She was a cowgirl, and when she wished, elegant, in dress and movement.

Aided by the exposure of Wild West shows, cowgirls and cowgirl fashion were very popular. The widely promoted and marketed images showing young women no longer riding sidesaddle but sitting astride galloping horses while outfitted in western ranch attire suited and described Ann Bassett perfectly. She came of age in the middle of it all. She was stunningly beautiful on the back of a horse, and she seemed to know it. Proud and well-aware of her abilities, Ann sometimes came across as uppity. Her temper which manifested so prominently after her mother's death didn't soften much as she grew. John Rolfe Burroughs wrote:

> Ann Bassett was not merely good looking; she was an extremely at-
> tractive young lady. Arriving at maturity, she stood five feet three inches
> tall, weighed a hundred and fifteen pounds and possessed an "hour
> glass" figure without the assistance of corsets, which, loathing them, she

220

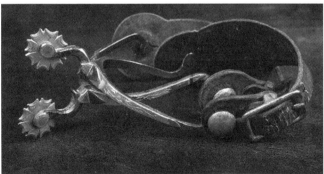

Top, Queen Ann Bassett, circa 1899. *The Museum of NW Colorado–Craig.*
Bottom, Ann Bassett's spurs. *Photo copyright Paul Knowles and the Museum of NW Colorado–Craig.*

seldom wore, and she had large, deceptively mild gray eyes and naturally wavy auburn hair. As spirited as she was high-strung, and highly intelligent, suiting her own convenience or caprice Ann could play the role of cultured young gentlewoman full to overflowing with gentility plus the innate Bassett charm; or she could be a perfect little hell-cat capable of throwing and breaking things. . . .[2]

Josie described her younger sister's wrath to be terrible and, at times, uncontrollable.[3] A combination of her temper and haughtiness initially earned her the title of "Queen."

A group of young adults, friends of Ann's as well as those of her brothers, commonly congregated at the Bassett Ranch and showed off their riding and roping skills. A cowhand began taunting Ann, joking about the way she rode. Some things Ann took in her stride; her talent for riding and roping were usually not among those things, for they were at her core. When the man took his mocking one word too far Ann angrily yanked off her fringed gauntlets and with the potency of fury, smacked the cowboy across the face. Rubbing his cheek the man said, "Well Queenie, at least you've got some spunk!"[4] Ann berated the man with a contemptuous dressing-down. Nonetheless, the royal title suited Ann Bassett so well that it affixed itself to her as a budding legend that was planted and left to grow and evolve from that day forward.

Another day and a different circumstance caused an altered reaction from Ann. Kid Vaughn was an extremely good looking champion bronc rider. Ann was love-struck. One day in Maybell she rode among several cowboys, including handsome Vaughn. Sitting astride a beautiful but skittish horse, Ann was feeling the glory of showing off when Kid Vaughn suddenly took off his hat and threw it. The hat sailed, twirling to land under the belly of her gelding. Her edgy horse was waiting for that excuse: he jumped sideways before dropping his head between his legs, bucking, and sending Ann flying. No romance developed between the two but when speaking about that day Ann would smile before remarking, "If that had been anybody besides Kid Vaughn, I would have killed him!"[5]

Ann's complexion was flawless and her thick hair gleamed reddish brown. She learned early on from her mother's regimen and continued to take immaculate care of her hair and skin.[6] Ann's sister, Josie, had a tiny waist and was more delicately built in every way than Ann, who was more rounded with a full bosom. Ann's face had a softer, prettier tone than Josie's and she

Kid Vaughn, champion cowboy. *The Museum of NW Colorado–Craig.*

carried a more charismatic impression. Josie, always serious-minded, was compared to a steam shovel in the way she went about her work while Ann was all about adventurous proficiency with horses and cattle.

When doing ranch work, Ann continued to most often dress in buck-skin trousers or waist overalls with the bottoms of the pant legs tucked into the tops of her boots. Although it wasn't often, she occasionally did take on the modern look of wearing a split riding skirt buttoned around her slim waist. With either style she wore a neck scarf, broad-brimmed hat, and a style of boot. Her hat had a slight curve in the brim and a crease down the center of the crown. Her ever-present buckskin gloves were either long-cuffed gauntlets or daintier riding gloves, depending on the weather and demands of the work. While helping her three brothers, Sam, Eb, and George run the ranch, Ann rode a double rigged saddle with a tall saddle horn suitable to support a rope's dally. Her coiled lariat sat attached to the right front saddlestrings and a pair of saddlebags rode behind the seat. A small bag rolled up in her slicker, also tied behind her saddle, contained personal items and a clean change of clothes. If she was going to be on the range overnight she also carried a bedroll on her saddle. Ann very often had a rifle scabbard holding a rifle on the left side of her saddle and kept a small handgun in her saddlebags when riding. When traveling other than on horseback, she transferred the handgun to her carpetbag.[7]

Ann was skilled at handling a bullwhip but only carried one on her saddle on certain occasions. However, she always rode with a shot-loaded leather quirt at the ready. The core of the quirt contained a leather bag filled with lead shot which gave important weight to the handle and aided in the quirt's action and accuracy. The leather popper on the other end was the noise maker. With the downward flick of her wrist Ann could "drop" the quirt to achieve the cracking pop. Other times she achieved the sound by slapping the quirt against the leg of her chaps. The sound was highly effective in either getting the startled attention of a misbehaving horse or, most often, in working and driving cattle.

❧ ❧ ❧

Although not as influential politically as the Wyoming Stock Growers Association, Colorado's Little Snake River Stock Growers' Association had sway over most of Routt County which took in land of northwestern Colorado from the Utah line running east 127 miles and over fifty miles south from the Wyoming border. The authority of this association came from a collective of several large ranches including: Ora Haley's Two-Bar operation; Charles E. "Charley" Ayer's Bar L7 Ranch; Jeremiah Pierce and Joseph Reef's Sevens Ranch; and Yampa Livestock (Two-Circle-Bar) belonging to Robert Cary and John S. Cary. In a continuing effort to dominate the range the Little Snake River Stock Growers' Association put its focus on range interference caused by the menace of small ranches and cattle rustlers.

The highly successful foreman for Ora Haley's Colorado holdings was a redheaded, blue-eyed cow man known as Hiram "Hi" Bernard.[8] He ran the Two-Bar extension of the Haley Livestock and Trading Company. Ora Haley was proficient in hiring competent managers and the Texas man, Hi Bernard, whom he hired in 1896, was his best. Bernard headquartered at Haley's recently acquired Salisbury and Major ranches located on the lower Little Snake River in Colorado, about thirty miles east of Brown's Park but butting up against Brown's Park range.

Hi Bernard was appointed to a cattlemen's committee along with Charley Ayer and Wilford W. "Wiff" Wilson. Ayer was already employed by the Little Snake River Association as a stock detective and acted as a captain in the Association's conflicts with sheep ranchers. Bernard, Ayer, and Wilson[9] followed the committee's directive to manage the range and oppose sheepmen and cattle rustlers. Hi Bernard, his squared faced ruggedly attractive but scarred by smallpox, rode into Brown's Park and met with Mat Rash, president of the Brown's Park Cattle Association, to make a deal. Bernard's intention was to work out an agreement with

Brown's Park ranchers, who in his opinion were underutilizing their range. He proposed that the Brown's Parkers simply run their cattle in common with the big outfits whereby the cattle would all be gathered in a general roundup. Everything, though, would be controlled by the big ranchers of the Little Snake River Stock Growers' Association.

Bernard told Mat Rash and members of the Brown's Park Cattle Association that all they would have to do is come get their stock after it was gathered, with no expense to them. He was surprised to find that Brown's Park wanted no part of his roundup or the concept of sharing the range. The Brown's Park ranchers didn't want to change the independent way in which they operated. They believed that if they didn't hold back the encroaching mass of cattle their range would be grubbed out with no way of stopping it. According to Frank Willis, about getting the cold shoulder Hi Bernard said:

> My offer was rejected with ceremonial courtesy. On that mission to Brown's Park I did not meet Ann Bassett, but I received a letter from her soon afterwards, advising that neither me or the Haley outfit were desirable. And when, and if, it was necessary for me to visit Brown's Park, would I please confine myself to road travel, for the tracks of Two-Bar Horses, or cattle, were obnoxious.[10]

Though Hi Bernard had not made the deal he wanted, he did reach an agreement concerning how Brown's Park herds would stay separate. A territorial boundary line called the divide was designated along a distinctive limestone ridge between Vermillion Creek and Little Snake River. Brown's Park cattle were to stay west of the divide and the Two-Bar cattle to the east. The association from Brown's Park soon built a cabin near the divide where riders were based to assure Brown's Park cattle didn't cross over and that Two-Bar cattle were pushed back.

About meeting Ann for the first time Hi Bernard said:

> The following spring I was making a tour of range investigation on the remote Douglas Mesa section, and I met Ann Bassett riding alone; a smallish imp of a girl sitting straddle of a superb horse, and fitted as if she had grown there.
>
> She was dressed in at least one gun, and reminded me of tales I had heard about the equally romantic, and lovable, Sitting Bull, mopping up at the Little Big Horn. My hands wanted to reach for something high overhead. I restrained them with difficulty and introduced myself,

and spluttered about the number of lobos inhabiting the range country. I got a salty reply that gave me the idea that grey wolves were natives, and belonged, while I was nothing but a worm crawling out of bounds.[11]

Ann didn't know the power this man with whom she was so dismissive would hold over her life. She was young, easily rankled, and obsessively protective of Brown's Park and its surrounding range.

The Brown's Park ranchers, though, exuded the unfortunate impression of being self-important and not cooperative, providing an easy next step for members of the Little Snake River Association to take action. Ora Haley, Hi Bernard, Charley Ayer, John C. Coble, and Wiff Wilson met in Ora Haley's office in Denver. Charley Ayer and Wiff Wilson specifically named Mat Rash and Jim McKnight as being the lead rustlers. They strongly condemned the valley of Brown's Park as a hangout for outlaws and rustlers. Either during this meeting or sometime soon after, Ann and Eb Bassett, the Davenports, and Longhorn Thompson were also disparaged by these men as suspected rustlers.

Frank Willis quoted Hi Bernard's description of the meeting [The variant spellings of names are as written in the original document]:

> Haley sent for me to meet him in Denver, I met him there and the question of range west of the divide near his Snake River ranches was discussed. Haley told me that Wiff Wilson and Charley Ayers were in Denver and they had given him a tip on Brown's Park conditions. Wilson and Ayers were prominent business and cattle men of Baggs, Wyoming. They each had ranches on upper Snake River, and were old timers in the range country of Routt County. A meeting was scheduled for nine o'clock that evening at Haley's office. We went to dinner and returned to the office; an hour or so later, Wiff Wilson, Charley Ayers, and John Cobel came in; Cobel was a man of affairs from Wyoming who had extensive range interests north of Cheyenne and he had been invited to attend the conference.
>
> The business at hand got underway immediately, with Wilson and Ayers bringing up the subject of range in Brown's Park. They condemned the place as an outlaw hangout, and a threat to the Haley interests. Both men stated what they knew about the reputation of the Park, and Wilson from personal experience, giving detailed information regarding his losses, he attributed to the thieves of Brown's Park and named Matt Rash and Jim McKnight as the individuals whom he knew were cattle rustlers.

Mat Rash was the president of the Brown's Park Cattle Association and attended parties and dances with Ann Bassett. *The Museum of NW Colorado–Craig.*

Brown's Park's reputation as a hangout for outlaws was far-flung. The sincerity and truthfulness of one of the speakers had never been questioned, so far as I knew. Their repeated accusations were convincing. John Cobel had like grievances in his part of the country, and he offered a solution to the problem that would wipe out the range menace permanently. He would contact a man whom he knew with the Pinkerton Detective Agency. A man that could be relied on to do the job and no questions asked. A committee was appointed. Wilson, Ayers and I were to act for the joint interests in our range section.

Cobel would take care of his part of the country. Tom Horn was the man chosen by Cobel. Horn was not at the meeting, and Cobel acting for him, said that Horn was to be paid five hundred dollars for every known cattle thief he killed. Haley was to put up one half of the money, and Wilson and Ayers one half. Wilson and Ayers agreed to handle the financial transaction with Horn. Haley nodded consent to the agreement but he did not commit himself in words, he instructed me to furnish Horn with accommodations and saddle horses at the

Two-Bar ranches. After the meeting was over and Haley and I were by ourselves he said to me: "Neither you or I can afford to lay ourselves open to this man Horn. I do not want him on my payroll to kick back, and collect money from me in a much more simple way than killing men for it."

Tom Horn was hired and given a free hand by the appointed Committee to make a thorough investigation of conditions in Brown's Park. [12]

It was thirty-nine years earlier that Tom Horn's dark journey to Brown's Park began. He was born November 21, 1860, free of life's persuasions and innocent of all that he would one day become. As he worked his way through life his ventures were varied, convoluted, and impressive. Each inched him onward from the affection-deadening harshness of his childhood to a life of an unashamed assassin capable of unbridling a sad wickedness in Ann Bassett's life.

By January 1900 Tom Horn was employed by the Little Snake River Stock Growers' Association to infiltrate Brown's Park. Members of the Association who directed Horn held pious justification for disdain. Brown's Park, after all, was well-known to be a notorious nest that sanctified train and bank robbers, murder, hangings, escaped convicts, cattle rustlers, horse thieves, and imagined no-accounts of every other sort.

The Association knew that in 1894 Mat Rash, now the president of the Brown's Park Cattle Association, was accused of unlawfully taking and driving away a branded steer from Nelson Morris. Mat was summoned by the judge to appear at Hahn's Peak where he was charged with grand larceny and then ordered to post $250 bond. However, all charges were ultimately dropped by the prosecution and there was never a trial.[13] The incident was likely seen as evidence against Mat Rash. Whether or not there was any truth to the accusation was of less concern.

Members of the Association were also aware that Justice of the Peace J.S. Hoy frequently referred to his neighbors, the Bassetts, as a gang. Hoy was often at his writing desk penning letters to newspapers about the lawlessness in Brown's Park.

No matter to the Association or its Cattlemen's Committee that the actual residents of Brown's Park combatted, worried over, and grieved about such things. No matter that they rode side-by-side with lawmen in posses while sometimes enduring dreadful conditions and sacrifice. No matter that J.S. Hoy was brilliant but troubled and eccentric and always spoke of each member of the Bassett family, individually, with high regard. None of it mattered now, for the shadowy detective and outlaw hunter Tom Horn was on his way, and the perfect storm was congealing.

⚜

Notes to Chapter Sixteen

1. "Brown's Park Items," *Craig Courier*, 9 Jan 1897.

2. John R. Burroughs, *Where the Old West Stayed Young,* (New York: Bonanza Books, 1962), 218, 220.

3. Josie Bassett Morris, interview with Messersmith, 17 Jul 1960, The Museum of NW Colorado–Craig.

4. Frank McKnight, *A Family Remembered*, (Salt Lake City: Ponderosa Printing, 1996), 65.

5. Patty Vaughn Miller, telephone interview with author, 27 Apr 2015.

6. Dick and Daun DeJournette, *On Hundred Years of Brown's Park and Diamond Mountain*, 225.

7. Frank McKnight, *A Family Remembered*, 111–112.

8. L.H. "Doc" Chivington, *Last Guard: The True Story of Cowboy Life, From Actual Experiences of L.H. "Doc" Chivington*, (Minneapolis: Celebrations of Life Services, Inc., 2015) 105, The Museum of NW Colorado–Craig. Doc Chivington, who rode with Hi Bernard, wrote: "Hi Bernard had been letting his whiskers grow until he looked like a redheaded woodpecker."

9. "One Land Mark Being Torn Down," *Craig Empire Courier*, 26 Aug 1931. The Museum of NW Colorado–Craig.

10. Frank Willis, "Confidentially Told, unpublished account as told by Hi Bernard, The Museum of NW Colorado–Craig.

11. Frank Willis, "Confidentially Told."

12. Frank Willis, "Confidentially Told."

13. The People of the State of Colorado v. Madison M. Rash, Routt County, First Judicial District Court, County Attorney William Wiley File, 20 Mar 1894, The Museum of NW Colorado–Craig.

CHAPTER SEVENTEEN

THE STRANGER

Neither Ann nor Josie liked or believed Tom Horn, who posed as Tom Hicks when he arrived at the Bassett Ranch during late winter or early spring 1900. Hicks claimed to be looking for some good horses or a ranch to buy. Handsomely well-built, the broad-shouldered man was over six feet tall with brown hair and eyes. At age thirty-nine, his weathered complexion was heavily tanned, his hands noticeably rough, and he walked with a slight forward stoop.[1] He asked if he could stay at the ranch and Sam, always welcoming, said, "Why, yes, you can stay here. We have horses to sell."

Several riders went along when Sam took Tom Hicks, who was loaned Eb's best saddle horse to ride, to Douglas Springs to show him a herd of Bassett horses. When they returned Josie took the first opportunity to voice her displeasure, saying, "Sam, you done wrong to let that fellow stay here. I don't believe he's a horse buyer; I think he's a horse thief. There's something wrong about him. He don't look good me."[2]

Mat Rash hired the newcomer as a camp cook and horse wrangler. Ann and Josie continued to sense an underlying vulgarity in Hicks which grated on them both, but appeared to go unnoticed by the men. Josie described him as being nasty in the way he asked how old she was. She went to her father and said, "That fellow is a mistake, that's all!"[3]

Ann deplored the way Hicks bragged in grisly fashion about killing Indians and she let him know it. Mat Rash put an arm around his fiancé and calmed her anger by making light of Hicks' boasting: "Most all of the big Indian battles were fought around the campfire as men smoked and talked."[4]

Josie had too much going on in her marriage to pay any more attention to Tom Hicks and instead ignored him. Josie, nor her husband Jim McKnight, found much happiness in their years together. Jim had just announced he was ready to leave ranching and Brown's Park, and he wanted to move Josie and the boys to Vernal where he would open a saloon. She staunchly refused, telling him he was on the wrong road. She hated all the whiskey business and told Jim to go ahead and leave and do whatever he wanted. She was going to stay put on Beaver Creek.

Exactly what Jim McKnight's reasoning was is uncertain, but he gathered up his two sons, Crawford and Chick, and took them to Salt Lake City where he left them with his sister, a kindly woman, Aunt Jodie Heath.

The end of March Josie, accompanied by her father, traveled to Craig and Steamboat Springs seeking legal representation for a divorce, including regaining custody of her children and maintaining her share of the cattle. This all led to an unforeseen calamity. Once again, bloodshed in Brown's Park was in the headlines:

SHOOTING AT BROWN'S PARK
James McKnight Probably Fatally Wounded
By Deputy Sheriff W.H. Harris

James McKnight, of Brown's Park, was shot and probably fatally wounded by Deputy Sheriff W.H. Harris, also of Brown's Park, on Wednesday evening, April 4, about 9 o'clock at the Edwards ranch on Beaver Creek.

Mr. and Mrs. McKnight have had some domestic troubles during the past year and Mrs. McKnight and her father A.H. Bassett, an old resident of Brown's Park, were at Craig and Steamboat Springs and commenced divorce proceedings against James McKnight. Mrs. McKnight retained attorney . . . and a summons and an order from the county court restraining McKnight from disposing of his property, and a bond for $2500 for his appearance were placed in the hands of Sheriff Farnham to serve on McKnight at Brown's Park.

The Sheriff arrived at Bassetts' on the 31st of March, a day in advance of Bassett and Mrs. McKnight. The Sheriff found that McKnight had already disposed of his property and left for Utah, not aware that he was just across the line and only a few miles away. Not knowing whether or not McKnight would ever return, Sheriff Farnham appointed W.H. Harris, formerly of Rock Springs, who was recommended to him, to serve the papers should McKnight return, then left for Craig. On April the 4th Mrs. McKnight sent word to her husband that she was very sick and wished to see him and "fix up matters." About dark he made his appearance. Those present at the ranch were: Miss Blanche Tilton, Miss Ann Bassett, Carl Blair, Larry Curtin, Geo.

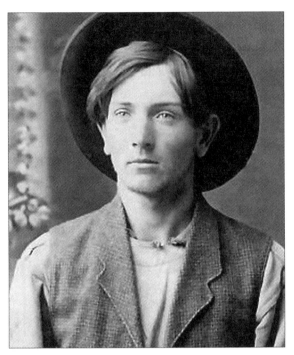

Joe Davenport was given notice to get out of the country. *Author's Collection.*

Bassett, Eva Hoy, Valentine Hoy [Junior], and Mrs. James McKnight. Mrs. McKnight was in bed and the women were giving her medicine and applying numerous mustard plasters. A little later Harris happened along and went into the house. McKnight said "How do you do, Harris?" and the latter replied "How do you do, Jim?" Miss Tilton then invited both men to remain overnight. Harris turned his horse in the corral and returned to the house and McKnight said he guessed he would go home, which was just across the line in Utah, and started for the door. Harris said, "Jim, I have a letter here for you to read" and handed him the summons which Jim read and threw them on the table and remarked "that is only a matter of form." He then started for the door and Harris asked him if he could give bonds for those papers. He said "yes!" and started for the door again and Harris said he would put him under arrest until morning. McKnight did not answer, but opened the door and went out. Harris followed and called to him three times to stop but [he] paid no attention to the command and Harris shot twice, one ball taking effect in the left side near the spine and glanced upward. Jim fell and called on Harris to shoot him in the head and finish the job. All rushed out of the house and excitement was at a high pitch. Miss Annie Bassett, sister of Mrs. McKnight, being very demonstrative about the misfortune which had befell her brother-in-law. Mrs. McKnight was quite ill and could not realize the gravity of the excitement. Larry Curtain and Carl Blair carried Jim into the house and then other neighbors were sent for. Carl Blair rode to Rock Springs for medical aid, a distance of sixty five miles, in eight hours, and twenty-four hours after the shooting Dr. Freeman arrived and extracted the bullet.[5]

Interestingly it was Tom Horn posing as Tom Hicks who made a fast ride to Vernal on Jim McKnight's behalf and wired the McKnight family in Salt Lake City.[6] Soon after getting the news, Jim's brother Frank arrived and stayed to look after Jim. On April 7, Jim signed the papers and Deputy Harris delivered them to Sheriff Farnham.

Although Ann was in full support of her sister, she was livid that the deputy used such terrible judgment in shooting Jim. All in Brown's Park felt the same way. The newspaper echoed that sentiment:

> The people of the valley are very sorry to hear of the shooting of Jim McKnight at Brown's park. We heard tonight that he could not possibly live. We would say to Ethan [Farnham] he had better serve his warrants himself.[7]

Jim McKnight did recover, though the earlier newspaper report was in error, the bullet was not removed and remained lodged in place. On June 16, the much publicized divorce was granted. Although all expected a bitter battle to ensue, Jim and Josie agreed to terms and all was settled. Josie agreed to accept $2000 permanent alimony and the custody of the children. Jim also gave Josie an additional $500 which the newspaper called a "present." Because interest in the case was strong, all was printed in the newspaper, including that the couple bade each other goodbye at Craig with best wishes for each other.[8]

Jim then began the paperwork to prove he met the terms of improving on and residing at his homestead on Beaver Creek to obtain a clear title so the ranch could be sold. One of his witnesses in this endeavor was Routt County Sheriff Ethan Farnham.[9] Josie carried with her a letter written by Jim to his sister when she went after her boys.[10]

Ironically, getting shot and divorced probably saved the life of Jim McKnight, most certainly the fact that he was in the process of moving from Brown's Park helped keep him alive. Tom Horn's attention may have drawn away from him and focused, instead, on Isam Dart, or Isam could have been part of Horn's hunt, all along.

Isam Dart was now around forty-two years of age. He was well-established in the area as a talented cowboy and a respected part of the community. Joe Davenport, one of Isam's young understudies, described Isam as "the greatest all around cowman I ever saw and a delight to watch while in the saddle. His narrow hips, long legs and massive shoulders made him an ideal equestrian and a picture on a saddle."[11]

Through the years after Elizabeth's death, Isam Dart occasionally rode for the Bassett and other ranches however he most often worked for Josie and Jim McKnight. Jim had taken an additional ranch on Cold Spring Mountain, where he put Isam to work building a cabin and corrals and generally improving the place by clearing and planting the land.[12] Isam was a trusted caregiver for the two McKnight boys; a fine cook, and all-around help for Josie at the place. The children, Crawford and Chick, knew Isam to be extremely kind to them and to the horses they watched him train.[13] Sometimes, just after dark, Isam would climb to the top of a high hill where he would build a large bonfire. Sitting beside the glimmer of the flames he stayed for an extended time playing his fiddle and harmonica and singing songs of the south.[14]

All the while, Isam was building a small herd of his own cattle and had several head of horses that he grazed along with the McKnight stock. Isam acquired most of his cattle by trading wild horses he caught, tamed, and trained into excellent saddle horses.

While working a roundup one fall for the G outfit south of Bitter Creek in Wyoming, helping gather hundreds of steers to be shipped on the railroad, Isam demonstrated his skill, dedication, and ingrained determination to do the job he was given.

Day herders had put together seven or eight hundred head of cattle when Isam and another cowboy went on duty about midnight as the nighthawks, or night herders. The two men circled the herd to prevent the cattle from straying and to guard against predators. Isam and his partner found the cattle to be distressed and thirsty. The country was rough, dry, and covered in tall sagebrush and although Bitter Creek ran through it, the day herders had not been able to get the cattle to go off the high and steep banks to water. Needing water, the milling herd refused to bed down for the night. Several big steers continuously tried

Josie Bassett McKnight at the Bassett Ranch with a pet deer named Bucker. *The Museum of NW Colorado–Craig.*

to break away. As soon as Isam and the other cowhand got one turned back to the herd, another steer or group of steers bolted.

This rigmarole continued through the hours until it was nearing time for the relief riders to be called. The man working with Isam heard whacking noises coming from the other side of the herd. He rode toward the sound and spotted a familiar white steer he'd chased many times that night, lying down on the ground with Isam grasping its tail between its hind legs in a manner that made it impossible for the steer to get either foot on the ground. In his other hand Isam had a good sized stick that he'd used to, "teach him some manners."

The cowboy was astounded to see that Isam had used every rope he could find to rope and hogtie the worst of the bunch-quitters. Because he'd already used up all the ropes when the white steer once again took off, Isam loped his horse alongside the steer, grabbed it by the tail and tipped the large animal over into a jumble. Swiftly dismounting, Isam held the critter there. When at last he let the steer get to its feet it ran straight back to the herd and stayed there. Isam's work partner said that the first thing the next morning Isam quickly ate breakfast before hurrying back to the brush to untie all the troublemakers.[15]

In 1897, Isam Dart entered a realm of newsprint sensationalism which linked his name with Butch Cassidy's and carried that linkage from Wheatland, Wyoming, all across the country in reprints. The article said

Isam Dart was part of Cassidy's criminal league of four hundred men that the newspaper described as the most powerful band of organized desperados to ever exist in America, who operated in the mountains of the frontiers of Utah, Colorado, Wyoming, and Idaho. Brown's Park was named as one of two chief headquarters.

It was back eight years, in 1889, when Isam walked away from the jail at Hahn's Peak after being involved in the fire at Harry Hoy's place. However, that appears to be the one true item picked up and used by the newspaper, although the over-the-top article was even wrong about the details of that escape. The dramatization said:

> A negro named Isam Dart, otherwise known as "Grubbed the Left," on account of having lost his left ear in a fight, is believed to be an important figure in the business of the gang. Dart holds out in Brown's Park on the Green river, and is thought to be a mediator between the Ute Indians and the outlaws in the exchange of stolen goods. The Indians each fall come over to Colorado to hunt, and last fall they are said to have taken back with them several thousand head of Colorado horses and cattle, for which the supposition is they gave Dart Utah horses and cattle that the brands might not be detected.
>
> A similar exchange is believed to be carried on between the Wyoming and Idaho gangs. Dart is a refugee from Colorado justice, he having made a sensational escape from the authorities at Hahn's Peak, Colorado, last year by riding ninety miles over the mountains between sunset and dawn without changing horses.[16]

Exaggerated articles like this one and others about Butch Cassidy and Cassidy's connection with Brown's Park reinforced the perception of the valley being an outlaw and rustler haven and a place in need of being cleaned out. After describing Butch Cassidy as the supreme power of a gang made up of five separate bands another article said:

> It is no idle boast to say that the leader of these notorious bands has 500 men at his beck and call. Marauding and murderous bands conduct their raids without restraint. The theft of livestock run into the millions. Ranchers are murdered and run out of business, and the officers of the law are powerless.[17]

On June 2, 1899, the Union Pacific Railroad was held up by Butch Cassidy's gang near Wilcox, Wyoming, and became one of the West's most infamous train robberies. Butch Cassidy and Elzy Lay had split up by then but a couple of months later, Elzy robbed a train near Folsom, New Mexico Territory, and was captured and charged with murder after a shootout with lawmen left Sheriff Ed Farr dead. Elzy Lay was locked up and out of the picture but Tom Horn and other lawmen tirelessly pursued Butch Cassidy and his men.

Angus McDougal, a longtime Brown's Park cowboy who got in trouble with Isam Dart over the arson at Harry Hoy's ranch and served a short stint in prison because of it, had immediately returned to Brown's Park upon his release. There he continued an honest life and became close friends with Ann and especially her friend Lizzie Brown. While building his own horse business, McDougal continued working for Brown's Park ranches.

About two months after the Wilcox train robbery, Angus McDougal was riding with Isam Dart during a roundup about thirty miles south of Powder Springs near Brown's Park when a man rode up showing clear signs of being worn out by hard riding. He had six well-shod horses with him and one loaded packhorse. Both Isam and Angus knew the man to be Tom McCarty. During McCarty's conversation with Isam he said, "Dart, I'm damn glad to see you. I've had a hell of a time since I saw you last." After first saying he was in British Columbia when the Wilcox robbery occurred, McCarty later came very close to admitting he'd been in on it and said, "I had a hell of a time keeping away from the hounds. Dart, you must not give me away to anyone, don't tell them I was here."[18]

McDougal soon made a trip to Rock Springs and informed the authorities about meeting up with Tom McCarty. On August 12, 1899, D.G. Thomas, Sweetwater County Prosecuting Attorney, wrote to U.S. Marshal Frank Hadsell in Cheyenne describing the encounter in detail. Thomas wrote that McCarty was believed to have remained near Powder Springs and that McDougal, if accompanied by Sweetwater County Deputy Sheriff Morton, would be willing to go after McCarty if a discreet agreement could be formed. There was fear for McDougal's safety if word got out.[19]

Angus McDougal surely didn't realize that in the backdrop, assassin Tom Horn was heavily investigating the train robbery; that he could be privy to the contents of the letter and be unhindered in drawing any conclusions he wished about Angus's friend of many years, Isam Dart. Nor could McDougal have foreseen that Horn would be handed an even higher priority in addition to his search for the outlaws and that would be the illicit cleansing of Brown's Park.

Tom Horn moved with stealth among the inhabitants of Brown's Park, rode beside them, ate and laughed with them in the course of his infiltration into their lives. Little attention was paid to his coming and going.

On or about May 6, George Banks, the twenty-year-old son of a rancher named John Banks, was at the livery stable in Craig when he accidently overheard a covert meeting between Hi Bernard, Tom Horn, and Two-Bar employee Mexican Pete. The Banks family had a ranch near Lay. Banks stated and later swore in a deposition that he heard Hi Bernard instructing Horn to kill Mat Rash, Isam Dart, and Longhorn Thompson and to give notice to Joe Davenport, Eb Bassett, and Ann Bassett to leave the country. A statement written in the hand of George Banks states:

> I the undersigned wish to put in, writing, a conversation which I overheard between three men one being H.H. Bernard, and one known as Hicks or Tom Horn, and one known as Mexican Pete, working for the two bar. I over heard the conversation on or about May 6 1900. I heard Mr. Bernard say now we have got to get rid of these thieves and he says to Mr. Hicks: you kill Rash and that negro and Thompson and notify Annie and Elbert Bassett, and, Joe Davenport: to leave the country, and you can get your pay anytime you want it, and Mr. Bernard says to Mexican Pete, we want you to look after some other certain men, and help us in case Tom fails or gets caught. Mr. Bernard pulled some paper out of his pocket and saying here is some men we want watched, and red [read] the following names the Barber Bro:s [Brothers] John Schoonover, and the Gint Bro:s, and Jim Hoy, and he handed one small sheet of paper to Hicks and one to Pete and said if they don't go careful we will wait on them the same way. Mr. Bernard, says you can notify An. and Eb Bassett, and Joe Davenport and Lew Herd: to leave the country and if they dont leave or close out, we will put them out of the way, and if they close out and dont leave we want them watched and we want them other three fellows put out of the way as soon as possible, so we turn the whole thing over to you fellows.
> George H. Banks[20]

Years later when Hi Bernard gave his account concerning events surrounding Tom Horn he told fellow cowboy Frank Willis the following:

> A bunch of twenty-eight head of well-bred heifers branded VD belonging to a man at Baggs, Wyoming, on upper Snake River, were missing. Horn reported that he followed the tracks of a small bunch of cattle from Snake River, by way of Powder Wash to Limestone Mountain, east of Beaver Basin.

> Wiff Wilson and I went back with Horn, and were shown parts of the cattle trail. It was an isolated country, the trail was old, but traces could be picked up in the clay soil. The cattle had been driven by two horsemen. They had camped and night-herded in a small canyon. Wilson and I did not go all the way to Beaver Basin. Horn's statements had been verified so far, and we instructed him to make an effort to locate the cattle. Horn reported back to the committee that he had found butchered hides bearing the VD brand. One of the hides was found at Jim McKnight's summer cow camp at Summit Springs, and one at Matt Rash's NS camp. Both places were at Beaver Basin. Rash and McKnight were using these summer places at the time and had done so for several years. Horn brought the pieces of hides for Ayers [Ayer] and me to examine. We wet and stretched the pieces of hide and found the VD brand on each piece. That looked like the boldest, most outrageous cattle rustling job I had ever seen or heard of.[21]

Not only would such a rustling job have been bold and outrageous, it would have been exceedingly foolish and completely out of character for such range savvy men as Mat Rash, Jim McKnight, and Isam Dart. Although it is impossible to know with certainty, it is reasonable to conclude that the entire affair was a deliberate ploy to use the cattle as bait to ensnare the Brown's Parkers. The plan was foolproof for Horn: taking a couple of hides as a show-and-tell made it easy to convince his employers that he had solid proof of barefaced rustling.

For her part, Ann claimed that in June 1899, twenty-one head of young cattle wearing the VD brand showed up in the Utah end of Brown's Park after straying in from the north by way of Willow Creek Canyon. Joe Davenport spotted the cattle in the canyon as they foraged along the creek and moved through a flock of his father's sheep while slowly making their way down the canyon. Before leaving the sheep camp, Joe gave instructions to the Mexican sheepherder to get the names of anyone inquiring about the cattle. When Joe made his return trip to the canyon, the herder said Charley Ward had been by saying some of his cattle had strayed away from Clay Basin, just outside of Brown's Park.[22]

Charley Ward was one of the cowhands working years ago for Jim Warren on Diamond Mountain when Matt Warner first arrived there. Ward was around Brown's Park on and off through the years and never seemed to accumulate much more than a saddle horse, packhorse, and some gear. His story about the cattle being his didn't ring true to Joe

From left: Bill Davenport, Bob Franklin, Charley Ward, Joe Davenport, Jim Warren—all Brown's Park cowboys. *The Museum of NW Colorado–Craig.*

Davenport. Joe decided to ride to the Bassett Ranch to talk the matter over with trusted advisors Mat Rash and Sam Bassett. When he arrived, however, he found Ann and some of her town friends there, but Mat and Sam were away, having gone to the summer range on the mountain.

As soon as Ann heard what Joe had to say, she jumped to the conclusion that Charley Ward must have stolen the cattle. The brand was unfamiliar. She guessed the cattle were out of Utah. To her it was a prime opportunity to take her visiting girlfriends along on a wild ride.

"Yippee! I've got a wonderful idea! The poor cattle are homesick, let's give 'em a leg over the river. The girls aren't being properly trained in roping. We will demonstrate on those VD cattle."[23]

Joe, who had grown up with her, wasn't at all enthusiastic about Ann's impulsive plan. Nonetheless Ann Bassett had the dominant behavior, as usual, and she gave Joe his orders: "Don't stand there, looking at me! Drag it to the pasture and run in a fresh string."[24]

Ann and her friends galloped and trotted their horses up the valley, to "stretch their hard-twist ropes" in what Ann believed to be the worthy cause of sending the cattle back to their home range. The riders found the little bunch they were looking for about four miles west of the Davenport Ranch grazing along the river. The cattle were branded with a connected VD on the left hip. It was evening by then, but Ann and her friends had a bit of fun practice-roping the VD cattle. Before long they rode back to the Davenport Ranch to spend the night.

Early the next morning the young women gathered up the herd and drove them to the Parsons Ford just across the river from the Parsons cabin and pushed them into the river, sending the cattle on a swim to the other side. The last they saw of the VD cattle they were headed past the vacant cabin, making their way into the boxelder and cottonwood trees along the creek and moving among the cedars on the hillside, which leveled off to a sagebrush flat at the foot of Diamond Mountain.

In reality, the VD cattle were owned by Doty Brothers, a horse and cattle outfit at Willows, Wyoming. When Ann found out that the owners sent out letters to different well-known ranchers, including Mat Rash, asking for assistance in finding any trace of the cattle, she was embarrassed and afraid of repercussions if she admitted what she'd done. When Joe Davenport asked her if they should tell what they knew about the cattle she said, "No, and do not so much as imply to Sam Bassett or Mat Rash that we ever heard of that stuff."[25] That was a critical mistake.

Mat Rash was fully aware of the perils of running a cattle operation in the present climate of guns, accusations, and tempers. In a letter he wrote on November 13, 1898, to Joe Martin Blansit he chooses his words carefully to avoid conflict. The letter, in part, reads:

> Friend Joe I will write you a few lines to let you know how I am getting a long this leaves me well hoping it may find you the same. I was over there this summer but you was not at home, we had dinner and fed our horses. Joe I saw Frank Temple at Hahn's Peak and he told me that Charlie had one or two head of cattle of mine and he didn't know whether he sold them or shipped them. I wish you would find out. I ain't uneasy about it. But the reason I want to find out he might of sold them to someone that was to settle with me. You find out and let me know but don't think that I am borrowing any trouble about it. I will be over some time after winter so write soon.
>
> And as ever your friend
> Mat [26]

A different explanation concerning the mysterious VD cattle came from Carl Davidson, a cowboy of the time from the Baggs area. Davidson said the following:

> Now I will have to tell you what I know about the VD cows. There were two brothers, John and Dow Doty. They had ranches between

Baggs and Rawlins. One was at the Willows which was halfway between Baggs and Rawlins and was the halfway stage station. The other ranch was east of there on Cow Creek.

They ran a good sized bunch of horses for some time. Their brand was VD connected. The spring of 1899 they went to Vernal, Utah, bought a bunch of cows and calves, and trailed them back. They crossed the Green River on the bridge at Bridgeport, which was the Charley Crouse ranch. They stopped there for noon, then drove off and left 23 head of cows and calves. [The] cows were branded but the calves were not. Crouse told me the cows were there all summer. He saw them every day. Then sometime in September Isom Dart and Queen Ann drove them down into Brown's Park. That was the last Crouse ever saw of them. Why did Doty go and leave them there? And why didn't they go back and get them?[27]

Carl Davidson went on to say that in October 1899, Charley Ayer told him that he planned to attend the big Two-Bar roundup on Little Snake River and was also going to Brown's Park to see about the VD cattle. However, his trip was cut short after he was seriously injured by a horse. Wherever the truth about the VD cattle lay, the animals were used by members of the Little Snake River Stock Growers' Association, specifically Charlie Ayer, Wiff Wilson, and Ora Haley, to elicit a move against Brown's Park. Unbeknownst to Ann, in a world away from Brown's Park, a cattlemen's committee had reached a consensus: "Acting for the general welfare of all range users adjacent to Brown's Park, the appointed Committee gave Horn the go ahead signal, and cautioned him to be sure he got the guilty men."[28]

According to Frank Willis, Hi Bernard later stated:

At the time I interviewed the Brown's Parkers on the range question, Sam Bassett, a very fine young man, was the only one of them willing to cooperate with me on the grazing problem. Sam was selling his cattle at the time and preparing to see Alaska, therefore he was overruled in the matter. McKnight and Rash were willing to use me as a buffer against sheep invasion, but insisted on a strict deadline against the Two-Bar Cattle. It looked like they could have something to cover up, and I could not make a personal investigation, it required a stranger to do that successfully. Wilson and Ayer claimed to know the facts concerning Brown's Park and I accepted their word on face value. If the information, regarding Wilson's experience in Brown's Park had been passed on to me at the time, as it was four years later, the entire affair might have been quite the reverse of what it was.

A group of northwestern Colorado cattlemen pose at Lakeside Amusement Park, Denver. From left: Hi Bernard, Frank Temple, Charley Ayer, "Doc" Chivington, Theodore Tucker. *The Museum of NW Colorado–Craig.*

Another angle of the case presented itself to me when Al McCarger of Baggs told me that several years before I came into Colorado, Wilson had bought a bunch of horses in southern Utah. The horses attempted to go back to their old range. They strayed into Brown's Park and were picked up late in the fall by Sam Bassett. The horses were in poor condition and Sam fed them all winter, and notified Wilson to come and get them in the spring. McCarger told me about making the trip to the Bassett ranch with Wilson, and he said: "We found the horses in good shape. We spent the night at the Bassett ranch, took the horses and returned home, I heard Sam Bassett refuse payment for the care of the horses and also for our meals while we were there." This information was given to me by McCarger in the presence of Wiff Wilson who admitted it was true. I am not offering this tale to justify my actions in the

Tom Horn case, but it does puzzle me, why Wiff Wilson and Charley Ayer were over-anxious to move in on Brown's Park for the kill.[29]

Although there is no doubt that all of Herb and Elizabeth's children were traumatized and their lives deeply altered by Elizabeth's death, surely it was no harder for anyone than it was for Sam. Nearly every day he rode at his mother's side and under her tutelage. She was his mentor and pattern for conduct. As he was growing up it was undisputed that his future was laid out and he would be commander and protector of the Bassett Ranch and its legacy. Now, he was nearly finished with it all; it was no doubt very difficult to be letting loose of his mother's vision. While his father was always a source of gentleness, intellect, and morality, he was never a source of strength. That had fallen to Sam. So much had happened; adversities were too many. His heart no longer held his mother's dream. Then the news that Mat Rash lay murdered in his mountain cabin hit Sam and Ann like a thunderclap.

<hr />

NOTES TO CHAPTER SEVENTEEN

1. Larry D. Ball, *Tom Horn in Life and Legend*, (Norman: University of Oklahoma Press, 2014), 255-256.

2. Josie Bassett Morris, interview with Messersmith, 18 Jul 1960, The Museum of NW Colorado–Craig.

3. Josie Bassett Morris, interview with Untermann, Mortensen, and Cooley, Sep 1959, The Museum of NW Colorado–Craig.

4. Ann Bassett Willis, "Queen Ann of Brown's Park," *The Colorado Magazine*, Jan 1953, 62.

5. "Shooting at Browns Park," *Craig Courier*, 14 Apr 1900.

6. "Shooting at Browns Park," *Craig Courier*, 14 Apr 1900.

7. "Shooting at Browns Park," *Craig Courier*, 14 Apr 1900.

8. "Mrs. McKnight is Divorced," *Craig Courier*, 16 Jun 1900.

9. Homestead Proof—Testimony of Claimant, James F. McKnight, Glenwood Springs Land Office; Testimony of Witness, E.A. Farnham, 5 Sep 1900, The Museum of NW Colorado–Craig.

10. "Mrs. McKnight is Divorced," *Craig Courier*, 16 Jun 1900.

11. "Isom Dart and Tom Horn," *Rock Springs Rocket*, 5 Apr 1929, The Museum of NW Colorado–Craig.

12. Ann Bassett Willis, unpublished fragment of her memoir, "Scars and Two Bars."

13. Crawford MacKnight, letter to Cary Stif, 12 Nov 1968, The Museum of NW Colorado–Craig.

14. J.A. McKnight, letter to Cary Stif, 12 Nov 1968, The Museum of NW Colorado–Craig. J.A. McKnight was Jim McKnight's youngest son and half-brother to Crawford and Chick.

15. Nellie Snyder Yost, manuscript 40-42, The Museum of NW Colorado–Craig.

16. "Great Robber Gang," *Wheatland World*, 10 Dec 1897.

17. "Cassidy A Bad Man," *Western Newspaper Union*, Salt Lake City, Utah, 20 Nov 1898.

18. D.G. Thomas, letter from the Sweetwater County Office of the County and Prosecuting Attorney to U.S. Marshal Frank Hadsell, 12 Aug 1899. Wyoming State Museum through The Museum of NW Colorado–Craig.

19. D.G. Thomas, letter from Sweetwater County Office of Frank Hadsell.

20. Statement of George Banks, undated, Folder 4, George Banks papers, 1898-2005, Collection Number 11450, American Heritage Center, University of Wyoming.

21. Frank Willis, "Confidentially Told," The Museum of NW Colorado–Craig.

22. Ann Bassett Willis, "Queen Ann of Brown's Park," 62.

23. Ann Bassett Willis, "Queen Ann of Brown's Park," 63.

24. Ann Bassett Willis, "Queen Ann of Brown's Park," p. 63.

25. Ann Bassett Willis, "Queen Ann of Brown's Park," 64.

26. Mat Rash, letter written to Joe Martin Blansit, 13 Nov 1898, The Museum of NW Colorado–Craig.

27. C.A. Stoddard, *Tales of the Old West Retold*, edited by Dan Davidson, Janet Gerber, Shannan Koucherik, (Montrose, Colo: Lifetime Chronicle Press, 2017), 221-222. Although Charlie Crouse was living at that location in 1899, the Bridgeport bridge didn't yet exist. Construction of the bridge didn't begin until after a survey was completed in Dec 1901. Charlie Crouse's new ranch where he was establishing Bridgeport was upriver a short distance from the Parsons ford, where Ann said she and her friends sent the VD cattle across the river.

28. Frank Willis, "Confidentially Told."

29. Frank Willis, "Confidentially Told."

CHAPTER EIGHTEEN

THE TEMPEST

On August 25, 1900, twenty-four-year-old Sam Bassett wrote out a five page letter explaining the death of Mat Rash, the man who had been his advisor and close friend and had shared with him the shockwave of the loss of Elizabeth Bassett, staying ever close to help the family in any way he could:

Ladore, Colo
Aug. 25, 1900

Mr. J.M. Blansit:
Dear Friend

Your letter of recent date came to hand and [I] was very glad to hear from you. Joe in regard to the killing of Mat I know but very little but neither does anyone else. He was found shot and who done it no one knows here. He was supposed to have been killed July 8th and was not found till the 10th. He was at his camp eating a meal and was shot in the back once and once in the breast. It is the supposition he was shot in the back first and fell and was shot the second time. The door is directly in front of the table he fell back in one end of the house and was undoubtedly shot the second time whare [where] he fell and lay there sometime for there was lots of blood there and one of the bullets a 30-30 Winchester was found in the wall. He must have survived for a short time and got to the bed. He was lying on the bed face to the wall and his sixshooter and a note book lay by him they were all covered with blood. He had $32.00 with him and that was under the head of the bed. One shoe was off and the other unlaced. A horse was also shot about 30 steps from the house not the one he was riding but a half broke one of Mats. Some think he was put on the bed bed (sic) but I think he got there him self. There has been some people suspected but no proof atall. His Father and one Brother are here but I don't know what their address is in Texas. But I think Mat came from Cleburne or somewhere near thare [there]. Mat had between seven and eight hundred head of cattle and good ones to. He was buried right there for his body was in a terriable [terrible] condition full of worms. He left here "our ranch" and went to the mountain the 8th of July and the supposition is he was killed that day but we cant tell exactly. Well Joe if you do come up here come and see me. I am still here on the old place. This damn country is just as bad as it used to be, rowing all the time between the cattle and sheep men. I think this is the cause of that killing. Well Joe this is all at present. Write soon again soon.

I am as ever

Your friend

Sam Bassett Jr.[1]

The *Rock Spring Miner* newspaper soon carried an account of the killing as told to them by Eb Bassett:

ANOTHER TRAGEDY
Matt Rash, of Brown's Park Shot and
Killed - A cold Blooded Murder -
No Clue to the Murder

Another tragedy is reported from Brown's Park. This time Matt Rash, the cattleman, is the victim. Ebb Bassett arrived yesterday with the news that Matt Rash was found dead in bed, shot through the back in two places, in his cabin at the old N.S. corrals on Coal [Cold] Springs mountain. The body was found by Felix Myers and Wm. Rife on the 10th inst. That night Ebb Bassett started for town and riding all night, arrived in town yesterday. Mr. Kendall telegraphed the news to the dead man's father in Texas, who replied to bury the body and take charge of his property. Tomorrow morning Mr. D.A. Reavill [Attorney-at-Law] starts south to have an administrator appointed and others will see to the safety of the property. Matt Rash had from 600 to 800 head of cattle and couple of ranches.

The shooting of Matt Rash cannot be explained. Future developments however, may clear up the mystery.

Mr. Rash spent the fourth of July in Rock Springs and started for home on the 5th, that night he camped with Willis Rouff and James Taggart on Red creek. The night of the 6th he spent at Bassett's ranch, Ladore, and about 4:30 on the afternoon of the 7th he started on horseback for his cabin, nine miles away, which was the last time he was seen alive.

On the 10th, about one o'clock p.m. his body was found, and as decomposition had set in he must have been killed either the night he got to camp or early the next day. His cabin door was open and at the corner of the house lay his saddle with his coat tied to it, and in a bunch of trees about 25 yards from the cabin his saddle horse lay dead, the animal having been, like his master, shot. Whoever did the deed showed determination to make thorough work of it. William Rife remained with the body, while Felix Myers rode over to Bassett's ranch with the news. John Demsher, George Bassett and Elbert Bassett returned with Myers to the dead man's cabin where by this time A.L. Sparks had joined Mr. Rife and then a consultation was held. As a result of it Elbert Bassett rode to Rock Springs, and George Bassett started for Craig to notify the coroner and sheriff, of Route [Routt] county, Colorado.

The body lay in bed, face to the wall, the head resting on his right hand. In front of Matt on the bed was his pistol and also the scabbard. One shoe was off and lying on the floor at the edge of the bed as if it had dropped from his foot. His hat was on the floor behind the chair, which was close up to the table. Near the hat was a pool of blood and blood tracks were traceable from the table to the bed showing that he was shot while eating. On the table was a can of tomatoes opened with part of them emptied into a plate. His gloves lay on the table, his vest hung at the foot of the bed. There were two bullet holes in his back about an inch apart.

Mr. Bassett could throw no light upon the deed, saying he knew of no one who held any grudge against Matt.

Matt Rash was well known in Rock Springs and regarded here as a quiet man. He has been about eighteen years in the country, and before he owned a brand of his own he worked for the "G" outfit, the Two Bar [Middlesex] and for Mr. Kinney. He has no relatives in the country, but has a father and sister in Texas and two brothers, one in New Mexico and the other in Arizona. The deceased was 35 years old.[2]

That summer day, July 10, became an indescribable horror for Billy Rife and especially Felix Myers, the fourteen year old step-son of stockman Antone Prestopitz. Carefree and enjoying the ride together the two cowhands decided to stop by Mat Rash's mountain cabin to say hello. The smell of carrion had the air well-coated and growing stronger by the time they spotted a sorrel bronc lying dead in the corral, surrounded by the hum of flies at work. Blood from a bullet hole just above the point of the horse's nose was dried dark and crusty. Perplexed, Felix walked to the cabin where the door was standing ajar.

Mat Rash's log cabin was fourteen feet square with a dirt floor. The door, made to swing inward, was located near the southwest corner of the building. On the opposite side of the cabin was a small window with a table just beneath it. A wood burning cookstove was located a short distance to the right of the table.[3] As Felix pushed on the door to open it wider, it bumped against the bed. The teenager stepped inside and was knocked backward by the sight and smell of death.

Another account was reported in the *Steamboat Pilot*:

The Killing of Rash.

Brown's Park, Colo., July 16th – Madison M. Rash, well known throughout the county and country generally, was found dead on Tuesday, 10th-of-July at his summer camp on Cold Spring mountain just north and overlooking the east end of Brown's Park. He was shot twice, once through the body above the hips and through the chest coming out low down near the backbone. Either one necessarily fatal. It is supposed he was killed on Sunday but the murder was not discovered until Tuesday. It was a murder most foul. Rash had from appearance sat down to eat, was shot in one side, fell, raised up and turned pretty near around and then was shot from the opposite side. A large pool of blood collected on the ground floor where he fell showed he must have lain there some time, yet he was found lying on his bed, his watch and memorandum book lying by his side and purse with $32 under his pillow. He was lying mostly on his face with his head on his arm in an easy, natural position. It seems impossible that shot as he was he could rise from the ground and lay his trinkets around him. Decomposition had set in and the body was in bad shape when found, and one can imagine its condition when buried on Friday, five days after being killed. The only thing to be done was to wrap the mattress and blankets about him and bury him near where he died. The cause of the delay for burial was that an effort was made to have an investigation by a coroner, the Justice of the Peace of District Court at Hahn's Peak. The killing and the cause therefore is a mystery and may remain so, as so far there is no clue and no conjecture.[4]

Those who carried the cattleman's body from the cabin wore bandages and handkerchiefs over their noses and mouths. The body, wrapped in the bedding, was carried by the feather tick mattress to the burial site nearby. Working as quickly and gently as could be managed, Mat's body was rolled into the grave.

There it was: the horrific and stark result of Tom Horn's occupation and enigmatic darkness sanctioned by those who paid him and the politicians who allowed the emergence of such campaigns. The once handsome president of the Brown's Park Cattle Association betrothed to the darling of Brown's Park, Ann Bassett, was found decaying, and teeming with the legless, soft-bodied larva of flies.

Felix Myers could not recover from the shock. He developed Sydenham's chorea, a disorder referred to as Saint Vitus Dance. The condition caused Felix uncoordinated jerking movements the rest of his life. Never able to fit in with society, he faced life alone.[5] The entire Brown's Park community was in shock and terrified, which was, of course, the exact reaction Horn's terror campaign was designed to inspire. If this could happen to Mat Rash who was known among the Brown's Parkers as "a prince of a man"[6] who was highly capable, respected, and the most prominent cattleman in Brown's Park, it could happen to any one of them.

Upon receiving word of Mat Rash's death, his sixty-six-year-old father, Samuel Rash from Acton, Texas, and one of Mat's brothers, William "Billy" Rash, who was a couple years younger than Mat and living in Double Mountain, Texas, traveled north to take care of Mat's affairs. They also planned to have the body removed to Acton, Texas.

On July 28, 1900, Mat Rash's bank, the First National Bank of Rock Springs, petitioned Judge Isaac G. Voice of the Routt County court in the matter of the estate of Madison M. Rash. The petition listed the following facts about what the estate was worth: The Rash Ranch was believed to be 160 acres of deeded land and with improvements was valued at $1500; six-hundred head of cattle were valued at $25 each or $15,000; six horses had a total value of $200; wagons, harness, hay, and other personal property of various kinds were valued at $300. The petition states that the bank held a balance on a note on the 600 head of cattle for $6,000 still owed. The bank stated that due search and inquiry was made and it was determined that Mat Rash died intestate, meaning without a will. The heirs at law were Mat's father Samuel, his brothers James, Charles, and William and sisters Cynthia Oldham and Lorena MacDonald. The bank asked the court to appoint Charles Crouse as administrator of the estate.[7] On July 28, William Rash petitioned the court in the matter of his brother's estate on behalf of his father and siblings as heirs.

Ann Bassett was wholly inconsolable after Mat's murder. Once again, in an instant, her life and comfort splintered. The constant of Mat Rash as an integral part of not only her life but the entire Bassett family was now irreversibly, painfully, empty. He, and all that defined him, was supposed to be hers in marriage. She and her family were there, not Mat's

Texas family, to support and help him build his ranch. She shared his pride, not them, when he bought the Goodman sheep outfit and got financing through a bank in Rock Springs to buy cattle and build the place into a cattle ranch. How could she accept being stranded with no right to any of it?

Accompanied by her father, Ann traveled to Steamboat Springs to obtain a lawyer. Herb and Ann registered at the Sheridan Hotel, the very hotel where Mat Rash's father Samuel and his lawyer from Rock Springs, D.A. Reavill, were staying.[8]

Ann retained attorney Wells B. McClelland of Steamboat. On July 30, she formally petitioned the court and was identified as the betrothed wife of Madison M. Rash:

> Petition of Anna M. Bassett in the matter of the last will and testament of Madison M. Rash, Deceased, for probate of will and letters testamentary.
>
> To the Honorable Isaac G. Voice, Judge of the County Court of Routt County, in the State of Colorado:
>
> The petition of the undersigned Anna M. Bassett respectfully represents that Madison M. Rash of Ladore in the said county of Routt and state of Colorado, departed this life on or about the 10th day of July A.D. 1900, leaving a last will and testament duly signed and published, and which is by her herewith presented to your honor for probate.

In the petition, Ann claimed that on or about May 20, 1900, Mat Rash wrote his will and signed it in front of witnesses and then gave it to her. Since his death, she had searched for the will but had been unable to find it. Witnesses, though, the petition stated, would establish the will's existence and contents. The petition went on to state that the terms of the will left all personal property to Anna Bassett for her own use and benefit, and to no one else. It offered a list of names of witnesses and requested that those on the list be summoned to give testimony; although the will was lost, these witnesses had knowledge that the will did exist. The list included neighboring rancher Larry Curtin, Brown's Park schoolteacher Blanche Tilton, Eb Bassett, E.B. Thompson, and Josephine McKnight. It was requested that William W. Bragg be administrator of the will.

The *Steamboat Pilot* reported:

> There is a romance, which makes more sad the tragedy of the murder of Matt Rash of Brown's Park. His will, which will be admitted to probate, leaves his property to Miss Anna Bassett, who was soon to have been his wife. A $5,000 insurance policy on his life goes to his father in

Texas. The estate is valued at between $15,000 and $20,000. There is no clue to the perpetrator of the foul Murder.[9]

The August 1 issue of the *Steamboat Pilot* reported that Ann's father's post office was closing and his position at the Bassett ranch ending.

A.H. Bassett and Miss Annie Bassett, of Brown's Park came up from the lower country Sunday on business. Mr. Bassett is one of the pioneers of Routt County, having lived in Brown's Park for twenty two years, and is now preparing to leave the country. He has leased his ranch to his sons and will spend the summers in Wyoming, later going to his old home in the south.[10]

Herb, an intensely devout Christian, had grown weary. Many things must have been causing him sorrow. His oldest son, six foot tall and handsome, kindhearted and a skilled cattleman was on the verge of leaving the ranch and going all the way to Alaska to live; Mat Rash upon whom he and his children had regularly relied was cruelly murdered; Josie was in a sensationalized divorce; and his dearest Anna Maria, whose future was dashed, was in the process of swearing a legal claim to a phantom last will and testament.

At the end of August the *Steamboat Pilot* reported: "S.A. Rash of Texas and Larry Curtain [Curtin] of Brown's Park are camping here until after Game day." Game Day was a multi-day event drawing about 3,000 people to Steamboat Springs to watch rough riding, steer roping, pony racing, shooting contests, running races, and dances.[11] The August 29, 1900, article went on to state that:

S.A. Rash, father of the late Madison M. Rash has added $500 to the $200 offered by the county commissioners for the arrest and conviction of the murders [murderers] of his son. The reward [is] now $700 for Mat Rash's slayer.

Mat Rash's banker in Rock Springs, Augustine Kendall, offered an additional $500 reward.[12] Newspapers ran the following notice about the Routt County reward:

REWARD

The Board of County Commissioners of Routt County Colorado do hereby offer a reward of two hundred dollars for the arrest and conviction of the murderers of Madison M. Rash of Brown's Park Routt County Colorado.

JOHN ADAIR,
Chairman[13]

There is little doubt that Ann and her father became acquainted with Mat Rash's father and brother. A story emerged that while they were all traveling together to Hahn's Peak for court, they stopped at a roadhouse in Lay owned by homesteader and wildlife photographers, Allen "A.G." and Augusta Wallihan. Supposedly, as they lunched, Ann was offered a $250 settlement if she would drop her claim against Mat's estate.[14] Whether this actually happened is unknown. It is true that Ann was left owing her attorney a hefty sum of money. Perhaps further pursuing a claim that she wasn't likely to win simply became too expensive. Whatever her reasoning, Ann took the legal steps to:

> ... move the court that her said petition and application be dismissed, and she hereby consents that said will and testament may be not probated and allowed and that judgment may be entered by the court disallowing and refusing the probate of said will and testament sought to be probated herein.[15]
>
> Anna Bassett

On September 24, 1900, in open court, the judge's statement included: "And the Court after duly considering the same motion does order adjudge and discern that said supposed last will and testament so sought to be probated by the said Anna M. Bassett in her said petition is not the last will and testament of the said Madison M. Rash."[16] It was over for Ann. She would have no say and little, if any, benefit. Samuel Rash was determined the sole heir.[17]

September 26, 1900, Tom Horn was in Hahn's Peak brewing what was most certainly another ruse by swearing an Affidavit of Charged Offense against Isam Dart. The affidavit stated that on June 8, 1900, Isam Dart rode away, with intent to steal, a ten-year-old sorrel horse belonging to Jim McKnight. Although Isam Dart was working for Jim McKnight and McKnight was in the process of moving away from Brown's Park, Horn named McKnight along with Henry Lang as witnesses. Interestingly, Henry Lang owned a ranch on the south side of the Little Snake River beside the Two-Bar holdings belonging to Ora Haley. Horn signed his given name, Thomas Horn, to the document.[18] It is probable that Horn did this because he was still planning to kill Jim McKnight and was creating a set-up where he could pin the murder on Isam Dart, who now appeared to have a motive. Such a plot would have the potential of eliminating both men. It's most certain that Isam was never aware of the

The Museum of Northwest Colorado displays a photograph of Isam Dart along with the leather cuffs that he frequently wore. © *Copyright Paul Knowles and the Museum of NW Colorado–Craig.*

charge against him. Nor could he have known about Tom Horn's scheme that would culminate just eight days later.

Isam Dart didn't own any land but had squatted on some acreage in Brown's Park and built a double cabin there. He had formed a partnership with twenty-five-year-old John Demsher, who was an Austrian immigrant.[19] They each had one-half interest in sixteen horses and a small bunch of thirty-six head of cattle.[20] Isam was continuing to oversee the bit of livestock Jim McKnight had remaining in the area, and he had some form of lease agreement on McKnight's summer range and cabin located just a few miles from where Mat Rash was killed.

❧ ❧ ❧

During October, cooling breezes of fall flutter the quaking aspen leaves on Cold Spring Mountain and they shimmer in the rising color along creeks, meadows, and slopes. Thick stands of white-barked aspen trees grew all about Jim McKnight's one room mountain cabin and were lavishly sustained by spring water.

The night of October 3, Sam Bassett and his youngest brother, sixteen-year-old George, accompanied by Louis "Lew" Brown, spent the night on Cold Spring Mountain with Isam at the McKnight cabin Isam had built by hand. Lew Brown had recently, on June 14, arrived in Brown's Park from Missouri and was working as a cowhand.

It was between eight and nine the next morning, October 4, 1900,[21] when Isam, accompanied by George, came out of the cabin. They picked up their bridles and headed to the corral to saddle up the two horses kept there overnight for use in wrangling the rest of the saddle horses from the nearby range. George walked just a little ahead and on Isam's right as they went to the horses. When they'd gone about two-thirds of the way, a rifle shot blasted from the stillness. George turned to see Isam falling. The top-hand cowboy said, "Oh, my God," before hitting the ground face first. George stood frozen for a moment, not knowing from which way the shot had come. Not seeing anyone, he ran with all his strength for the cabin where Sam and Lew stood at the door. Upon reaching the cabin George uttered, "Someone killed Isam!"[22]

Sam, George, and Lew got their guns and then stood near the door, which faced east, watching and waiting. Seeing no sign of anyone but continuing to fear an ambush they decided to vacate the cabin by climbing through the window which was on the south side of the building.[23]

Their first steps outside the cabin were ones of trepidation. They walked toward Mat Rash's cabin, knowing there were men there. They met up with Larry Curtin, Mat Rash's brother Billy Rash, and Charlie Neiman. Neiman's term as Sheriff of Routt County had ended the previous year. On September 8, at the request of Samuel Rash, he'd been appointed to collect and administrate the estate of Mat Rash.[24]

Larry Curtin, Billy Rash, Lew Brown, Sam, and George, went in a group to where Isam lay. Neiman rode to round up Isam Dart's saddle horses and bring them to the corral.[25] While some stayed with the body, others soon rode out to spread the word.

Justice of the Peace J.S. Hoy quickly impaneled a jury to hold an inquest with the group gathering at the site of the killing. The assassin had come from the east and ridden to within three hundred yards of the cabin where he tied his horse to a tree before moving up to within a few yards of the corral. There he stationed himself behind a tree, apparently resting his gun on the poles of the fence. The tree he hid behind had been used as a post in the fence line. He waited until Isam was about 120 yards away from him before he fired. It was concluded that the gunman was familiar with Isam Dart's habits and timed his arrival accordingly. The prints of the horse hooves revealed it had been tied only a short time.[26]

The jury observed Isam's body as it lay in the box of a wagon. He had dressed himself in a heavy suit of underwear beneath a layer of two shirts.[27] Using a probe to learn how the bullet traveled, jury member Billy Bragg placed the end of it into the wound that was an inch to the left of the right nipple. The ball had ranged downward and lodged near the spinal column. On October 5, as Isam was prepared for burial, his well-used leather cuffs were removed from his wrists.[28] Snowflakes fell as Isam Dart was buried nearby, in a serene setting among the aspens overlooking Beaver Basin.[29] In the far distance, Sam Bassett and Billy Bragg were on the trail, following the tracks of a well-shod horse that carried the assassin away. After following the tracks in the storm east for eight miles, the two gave up and turned back.[30]

Years later, Joe Davenport was interviewed about Isam Dart. The article by George L. Erhard, in part, states:

> Of Isom Dart, negro cow-puncher of early days, old-timers speak reverently. He was in a way the Gunga Din of Brown's Park during the 80s and his engaging personality was such that he left an ineffaceable

imprint in many minds both for his daring deeds and his unswerving integrity. Joe Davenport, local patrolman [is the] last survivor of the intrepid five who captured Harry Tracy after the latter had murdered Valentine Hoy and in a talk with the writer this week, Davenport extolled his old riding companion with a Wild West eulogy that appealed:

"I worked side by side with him for years and he taught me all the tricks of riding. Isom was the most polite man I ever met and was a courtier supreme in his respect for women. I have seen all the great riders. But for all-around skill as a cowman, Isom Dart was unexcelled and I never saw his peer."[31]

Joe Davenport's depiction of Isam Dart, a man he so admired, offered a sobering conclusion: "He kept his place and invariably ate his meals in silence alone, although not a cowman, ever, objected to his company."

Tension from the assassinations reverberated throughout the country. On October 20, 1900, the Craig newspaper startled readers with a report that a letter was found among the effects of Isam Dart warning Sam, Eb, and George Bassett along with Joe Davenport to leave Brown's Park inside of sixty days or suffer the same fate which befell Mat Rash and Isam Dart.[32] However, on November 3, 1900, the newspaper carried a response from Sam disputing the story:

Shortly after the killing of Isam Dart in Browns Park statements were published in various papers reporting that a letter warning the Bassett boys and others to leave the Park was found among Dart's effects. Samuel Bassett writes from Brown's Park saying that no such letter was found as far as he knows and that the Bassett boys have not been warned to leave that section.[33]

As the estates of Isam Dart and Mat Rash were argued and resolved, it's curious that on November 6, 1900, Henry Lang, the Little Snake River rancher and neighbor of Ora Haley who signed his name as a witness for Tom Horn in the affidavit stating that Isam Dart stole one of Jim Mcknight's horses, visited Justice of the Peace James H. Templeton to make a claim against Isam Dart's estate. Lang swore he was owed two horses worth $50 each and another worth $25 for a total of $125.[34] It is not known whether Lang collected or, for that matter, if he had ever had any dealings at all with Isam Dart. Though the paperwork was filed, there is no mention of Lang in the final accounting of Isam's claimants.

On November 2, 1900, a correspondence was sent from Brown's Park to the *Steamboat Pilot*:

Mat Rash's cabin on Cold Spring Mountain with Arthur Sparks looking on, taken in 1915. *The Museum of NW Colorado–Craig.*

On the 30th of October a party of men assisted Mr. Rash senior to disinter the body of his son, M.M. Rash, and place it in a coffin for shipment to his old home in Texas.

The remains were in no worse condition than when buried. It seems that when the body was put under ground decomposition was partially delayed.

Both of the Rashes have departed for Texas. The way the bills came in it began to look as if they would not have money enough to take them home.

Late developments have convinced a number of people that the same man murdered both Rash and Dart, and the assassin came from the outside. One thing is almost certain, that the murderer of Dart was not a citizen of this section as there are so few men here it is an easy matter for each man to show where he was when Dart was shot.

The "lone horseman" that was seen riding east after Dart was killed was tracked miles from where he stood when he fired the fatal shot, east into the Bad Lands on his way in the direction toward Snake river. I suppose none of us here are any better than we ought to be, but I am loth to believe there is anyone who would deliberately shoot down in cold blood, as Rash and Dart were, and if the murderer of these two men is ever known he will be an outsider. The fact is, nearly all the serious crimes committed here have been done by outsiders.

B. B.[35]

At last, Mat Rash was buried by his family in the Acton, Texas, cemetery. A tall and stately headstone stands in memoriam and reads:

M. M. Rash—Jan. 4, 1865—Murdered in his cabin on his Ranch on Cold Spring Mt. Routt Co. Col.—July 8, 1900—A dutiful son—A faithful friend–A worthy citizen

❧ ❧ ❧

Ann suspected Tom Hicks was the killer but still didn't know Hicks was actually Tom Horn. Tom Horn, however, was revealing himself to be a braggart who was defaming Mat Rash, Isam Dart, and Brown's Park, in general. Ann believed the rumors that the entire bloody affair sat at the feet of Ora Haley, a baron who wanted the prized Brown's Park rangeland. She told all who would listen of her suspicions. She begged her neighbors for help in patrolling the designated divide. However, she found her community and even her brothers feeling bewildered and afraid; the risk just too real and menacing.

The storm had come on bitter winds and bold and twisted words, all merging into a tempest to take the lives of Mat Rash and Isam Dart. It came with the force of night terrors ripping at the future which Ann Bassett thought she knew. Brown's Park shuddered, Ann Bassett wept, and a well-schooled assassin collected on the payment he was due.

NOTES TO CHAPTER EIGHTEEN

1. Sam Bassett, letter to Joe Martin Blansit, 25 Aug 1900, The Museum of NW Colorado–Craig.
2. "Another Tragedy," *Vernal Express,* Jul 21, 1900, reprinted from article in *Rock Springs Miner.*
3. William D. Tittsworth, transcription of taped interview with C.A. Stoddard Jr., 1998, The Museum of NW Colorado–Craig.
4. "The Killing Of Rash," *The Steamboat Pilot,* 25 Jul 1900.
5. Hazel Teters Overy, interviews with author, 1981-1987.
6. "Mystery Murders of Matt Rash and Isom Dart Now Believed The Dastardly Acts of Tom Horn," *Rock Springs Rocket,* 5 Apr 1929, The Museum of NW Colorado–Craig.
7. Petition of First National Bank of Rock Springs, Wyoming, In the Matter of the Estate of Madison M. Rash, 28 Jul 1900, The Museum of NW Colorado–Craig.

8. *The Steamboat Pilot,* 1 Aug 1900.

9. "Sayings of Others," Vernal *Express,* 11 Aug 1900, reprinted from *The Steamboat Pilot.*

10. *The Steamboat Pilot,* 1 Aug 1900.

11. Steamboat Springs Pro Rodeo Series, www.steamboatprorodeo.com/history, accessed 14 May 2017.

12. "Reign of Terror," *Laramie Republic,* 18 Dec 1900.

13. *The Steamboat Pilot,* 29 Aug 1900.

14. John R. Burroughs, *Where the Old West Stayed Young,* (New York: Bonanza Books, 1962), 222.

15. Withdrawal of Petition to Inherit by Anna M. Bassett, The Museum of NW Colorado–Craig.

16. Judge's statement denying petition of Anna M. Bassett, 24 Sep 1900, The Museum of NW Colorado–Craig.

17. Petition for Letters of Administration to Collect, Samuel A. Rash in the matter of the Estate of Madison M. Rash to Judge Voice, 9 Aug 1900, The Museum of NW Colorado–Craig.

18. Affidavit of Charged Offense filed by Thomas Horn against Isam Dart, 26 Sep 1900, The Museum of NW Colorado–Craig.

19. U.S. Census 1900; Isam Dart's estate documents, The Museum of NW Colorado–Craig.

20. Isam Dart's estate documents.

21. Affidavit of Decease for Isam Dart sworn by William H. Blair, 3 Dec 1900, The Museum of NW Colorado–Craig.

22. "Murder of Isam Dart," *The Steamboat Pilot,* from the sworn testimonies of George Bassett and Lewis Brown, 17 Oct 1900.

23. "Murder of Isam Dart," *The Steamboat Pilot.*

24. Letters of Administration to Collect, 8 Sep 1900, The Museum of NW Colorado–Craig.

25. "Murder of Isam Dart," *The Steamboat Pilot.*

26. "Murder of Isam Dart," *The Steamboat Pilot.*

27. William D. Tittsworth, transcription of taped interview with Stoddard, The Museum of NW Colorado–Craig.

28. Crawford MacKnight, letter to Cary Stif, 12 Nov 1968; the cuffs are on display at the Museum of NW Colorado–Craig .

29. "Murder of Isam Dart," *The Steamboat Pilot.*

30. "Killing in Brown's Park," *Craig Courier,* 13 Oct 1900; "Cold Blooded Murder," *Vernal Express,* Oct 1900 ; William D. Tittsworth, transcription of taped interview with Stoddard, The Museum of NW Colorado–Craig.

31. "Mystery Murders of Matt Rash and Isom Dart Now Believed The Dastardly Acts of Tom Horn," Rock *Springs Rocket.*

32. "Dart Killed," *Craig Courier,* 20 Oct 1900.

33. "Dart Killed," *Craig Courier,* 3 Nov 1900.

34. Creditor's Claim by Henry Lang against the estate of Isam Dart, 6 Nov 1900, The Museum of NW Colorado–Craig.

35. Correspondence from Brown's Park, *The Steamboat Pilot,* 14 Nov 1900.

CHAPTER NINETEEN

RIDING INTO LEGEND

Brown's Park witnessed Ann Bassett's mounting obsession for vengeance, as her grief turned to fury. The violence that slammed into her valley fragmented the Brown's Park Cattle Association. The men ceased sending anyone to the divide to hold back Ora Haley's herds. Enraged and grim-faced Queen Ann saddled her horse. The young woman rode alone through pine, sagebrush, grasslands, and cedars to defend her valley. Steeped in the gloom of anger and sorrow, she kept a rifle strapped to her saddle. Ann traveled against the winds, some shaped by nature and others by circumstance, while doing her best to hold back what she saw as an avalanche of despised Two-Bar cattle. Moving in rhythm with the horse beneath her, this daughter of both Brown's Park and the cattlewoman Elizabeth Bassett was in the throes of becoming a legend.

As for Tom Horn, by November, he was in Cheyenne, apparently basking in a state of glorified invincibility; an attitude gifted to him in large part by men of wealth and high office who praised, encouraged, and enabled him to be, on his word alone and for money, a judge and executioner of his fellow man. Horn consented to an interview with George H. Evans in Cheyenne and the resulting article in the *Wyoming Tribune* reveals much about his depravity. His pathological falsehoods were presented as fact, and, regrettably, exalted by the writer.

A RUSTLER CHIEF
Sensational Developments Surrounding the Death of Matt Rash and
His Partner Isham Dart.
Their Ranches the Rendezvous for Train Robbers and Horse Thieves
When Hard Pressed by Officers Were Thought to be Respectable Citizens.
But in Reality Were Outlaws and Desperados.

Colonel Tom Horn, the noted scout and Indian fighter, has just returned from a trip through the Brown's park country on the Wyoming-

262

Utah-Colorado line in the Sierra Madre mountains, the notorious rendezvous for outlaws, train robbers and murderers, and tells an interesting story of that section, its lawless inhabitants, and how the gang of bandits was finally broke up almost a month ago. . . .

A few weeks ago Matt Rash, a ranchman living in the Brown's Park country, who had been suspected for some time of cattle stealing and harboring train robbers and outlaws, was killed in his cabin on Cold Spring mountain. He was found one morning with a bullet in his brain, and a week later Isham Dart, colored, a partner and neighboring ranchman, was killed in the same manner. A report reached the railroad that the stockmen had been murdered by rustlers but Colonel Horn says the dead men were leaders of the rustler bands, instead of respectable ranchmen, as had been supposed. In speaking of the two men Colonel Horn said:

"I know Rash and Dart well, and two more notorious rustlers never infested the Rocky mountain country. Both men came from Texas sixteen years ago. Rash was for a number of years employed by Tim Kinney, the sheep king, who was then in the cattle business, but he branded so many of Kinney's calves for himself that Kinney discharged him. Dart secured employment on ranches in Southern Wyoming. Eastern Utah and Northern Colorado, and, like Rash, branded other men's calves and became a cattle thief.

'Dart and Rash, who had been cowboys together in Texas, fled to the Brown's park country when the range became too hot to hold them and there formed a partnership. With the money received from stolen cattle they established two "peanut" ranches, which soon became the rendezvous for one of the worst bands of outlaws that ever infested the western country. It was at Rash's and Dart's places that train robbers, bank robbers, cattle and horse thieves and all classes of criminals found refuge when hard pressed by sheriff's posses and United States officers, and it was these two men that furnished fresh horses, food and ammunition to the outlaws. . . .

'Rash and Dart were ably assisted in their nefarious work by a man named Joe Davenport and the Bassett brothers three in number. These men, as soon as they learned of the death of the two leaders, fled from the country, not stopping long enough to round up what horses and cattle they claimed to own, but which had been stolen.

'At the time Rash was killed he had about 650 head of cattle, 100 head of horses and about 200 head of calves. Dart, who was not as thrifty as Rash, and who spent most of his ill-gotten gains in drink and cards, had less than 200 head of cattle, about 10 head of horses.

'Now that Brown's Park has been freed of its undesirable residents, respectable stockmen will go in there," continued Colonel Horn, "and settle the country. Brown's park is a beautiful valley between high mountains, about forty miles long and eighteen miles wide, well-watered and level. It is one of the best stock sections to be found in the entire Rocky Mountain range. When once the cattleman gets possession, outlaws had better give the place a wide berth. There have been numerous murders in that section during the past few years and ranchmen living just outside of the park have lost hundreds of head of cattle and horses, but they will not be molested from now on. . . .[1]

Tom Horn's slurs and grandiose expressions are quite remarkable. It's important to note that Tom Horn never held the rank of colonel. Mat Rash did work for Tim Kinney, but Kinney backed Mat financially in helping the young man enter the cattle business when Kinney sold his cattle and bought sheep. There is no evidence that Mat Rash or Isam Dart ever harbored, partnered with, or had financial dealings with rustlers and outlaws. Mat Rash owned six horses not one hundred and he bought his cattle herd, which at his death numbered six hundred head, with financing from the First National Bank of Rock Springs, Wyoming. Isam Dart was not a drinker or gambler. Of course, Horn's slander against Sam, Eb, and George Bassett as well as Joe Davenport was described as absurd by those who knew them.

Apparently another detective was sent to take the place of Tom Horn in northwestern Colorado. Some surmise that the replacement was Horn's friend and fellow lawman, Bob Meldrum. An attempt was made on Longhorn Thompson's life but the bullet didn't find its mark. Longhorn survived to return home to Armida and his two children. Rather than live in daily fear, the Thompson family left the ranch and went to Craig.

"It all sums up to the question of ground," Two-Bar foreman Hi Bernard said, "the question that started when the first white man advanced westward. First, we killed the Indians to get it, now we kill each other for the same reason."[2]

In late November or early December, George Banks, the young man who overheard Hi Bernard, Tom Horn, and Mexican Pete in the livery stable, came very close to losing his life. Early morning the young man saddled his horse and rode out to bring the milk cows to the corral. Suddenly a bullet cut through his shirt near his heart before tearing into the lapel of his vest and ripping the shirt off his arm. George quickly drew his rifle from its scabbard and returned fire as the assailant rode away over a hill. George gave chase but his horse was no match for the gunman's and was soon outdistanced. George Banks said the man rode in the direction of Craig.

In reporting the incident, a newspaper described the Banks family as one of the most respectable in Routt County who had been residents of the county for seventeen years. It went on to state that the assassin was no doubt connected to those who killed the men in Brown's Park.[3]

It has often been written and long held as fact that before the killings of Mat Rash and Isam Dart, they—as well as the Davenports, Longhorn Thompson, and Eb Bassett—awakened to find unsigned notes of warning at their doors stating that those named were to move out of the valley in thirty days or suffer the consequences. However, evidence to substantiate the existence of any such notes is elusive. The only warning note mentioned in the newspapers which were reporting on every aspect of trouble in Brown's Park at that time was the one that was supposedly found in Isam Dart's effects. The existence of that letter was immediately refuted by Sam Bassett and the newspaper printed the correction.

William D. Tittsworth, son of Billy Tittsworth, moved to Brown's Park in May of 1899. While some of his recollections in a recorded interview looking back many years may be valuable, other things are not based in fact, such as his claim that while Mat Rash was in Rock Springs just days before his death, Rash received a letter from Tom Horn telling him to leave the country or be killed. Mat Rash was well-known in Rock Springs. If he had received such a letter, he would have undoubtedly told his close associates as well as the authorities.

However, warning letters were received by both Ann and Eb Bassett, postmarked from Cheyenne. Who wrote them is a mystery but their physical evidence is well-documented. Dated November 12, 1900, the letter addressed to Ann read:

> Anna Bassett, Ladore, Col.
>
> You are requested to leave that country for parts unknown within thirty days or you will be killed—thirty days for your life.
>
> Committee

Ann shared her letter with the *Craig Courier* and the newspaper printed it in the December 8 edition. The accompanying article went on to say:

> Our correspondent states that the envelope enclosing the above letter when received by Miss Bassett was endorsed on the back: "Received

under cover, P.O. at Cheyenne, Wyo." The envelope also bears the Cheyenne postmark of Nov. 15, 1900.

Elbert Bassett also received a similar warning to that contained in the above letter upon the same mail and from the same source.[4]

Nerves were raw with fear. Within that trepidation, the people of the valley and surrounding area held a disheartening sense of being isolated in their suffering. Then, a brave and moving voice arose in the form of the *Steamboat Pilot*, advocating for those in Brown's Park who were at a loss in knowing how to stand against the terrorism inflicted upon them. The commentary described a reign of terror in Brown's Park where residents awaited in fear and mistrust for the next blow to fall. It told of whispered statements of the involvement of powerful influences that reached up to the very head of government in three states. The writer continued:

> . . . It is asserted that men who had the ear of the governors told them that certain settlers were the aiders, abettors and protectors of the outlaws. That they were themselves cattle rustlers and should be cleaned out. What the officials themselves did is not known, but they at least encouraged powerful interests which are antagonistic to the rustlers, if such they be, to employ a detective to enter that section. What his instructions were none may know. But his deadly work speaks for itself. In this remarkable story the assassin's name is even mentioned. According to the story he sat with Rash at his table and partook of his hospitality. He then murdered him like a dog. He was seen going from the place where Dart met his sudden fate a few weeks later.
>
> This man was spotted and a new one came to take his place. The first man openly boasted in Cheyenne and his interview was published in the Denver papers that the "rustlers" would soon be cleaned out of Browns Park and it would be a safe place in which to live. The second man is in the country now. He is evidently not as good a shot as the other. Twice he has tried and failed. There are said to be seven names on the death list carried by these men.
>
> The people of this county have been shocked beyond measure by this horror, and they want a stop put to it. We have given the story as it comes to us. It is goulish [ghoulish], ghastly, but does anyone suppose that these murders have been committed without leaving evidence? It is impossible. It is fear on the part of people living in the vicinity that prevents the whole facts from being known—a fear which is well founded. It does not pay to know too much when death lurks in the shadows. We repeat, for the good name of this county, this awful thing

must cease. If local officers are unable to cope with the matter, then some other means should be taken to make life more secure in the western end of Routt county.[5]

Sheriff Ethan Farnham was no doubt insulted and possibly embarrassed saying, "If the parties have such positive information regarding the perpetrators of the crimes in Browns park and who unbosomed their evidence to the *Pilot* would swear out warrants and give the 'local officers' a chance, something might be accomplished. As it is I can do nothing without proper papers and authority from the board of county commissioners."

The sheriff's response caused the *Craig Courier* to conclude that the work of assassination in Brown's Park was evidentially going to continue, to the disgrace of Routt County. It went on to say: "That the citizens of Brown's park are highly wrought over the situation is putting it mildly, yet Sheriff Farnham declares that no appeal for assistance or protection has been made to him by anyone and that he is entirely in the dark as to the facts in any of the cases." Sheriff Farnham was then quoted as saying: "I am perfectly willing to render all the assistance in my power to the citizens of Browns park and am ready to perform my duties."[6]

The public's clamor for the law to take action grew all the louder when the *Denver Post* picked up a December 20, article from Hayden, Colorado, and reprinted the article:

War on Woman
New Feature to the Routt County Trouble
Outlaws Growing Bolder
They Warn Miss Anna Bassett to Leave the Country Within
Thirty Days or Suffer the Consequences.
The latest development in connection with the reign of terror in
central and western Routt County is the publication of a warning letter
to Miss Anna Bassett who has until recently been living with her father
who is postmaster in Lodore and assisting her brothers in their ranch
and range work...

The way the murders were being handled by the law left speculation, true or not, that there was influence to stand down coming from somewhere. Tom Horn would have had little reason to imagine his fortune was, within a year or so, going to take a downward turn. With his services still in demand he went about his business as the intimidating and unstoppable range detective. However, voices of concern in the press held the power of cracking through walls of those not wanting to be exposed. The string of articles printed in December along with the extraordinary interview Tom Horn gave to the *Wyoming Tribune* a month earlier in November must have combined to cause some anxiety among Horn's backers and possibly Horn, himself.

WYOMING IN IT

Brown's Park Conspiracy Points Toward This State

CATTLEMEN MAY BE MURDERERS

Says the Denver Evening Post
Corpse of Old Cattle Trouble Comes to Life
Wyoming Corporations Alleged to Be Prime Factors in the Trouble
Best Way to Remove Rustlers
Threatening Letters from Cheyenne

The trouble in Brown's Park, Colorado, is assuming an interesting phase to citizens of Wyoming, and Cheyenne in particular, as all the threatening letters received by residents of the Park bear a Cheyenne postmark. The murders of Dart and Rash are still fresh in many peoples' minds and the following dispatch to the *Denver Evening Post* throws some light on the subject:

"Craig, Colorado, December 22, 'The Brown's Park conspiracy,' as it is now generally called, seems is really to be a final chapter of the old cattle disputes which have been the cause of so many tragedies in Wyoming and Colorado.

"The men who are guilty of the various outrages in Brown's park are said to be detectives imported by cattlemen to run the cattle rustlers out of the country, who seem to have chosen assassination as the quickest and surest method of accomplishing their task. Cattlemen declare that not only Rash and Dart but the Bassett boys, Davenport, Tom Kimbly and E.B. Thompson have been cattle rustlers for years, and point to the statement of Judge Rucker made in court at Glenwood Springs a short time ago that it was impossible to secure a conviction in cattle rustling cases and that the cattlemen should combine for their own protection, as an excuse for the present condition of affairs.

"Friends of the murdered Rash and Dart, and of the other settlers now living in persecution, however, say that these men are no more guilty of rustling than the big cattlemen in the west, the branding of mavericks being a practice of long establishment and recognized as practically lawful by local custom.

"It is now stated that the murderers are not only known to the sheriff, but to the whole county, and that only fear of vengeance from the detectives and the Wyoming corporation which employs them, prevents their names from being openly published.

"…it is even reported that the sheriff gave the man who shot Rash a warrant for the latter's arrest, and was cognizant of the whole affair, and of the other acts of the alleged conspirators since.

"…the sheriff as yet has made no move, but the series of murders has so injured the reputation of the county that great pressure has been brought to bear upon him…"[7]

The law had not come to the aid of the Brown's Parkers. The sheriff of Routt County, Ethan Farnham, hadn't ventured near Brown's Park since the killings and there was no official investigation.

Then a terrorist came to call at the Bassett Ranch. Ann wrote:

I sat at a table in the living room playing solitaire. Four young boys, Carl Blair, Gail Downing, and my brothers George and Eb Bassett, were lunching in the adjoining kitchen. Suddenly the night was shattered by blasts of gunfire. Two bullets came splintering through the door, imbedding themselves in the opposite wall, less than six inches from where I had been seated. There could be not the slightest doubt for who these bullets were intended. I dropped to the floor and rolled under the table. The boys doused the lamp and jumped to a side window, to shoot out into the night in the direction the gunfire had come.

We remained in the darkened house and speculated on why our shepherd dog had not given the alarm of a night prowler's approach; he did not bark all during the night, which was most unusual. That faithful old watch dog never barked again, he had been strangled to death by the spiteful marauder.

Fearful of being clipped by shots from ambush, we stayed in the house under cover until eleven o'clock the next day, when two ranch-men, Pete Lowe and Harry Hindle, drove up to the corral in a wagon. We called to them to watch out for gun snipers. They crouched down in the wagon box, and drove on to the house. When we told them of the night's happenings they helped us in making a search of surrounding hills. We found a man's boot tracks in the mud and leading to a hill overlooking the house. A horse had been tied there for several hours, the horse ridden away on the jump traveling in an easterly direction, all intervening wire fences having been cut for him to pass through.

Eb Bassett and Carl Blair rode to Zenobia Basin when they were joined by Will Morgan and my brother Sam. The four of them followed the horse tracks of the would-be killer over the sand hills to the [Charley

Ayer] L7 ranch fifty miles from Brown's Park. There they found a very tired horse near the corral and indications that a fresh horse had been ridden away, toward Baggs, Wyoming. In the little village of Baggs they lost all trace of the horse and rider.[8]

Edwin Vernie "E.V." "Ed" Haughey (pronounced Hoy), a twenty-three-year-old cowboy working for the Two-Bar, said that it was Charley Ayer of the L7, not Ora Haley, who first brought Tom Horn into the area. He observed Hi Bernard ride away from the Two-Bar one evening leading two or three of the best horses owned by the ranch. Bernard returned before daylight the next morning but was without the horses. Haughey said word soon arrived that there had been a killing. Ed Haughey helped gather those Two-Bar horses off the range during the fall roundup.[9]

Wrapped tightly in the cold of January, the new year of 1901 arrived. The near miss of a bullet along with the chilling letters of warning Ann and Eb received served to tamp down Ann's bluster, just as they were designed to do. Although her fervor was still filled with pain, the young woman was forced to let it subside into some form of acceptance.

NOTES TO CHAPTER NINETEEN

1. "Was A Close Call," *The Steamboat Pilot*, 5 Dec 1900.

2. Frank Willis, "Confidentially Told," The Museum of NW Colorado–Craig.

3. "Was a Close Call," *The Steamboat Pilot*, 5 Dec 1900.

4. "Sheriff Farnham On Brown's Park Assassinations," *Craig Courier*, 8 Dec 1900.

5. "The Assassination of Citizens Must be Brought to a Close," *The Steamboat Pilot*, 5 Dec 1900.

6. "Sheriff On Assassinations," Craig *Courier*, 8 Dec 1900.

7. "Wyoming In It," *Wyoming Tribune*, 23 Dec 1900.

8. Ann Bassett Willis, "Queen Ann of Brown's Park," *The Colorado Magazine*, Jan 1953, 66-67.

9. E.V. Haughey, "E.V. Houghy [Haughey] Account," Jay Monaghan transcription, original at the Colorado Historical Society, The Museum of NW Colorado–Craig.

CHAPTER TWENTY

AN UNSAVORY DEN

Perhaps it brought some relief, letting loose of the crushing grip of inflamed emotions. The hour had come for Ann to focus on new plans to spend time away and leave behind the dread of the last six months. Eb and George were also leaving, going off to school in Chillicothe, Missouri, where Eb would be attending college at the Chillicothe Normal School and Business Institute. Sam, not yet ready to move away would manage the ranch alone for a while. Just before their trips began, Ann and Eb left home together and went to Craig to stay for a couple of weeks.[1]

Ann was not feeling at all well when she climbed aboard the stage for the first leg of her trip from Craig to Texas with plans to visit in Grand Junction and Denver along the way.[2] By the time she reached Grand Junction, she was very ill. The newspaper said:

> Miss Annie Basset[t] is reported to the hospital at Grand Junction suffering from an attack of pneumonia. Miss Bassett was just recovering from a case of grip when she left Craig two weeks ago. Her condition is not considered dangerous and as she is receiving the best of care will no doubt soon recover, when she will resume her journey to Texas.[3]

The aging father of the Bassett children was trying to decide what to do with himself in the remaining time of his life. Although he had no choice but be resigned to what had happened, it appears that he felt sad and ill at ease, as he so often had since his wife Elizabeth's death. He talked often about returning to Arkansas, at least for a visit. He stopped by the newspaper office in Craig which resulted in the following article:

> A.H. Bassett, the pioneer of Brown's Park was a pleasant caller at this office last Tuesday. Mr. Bassett has resided in the Park twenty-two years and many is the traveler that has partaken of the hospitality of his ranch at Ladore during all these years. He is a genial whole-souled

271

man, with a fund of good stories of pioneer days and ever ready to extend a welcome hand to the stranger who is "just looking over the country" or to the weary cowpuncher who finds his way to Ladore. Mr. Bassett contemplates leaving Brown's Park and returning to his former home in Arkansas where he was a prominent figure during the war and for a number of years after the "unpleasantness" [repercussions of the Civil War]. He has been postmaster of Ladore ever since the office was established ten years ago. Mr. Bassett recently resigned his position of postmaster and Mrs. W.H. Blair has been appointed his successor. The post office will be moved to the Blair ranch on Green river, about five miles from its present location.[4]

Although Ann would be back in Brown's Park by Christmas, during November 1901, she was in Chickasha, Oklahoma. Founded in 1892 with the arrival of the Chicago, Rock Island, and Pacific Railway, the town was growing rapidly with a population of just over four thousand. Chickasha, in the fertile Washita River Valley, was two miles east of the Comanche Reservation in what was called Indian Territory.

While Ann was staying in Chickasha, she wrote Eb a letter. It reveals the tenderness she felt for her brothers. The return address in the heading must have made Eb chuckle:

Chicka(shit) Ind. Terr.
Nov. 8, 1901

Your letter came yesterday and glad to hear from you. Yes it is a wise idea for you to stay and go to school, of course you will meet a great many obstickles, but be brave and "never dispare" for unless you can do this you never can hope to be successful every one has their trials and drawbacks but walk over them with a view to better time, study hard, take all into that head it will hold. There is plenty of room for knowledge and you are naturally smart, so don't kill any time. You can't afford to for there are so many many things to learn, it will take a life time [to] find out we don't know any thing, but just keep grinding and get all out of life you can. Make your self useful, etc.

You never said a word of George, isn't he there? Keep him with you—he will make a fine man if he has any encouragement, don't neglect your duty toward him—for his caracter isn't yet formed now he needs advice and friendly little talks. If he doesn't do just right talk nicely to him, he is only a boy and its not his fault he gets off. Tell him to write me I wrote last, but will write again. You spoke of Lizzie having fits, what do you mean? Tell me about it, who did you see in

Ann Bassett poses for photographs as a young woman. *Photograph on left courtesy of Jo Semotan; on right, The Museum of NW Colorado–Craig.*

town? How is Sheridan? Write me all about Chillicothe, and do send a picture. The last one George sent does me a world of good. I keep it on my dresser to look at, and I want yours on the other side—be sure and dress in the latest style—and look pretty.

Love to both of you—Stay together
Anna[5]

Whenever Ann was back home in Brown's Park she still took every opportunity to help rid the Brown's Park range and especially her valley, of trespassing Two-Bar cattle. However, the vendetta launched by Ann Bassett against Ora Haley was likely never as extreme as it would come to be portrayed. Almost certainly Ann wasn't guilty of certain lawless acts attributed to her in myth, such as the shooting of invading cattle when they strayed across the divide. Ann knew all too well that a gunman, most likely hired by Haley and his ilk, could on any given day be lurking in the vicinity. Also, there was the inconvenient reality of unavoidable evidence that dead cattle lying in the brush would create. What she *did* do, for years to come, was to take encroaching cattle on a hard lope to the banks of the Green River and force them into the water to swim for their lives; what she hoped was the outcome of this swim is unknown.

❦ ❦ ❦

Thirteen-year-old Leath Chew's father, John "Jack" Chew, had been employed by some Utah stockmen to put their cattle herds together and graze them in common. It was up to Jack, and in that he included his wife and the children, to take care of the herd all year around. The Chew family kept the cattle on good feed on the open range during the summer and then fed them hay in the winter, usually on the hay ground around Vernal. The family had a small bunch of their own cattle and rather large herd of horses that grazed within the managed herd.

Leath wrote in her memoir that as her family headed to Brown's Park in 1901, the children were a motley but organized bunch of nine towheads ranging in age from nineteen years to an infant.[6] Leath depicted their home of a couple of months on Diamond Mountain near Pot Creek to be at an elevation of eight thousand feet where to her the air felt dry but invigorating. The young girl went about exploring all the little valleys and admiring the sidehills covered with wildflowers of blue larkspur and Indian paintbrush.[7]

One day in June 1901, Leath left camp on another of her escapades of discovery. She rode bareback on a brown mare named Smarty. Leath followed the Hoy trail off the mountain to Brown's Park. She described that the canyon walls abruptly fell away from the trail to reveal a spell-binding view of river and valley. In the distance she saw dust:

> Across the river, in the low hills to the east, a dust began to rise. The cause of the dust was at first hidden. As I watched, a small herd of cattle came into sight and rushed for the river. They were followed by four riders, swinging bullwhips or lariats, whooping and yelling. The cattle rushed into the swift water of the river without slacking pace. They were soon in swimming water. Many were carried downstream a considerable distance before gaining the opposite shore. There were doubts in my mind that all would reach my side and I watched and wondered. Dad didn't handle cattle in that fashion.[8]

The riders halted their horses at the edge of the river and waved to Leath as they called out greetings. On impulse, the youngster rode upriver about two hundred yards and urged Smarty off the riverbank and into the water. The mare was soon in swimming water. Leath gripped hold of

Young Leath Chew. Later she changed her first name to Avvon.
Courtesy Jo Semotan.

Smarty's mane in the same hand with which she held the bridle reins and floated off the mare's back. Although Smarty was a strong swimmer, the current was swift and it carried the pair downstream. The riders had their ropes ready in case the horse couldn't make the swim but the mare reached solid footing and she pulled Leath up the bank to where the riders were waiting. An attractive young woman spoke first. "Crazy stunt," she said. "What's your name?"[9]

Suddenly self-conscious Leath retorted, "Smarty kin swim and so kin I. I'm Leath Chew." The cowgirl smiled, mentioned knowing one of Leath's brothers, and introduced herself as Ann Bassett. Ann presented the other riders to Leath and told her that they were visiting from Chicago. She then showed Leath a nearby ford and said it was a much safer place to cross the river.

Leath later said that Queen Ann Bassett was the first woman she had ever met whom she both liked and admired. The two developed a lasting friendship. At times Leath helped Ann chase away Two-Bar cattle. Leath

Elbert "Eb" Bassett had a lifelong admiration of Leath Chew. *Courtesy Jo Semotan.*

wrote in her memoir that Ora Haley would sometimes have two or three hundred head of Two-Bar cattle driven past the divide and then left to drift along Vermillion Creek and into Brown's Park. It was Ann's custom, Leath said, to drive the trespassing cattle into the Green River, often using the help of young people with whom Queen Ann was always a favorite.[10]

By the fall of 1901, Leath's father was no longer employed as a herdsman but had one hundred fifty head of his own cattle and one hundred head of horses. The Chews picked out a home site at the foot of Douglas Mountain at Currant Springs. Although Jack Chew was continually taking Leath and her siblings out of school whenever he needed them for one task or another, the kids managed a few weeks of school at the schoolhouse on Beaver Creek in Brown's Park.

When the Christmas season arrived, the Brown's Park settlers took time to feel joy, far removed from the ugliness of the previous year's assassinations. They came together in the familiar way they'd done for all of Ann Bassett's life which had served to keep them a steadfast community, in spite of occasional disagreements. A party turned out to be a life-altering experience for young Leath Chew, a preciously shared moment in time, with the distinguished and very handsome Eb Bassett

J.S. Hoy held a Christmas celebration and dance at his ranch with the offering of a barbequed beef for the guests. Friends and neighbors from as far away as sixty miles brought a variety of salads, sauces, and desserts. Ann and Eb arrived on horseback while Esther Davenport and Josie McKnight rode in a buckboard and brought offerings of fresh baked bread, pie, and cake. Leath wrote:

> The evening began for me when I caught my first raptured glimpse of Eb Bassett, glamorous in store clothes, having that very day arrived from Chillicothe College. He was about five feet eight inches tall, black hair, and had large gray eyes with black eyebrows. His features were classic and he had the kindest mouth I had ever seen. I could not take my eyes away from him. I knew he was Queen Ann's brother. I had heard her speak of him, but she never told me he was the very handsomest man in the whole world. How I envied her and I took a very disparaging glance at my own towheaded, unpolished, unhandsome brother, and wondered why some people have all the luck. My gaze returned to this old man of twenty-one, and I continued to marvel at his perfection. I was so engrossed I could scarcely attend to the business of dancing.

Leath danced with Eb several times and each time she felt transported. Around midnight, Eb was teaching her the steps to the cakewalk when he asked Leath her age. Breathlessly she responded that she would soon be fourteen. Eb looked into her eyes and said, "Now, I wanted to ask you, if I wait until you grow up, will you marry me?" The young girl felt nearly paralyzed with emotion as she nodded her head.[11] Leath wrote:

> When the music stopped, Eb detained me on the center of the floor until the other dancers were ranged around the walls. Holding my hand in his, he said, "Folks, I have an announcement to make. Leath and I are engaged. As soon as she grows up, we are going to get married." His face was serious and he dropped an arm around my shoulders, protectively. Everyone applauded loudly and when the noise subsided somewhat, John Jarvie presented Eb with a band from a cigar.
>
> "Here's a ring, Eb, to make it official."
>
> Eb solemnly placed the ring on my finger and sealed it with a kiss. The noisy hilarity ceased instantly. After a moment Joe Davenport, who was from Willow Creek, said wonderingly, "You know, the guy means it."[12]

❧ ❧ ❧

Within four months after Tom Horn was arrested for the murder of the teenaged boy Willie Nickell on January 13, 1902, the Bassett Ranch was leased to new arrivals W.E. and Annie Grimes. In May, Sam finally left for Nome, Alaska, to meet up with his partner Griff Yarnell.[13] Not even once in his lifetime did Sam make a return journey to Brown's Park. His life there on the back of a horse as a cattleman was forever finished.

Without Sam to lean on, his siblings must have felt a sense of uncertainty when they returned to the ranch. Josie was also gone and had been since shortly after her divorce. Although she argued against it and would have rather stayed at the Bassett Ranch, Herb insisted that as a single woman with two children, Josie should move to Craig where she could make her way. She leased the Craig Hotel where she made a living cooking and cleaning for guests. She despised it. On April 26, 1902, she married Charles "C.A." Ranney. Charley Ranney was a druggist from one of the prominent families of Craig. While he, Josie, and the boys lived in a very nice home, almost immediately Crawford and Chick were miserable. They found their stepfather to be an unyielding disciplinarian.

After the Grimes' lease of the Bassett ranch was up, Ann went back to helping her brothers Eb and George on the home place. Their operation was no longer a large one but there was always plenty to do.

Brown's Park ranchers, including the Bassetts, decided something official had to be done to combat wolves, so in 1902 the Brown's Park Ranchmen's Association was formed for that purpose. The packs had grown to a fierce number, and the toll on livestock was terrible. Besides trying to kill any of the wolves the stockmen saw, lanterns were hung around corrals at night in an effort to save the calves and colts within; numerous tin cans with small rocks inside were hung on barbed wire fences. They rattled if the wire was disturbed with the hope that the noise would scare off the predators and prevent them from entering enclosed fields. The Brown's Park Ranchmen's Association members contributed to a fund to offer a large bounty of $20 per wolf hide.[14]

Ann grew impatient when, even with the bounty in place, wolves seemed to be increasing. She was witness to some terrific devastation being done to cattle and horses. One day early in the month of March she was riding on the Douglas Mesa accompanied by a six-year-old girl named Doris Morgan, when Ann spotted a wolf den.[15] Ann wrote:

George Bassett was the youngest of the Bassett siblings (circa 1900). *The Museum of NW Colorado–Craig.*

We came to a place where the wolf tracks circled the head of a rough gulch. When we found that circle of tracks, I knew the den was near. I also observed the fresh traces of two grown wolves. The paw marks were deep in the soft sand where they had jumped and run away only a few minutes before.

I rode fast in the direction taken by the wolves fleeing when they caught the human smell. After following the trail a short distance it became apparent they were out of sight and out of gun shot.

I went back to the gulch to a mound of earth that had been thrown out, and found the den. These tunnel-like openings are dug slope-wise in the soft sand or silt between ledges of rocks and are a tight squeeze for the wolves to enter. I prepared to bring the pups out and kill them. Tying my horse to a tree, I broke off a long cedar limb to tangle in the pups' fur and drag them out.

Ann happened to be dressed in a lovely riding skirt. After standing her rifle near the den opening, she stripped off the garment and spread it across a bush. Then she wrapped a neckerchief about her hair. Ann retrieved a muslin tobacco pouch filled with matches from her saddlebag and attached the pouch to a stick. The matches would be her light source.

Headfirst with her arms stretched out in front and each hand holding a stick, Ann entered the narrow den and began wriggling and twisting her way forward. The darkness deepened as she went until at last it was a blackout. After retrieving a match Ann struck it to a burst and was instantly startled to see what lay ahead. In a rounded dugout the wolf pups were much larger than the tiny pups of early spring she was expecting. Indeed, they were quite large and all of them were now snarling. Ann began shoving herself backward an agonizing few inches at a time:

> I had to hold my arms forward and slide. The going was not good and very soon I hit a tighter place. The slopes of the rock reefs were pointed and the jagged edges caught my corset stays. I could not get my hands back to loosen the hold and I was not strong enough in that position to break either the stays or the rocks. I was held fast in a trap, with the parent wolves lurking somewhere near on the outside, and the big pups glaring and snarling close ahead in the den.
>
> I called to my little companion who sat her pony standing guard at the entrance of the den. When she heard me call, she dismounted and came to the mouth of the passage. I told her I wanted to stay in the hole—just then those words "wanted to stay" almost strangled me, for by that time I was numb with fright. I instructed Doris to ride back to the ranch, reckoned to be about eight miles. She should back track our shod horses, the tracks we made that morning in the soft earth. I cautioned her to be sure that the tracks she followed had shoe marks, that being very important.
>
> I was fearful of betraying my trapped condition to the small child who was all I had between me and the jaws of a mother wolf. If Doris became frightened, or lost, we were both sunk. There were no other people near; no fences or roads to guide her over endless hills, but she was a child of the hills with natural instincts of direction and could be relied upon to do as she was told. With only shod tracks to direct her, the brave little crusader went cheerfully on her way, alone.
>
> Lying there in a helpless position stretched out like a string in that unsavory den, was nothing to be enthusiastic over. With the eyes of the big pups glaring at me from the front and expecting the enraged mother to chew on me from the rear was not a pleasant situation.
>
> Nothing could be done about it. I was forced to lie motionless and wait for one of two things. If help came all would be well, otherwise the wolves would make short work of me. The welfare of the little

child was a cause for much anxiety. The child I had led into this uncanny circumstance in a head-on enthusiasm of wolf phobia. If the child became lost in her direction, it was reasonable to suppose that the old horse she was riding would eventually go to the ranch when he felt the urge to have the saddle removed. He would, of course, take his own time to do that and when night came on the tracks to the den could not be found.

After several hours, that seemed years, I heard my saddle horse call and he began to stomp and walk around in a nervous, uneasy manner. I knew instinctively that other horses were approaching.

I was filled with joy almost to the bursting point. After a short time all was quiet again. No sound of voices or footsteps came near the den. I slumped. The walking around of my horse was caused by range horses passing somewhere close and he had either seen or smelled them.

All hope was vanishing fast; utter despair was creeping over me. I was too weak to cuss, misery had completely engulfed me.

At last, I heard the ring of steel from a pick striking rock as it was thrown to the ground. And a voice said, "I'm here now, you can come out."

"Come out, hell! I'm caught in here, fastened tight as a wedge!"

Ann's old friend and disciplinarian, Jim, had come to her rescue and apparently was unable to resist teasing "his" Annie about being caught in such a predicament. Shortly he was at work picking and shoveling. After nearly an hour, Jim finally widened the tunnel enough that it released its grip. Ann awkwardly crawled out from the dirt, fully disheveled. She described herself as looking like an animated clod covered over with cactus and wolf hair. Quickly retrieving her skirt from the bush, she hurried behind a cedar to put the skirt on and take off the despised corset. She said she left the corset behind, "to 'rust' in peace in a quiet spot on the Douglas Mesa."[16]

❧ ❧ ❧

In the spring of 1903, Ann, Eb, and George hosted a large get-together at the ranch. They were saddened that John Jarvie, who was always entertaining, couldn't attend. He'd just been thrown from a horse, leaving his head and back badly bruised. A huge crowd danced and played cards and other games. Special guests being entertained at the Bassett home were none other than the prominent lawyer who had served as Butch Cassidy's attorney, Douglas Preston, accompanied by J.J. Jones.[17]

Two months later, during Decoration Day, 1903, Herb Bassett was in California to partake in the grand parade and its accompanying celebrations to honor the Civil War dead and put flowers on their graves. It was a splendid affair with the veterans dressed in full uniform. Throughout the morning, artillery fired thirteen guns at intervals of eight minutes until the close of the morning ceremonies. Herb was deeply moved. His sensitive nature is fully revealed in a letter he wrote to Josie:

> Soldiers Home
> Los Angeles County
> California
> May 30, 1903
>
> Dear Josie
>
> Today I received a letter from you and one from Eb. This has been the best day to me for a great many years—Decoration Day—This is my first attendance on this Memorial day and you may bet I had a great big cry all alone. I was attending a Nazarene meeting a few nights ago and sat in a draft and caught cold. I was excused from marching in uniform and standing so long—all too much formality—So I took my time and went to the cemetery and out to a field of hay cut and cocked up and there I took in the whole proceedings.
>
> The Procession came from Depot with the delegation of young ladies from Los Angeles all dressed in white. They looked splendid, and each one of the United States and other Territories were represented by a certain girl, but I could not discover any way that the representation was made.
>
> The drive way up to the cemetery was between rows of pepper trees, at the top, near where I sat. The driveway turned to the left from me and went to flagpole about 200 yards from me. There was a speaker stand and a big cannon, the minute men fired often, but not that regular. The old boys and the Marines formed two lines, one each side of the way. The flags from the head of each column nearly touched and the procession passed under the flags and filed left and went to the flagpole. The procession reached nearly to the cars half a mile long. I saw the old blue coats and gray beards and the canes to support them now, 40 years ago they stood shoulder to shoulder fighting to sustain the best Gov't on earth, today. They are shoulder to shoulder again probably for the last time, to contribute to the memory of their dead comrades. Very few of those remaining are Soldiers of the Cross and ready for their last roll call. These few serious thoughts, together with, the minute gun firing and the flags and flowers at all the graves gave me a good opportunity for a real genuine cry, and I'm provided the opportunity and more from just hearing of the great wagon load of flowers being then strewn upon the waves of the ocean out from Santa

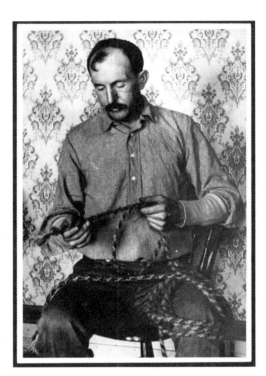

Tom Horn braiding a lariat while being held in the Laramie County jail in Cheyenne. *American Heritage Center, University of Wyoming.*

Monica, in memory of the Marines who had been buried in the deep Sea and who had died for their country! Well, I had never heard of such proceedings! But it's perfectly right all the same.

Well, I struck out for the dining hall and of all the women and girls I've ever saw at one dinner, this took the cake! The first table seats 78 and it was nearly filled by the girls and women. Then the Lieutenant of the dining hall called in about 100 or maybe a few more men to fill first table. Still there were enough girls and women in the home grounds in groups eating their own dinners, to more than fill the first table. So that was the biggest woman feast I ever saw. Uncle Sam was the only one able to Set-Em-Up for that crowd! Then at Memorial Hall there was speaking, but the crowd was too many for me. I heard patriotic songs and women orators. . . .[18]

In October, Ann made a strenuous protest to the Craig newspaper regarding an article printed in the *Steamboat Pilot.* The writer wrongly placed a killing in Brown's Park when it actually occurred at Juniper Springs, seventy miles away. The Craig paper responded: "We heartily agree with Miss Bassett in this regard. Browns Park has had troubles enough of its own the past few years without loading every fracas that occurs west of Hayden canon to Provo, Utah, onto its shoulders."[19]

Tom Horn was hanged on November 20, 1903, but his death did nothing to lessen the damage he'd inflicted on the Bassetts, leaving in his wake a severely altered future without Mat Rash, especially for Ann and Eb. In September Ann's former lawyer, W.B. McClelland, who represented her in petitioning the court concerning Mat Rash's estate, took her to court for unpaid legal fees. In October, McClelland won a judgment against her in the amount of $1,130.12.[20] Six days after Tom Horn's hanging in Cheyenne, Eb was sued by Annie E. Grimes for $70 she said was due her in connection with the lease she and her husband held for a short while on the Bassett Ranch.

Eb tried to head things up at the ranch. He worked hard but never had the business sense or aptitude for ranch management his brother Sam and Mat Rash possessed. This trait along with others unforeseen will, in droplets, drain the Bassett Ranch away.

<hr />

NOTES TO CHAPTER TWENTY

1. *Craig Courier*, "Happenings At Home," 5 Jan 1901.

2. *Craig Courier*, "Happenings At Home," 26 Jan 1901.

3. *Craig Courier*, "Happenings At Home," 9 Feb 1901.

4. *Craig Courier*, "Happenings At Home," 2 Jun 1900.

5. Letter from Ann Bassett to Eb Bassett, 8 Nov 1901, The Museum of NW Colorado–Craig.

6. Avvon Hughel, *The Chew Bunch of Brown's Park*, Prologue. Leath later changed her name from Leath to Avvon.

7. Avvon Hughel, *The Chew Bunch of Brown's* Park, 62.

8. Avvon Hughel, *The Chew Bunch of Brown's Park*, 63.

9. Avvon Hughel, *The Chew Bunch of Brown's Park*, 63.

10. Avvon Hughel, *The Chew Bunch of Brown's Park*, 64.

11. Avvon Hughel, *The Chew Bunch of Brown's Park*, 75.

12. Avvon Hughel, *The Chew Bunch of Brown's Park*, 75, 76.

13. *Craig Courier*, "Happenings at Home," 24 May 1902. Sam Bassett and Griff Yarnell joined the rush for riches after the discovery of gold on a

tributary of the Klondike River in Alaska in 1896. There, in Nome, in 1905, Sam was married to Alma Karja, a young woman from Finland. On March 16, 1907, in Nome, their first child Samuel Clark Bassett was born. Other children were Louis Herbert (1908), Emerson (1911), Roy Cary (1912) and Alma (Oct 29, 1913). Alma died at age nine on March 29, 1923, in Olympia, Washington, where the family remained.

14. Frederic J. Athearn, "An Isolated Empire: A History of Northwest Colorado", BLM Cultural Resource Series, 1977.

15. Ann Bassett Willis, "The Gray Wolves," condensed version, Author's Collection.

16. Ann Bassett Willis, "The Gray Wolves," condensed version, Author's Collection.

17. *The Miner*, "Brown's Park News," 27 Mar 1903.

18. Herb Bassett, letter written to Josie, 30 May 1903, courtesy of Tracy McKnight.

19. *Craig Courier*, "Brown's Park Paragraphs," 16 Oct 1903.

20. Transcript of Judgement Document, Book 11-24, Judgement Debtors Annie M. Bassett, Judgement Creditors W.B. McClelland. The Museum of NW Colorado–Craig.

CHAPTER TWENTY-ONE

THE TWO-BAR FOREMAN

Ann Bassett made a decision. In the spring of 1904 she was leasing and living at a ranch at the base of Douglas Mountain. The place was once Griff Edwards' sheep ranch and was known locally as the smelter, named for its bromide mine and copper smelting operation. The process left behind several coke ovens, large beehive-shaped rock structures that stood idle. Ann was dividing her time between the ranch in Brown's Park where she spent the winter months and the Douglas Mountain ranch on the summer range. She contemplated her life; then decided to invite the Two-Bar foreman, Hi Bernard, to come see her.

In "Confidentially Told," a manuscript written by Frank Willis,[1] Willis attributes Hi Bernard with the following quote:

> Ann Bassett grimly rode herd over her favorite hunting grounds, to be sure that Two-Bar cattle did not eat the grass west of the divide. I was not in the mood to put my neck into another loop. Responsibilities kept me around Snake River for one reason—there was a slight tinge of sentiment in the direction of Brown's Park, quite justifiable and excusable in view of certain facts. Sitting Bull did not have green eyes or reddish brown curls. You must remember, that we are men after all, and savage looking girls can be attractive, very attractive, especially so if they happen to be the first of the kind you ever saw, and the last of the kind too.
>
> At that time I was thinking seriously of throwing my Colorado job overboard to try my luck in Oregon. Then I received a message, delivered by Tom Armstrong, an odd character, who was building fence for me west of Snake River. The message was a note from Ann Bassett, requesting me to meet her at the Douglas ranch. The message confused and pleased me at the same time. I didn't know what to expect, but I did know that little things like bullets were a minor consideration and would not stop me from trying to reach the Douglas ranch. I rounded up my courage and sloped[2] out to keep the appointment.

Ann Bassett (in white dress) is shown at the Douglas Mountain Ranch with dogs and visitors. Others are unidentified. *The Museum of NW Colorado–Craig*

When I arrived at Douglas, Ann Bassett was there. Not the stern little gun-toter I had seen patrolling the range on Douglas Mesa, but a girl wearing a pretty blue dress that went well with shiny hair. I was invited into a cozy cabin and frankly told why I was sent for. Ann was contemplating a partnership arrangement to stock the Douglas range with cattle, using the Bassett ranches as a winter base. She outlined the program in a very businesslike way and said, you are a cow man, and if you are interested just think the matter over and advise me of your decision at some future date. As simple as that. By that time cattle and range was the last thing on my mind. When we were called to dinner I had turned to ashes, and I did sure need a bracer of strong coffee to pick me up, for I had a counteroffer to make, and it needed a lot of back bone that I was unable to locate just then.

So far the most important part of the contract had been overlooked. I did not intend to let that slip away from me. It was not Brown's Park and a jumble of sand hills I was after; it was a wife. I braced myself and boldly said so. It seemed the most natural thing in the world for a man to fall in love with a striking young woman and want to marry her. She was not a kid but was well along toward her thirties. She was a capable woman with a mind of her own; she meant something more to me than a toehold on any country. The woods were full of men and I was flattered to be chosen as her partner. It was strictly cattle to Ann and she did not pretend otherwise.

When Ann revealed to Josie that she was marrying Hi Bernard, Josie was in disbelief. Hi Bernard's involvement with Tom Horn still hung in the air. Josie could hardly comprehend this. Josie later said: "Hi Bernard was the Two-Bar foreman, and the Two-Bar was helping Tom Horn, furnishing him homes and horses to ride when he was a cold blooded murderer."[3] For Ann, though, it was a matter of survival. Not only was the threat and provocation of her nemesis Ora Haley hounding her mind, she very likely still owed a great deal of money to the lawyer who won the judgment against her for fees that had accumulated when she contested Mat Rash's estate. Everything else aside, in Hi Bernard she saw an exciting partner who could help her achieve a ranch operation as successful as the Bassett Ranch had once been, under the authority of her mother.

While Ann and Hi Bernard were making plans for the upcoming wedding, Ann received word that her best and dearest friend, Lizzie Brown, was very ill. Lizzie still lived in Rock Springs and for the last five years had been employed by what was originally Beckwith, Quinn & Co. Beautiful and capable Lizzie helped with the company's transition into Boeman & Neuber Mercantile. Throughout her life Lizzie spent as much time as she could in Brown's Park, riding with the Bassetts and helping with all aspects of ranch work. Lizzie and her mother, Annie Brown, grieved with Ann and held her hand through Ann's saddest losses. On Friday, March 18, 1904, Lizzie fell ill. It wasn't until the following Tuesday that she was taken to the hospital after her condition suddenly grew worse. At four the following Friday afternoon, Lizzie died from what was diagnosed as typhoid-pneumonia.

Ann attended Lizzie's funeral at the Catholic Church in Rock Springs where High Mass was sung. The Reverend Father Dreyer conducted a lovely sermon on Lizzie's life. As Ann stood up and then passed with the other mourners from the church, she listened to a sorrowful rendition of "Nearer My God to Thee."[4] This death—this loss—was another transforming episode in Ann Bassett's life. Lizzie was her, and she was Lizzie. Now she must ride alone in her memories of shared adventures on the rangeland, many involving sending Two-Bar cattle away in a rolling dust.

Just two months before Lizzie died, Ann cried over another profound loss when Mary Crouse had died. Mary was Ann's mother's dear friend for many years, and she was one of Ann's most treasured examples of womanhood. About five years earlier Mary was terribly injured when the horse she was riding fell and rolled over her.[5] Being the determined center of her family, she overcame most of her injuries.

By 1903 Mary and Charlie Crouse were living at Bridgeport in Brown's Park, a spot just down the river from John Jarvie's store, where they planned a ranch and hoped to establish a townsite. As they built their ranch, they and their hired men put in over fifty acres of hay meadows and built an impressive irrigation ditch to water those acres and more. The Crouse's had a toll bridge constructed across the Green River, and they opened a small store. Their lovely daughter, Minnie, had completed her elementary education in Avoca, Iowa, while living with her aunt and uncle, Billy and Jean Tittsworth. She then gained her higher education at Saint Francis Academy in Council Bluffs, Iowa. On June 18, 1903, she finished the final year of her formal education before returning to live with her parents at Bridgeport.[6]

When Minnie arrived home, she found that her mother had been quite ill, suffering from quinsy, also known as peritonsillar abscess, a rare but serious complication of tonsillitis. Mary's health was up and down throughout the summer and fall. However, on January 31, 1904, Mary Crouse suddenly died.

Although Charlie Crouse and John Jarvie had been competitors in business, they remained close friends. John Jarvie, his long hair and beard now the purity of white, spoke most eloquently over Mary's grave at Bridgeport beside the peaceful flow of the icing river. Ann, all of Brown's Park, and others from beyond, stood in silence and listened to John Jarvie's words heavily laced with his Scottish brogue:

> Here in this world where life and death are equal kings, all should be brave enough to meet what all have met—from the wondrous tree of life the buds and blossoms fall with ripened fruit and in the common bed of earth patriarchs and babes sleep side by side.
>
> It may be that death gives all there is of worth to life. If those who press and strain against our hearts could never die, perhaps that love would wither from the earth. Maybe a common faith treads from out the paths between our hearts and the weeds of selfishness and I should rather live and love where death is king than have eternal life where love is not.
>
> Another life is naught, unless we know and love again the ones who love us here.

> The largest and nobler faith in all that is, and is to be, tells us that death, even at its worst, is only perfect rest—we have no fear; we all are children of the same mother, and the same fate awaits us all.
>
> We, too, have our religion and it is this: Help for the living. Hope for the dead.[7]

❦ ❦ ❦

Ann was not quite twenty-six (her birthday would arrive a month later on May 12) when she married Hiram H. Bernard in Craig. The next day, the following notice appeared in the *Routt County Courier:*

Nuptial Ceremony

> Yesterday evening, April 13, 1904, at the home of Mr. and Mrs. Frank Ranney, were united in marriage Miss Ann Bassett of Brown's Park and H.H. Bernard. Rev Anderson officiated during the ceremony. The bride and groom are both well-known residents of western Routt County. Miss Bassett's name has been heralded in many parts of the country as a member of the Bassett family of Brown's Park, most of the stories, however, being imaginative newspaper talk and entirely unauthoritative. Miss Bassett, herself, is an amiable lady who has many fast friends in her home locally. Of Hi Bernard, it is said, he is first in one thing at least, and this is the management of cattle. Mr. Bernard has no equal in this line in Northwestern Colorado. Every foot of the range is familiar to him, and during roundup season he is king. His qualities in this line are attested by the position of foreman he has held with Mr. Haley for several years. The *Courier* extends to the new couple most sincere wishes for future welfare and happiness.[8]

The newlyweds were guests of honor at a celebration of their wedding given at the Two-Bar headquarters on Little Snake River. It has often been written that Hi Bernard was immediately fired when Ora Haley learned that he had married Haley's enemy, Ann Bassett. In fact, Hi Bernard was still working for Haley six months later when he went on a cattle drive with a shipment of Two-Bar cattle heading to Wolcott.[9] How long Hi Bernard continued as Ora Haley's Two-Bar foreman is unknown, but it is doubtful he was ever fired. Rather, his and Ann's decision to expand their cattle operation probably demanded his full attention and led to his decision to quit his job. Hi Bernard said he and Haley had a hearty row when he quit, and the two didn't see each other afterward.[10]

Hi and Ann complemented each other in their knowledge and abilities with cattle. Their social life expanded to include Brown's Park events which were new to Hi Bernard and Little Snake River affairs,

Willa McClure (left) and Ann Bassett (right) on a successful deer hunt. *The Museum of NW Colorado–Craig.*

new for Ann. In December it was reported in the *Routt County Courier* that the couple made a flying trip to attend a dance at Dixon on Little Snake River.[11] Hi Bernard was in love and took pride in having Queen Ann at his side. Ann was very fond of her husband, though it is not known if she ever truly loved him. There is little doubt she enjoyed the position he commanded as a respected cowman and ranch manager. It is possible he worked for Ora Haley until the fall of 1905 when on November 30, it was reported: "H.H. Bernard has moved into his new house and got down to permanent housekeeping in the park. He has bought hay from Harry Hoy and will feed about 100 steers this winter."[12]

Hi Bernard had lived a fascinating life and it is no wonder Ann was attracted by the sheer presence he presented and the tranquil blue eyes with which he gazed upon her. Frank Willis quoted Hi Bernard as saying:

> I was born in 1854 near Knoxville, Tennessee. My father went away to become a soldier in the Rebel army, mother was left with my baby brother George and me, on a farm to make our living, with no

help but an aged Negro woman. In the beginning we had some stock and could raise vegetables and fruit to supply our needs. Then the Union Army came by our place on a raid and took most of our stock. Later they returned, gathered our crops for themselves, and took away our last cow. How we managed to live I do not know. Father came home wounded by a Minnie ball. He traded the farm for a team of mules and an old covered wagon. Our household goods that could be hauled, were loaded on the wagon and we started west, on a long slow journey to Texas.

Some young boys might have enjoyed this trip as an adventure, but it will always remain a horror to me. I can remember my mother in a faded and patched calico dress, cooking our scant meals over a smoking campfire, and washing our ragged clothes by a creek. When we reached Texas father rented a small farm near Houston on shares. I came down sick with smallpox. I had to lie on a hard pallet in a desolate old adobe house, alone most of the time with nothing to do but count the bedbugs crawling up and down from one crack to another.

Hi Bernard was hired at age twelve to rope and gather wild cattle that came out of the brush to graze by the moonlight. At fifteen he helped drive a herd of eight thousand steers to Wyoming and by the age of seventeen, Hi was riding as trail boss. His successful career as a range foreman began with the Goose Egg Cattle Company in Wyoming. He could, without conscience, force homesteaders, squatters, and small-time ranchers off their places. To Hi Bernard who was a manager of ranches, these folks were all merely trespassers against his employers.

Frank Willis further quoted Hi Bernard:

I worked for their interests to the extent that no outfit under my management ever went broke. When small ranch seekers came to squat on our ranges I was not in sympathy with them and used every means in my power to move them on, using force if need be. Every poor family moving in a covered wagon, to settle on a lonesome claim with family, to chuck into a little rough dugout, or a dirt-covered log shack, brought back memories of bed bugs, my childhood and my little sad mother in poverty, drudging wearily along, and bravely enduring such an existence.

I came into Routt County, Colorado, and bought several hay ranches for [Ora] Haley. These ranches extended over a wide public domain, a choice range, and with few fences to hinder the movement of cattle for a distance of about one hundred miles in all directions that constituted a pretty layout, and easy to handle.

It proved to be good. Haley made over a million dollars profit on his Routt County investment in less than ten years. And, in that time he never saw the range end of the business but three times. He did not know a thing about it for he was not a range man.

Haley was a smart, and a lucky, financier. He came to Wyoming a bullwhacker, and started in the cow business in Laramie with three old dairy cows. He was smart enough to see opportunities and capitalize on them, lucky to find a sucker to handle a range cattle business better than he could, and he was wise enough to keep from meddling with the range end, where the payoff came from. That is a rare combination of human character.

After the arrest of Tom Horn, a hush settled over the range country in northwestern Colorado and along the southern border of Wyoming. The big cattle outfits were slowed down and satisfied to stay all in one package, if we could, for we were skating on thin ice until Horn was put out of commission.

Just after Ann and Hi Bernard were married, they formed a partnership called the 7L with Ann's brothers, Eb and George. Together they purchased Henry Templeton's entire herd of cattle and branded them all with the 7L.[13] Upon entering Ann's world Hi Bernard formed impressions of some of those he came to live among in Brown's Park:

A few of the old pioneers were in Brown's Park when I came to live here in 1905. Charlie Crouse was one of them. He was a regular westerner, enterprising and well-liked by all his neighbors, except J.S. Hoy. Another was Uncle Sam Bassett; a grand old man, a bachelor who had made several fortunes in mining at various camps over the west. He mined at Virginia City, Nevada, and he picked up gold nuggets at Sutter's Mill in California's boom days. A miner at heart, [he] remained a miner to the end of his days.

Sam Bassett junior became interested in mining in Alaska. He is married and lives there. The [friendliest] one of the immediate Bassett family now living in Brown's Park is Eb Bassett. He lives generously, is kind to the human race, and has not dedicated himself to animals. George Bassett's chief concern is in being unconcerned and he mosies about the business of life in his individual way.

The entire Bassett family is devoted to their father. I never could get acquainted with Mr. Bassett for he is a religious man and is away over my head. He peeps over his specs at me and seems to be smiling behind his long white beard as if he was amused at the antics of some strange insect he had come upon by accident.

> Mountains of hokum has been peddled far and wide about [my marriage to Ann], made up by nose-ins who are setting up their own standards and jumping at their own conclusions regarding a private affair that they were not consulted about. [J. S.] Hoy and his tribe of gabbers did not dare to approach Ann on the subject. She hazed the rattle tongues to cover, and dealt them to a sizable cussing a time or two, for she understood the situation and was loyal about it. Loyalty is one of her admirable traits.
>
> Together [Ann and I] built up a prosperous cattle business in Brown's Park. Ann rode the range with me, and that was not the hardest job I ever did. Ann can qualify as an expert in handling livestock of any kind and she knows more about cattle than they know about themselves.

❧ ❧ ❧

In the early spring of 1905, Rosalie Miles moved into Brown's Park with her family. Her homesteading father, Charles Miles, had formed a strong desire to remove his family from a near poverty situation in Kentucky. He arrived in Brown's Park first, to prepare a place for his family. By the time Rosalie's mother, Addie, and the children got to Brown's Park, Charles had a two-story house with seven rooms built on their new homestead. Nine-year-old Rosalie took in the unfamiliar remoteness of her surroundings and wondered what course her life would take in such a place. She described what happened next:

> My thoughts were interrupted by the sound of the steady rhythm of horse hoofs traveling swiftly over the sage-covered hill. I'll never forget seeing this beautiful woman riding her horse as if molded to the saddle. Thick, reddish-brown hair peeked out from under a large white scarf tied beneath her chin. Her skin was flawless with shining eyes which flashed with fire and life. Her hands were covered with a pair of dainty leather gloves. This was my first glimpse of Queen Ann, but it wouldn't be the last. Every nine-year-old has an idol: this lovely lady of twenty-seven years became mine immediately. I was glad we didn't live too far from the Bassett place.

One year a number of local ranchers' cattle were left behind during the fall gathering from the summer range, and they remained on-the-loose for a couple of years. The cattle, and especially the bulls, turned wild and dashed away at the first sight of a rider approaching. Ranchers George and Bill Kennon made a sport out of trying to gather the bulls. They had fun but little success and left the bulls scattered over a large area.

Ann Bernard took over the job and soon had the bulls under control and back to their owners. She was then hired by the local cattle association to be its bull herder.[14] Rosalie Miles further described her idol:

> The Brown's Park Cattle Association hired Queen Ann to herd their bulls. There were no fences back in those days, so it was quite a job to keep the bulls from straying away and hunting the cow herd. I immediately decided I wanted to help Queen Ann and she took a shine to me.
>
> It was a spectacular sight to watch Ann handle the bullwhip. I remember some of the bulls were spotted in color. When they started fighting or straying away over the grass valleys and sage hills, Ann could handle that whip and put them in their place.
>
> Ann had a horse that no one else could ride. Sometimes Ann would wear Uncle Hi's overalls [Levi denims] when she rode horseback. Queen Ann loved to wear buckskin britches and so of course I had to have some just like hers.
>
> After a day of herding bulls, we would go back to Queen Ann's [and Hi Bernard's] cabin. She would always cream her face and take care of her beautiful hair. I loved to listen to her tell stories of the outlaws and the Indians who had roamed in the Park.

Rosalie said that her parents believed Brown's Park to be the Promised Land with its mild winters, abundance of game, and meadows thick with grass along the Green River. Because of Queen Ann, Rosalie learned to deeply value the beauty of it all. Ann expressed to Rosalie her own love of Brown's Park, its native people, and early settlers, and articulated to her the loveliness of nature. Rosalie's sentiment was: "*Thank you Queen Ann, thank you for being so kind to me. You helped make Brown's Park my Garden of Eden.*"[15]

❧ ❧ ❧

During the summer of 1906, Ann, her brother George, and Hi Bernard rode horseback working a large herd of their 7L cattle near Little Snake River when, about noon, Ann noticed a covered wagon in the near distance. It came across the lower bridge at the river and then made its way into a grassy bottom where it pulled to a stop. Ann observed a young couple and two little kids emerge from the wagon. The matched pair of team horses colored light grey and a bald-faced bay saddle horse all grazed as the travelers lit a campfire. Ann left the men to take care of the cattle and urged her horse into a trot toward the wagon.

Nina and C.M. Taylor moved from Nebraska to the Brown's Park valley in 1906. *Author's Collection*

A close friendship began when Ann, wearing her chaps, spurs and wide-brimmed hat, reached the campsite and stepped off her horse. After taking off her gloves she stuck out her hand and said, "Hello there, I'm Anna Bernard."

Charles Melvin "C.M." Taylor, his wife Nina, and their children, five-year-old Jesse "Jess" and two-year-old Nancy had traveled from Nebraska in search of their dream of owning a cattle ranch in the mountains.

Ann remained with the Taylors for quite some time, sharing a lunch of biscuits topped with pickled herring served from a two-gallon wooden keg. Ann delighted in telling the Taylors all about her valley where, she said, she had spent her lifetime cattle ranching in the mountains. C.M. and Nina eagerly absorbed every word the charismatic cattlewoman had to share. In turn, Ann listened with great interest as they explained their excitement about the unexpected turn their journey had taken.

For quite some time, C.M. had been corresponding with postmasters in Rangely, Colorado, and Vernal, Utah, about the appeal and opportunities of the different communities. The Taylors had decided to sell their farm in Ainsworth and head for Vernal. Their first glimpse of the Rocky

Mountains astounded the flatlanders. When they saw the mountains far in the distance, it still took days before they could be sure that what they were seeing were not clouds on the horizon, but the majesty of mountains. They'd had quite a journey over the mountain pass after leaving Fort Collins. Deep drifts of snow covered the country, and they were forced to unload the wagon several times so the horses could pull it across the crusted snow.

When the Taylors reached Maybell, the bridge across Bear River was washed out, preventing them from continuing to Vernal. C.M. and Nina had no idea what they were going to do when forty-eight-year-old Billy Braggs rode into their camp, leading a packhorse. They discovered he was heading home from a place called Brown's Park. The Taylors invited Billy to share supper and to camp with them overnight. C.M. and Billy stayed up half the night with Billy telling him all about the valley on the Green River where he grazed his cattle. By morning when Billy Braggs departed, the Taylors had a new destination.

❧ ❧ ❧

Ann adored youngsters. The previous April, she had hosted a large party at the ranch, just for children.[16] It is a shame that she would never have any of her own. On the other hand, many young people just like Rosalie Miles and Leath Chew saw Ann as nothing less than an idol. Young Jess Taylor was instantly in awe of Ann. From that first moment when she rode up to their covered wagon, and throughout his long life, Jess had great admiration and love for the refined and gracious cowgirl he knew as Queen Ann.[17]

***

NOTES TO CHAPTER TWENTY-ONE

1. Compelling evidence that Frank Willis authored "Confidentially Told" and that the words Willis attributes to Hi Bernard are accurately quoted can be found in the following: In a letter to Duward and Esther Campbell dated August 4, 1950, Ann Bassett Willis wrote, "Frank's story of what Hi Bernard told him I typed without a change. Frank is a better writer than I am and remembers to a letter what he hears." Josie Bassett Morris and others said that Frank Willis had a remarkable memory. In Josie's July 18, 1960,

interview with Messersmith, Josie said that the things Frank Willis told were, "absolutely right."

2. The slang word "slope" means to make one's way out furtively or slowly.

3. Josie Bassett Morris, interview with Messersmith, 18 Jul 1960, The Museum of NW Colorado–Craig.

4. "Death of Lizzie Brown," *Rock Springs Miner*, 31 Mar 1904.

5. *Rock Springs Miner*, 14 Sep 1899.

6. Mary Crouse, letter to Billy Tittsworth, copy in Author's Collection; De-Journette, *One Hundred Years of Brown's Park and Diamond Mountain*, 54.

7. "Eulogy for Mary Crouse," John Jarvie, Author's Collection.

8. "Nuptial Ceremony," *Routt County Courier*, 14 Apr 1904.

9. "The Local News," *Routt County Courier*, 20 Oct 1904.

10. Frank Willis, "Confidentially Told," The Museum of NW Colorado–Craig.

11. *Routt County Courier*, 1 Dec 1904.

12. "Brown's Park News," *Craig Courier*, 30 Nov 1905.

13. Crawford MacKnight, (Josie's son Crawford used the Scottish spelling of McKnight), letter written to his cousin, Edna Hayworth, Oct 1961, The Museum of NW Colorado–Craig.

14. Ann Bassett Willis, letter to Duward and Esther Campbell, 2 Mar 1951, Museum of the West through The Museum of NW Colorado–Craig.

15. Dick and Daun DeJournette, *One Hundred Years of Brown's Park and Diamond Mountain*, 224-246.

16. "Harry Hoy Dead," *Rock Springs Independent*, 13 Apr 1906.

17. Jesse Taylor, interviews with author 1981-1982.

CHAPTER TWENTY-TWO

IN SHEETS OF ICE

Ann grew concerned about Charlie Crouse when Nina Taylor and her two young children, Jess and Nancy, came to visit, driving a newly purchased buckboard. The Taylors were now living in the three-room cabin at Joe Tolliver's old ranch. Nina and C.M. recently purchased the charming place from Charlie Crouse, as the start of their new cattle ranch. The Tolliver place was on the other side of the river from both Bridgeport and John Jarvie's store, up against the base of Diamond Mountain. Nina spoke to Ann of how she and her family were greeted warmly by Charlie and his daughter, Minnie, when they first arrived in their covered wagon at Bridgeport, a place now consisting of a nice home, corrals, bunkhouse, blacksmith shop, meat house, and dugout cellar. Charlie immediately hired C.M. to do some work for him and by the next morning C.M. was using his grey team to pull a Mormon scraper while helping two other hired men, Bill Aines and Gus Beard, clean river trash from Charlie's large irrigation ditch.

The Taylors were fascinated by a large number of Utes camped along the river surrounding Bridgeport. The Utes traveled freely between reservations and often stayed in Brown's Park for extended periods. Charlie Crouse's corral was filled with Ute ponies of all colors. After Charlie and Minnie invited the Taylors to dine with them, Charlie shot one of his large steers grazing nearby on Bake Oven Flat. The Utes hurried to the downed steer and with precision dressed it out. The established routine allowed that Charlie took only the best of the meat and gave all the rest to the Utes. After the Utes carried their share, including entrails, to the river to thoroughly wash everything, they built a large bonfire and had a festive feast.

Nina enjoyed hearing Ann's stories about the Utes, including that a young Ute mother had so generously shared herself to sustain Ann, a tiny white baby. Ann explained how connected she felt with the Utes and how glad she was to have families of them still fixtures in Brown's Park, even though they could no longer call it home.[1]

Ann had not had the opportunity to see the Crouses for some time and was saddened to hear from Nina that Charlie Crouse was still thoroughly devastated by the enormity of Mary's death and that he was drinking heavily. Although he continued to maintain his place at Bridgeport, he didn't have the heart to have his toll bridge rebuilt since it had been destroyed by an ice jam. The plan for forming a town at Bridgeport had lost its appeal, and Charlie no longer pursued it.

Both Charlie Crouse and John Jarvie were extremely kind and welcoming to not only Nina and C.M. but to the children. John Jarvie, whose four boys were grown and gone from home, read to Nancy and Jess, played his instruments for them, recited poetry, and told stories. He challenged Jess to foot races that caused Jess to laugh as he tried to keep up with the older man bounding over sagebrush like a deer. The Taylors admired John Jarvie's wit and scholarly knowledge, and the kids loved watching in the wintertime when, with his mane of wavy white hair and full beard flowing, Mr. Jarvie swiftly glided along the river ice on skates. Charlie Crouse passed along advice to the Taylors about maintaining a great respect for the river and all things Brown's Park. He taught Jess to whittle and then, the last time Jess would ever see him, gave the boy his pearl-handled pocketknife.[2]

Both Charlie Crouse and John Jarvie hired C.M. to haul freight. On one freighting trip to Rock Springs, Charlie accompanied C.M. with a second supply wagon. The two men camped just outside Rock Springs, near the stockyards. A little before dark, a Pinkerton detective rode up and got off his horse. Ignoring C.M., the detective walked up to where Charlie was sitting beside the campfire. C.M. later told Nina the detective was arrogant and overbearing when he spoke to Charlie saying, "Well, hello again Mr. Crouse."

Charlie answered the man with a slight nod. The detective began questioning Charlie, demanding to know the whereabouts of certain men who were wanted in connection with a recent robbery. Charlie merely shrugged his shoulders and several times in a soft voice replied that he didn't know.

The detective grew more aggressive and spat out the words, "Are you aware, sir, that I have the authority to put you in jail if…" Cutting the

Nina Taylor and daughter Nancy. Nina is wearing gauntlets which were a gift from Ann Bassett. *Author's Collection*

detective off Charlie jumped to his feet and snarled directly into a startled face. "Listen here, you son-of-a-bitch, I said I don't know where those men are. Even if I did, you don't need to think I'd tell you! Now get the hell out of here!" Without another word the lawman mounted his horse and left.

A part of Charlie Crouse was still the young man who endured the rigors of the Civil War and Indian Wars before settling a young and tough frontier, all in his own way. He had seen much death and been the cause of some. Now he was heavy-hearted and sorrowful about much in his life and said he felt old and tired since Mary's death. He talked to C.M. about his brother Joe Tolliver's suicide saying, "I always accused Joe of having no nerve. You know, I believe he had more nerve than any of us. I've tried to kill myself a dozen times."[3]

More and more often when Charlie went to visit the Taylor home, he sat on the hearth in front of the stone fireplace with his whiskey jug at his side and talked about Mary. He had never imagined anything happening to her and had taken her loyalty and comforting presence for granted. He said, "My goodness, Taylor, I had a good woman and I treated her bad."

Nina told Ann that after drinking deeply from his jug, Charlie always passed out across the hearth. During his troubled sleep, he at times appeared to stop breathing. Then, with a whimper, he would start breathing once again.

Nina, just four years younger than Ann, brimmed with energy, and she willingly helped with the cooking and other chores. Ann made sure the children felt an important part of the visit. Nancy, her brown curls bouncing in long ringlets around her chubby face, was her brother's constant companion, and Jess called his little sister his very best friend in the world. When at last it was time for Nina to drive her buckboard on the long journey home to the upper end of Brown's Park, Ann gave the children treats for the trip and thrilled Nina with a new pair of gauntlets.[4]

Not long after that particular visit with Ann, Nina Taylor helped Minnie Crouse pack up her things to leave Brown's Park to live on her new homestead at a place on Spring Creek called "the gap" about twelve miles west and a little north of Brown's Park. The ranch became known as Minnie's Gap. The following spring, in 1907, Charlie sold his Bridgeport Ranch and implements to the First National Bank of Rock Springs[5] and went to live with Minnie. Although Charlie's health wasn't good, father and daughter returned regularly to visit friends and check on Charlie's elderly mother, Sarah Tolliver, who was doing fine and still living on her little place on Beaver Creek.

❧ ❧ ❧

Ann continued to enjoy her visits with the Chew family because she delighted in the antics of all those children. She and Leath, who now insisted on being called Avvon, rode a lot of miles together. Ann adored Mrs. Chew. She had the same first and middle names as Ann's mother, Mary Eliza, and she worked hard each day as a ranch wife and mother of an ever-increasing number of children.

Mid-July 1907, Ann stopped by the Chew home on Currant Springs. Avvon's sister, Enola, was about three-and-a-half years old at the time. Ann sat down with the family for the noon meal, a tasty spread of chicken and dumplings, new garden potatoes creamed with fresh peas, leaf lettuce, green onions, and radishes. Enola further described the meal:

And, there was strawberry shortcake with bonafide whipped cream. The big old cookstove had what I remember being called a hearth. At any rate it was at the end of the stove, under the fire box, and jutting out to make a shelf, with a cover or lid that lifted up so that the ashes could be removed. I don't remember who else was there for dinner besides Ann, but the large table was filled to capacity and three of us were given our filled plates and told to put them on the hearth where we kneeled or squatted to eat our dinners. I was in the middle, Ralph on one side and Douglas on the other. I think Ralph started it as he usually did, reaching across my plate to take something off Douglas's [plate]. Douglas grabbed it back, and for a time, I was unable to get a spoonful of anything to my mouth on account of the ruckus going on between them. Finally, with a spoonful of potatoes and gravy hoisted, I whanged each of them in turn with my loaded spoon and yelled: "Maw, make these little sons-of-bitches stop fighting over my plate!" I was subdued by Ann's gales of laughter.[6]

❦ ❦ ❦

The following September Ann and Josie were involved in a squabble with Annie Grimes. Luckily for all, it ended up to be more comical than serious. Annie Grimes, who earlier sued Eb Bassett over a lease, was described by Josie's son Crawford MacKnight as being "… a little ole Spaniard who was rank poison."[7] The Grimes place was located not far from the Bassett Ranch with a cabin sitting very near where Vermillion Creek flows into the Green River. The couple ran a small outfit of about one-hundred head of cattle. The *Routt County Courier* reported:

SHOOTING IN BROWN'S PARK

Word just reached Craig today of a sensational shooting scrape that happened in Brown's Park some days ago. The participants were all women. It seems that Mrs. Annie Grimes had been peddling gossip regarding Mrs. Hi Bernard, Mrs. Charley Williams [Josie] and Miss Ethel Chew. These three were at the Bassett ranch one day recently when Mrs. Grimes passed there in a wagon. They stopped her and commenced a talk during which Mrs. Grimes, through fear or rage, drew a gun and commenced shooting at the trio. They had the nerve, however, to hold her there until the conversation was exhausted and then went before Justice Hoy and swore out a complaint. Mrs. Grimes was arrested and Hoy fined her $60.[8]

By this time Josie was on her third marriage, having left Charles Raney in 1906 to be with another man. She moved across the Wyoming line to Baggs to open another boarding house and married Baggs resident Charles Williams as soon as she was free to do so, on July 12, 1906. Josie's sons, Crawford and Chick, described Charles Williams as a promoter and prizefighter, railroad man, and pharmacist. A local article reported that "Charlie Williams, well known in this part of the country and on Snake river knocked out Jack Christie of Salt Lake in six rounds at Rawlins."[9] Although the new husband was kind to the boys and agreed to move to Brown's Park, Crawford and Chick immediately observed that he was obviously a city man who didn't like being in the country. Only four months after the marriage, Charles Williams left Brown's Park and his marriage to Josie.

During the winter of 1906–1907, Ann and her husband were living at the Bassett Ranch in Brown's Park. Ann was now twenty-eight and Hi Bernard fifty-two. When a plea to help Mary Chew came to Ann from Mary's husband Jack, Ann quickly saddled up, as did her husband. The drape of time is lifted by these words of Hi Bernard, quoted by Frank Willis:

> There was a heavy snowfall and very cold weather in December; then came the January thaw which often happens in the Park. The warm Chinook winds blew for several days and melted the snow, broke up the ice in the streams and turned them into raging torrents of muddy water carrying great floating slabs of ice.
>
> Mr. Bassett [Herb] had stretched a wire cable across the Vermillion for the purpose of getting mail to and from the Star Route [Service] carrier. The mail carrier came once a week to the Maybell post office sixty miles to the east. Bedding and food for the mail carrier and feed for his horse was sent across the Vermillion by cable when the river was not fordable.
>
> One afternoon during the high water period, we saw a man on horseback riding up and down the banks of the Vermillion directly opposite our house. It was evident that someone wanted to communicate with us. I saddled a horse and rode to where the cable was anchored. I soon discovered the horseman to be Jack Chew; he was a recent settler who with his wife and several small children lived fifteen miles [southeast] and near the foot of Douglas Mountain. They were without neighbors at that time of the year. The roaring water of Vermillion was deafening. We could not hear a word spoken. I beckoned Chew to the cable and by motions instructed him to wind the ropes when I fastened pencil and paper to the pulleys. Chew's message came back that his wife had given birth to a baby the evening before. The baby had died. His wife was in a very bad condition and they needed immediate help.

I sent a note over to Chew, advising him to return home, and we would be with them as soon as the night air checked the thaw from the incoming streams and lowered the wild Vermillion so we could cross.

I hurried back to the house and broke the news to Ann. We selected our most dependable grain fed saddle horses and got ready for an early start the next morning. It was necessary to take a packhorse to carry warm blankets, food and medicine, and grain for our horses. The only crossing on the Vermillion with good landings was within fifty feet of a falls where the water dashed over a rock ledge to a lower level a hundred feet below.

We arranged to have several ropers—among them George and Eb Bassett—stationed on the bank where we were going to attempt a crossing. If a horse failed to swim, or became tangled in the debris and ice, it was possible for a horse and rider to be caught before going over the falls to sudden death.

When we were all set to take the plunge into the ice-jammed water, I stepped my horse in and he swam high and easy. Then the cowboys shoved the packhorse into the water. By dodging ice and swimming strong he made the landing. Ann came last; her horse reared back and refused to take the plunge. He was a spirited animal, and when she raked him with her spurs he made a long jump and went under water and struggled frantically downstream. He gained balance and treaded ice and swam low to my horse on the right bank.

The horses were cold and scared and we lit out on a keen run and kept the pace for a mile. With cold air fanning our wet clothing we were soon covered with solid sheets of ice. I roped the packhorse and built a fire in a cedar gulch to warm up a little. We removed our heavy coats and chaps from the pack, where we had them wrapped in a water-proof tarp. We put our dry things on top of our wet clothing and rode on toward the mountains.

The shock of seeing Ann's horse go under water so near the falls almost floored me. That was the first time I realized I had a bad heart. I damn near died and thought I could not hold out to reach the Chew dugout fourteen miles away. When we hit the dreary Lone Cedar Flat the snow was deep and crusted, and going was slowed up. I believe the only thing that kept me alive that day was Ann riding in the lead with her head thrown back in defiance of obstacles. On a mission of mercy bent and determined to reach a sick mother in time to help if possible.

We arrived at the Chew camp about four o'clock in the afternoon and found Mrs. Chew very weak and having chills as she tried feebly to feed her hungry brood. I immediately gathered wood and soon had a roaring fire. We heated rocks to warm the bed and gave her a stiff hot whiskey toddy.

When Mrs. Chew was made comfortable, Ann pitched in and put the dugout in order. She prepared supper for the children and put them to bed; then she took the only blanket we had to roll up in, and put it over her saddle horse. We sat around an old caved-in fireplace, in a muddy dugout and watched over Mrs. Chew that night, and for several days and nights, until we knew she was out of danger.

I have never regretted that experience, Mrs. Chew is a noble woman, and a splendid pioneer mother who is worthy of any kindness that can be bestowed upon her.[10]

Hi Bernard said he never revealed to Ann the fear he had of his heart giving out that day. He believed one simply didn't tell Ann that sort of thing. He knew his young wife would take such an acknowledgment as a mark of weakness, because to her way of thinking, a full grown man was not supposed to get sick. He said, "She takes life on the bounce and expects a man to do likewise. I still carry in memory that scene of Ann's unbeatable courage in swimming the river, and making that long, cold ride which she completely ignored at the time, and no doubt has long since forgotten."[11]

In the fall of 1908, Ann was overcome with sorrow when she received the news that C.M. and Nina Taylor's little four-year-old daughter, Nancy, was dead. Ann wept with Nina when she learned the details. After Charlie Crouse sold Bridgeport, the King family leased the place. The Taylors were there at Bridgeport in November when first Harold King and then his two boys followed by young Jess complained of sore throats and nausea. Nina and Mrs. King understood they were in for a bout of something so they busily made up sick beds. They nursed the patients with ginger tea sweetened with a little honey for the sore throats and upset stomachs and quinine was given for their fevers. All three soon began to recover.

Although Nancy seemed well at first, Nina wasn't surprised when she found her sitting quietly against the wall in the space behind the wood burning stove in the warmth. But Nina grew startled when her daughter looked up at her. Nancy's teeth chattered and her eyes drooped and burned with fever. Nina held her daughter as Nancy cried and vomited into a bucket. The ordeal that was coming would be one of horror for the Taylor family, dreadfully surreal.

Nancy's throat was red and swollen with pockets of pus. As the hours passed and throughout the night the little girl's symptoms intensified: Reddish pink pin points, sandpaper-like, formed on her neck and chest moving rapidly to her abdomen, forehead, and to the bridge of her tiny nose. The scarlet red was absent around her mouth leaving a pallor surrounding her dry lips. The odd greyness of her tongue disappeared as its color turned red and raw, resembling a strawberry. Nancy pulled at her severely burning and aching ears. Then, Nancy's temperature spiked to a wicked degree as her throat became so obstructed that she could hardly breathe. Her pretty blue eyes glazed with suffering. The strep bacteria invading her blood was lethal. Nancy convulsed and died. Born on February 16, 1904, her life ended on November 7, 1908.

By the time Ann learned of Nancy's death, the child had already been buried beneath the cottonwoods near the Taylor home in a wooden coffin constructed by her grieving father. This was the harsh reality of scarlet fever, a leading cause of death in children until the discovery of antibiotics in 1928.

The next month a large dance to celebrate Christmas was planned at Bridgeport with guests coming from as far away as Little Snake River and Rock Springs. However, it was suddenly cancelled when Brown's Park received word that Charlie Crouse had passed away. After making a trip to Rock Springs, Charlie had headed home and was about fifteen miles from town when he fell ill. A local rancher found him slumped in his wagon seat, alive but nearing death. The rancher took him back to his ranch house, and he and his wife took care of Charlie until he passed away. Charlie was buried in Rock Springs. In February 1911, Charlie's son Stanley exhumed his mother's remains and placed them beside his father.[12]

❧ ❧ ❧

Two-Bar cattle continued to steadily encroach on the Brown's Park rangeland, sometimes badly overgrazing an entire area before anyone noticed. This caused consternation and ongoing hardship for those Brown's Parkers counting on the grass. On Christmas Eve, three cowboys trying to run Two-Bar cattle away in the manner used by Ann Bassett Bernard had disastrous results.

Heavy rains from the summer past brought floods of water and mud down Vermillion Creek and the silt ran into the Green River in a manner that formed a ridge two or three feet high along the bottom of the river. It

Charlie Crouse grew unhappy and remorseful after his wife's death. *Author's Collection.*

held the water back a bit causing a large standing pool between seven and nine feet deep. The three cowboys didn't realize the mild weather had weakened the ice when they pushed the herd, numbering well over one hundred, onto the ice in an effort to send the cattle across the river. Quite a few of the cattle made it safely across but the weakened ice shifted under the weight and cracked and dipped. The panicked cattle crowded each other into a bunch until the weight forced the ice to give way. Moments later over sixty head of cattle broke through.

The pool prevented most of the cattle from immediately being swept beneath the ice by the current. A call for help was quickly sent out and neighbors rushed to the site. Using poles and ropes, they did all they could but only saved a few head. Crawford MacKnight was there and said, "Everybody was kind of indifferent about the Two-Bar but there wasn't a person in Brown's Park that didn't help try to get those cattle out of danger, but we didn't have much luck."[13]

The *Routt County Courier* said:

> Deputy Sheriff Frank Temple came in from Brown's park Sunday with Homer Walker and John Cantler, charged by the Two-bar outfit with running cattle off their accustomed range. This was the case resulting from the drowning of sixty head in Green River at Christmas

time. A hearing had previously been had before J.S. Hoy in the park, but the evidence not being considered sufficient the prisoners were released. The case was then taken up in Justice Haubrich's court but was settled outside of court and dismissed yesterday, Mr. Haley paying the costs. The exact terms of the settlement have not been given out but it is generally believed that Mr. Walker is to reimburse the Haley people for the loss of the steers. . . .[14]

Then, in the spring, Ora Haley was finally successful in getting a legitimate toe-hold on the Brown's Park rangeland he had long desired. The *Laramie Republican* reported:

Haley Preparing to Extend His Ranching

Ora Haley, the heavy cattle operator of Routt county and the Laramie plains says the Denver Field and Farm, is preparing to extend his ranching interests by recently purchasing the Valentine S. Hoy ranch in Brown's park consisting of 1,160 acres along the river. The price paid by Mr. Haley was $8,000.[15]

This latest blow from Ora Haley must have affected Ann deeply. By this time, though, she'd grown accustomed to having to accept many things over which she had no control. The Two-Bar operation hired several Brown's Park men for cattle work as well as for constructing new ranch buildings. Apparently among those employed for a time by the Two-Bar were Avvon's father Jack Chew as well as Hi Bernard. According to Enola Chew:

Although there were many times when Ann stopped by our place, or when we went to the Bassett place in Brown's Park, the next incidents I remember occurred at the Hoy house which was then part of the Two-Bar holdings. Ann and Hi Bernard lived in part of the house and the Chew mob lived in the other part. Burton was born there on March 12, 1909. I recall that shortly before he was born, I saw a Two-Bar cow bogged in the quicksand and hurried to tell Ann about it. Later that day Hi, using a team, dragged her [the cow] out, but [she] was too weak to get back on her feet, even with his help, so he batted her in the head with an axe and sent me to the house to tell Ann to come and help. Meantime he had ripped the cow open and had taken the calf which Ann carried to the house, scrubbed [the calf] up with a gunnysack and kept [it] warm behind the stove.

At the same time and with a great air of conspiracy she bet me she was going to be the first to know when a certain little heifer of hers was going to calve. I flew back to the shed and maintained a vigil on the heifer until the calf was born; then I rushed to the house to tell Ann. She was delighted and paid her bet (I think it was a cookie), gathered up the orphaned calf in her arms and toted it to the shed where the young cow was tidying up her own calf, and [Ann] soon persuaded [the cow] that she had two babies to tend. I didn't get to watch this maneuver; my female elders thought I'd spent enough time with Ann for one day.[16]

Early summer that same year, 1909, Nina Taylor and Jess arrived to spend a couple of days with Ann and also visit the Chews. Nina was eager to share with Ann, who had been so compassionate, the news that she was once again with child. Although the sadness Nina felt over losing Nancy had not passed, her fear about another loss was subsiding and she had begun to look forward to another child.[17] Nina brought along food items to share including a few jars of chokecherry jelly and two freshly baked coffee cakes. The cakes were deeply flavored with cinnamon and clove and raisins that had simmered in black coffee.[18] That evening while Ann and Nina prepared supper, Jess played outside with Doug Chew.

Herb, now seventy-five, was staying with Ann for a while before taking another of his trips. Although he occasionally had bouts with his asthma, he was still spry and helped out by doing certain morning and evening chores. Jess and Doug paid little attention when Mr. Bassett turned the milk cow out of the corral so that she could go to the nearby river and get her drink for the night. Fat and tame, the cow sauntered along the riverbank until she came to the well-worn pathway leading down a steep trail to the water. The milk cow was in no hurry and drank the water in long, lingering gulps.

After some time passed Herb grew impatient and seemingly decided the cow was taking too long. "Oh, you old fool," Herb said "Come outta there! Gonna drink that thing dry, are you?"

Naturally, the cow paid little attention and continued to drink. Herb started walking along the bank trying to shoo her back up the trail. Suddenly he lost his footing and stumbled awkwardly. Jess and Doug were shocked when Herb, his arms flailing, tumbled off the bank and landed in the river with a loud splash. The boys ran to look over the edge of the bank and watched as Herb's drenched grey head popped out of the water. Sputtering and wheezing, Herb made his way to dry ground and pulled himself up the trail. As he hobbled toward the house, trickles of water trailed along behind him.

After Herb disappeared into the house the boys heard Queen Ann expressing alarm at the sight of her father. The boys began giggling. Before long they were bent over with laughter. "Why didn't he just leave her alone and let her drink?" Doug said. Holding his stomach Jess nodded and said, "Yeah, she knew how much she wanted." Inside the house, as poor Herb was helped into dry clothes he had to suffer a scolding from his Anna.[19]

Then, not even a month later during the first week of July 1909, Ann, as well as all of Brown's Park and far beyond, was stricken with another shock that was beyond comprehension. The much loved and admired John Jarvie was dead: robbed and murdered. Ann and Hi Bernard were in disbelief for the very morning of the murder, July 6, Hi Bernard had stopped by Jarvie's store and all was well.[20]

During the late afternoon of July 6, John Jarvie's youngest son Jimmy frantically rode up to the Taylor home and pleaded with Nina to give him a gun. C.M. wasn't home because he was working for Martin Whalen as foreman at Charlie Crouse's old place, the Brown's Park Livestock Ranch. C.M. was on the bench above the ranch house in the hayfields with Gordon Wilson. Jess was nearby with Walter Hanks, Jr. hunting rabbits. Into sight came Bill Lookingbill galloping towards them with the news that something frightful had happened to John Jarvie.[21]

Jimmy Jarvie had gone to visit his father earlier in the afternoon. When he stepped into his father's house he was stunned by the mess. A meal fixed sometime earlier had never been cleaned up, including three plates and an open jug of whiskey on the table. The store and house had been ransacked.

Jimmy hurried outside and called for his dad. He was stopped short by the sight of drag marks and dried blood clumps on the pathway before him. He quivered with a sickness growing inside as he spotted patches of white hair snagged on bushes along the trail leading to the river. In a panic he looked no further but got on his horse and rode to the Taylor ranch where he found Nina home alone.

Throughout the night, word spread that something had happened to John Jarvie. By morning, most of the Jarvie boys and a sizable crowd of ranchers and ranch hands had gathered at the Brown's Park Livestock Ranch a few miles downriver from the Jarvie home. Although they all had guns, they were confounded that they had very little ammunition among them. Nonetheless, the men were determined and early that

John Jarvie was much beloved in Brown's Park. *Author's Collection.*

morning the unofficial posse, including eight-year-old Jess riding an old mare loaned to him, rode in a group to the Jarvie place.

When they arrived at the scene they learned that the day before Bill King had seen George Hood, an evil-looking fellow from Rock Springs whom C.M. and the others knew slightly. He and George Hood's brother-in-law, McKinley, walked out of Jesse Ewing Canyon and headed across Bake Oven Flat toward Jarvie's. It was surmised that it was these two who had partaken of John's hospitality then apparently assaulted, robbed, and killed him.

The group of men saw where Jarvie had been dragged to the river. The damp sand along the bank revealed where his body had lain, showing even the pattern of the rivets in his pants and what was feared to be a hole in the back of his head. Because Jarvie's rowboat was missing, they concluded that the body had been placed in the boat to either sink in the river or drift into the rapids of Lodore Canyon.

Tempers flared. The men agreed that when they found the killers they would take them to the willows on the riverbank near the Brown's Park Livestock ranch house where the mosquitoes were relentless. The killers would be stripped and forced to stand naked "for the mosquitos to eat on" until they confessed. When the scoundrels finally admitted the deed, the ranchers agreed, they would hang "those two birds" from the ferry cable post nearby.[22]

Tracking the two men and John Jarvie's stolen saddle horse, the ranchers discovered a pile of goods including hobbles and ropes in a heap about a mile downriver. The group surmised the culprits had planned to steal more horses but had abandoned the idea along with some of the loot in their hurry to escape. The tracks turned northward into the mouth of Jesse Ewing Canyon where C.M. and the others pulled up their horses. The opportunities for being ambushed through the steep, roadless climb were endless. Continuing would be foolhardy. Instead, they decided that John Jarvie, Jr. would travel alone by way of nearby Red Creek Canyon and ride hard to Rock Springs to alert the authorities. None of them knew it then, but the murderers had arrived in Rock Springs about midnight and stayed a few hours in a room at the Valley House before leaving on the 11 A.M. train east. John, Jr. rode into Rock Springs about ten that morning, but it took him about an hour to find the law officers. Hood and McKinley were never apprehended.

The ranchman's posse went back to Jarvie's to build a raft and drag the river. However, it wasn't until eight days after the murder and over twenty miles downstream, that Archie Jarvie found his father's severely swollen body that had at first been tied in the rowboat by a piece of clothesline from the store. Then the boat must have jettisoned the body into the river. The flow of the river water had stripped John Jarvie of his clothes except for his shirt which was turned inside out and over his head. The shirt was snagged on a piece of anchored driftwood and one of Jarvie's arms was tangled in a clump of willows. The driftwood and willows held John Jarvie in Brown's Park and prevented Lodore Canyon from claiming him. The overturned rowboat was found in a ditch among a tangle of driftwood about two miles upriver.[23]

At last the murder could be reconstructed. Intent on robbery, Jarvie's attackers apparently struck him over the head. As he stumbled outside and tried to make his way across the small bridge over the irrigation ditch, they shot him between the shoulders. Then at close range, they shot the wounded man through the temple. Hood and McKinley then dragged John Jarvie by his heels along the pathway and on to the river, tethered his body in the rowboat, and pushed it away from the bank and into the current.

Hood and McKinley then ransacked the store and rifled through Jarvie's personal belongings. Since Jarvie had recently taken his profits to the bank in Rock Springs, the Jarvie boys believed that a one-hundred-dollar bill and their father's pearl-handled revolver were the lone contents of the safe. The murderers loaded Jarvie's old horse with a variety of things including a new saddle, hobbles, ropes, foodstuff, gloves, shoes, and other clothing. It was later learned that the suspects got off the train at Point of Rocks, Wyoming, for a short stop where they pawned a pearl-handled .44 six-shooter and a new pair of shoes. Hood tried to change a hundred-dollar bill.

Tributes in various newspapers throughout the region praised and mourned John Jarvie. The July 30, 1909, *Vernal Express* declared on its front page, in part:

> It is hard to imagine John Jarvie dead. Harder still to think of him murdered. He was the sage of the Uintahs, the genius of Brown's Park. He could almost be called the wizard of the hills and river. He was not only a man among men but he was a friend among men and a Good Samaritan ever.
>
> He kept a ferry; but he was more than a ferryman; he kept a store, but he was not circumscribed by the small scope of a storekeeper.
>
> He was a good neighbor, a true friend. His Scotch brogue but added to the earnestness of his speech and enhanced his qualities. He read the book of nature from the wonderful hills that surrounded him.
>
> Nothing can be said which will enrich Mr. Jarvie's name nor which will enhance his worth; those who knew him loved and respected him. He was greater than the country in which he lived. We could have wished the grey haired veteran a peaceful ending.
>
> He was as broad and generous and far reaching in his good deeds as the stream which he knew and loved as a brother and over whose turbulent waters he had helped so many travelers and upon whose un-willing bosom he was set adrift to seek an unknown grave.
>
> May his body rest in peace near the Green River and in the pleasant vale between the hills, where history will be incomplete without the last thirty years of the life story of John Jarvie.[24]

Two five-hundred-dollar rewards for the killers were established, one by the people of Rock Springs and the other by Governor Cutler of Utah, to no avail. Archie and Jimmy Jarvie vowed to track down Hood and McKinley and bring them to justice, but it would not be. Brown's Park

Left: Ann found a savvy partner in Hi Bernard. *The Museum of NW Colorado–Craig.* Above: A rare look at Hi Bernard's gold pocket watch. The initials are beautifully engraved in purple. *Photo by Paul Knowles used with permission of a private collector.*

mourned again when Archie was killed in a mysterious coal mining accident in Idaho. Alone but resolved Jimmy followed the trail to the eastern United States and then back to Jackson Hole, Wyoming. The chase then took him into Idaho where he was pushed head first from a second-floor hotel window. A broken neck killed him instantly.[25]

Ann stated that next to her father, John Jarvie was the person most perfect.[26] It is likely that she was there with Nina, Minnie Crouse, and others who came together to put John Jarvie's plundered home back in order. The emotional task was made even more so when the women discovered Nell's clothes hanging neatly in the closet and her personal items on the dresser top where they had remained undisturbed for the past nineteen years.[27]

Later that summer in August, Hi Bernard was on the summer range on Cold Spring Mountain tending cattle when he was badly injured. The *Routt County Courier* reported:

Hi Bernard Reported To Be Seriously Injured

Word reached here the first of the week that H.H. Bernard of Browns park is in a very critical condition in a hospital at Rock Springs, Wyo., and that there is very little hopes for his recovery. About two weeks ago, Hi was shoeing a horse at the camp on Cold Spring mountain and as he started to pick up one of the horse's hind feet the animal, evidently not knowing anyone was about, became startled and pulled back, breaking the post to which he was hitched, the post striking Hi across the small of his back with considerable force. Mr. Bernard realized that he was hurt pretty bad, but as he was able to move around he didn't think it anything serious and in the evening he went to a dance, which was being held at the Moss ranch. The next morning he was unable to leave his bed and his condition became so alarming that he was taken to Rock Springs for treatment.[28]

It is unknown how severe Hi Bernard's injuries were, or how long and difficult the convalescence was for him. Without a doubt, it took a heavy toll on him. Clearly, from the beginning of their relationship, Ann made up her mind to not blame Hi Bernard for his part in Mat Rash's murder. Instead she chose to believe that her husband was caught up in the "dementia" of representing the vision and will of Ora Haley and other cattle barons.[29] It can only be presumed that Hi Bernard's mounting age and Ann's perception of her husband's waning strengths might have put a strain on the marriage. That she remained childless may have been another chink in the relationship. What is a certainty is that Ann grew more and more dissatisfied. The exact reasons the pair initially came apart can't be known. Perhaps they didn't even know themselves. As for Queen Ann, she was about to enter into infamy.

NOTES TO CHAPTER TWENTY-TWO

1. Nina Taylor, as told to the author, Nina's granddaughter; Jesse Taylor, interviews with author, 1981-1982.

2. Jesse Taylor, interviews with author.

3. Jesse Taylor, interviews with author.

4. Jesse Taylor, interviews with author.

5. "Brown's Park Happenings," *Routt County Courier*, 4 Apr 1907.

6. Enola Chew, letter to Kristy Wall, Feb 17, 1972, The Museum of NW Colorado–Craig.

7. Crawford MacKnight [Crawford used the Scottish spelling of McKnight], interview with Glade Ross, The Museum of NW Colorado–Craig.

8. "Shooting In Brown's Park," *Routt County Courier*, 19 Sep 1907.

9. "Local Mention," *Route County Courier*, 7 Jul 1907.

10. Frank Willis, "Confidentially Told," The Museum of NW Colorado–Craig.

11. Frank Willis, "Confidentially Told."

12. *Routt County Courier*, 31 Dec 1908; "Brown's Park," *Moffat County Courier*, 18 Feb 1911.

13. Crawford MacKnight, interview with Glade Ross.

14. "The Browns Park Case," *Routt County Courier*, 14 Jan 1909.

15. "Haley Preparing To Extend His Ranching," *Laramie Republican,* 10 Apr 1909.

16. Enola Chew, letter to Kristy Wall.

17. Nina Taylor, her story to author, circa 1960.

18. Jesse Taylor, interviews with author.

19. Jesse Taylor, Interviews with author.

20. "Murder Mystery in Brown's Park," *Routt County Courier*, 15 Jul 1909.

21. Jesse Taylor, interviews with author.

22. Jesse Taylor, interviews with author.

23. "Wedding in Browns Park and Other Notes of Interest," *Routt County Courier*, 5 Aug 1909.

24. Frank M. Young, "Tribute to John Jarvie," *Vernal Express*, 14 Jul 1909. Young was the Secretary of Uinta County Farmers Association and County Superintendent Of Schools,

25. Jesse Taylor, interviews with author 1981-1982; William L. Tennent, *John Jarvie of Brown's Park*; "Murder Mystery in Brown's Park," *Routt County Courier*, 15 Jul 1909*;* "Body of Jarvie Discovered," *Routt County Courier*, 22 Jul 1909; "Brown's Park News," *Routt County Courier*, 29 Jul 1909.

26. Ann Bassett Willis, letter to Duward and Esther Campbell, 3 Mar 1953, Museum of the West through The Museum of NW Colorado–Craig.

27. Jesse Taylor, interviews with author 1981-1982.

28. "Hi Bernard Reported to Be Seriously Injured," *Routt County Courier*, 2 Sep 1909.

29. Ann Bassett Willis, "Queen Ann of Brown's Park," *The Colorado Magazine*, Jan 1953, 70.

CHAPTER TWENTY-THREE

QUEEN OF THE CATTLE RUSTLERS

In the winter of 1910-1911, Hi Bernard spent time in Denver, possibly to receive medical treatment, and Ann remained at their Douglas Mountain Ranch. The 7L partnership with Eb and George had dissolved in 1909.[1] Still, as always, hired men and range use between Hi and Ann's operation and that of Ann's brothers were interchangeable, depending on the time of year and tasks needing to be done.

Ann's emotions must have run strong when her two younger brothers made the decision to demolish the Bassett ranch house.[2] The low and rambling house built by Herb was surely groaning as Eb and George worked to tear it down from around the years of voices and memories that saturated the logs from the inside out. However, the home had deteriorated and fallen into disrepair in the years since Elizabeth's death and the two decided it was time for new. Eb and George also tore down the sheds and corrals and moved them farther back in the pasture, altogether changing the appearance of the original ranch. The Bassett boys were moving forward with their plans for improving things.[3]

George, the youngest of Herb and Elizabeth's children, was now six feet tall, grown, and married. He had a lovely two-story house on his own land just a ways east of the Bassett ranch house. George married school teacher Alma "Ruby" McClure in July 1909. They had a baby daughter, Georgia Edna, whom was always called Edna, born in Craig the following spring in March 1910. Ruby and the baby stayed with Longhorn and Armida Thompson until they were able to safely travel back to Brown's Park.[4]

Photos reveal Eb's new house which replaced the original ranch house to be a smaller, one-story version of George's home. Eb's house was either built on site where the first house stood, or was one that once served as Sam's home and was moved there by Eb and George.[5]

Eb Bassett and most likely his niece Edna Bassett play with the dog and cat in front of his new home. *The Museum of NW Colorado–Craig.*

Herb was on a trip east and wouldn't return home until June. Josie lived in Brown's Park and leased the old Tom Davenport place on Willow Creek which had been turned back by the Davenports to the Rock Springs National Bank in Rock Springs. Josie had been taking care of Uncle Samuel Clark Bassett after he had a stroke until he passed away the previous fall in the arms of Josie's son, Crawford.[6] Josie was now on her fourth marriage, having married Emerson "Nig" Wells. Nig was said to be a good man, well-liked, and a capable rancher. Unfortunately, he was a binge alcoholic.

Because of the demolition and construction going on at the Bassett Ranch, Ann, who was then thirty-two, was spending the winter at her and Hi Bernard's summer ranch on Douglas Mountain instead of moving to the home ranch in Brown's Park during the coldest and snowiest months, as had always been the custom.

A cowboy named Wilson Steel, whom Ann knew to be a man of principle, was employed by Haley's Two-Bar. During the summer he rode in to the Douglas Mountain Ranch to ask Ann for a favor. Ann wrote:

> While ramrodding with the Two Bar, he asked permission to camp in one of my pastures with his outfit. Permission was granted purely

out of compassion for the tired, jaded horses, and as a personal courtesy to Steel. After dark and unknown to Steel, who had gone on to other duties, some of the smart boys turned the entire horse cavvy into my small meadow in which the hay was being harvested.

The meadow was a mile from the house, and the horses were not discovered until daylight. When I found them in my hay I took over by putting them all in a corral. When the cow punchers came for their horses I used pretty strong words. Some of the more venturesome, believing in the safety of numbers and cedar trees attempted a flank attack in mass formation to repossess their mounts. Their retreat became a stampede, boosted by [my] bullets cutting too close for comfort. They left the horses in my care, apparently well satisfied, for they didn't even look back to see what made things tick.[7]

However the event transpired, it's doubtful that Ann actually tried to shoot the men but she may have sent a couple of rounds in the cowboy's direction to emphasize her anger. Ann said that the tug of war between her and the Two-Bar continued for the next few months. The plentiful water supplied to her ranch from natural springs was something that the Two-Bar coveted because water was almost always in short supply for the rangeland surrounding the Douglas Mountain Ranch. The thousands of Two-Bar cattle were everywhere, and Ann felt them crowding her both day and night.

In the meantime, Charley Ayer of Dixon, Wyoming, the same man who encouraged the hiring of Tom Horn in order to "clean out" Brown's Park, hired another stock detective, F.W. Nelson of Cripple Creek, Colorado. Nelson was formerly with the Thiel Detective Service Company, a private detective agency in Denver. Ayer directed Nelson to investigate cases of cattle rustling in the Brown's Park country. Although it was Ayer who hired Nelson, it was obviously done with the support and backing of the Two-Bar and possibly other members of the Cattlemen's Association. On March 15, 1911, Nelson arrived at Ann's summer ranch under the guise that he was a mining man looking over formations in the area.[8] Ann welcomed him to stay, as was the custom, and put him up in the guest cabin. He eagerly drank her coffee and sat at her table and dined on beef for supper, along with Ann and Douglas Ranch foreman Thomas "Tom" Yarberry, who was co-running cattle with the Bernard cattle. Also there were cowhands William "Bill" Malone and Mat Morelock.

When Nelson left the Douglas Mountain Ranch he rode straight to Ora Haley's Two-Bar on Little Snake River and reported to the foreman

William "Bill" Patton that he had been served fresh beef at the Douglas Mountain Ranch and had discovered three-fourths of a beef hanging in the smoke house. Whatever else was said, it was enough to give Patton the justification to investigate further.[9]

Soon afterward newsprint was being devoured throughout a wide area as reports relayed the shocking news of the arrests of Ann Bernard and Tom Yarberry on a charge of cattle rustling:

UNDER ARREST FOR CATTLE RUSTLING

Craig, Colo., March 27—As a result of a warfare between large and small cattlemen of the western part of Moffat county, which has been waged at irregular intervals during the last quarter of a century, Mrs. Ann Bernard, known throughout the cattle district of Colorado, Utah and Wyoming as "Queen Ann," is under arrest charged with killing beef cattle that were the property of others.

With her is Tom Yarberry, another old-timer of the Browns park section, whom the Routt County Cattlemen's association has long suspected, it is said, of carelessness regarding ownership of range cattle. The specific charge is that "Queen Ann" and Yarberry butchered some steers belonging to the Two Bar, one of the Haley Livestock company's properties in Colorado, the formal complaint having been signed by W.M. Patton, foreman of the Two Bar.

Friends of "Queen Ann" assert that the arrest is only another scheme of the big cattlemen of northwestern Colorado to drive out the small stock-raisers and believe that their heroine and Yarberry will be freed at the preliminary hearing, which is to be held here Friday.

Mrs. Bernard is 30 years old, decidedly prepossessing and fascinating. Although born and raised in the wilds of the mountains, she received a college education, has traveled extensively and is said to be as much at home in a society drawing room as astride a broncho [bronco] on the range. She has stood her watch with other cowpunchers on the roundup and generally has the reputation of [being] the best pistol shot in the bunch.

The arrest was made by John S. Ledford, who is to be the first sheriff of Moffat county when it is formally organized. He also arrested Bill Malone and Mat Merdock [Morelock], who he said tried to prevent "Queen Ann" being taken. As Moffat county has no jail the prisoners are being kept under guard at the hotels in Craig.[10]

The Cheyenne State Leader picked up the story and printed it under the bold headlines: "QUEEN ANN IS BEHIND BARS FOR RUSTLING: Famous

Cow Woman of the West is Charged With Stealing Cattle"[11] On April 1, 1911, the *Craig Empire Courier* gave more details, however was incorrect in stating that Ann and Yarberry were charged with killing two beeves. The charge against them was for killing one Two-Bar heifer. Also, the arrest was not made at the Bassett Ranch in Brown's Park, but at the ranch on Douglas Mountain. The Craig paper printed an article that, in part, read:

FAMED CATTLE QUEEN HALED [HAULED] INTO COURTS

Mrs. Ann Bernard and Tom Yarberry Accused of Slaughtering Beeves From Herd of the 2-Bar Ranch IN DISTRICT COURT NEXT AUGUST— On complaint of W.M. Patton, foreman of the 2-Bar ranch.

Mrs. Ann Bernard, known throughout Northwestern Colorado as "Queen Ann," was arrested last Saturday at the Bassett ranch Brown's Park, and brought to Craig. It is charged that she and Tom Yarberry butchered two beeves belonging to the 2-Bar, the big Moffat county ranch of the Ora Haley Live Stock & Trading Company.

The complainant alleges that Yarberry drove up the animals and did the butchering after Queen Ann had shot them with her trusty rifle, all being done in full view of a detective engaged for the purpose of getting evidence against the Bassetts. The accused admit many of the acts as charged but deny the allegation of ownership of the cattle in question. At the preliminary hearing on Thursday Mrs. Bernard and Yarberry waived examination and were bound over to district court.

The case attracted widespread attention, and people came for miles around to be present at the hearing. Ora Haley, owner of the 2-Bar, came from Laramie, and Jerry Pierce, another of Northwestern Colorado's biggest cattle raisers, arrived from Denver. Hi Bernard who had been in Denver for several months got here with all possible speed, to be with his wife in her time of trouble. Craig citizens "chipped in" and rented the opera house so that all might have opportunity to hear the evidence.

Interest naturally centered on Mrs. Bernard, who is really a remarkable personage. Raised in the wilds of Northwestern Colorado, trained from childhood to ride and shoot, she has a splendid education which has been intensified by extensive travel. She is said to be as much at home at a swell social function as while taking her regular "watch" with other cowpunchers on the roundup. As she appeared in court Thursday she looked the part of "Queen Ann," with her wealth of brown hair, stylish attire and stately carriage.

The big cattle men claim they have for years been victims of pilfer-ings by the Bassetts and other Brown's park people, and that they now have evidence to convict. Others assert that it is only one of many schemes to drive out settlers, so that the big stockgrowers may have full possession of the range. And there the matter rests until decided next August by the term of District court for Moffat county.[12]

Judge Crowell fixed the bonds at $1000 each for Yarberry and Ann Bernard. Bond was posted for Tom Yarberry by Eb Bassett with bondsman J.J. Jones. Eb, ever loyal, also posted bond for his sister along with bonds-man M.H. Smith. The case was then closed until district court in August. At last Ann was released to return home, where the next month she had her thirty-third birthday.

There was confusion in an article about the arrests of Ann and Yarberry that said a Mrs. Hurd, which was a misspelling of Heard, was suspected of altering brands. The article mistakenly concluded that Mrs. Hurd was making her home with Ann Bernard and that Hurd had also been arrested after having been investigated by Detective Nelson.

The confusion arose from the fact that arrest warrants for Al and Harriet Hund, also a misspelling of Heard, accompanied the arrest war-rants for Ann and Thomas Yarberry. More confusion: Al and Harriet Heard had a ranch on Little Snake River where the Two-Bar foreman suspected brands were being changed. However, the Heard ranch had been leased to others and Al Heard was living and working in Brown's Park and Harriet Heard was living in Maybell. The month before the arrest warrants were issued, the February 18, 1911 *Craig Courier* said:

> Some parties who had leased the Mrs. Heard place on Snake river, found a note pinned on their door warning them that their work was too course [coarse] and to quit the country, or they would get killed. No attention was paid to the note, but while out after a load of wood, another note was pinned on the door and at once they saddled their packhorse and struck out. It is believed that they are laying in the hills waiting a chance to fix a certain foreman who as it appears, seems to be the sole offender.[13]

It was just a short time until the misunderstanding was cleared up and Al and Harriet Heard were no longer involved in the case. Those warrants were cast aside and the accusations dropped. It became clear that Harriet Heard never resided at the Douglas Mountain Ranch with Ann.

The Two-Bar Ranch on Little Snake River had a substantial headquarters. Taken July 7, 1918. *The Museum of NW Colorado–Craig.*

Although some have written that there was a romance between Queen Ann and Tom Yarberry, there is no hint of such an affair in any of the news coverage of the day. Another salacious but illogical story has been published concerning the way Ann retained the legal services of leading defense attorney, Judge A.M. Gooding of Steamboat Springs. The account claims that when Ann went to his office to ask Judge Gooding to represent her, Gooding didn't want to become embroiled in such an affair and therefore set the fee for his services at the high amount of $1000. Supposedly, upon hearing the demand, Ann coyly lifted her skirt and went about extracting ten hundred-dollar bills from the top of her silk stocking. Purportedly the judge was unable to resist such a gesture and capitulated. The story is almost certainly untrue and is not typical of either Ann Bassett Bernard's personality or finances. Hi Bernard paid Ann's legal fees.

Throughout the summer the court date in August must have hung heavily about the neck of not only Ann but those of her family. Ann received strong backing from the Brown's Parkers, and she especially reveled in the staunch support of the women. When at last the date of August 8, 1911 arrived, the trial began, the first criminal trial to be held in the newly designated county of Moffat which was formerly a portion of Routt County.[14] The defense team was prepared but so was the prosecution. Reporting stated: "It is evident that a great legal battle is to be pulled off today and tomorrow. M.G. Saunders, an able criminal lawyer of Pueblo and Judge Gooding of Steamboat [Springs] represents the defense while District Attorney Gentry of Meeker and Judge Wiley of

Craig are conducting the prosecution."[15] W.B. Wiley was the attorney for the Cattlemen's Association.

The trial began on August 9, 1911. Ann and Tom Yarberry were arraigned in the morning and both entered pleas of not guilty to the charge of: "The larceny of one heifer from the Haley Live Stock and Trading Company, about March 15, 1911." The clock finally ticked down to 3 P.M. and the trial began in a packed courthouse in Craig with Judge Shumate presiding. Agreement in picking a jury proved to be an exhausting exercise. At last a jury was seated. Those named included: A.J. Sulser, W.T. Stillings, Peter Bogenschutz, James M. Hart, A.J. Robinson, Lee Winslow, John Mack, J.E. Kellogg, E.A. McCann, Garfield Canon, Zene Maudlin, and Hugh Gilna.

In outlining the prosecution, District Attorney James C. Gentry said he would endeavor to prove that the defendants were guilty of the charged crime. He stated that because of frequent depredations, the Cattlemen's Association had engaged detectives to run down outlaws who were stealing cattle belonging to the big outfits.

Detective Frank Nelson gave testimony about his directive from Charles Ayer to investigate the Brown's Park area for rustling. He said he went to the Bernard ranch on March 15 and requested to be taken in as a boarder, saying that he was a mining man. That night for supper, fresh beef was served. He remained at the ranch for three days. He saw wagon tracks leading to the meat house and in the meat house saw three-fourths of a fresh beef hanging. Also on the back porch of the ranch house he saw a pair of women's overshoes with blood on them. Although he was free to roam the place he made no effort to find evidence of butchering. On March 18, Nelson said he went to the Two-Bar Ranch on Little Snake River and reported his findings to William M. Patton.

W.M. "Bill" Patton took the stand and testified that he along with John Patton and Ora McNurlen rode to a point near the Bernard ranch on the night of March 21, camping in the cedars about two miles from the Bernard house. The next morning at daylight they arrived at the Bernard ranch to search for evidence. Bill Patton stated that about four hundred yards from the Bernard house they found the hide and offal of a spayed heifer[16] and that he saw wagon tracks leading from the hide to the meat house. He said a place on the right hip where the brand might have been was cut from the hide and the right ear was missing, which could have showed the Two-Bar earmark. The left ear, however, showed the Two-Bar mark, which was an underbit. He went on to state that he and McNurlen took the hide up into the cedars to hide it until they returned with Sheriff Ledford.

Sheriff Ledford testified he carried a shotgun to make the arrest. He said he had sent Ora McNurlen and Fred Yoast back to the Bernard ranch to secure the hide and to saw bones off the quarters of meat in the smoke house, which had since been in his possession and were introduced as evidence. Fred Yoast testified about going with the party to make the arrest and of going back for the hide and hock bones on March 26.

When Ora McNurlen took the stand he gave his place of residence as "with the roundup wagon." He reiterated what Yoast said. On cross-examination he admitted that the others had made no effort to conceal the hide and offal, which could be seen from about fifty yards. He said a corral was nearby and a road fifty yards distant.

Bill Patton was recalled and he stated that he had compared the hock bones and was certain they belonged to the hide found near the Bernard house. He identified the spay scar and swore the animal was one of 800 he had helped to spay in 1909. Patton was then questioned about statements he was purported to have made to cowboys Chick Bowen, Emery Clark, and Lou Clark about his desire to run Bernard and Yarberry from the country because they had taken up land where springs were located. He denied having said that Queen Ann was in the way and that he would get rid of Tom Yarberry if he had to put up a job on him.

Judge Shumate delivered a brief but pointed lecture to the jury as to what was proper conduct between court sessions. Court was adjourned for the day.

John Patton was first on the stand the next morning. After giving testimony similar to those who had preceded him about finding the hide, he added that he observed footprints he believed to be those of a man and a woman. Although he admitted that he was not a practical cattleman nor was he a butcher, he said he noticed in particular the hock joints matching and a spay mark on the hide.

William A. Wear, cattle foreman for the Sevens Ranch, testified that no outfit was running spayed heifers except the Haley Company. He said Tom Yarberry told him that Yarberry was leasing the Bernard ranch and was running cattle there. Doc Chivington and George Long gave corroborating testimony about brands and spayed animals. William Brewster stated he'd been on the range twenty-two years and only knew of one other area rancher, Aylesworth, who branded on the right hip.

Ora Haley, president and manager of the Haley Livestock and Trading Company, took the stand and testified as to the brands and earmarks of his company and as evidence presented articles of incorporation. Haley stated that he had been connected with cattle business on the range for forty years and knew that a spay mark would always remain and be easily distinguished from a wound made in any other manner.

After the lunch recess, Ora Haley finished testifying and the defense called Two-Bar foreman Bill Patton back to the stand. Attorney Saunders asked him about the statement made by Emory Clark that Patton said he wanted to get rid of "those two sons-of-bitches" in reference to Mrs. Bernard and Yarberry. Patton denied making the statement. The attorney asked Patton if he had made threats against Mrs. Bernard and made statements that the Two-Bar needed her ranch for the water on it. Patton denied making any threats.

W.A. Wear was recalled and asked by the defense if during the recess he had admitted to being "balled up" in his testimony about Yarberry and saying things that weren't true. Wear answered that Yarberry asked him something while he was busy talking with someone else and he was not sure how he had answered. However, he didn't wish to make any changes to his testimony.

The Prosecution rested its case.

The afternoon session turned to the defense. An opening statement was made by Attorney Miles Saunders acknowledging that a beef was killed on the Bernard ranch at the direction of Mrs. Bernard on March 13, that Yarberry roped it, and Eb Bassett shot it. Ann Bernard was there and saw the operation. However it was not a Two-Bar heifer but one bearing the 7L brand which belonged to Eb Bassett, brother to Ann Bernard, who ranched about eighteen miles from his sister. The beef, Saunders said, was driven from Eb Bassett's place with some other cattle to the Bernard ranch to be butchered and that the heifer was killed on March 13. The meat was dressed and smoked and no attempt was made to conceal anything because those involved had a perfect right to the animal.

Eb Bassett took the stand and testified that he went to the Bernard home about noon on March 13. His sister informed him that she was

Queen Ann in Mexico, 1912. *The Museum of NW Colorado–Craig.*

about out of fresh meat. He told Yarberry to bring in the heifer they had been saving to butcher. Yarberry brought the heifer in and Eb shot it. Eb said the heifer did not carry the Two-Bar brand but was branded with the 7L, a brand he'd been using for about seven years but hadn't registered. He said the heifer had also been branded with the Heart M brand which belonged to Tom Yarberry. Eb said he and Yarberry removed the entrails and hide which were all left on the spot. Mat Morelock and Bill Malone brought the wagon over to load the beef to take it to the smoke house. Eb said that the hide was left on the ground, where it could be seen from the road. He denied mutilating the hide in any way.

When Ann took the stand the room was filled to "suffocation" with a great many observers coming from Brown's Park. Ann was beautifully dressed and her thick hair stylishly coiffed. She carried herself with the grace that came so naturally to her. News reports stated that Queen Ann spoke clearly with no sign of anxiety. She agreed with the testimony given by her brother and went on to say that Detective Nelson stayed four days at her place. Ann stated that the ranch was made up of some five hundred acres which contained several springs. She explained the ranch had always been a common watering place for livestock. She said she witnessed the killing and butchering of the heifer, and she saw no effort to conceal anything. The head and hide of the animal were left intact.

Mat Morelock and Bill Malone took the stand to corroborate the testimony surrounding the butchering of the heifer. Then, Hi Bernard took the stand in defense of his wife.

Hi Bernard stated that the mark found on the hide of the heifer may not have resulted from the animal being spayed but could have been caused in a dozen other ways. He said the scar could have been left by a wolf, a goring from other cattle, or an injury from a snag.

A cowhand named Dick Brown who had worked for the Two-Bar testified that the past spring, just before the arrests of Mrs. Bernard and Tom Yarberry, Patton told him that Mrs. Bernard was in the way and that he needed the water on the Bernard ranch. Dick Brown went on to say that Bill Patton also made the comment that he would get Yarberry out of the way even if he had to put up a job on him.

Another cowboy, Emory Clark, who was part of the Two-Bar roundup in the fall of 1910, testified that Patton said that he wanted to get rid of those two, referring to Mrs. Bernard and Tom Yarberry.

Ann was called back to the stand at the close of the case. When asked, she said that she did not at any time have anything to do with the stealing or killing of a Two-Bar animal.

At this point the defense rested and the testimony ended. Attorneys made closing arguments and the judge gave lengthy instructions to the jury. The judge explained to the jury that they could bring in a verdict of guilty or not guilty against one or both of the defendants. The case was given to the jury on August 11, 1911, at 4:30 in the afternoon.

A special to the *Steamboat Pilot* stated: "The consensus of opinion here is that the personnel of the jury selected to hear the evidence in the Mrs. H.H. ("Queen Ann") Bernard–Yarberry alleged cattle rustling case, and the evidence so far introduced, looks very favorable for the defendants. Opinion, of course, is widely different as to the outcome of the trial."[17]

Ann wrote to Mrs. Baker asking her to reserve a room for her upcoming trial for rustling. *The Museum of NW Colorado–Craig.*

The jury spent most of the night in what was described as heated argument. Later reports said that a majority of the jurors were for acquittal throughout the balloting. However, the holdout or holdouts for a conviction would not be persuaded. At nine the following morning, the jury informed Judge Shumate that it was impossible to arrive at a verdict. The judge sent them back to the jury room to try again. At 10:35, after deliberating for a total of thirty-six hours, the jury reported that their differences were irreconcilable. The jury was discharged.

Judge Shumate ordered a retrial to be conducted during the next term of court in February 1912. The judge also ordered that the defendants be admitted to bail in the sum of $1000 each until then.

Ann and her husband spent only a month, or at the most two, together before Ann left Colorado. Apparently there was a discussion between them about Ann fearing for her life.[18] She was scared and apprehensive. Not only did she have a trial for rustling pending, she was frightened about what Ora Haley and Charley Ayer might be planning next. She may have been wise to leave. Chick Bowen, a witness who said he heard Patton threatening to get rid of Ann, was killed on January 12, 1912, by stock detective/gunman Bob Meldrum.[19] Bowen was killed the month before the new trial was set to commence. Cowhand E.V. "Ed" Haughey worked for Haley's Two-Bar at the time of the killing and stated, "Bob

Meldrum killed Chick Bowen in Baggs to keep him from testifying in the Queen Ann case."[20]

By November 1911, Ann had gone south. While she may have first traveled to El Paso where she had relationships built since she was young, she was soon living in Douglas, Arizona, on the border with Mexico. Both she and Hi Bernard expected her to return for court in February. As it turned out, though, the case was continued by the court to August 1912. Ann did not come home that winter.

In July 1912, Ann lived in Sonora, Mexico, and worked for a copper mining company. In making preparations to return to Colorado for the August trial, she wrote a letter to a rooming house in Craig asking for accommodations:

> Abundance Copper Camp
> Sonora Mex. 7/17/12
>
> My dear Mrs. Baker,
>   I expect to be with you about first of Aug. and hope you will have me a room in the annex. The one I had last year if conveniant [sic]. I am enjoying my life in Mexico—and find many things of intrest [sic] here. I am not so troubled as last year, and fat as a pig. Altho havnt felt quite well for two or three days.
>   We start on a camping and hunting trip into the Gardo Mountains tomorrow. The Supt. and wife—a niece of theirs and the contractor, and me.[21]

After leaving Douglas, Arizona, Ann was on her way to El Paso, Texas, heading to Colorado when she became ill. As it turned out Ann was terribly sick with a ruptured appendix. As Ann recuperated from surgery it was likely on her mind that she was within a year of the same age her mother was when a ruptured appendix was attributed to taking her life. Ann was bedridden for several days and under a nurse's care for a full ten days. It was another ten days before she could travel.[22] By then her case had once again been continued. Hi Bernard's wife still did not come home to him or their marriage. She had just barely kept in touch with him. Now, her trial was not set to come up for another full year, in August 1913.[23]

Ann went back to Arizona from Texas. Since 1880 Arizona had been the prescription for patients with tuberculosis. During her stay in Tucson, Ann worked in a consumptive colony where treatment included pure air, maximum sunshine, clean and comfortable accommodations, and nutritious food. After several months in Tucson, Ann returned to El Paso. Her father, Herb, made a trip there to visit his daughter. During this time Hi Bernard filed for divorce. The surprise of it was in the "Local Mention" column of the *Moffat County Courier*:

> A.H. Bassett arrived from El Paso, Texas, Tuesday on the way to his home to Brown's Park. Mr. Bassett has been visiting his daughter, Mrs. Hi Bernard, and appeared quite surprised in looking over the *Courier* to find that Hi had applied for a divorce, as Mrs. Bernard had heard nothing of it at the time he left her. She has regained her health and has been employed some months as a nurse in one of the consumptive colonies of southern Arizona, but is at present back in El Paso.[24]

On May 23, 1913, Ann once again was in the newspapers:

Cattle Queen Facing Divorce

"Queen Ann of the Escalantes," famous through two consecutive trials on the charge of cattle rustling, both of which resulted in hung juries, [There had only been one trial.] and who is scheduled to appear for a third trial at the next term of the district court, is being sued for divorce by her husband, H.H. Bernard. The papers were filed in Craig, and the charge desertion.

Mrs. Bernard is a comely woman of unusual talent and charm, and she is popular throughout northwestern Colorado. Her arrest several years ago on the charge that she was the leader of a notorious rustling gang created a furor. The trials which followed were sensational.[25]

The *Aurora Democrat* reported: "Mrs. Anna Barnard [Bernard] known as 'Queen Ann' and conceded to be one of the most beautiful women who has ever lived in northwestern Colorado, has returned from Texas to face a second trial."[26]

Ann was finally home and duly present when her trial resumed on Wednesday, August 13, 1913. The divorce case had been postponed until after the cattle rustling trial. Ann was to be tried alone because Thomas Yarberry was nowhere to be found. She was once again represented by Judge Gooding from Steamboat Springs who was this time assisted by his partner, former Police Judge W.F. Chambers. Miles Saunders from Pueblo was again there to assist. Jury selection went far quicker than the first trial and those sworn in were: N.N. Chapman, Robert Humphrey, H.C. Rogers, George France, C.E. Jacobs, F.P. Aleshire, Henry Redmon, C.A. Snyder, Albert Taylor, A.T. Knowlton, W.C. Henning, and Ernest Butts.

According to the *Craig Empire*, "The court room was packed at all times during the trial by interested spectators and the many friends and well-wishers of Mrs. Bernard. The case brought to Craig probably the finest collection of legal talent ever heard in Northwestern Colorado."[27] District Attorney J.C. Gentry led the prosecution accompanied by W.B. Wiley, attorney for the Cattlemen's Association.

The trial introduced very little new evidence, but some interesting moments emerged. The first thing that morning, cattle baron Ora Haley was ordered from the enclosure near the jury box after the defense counsel objected to his close proximity to the jurors. When Haley was later called to the witness stand: "he became considerably balled up in regard to the manner in which the brand was placed upon the Haley cattle."[28] Haley also made other contradictory statements about the usage of the Two-Bar brand. Then, he caused a stir when he said that in the spring of 1911, he ran 10,000 head of cattle on the Brown's Park rangeland. Just recently, Haley had been threatening to sue the county for the recovery of taxed assessments, arguing that the number of Two-Bar cattle on the Brown's Park country at that time was considerably fewer than 10,000 head.

Hi Bernard testified in full support of Ann, although everyone knew he was divorcing her. She was exceedingly fortunate, for one wrong word from him could have convicted her. Instead, he was an impressive witness for the defense. He did not claim to be an expert on spaying heifers, but said he had spayed some 4,000 head without assistance. The cow man acted as an expert witness and gave valuable data regarding brands running in the Brown's Park section which was in direct contradiction to that of Bill Patton, the Two-Bar foreman during the arrest and first trial.

When Ann took the stand newspapers reported that she gave her testimony with no hesitancy and in a clear voice. She testified that the beef found in the meat house was from a freshly butchered animal, and that on March 13, 1911, she, accompanied by Tom Yarberry, Bill Malone, Mat Morelock, and Elbert Bassett killed a two-year-old heifer belonging to Elbert and bearing the 7L brand.

Neither Bill Malone nor Mat Morelock testified for the defense. Morelock had been found guilty of killing a horse and did a term at the state reformatory and didn't return to the area, and Malone was suspected of stealing sheep before he disappeared.

During closing arguments the next day on Saturday, August 16, 1913, defense attorney Miles Saunders made a strong and eloquent plea to the jury. In it he stated, positively, that the hide bearing the 7L brand was removed by Detective Nelson and that the Two-Bar hide was substituted.[29]

The jury deliberated just a few hours before it settled on a ruling. In the late afternoon when Ann was declared not guilty, the crowd in the courtroom stood and applauded. It can only be imagined how relieved and ecstatic the Brown's Park cattlewoman was at that moment. She was immediately surrounded by celebratory friends and family. Ann procured the Opera House, where her trials had been conducted, and invited all her friends to attend a celebration.[30]

Ann barely caught her breath from the cattle rustling trial when on August 23, 1913, she was back in court. She was now confronted with the civil matter of divorce, filed by the man she'd been married to for the past nine years. Interestingly, A.M. Gooding once again represented Ann, but Hi Bernard's lawyer was W.B. Wiley, the attorney who represented the Cattlemen's Association during the cattle rustling trial. Court records for the civil trial reveal the following:

H.H. Bernard Complaint: "First: That the amount of alimony claimed in this action does not exceed two thousand dollars, No alimony being asked or demanded. Second: That plaintiff now is and for more than one year last past has been a bona fide resident of Moffat County, state of Colorado. Third: That plaintiff and defendant were married at Craig, in Moffat County Colorado, on or about the 13th, day of April, A.D. 1904, and now are and ever since have been husband and wife. Fourth: That without any just cause or reason the said defendant has and still does absent herself from this plaintiff and refuses to live with him as a wife, for more than one year last past, That she has absented herself from the state of Colorado and deserted the said plaintiff for more than one year last past without any fault on the part on this said plaintiff." Hi Bernard asked that the now existing bands of matrimony be dissolved and a divorce be granted.[31]

H.H. Bernard Affidavit: Hi Bernard swore "that he is not an able bodied man, that he is fifty-five years of age and upon the account of occupation that he has led or followed he is broken down in health and is unable to earn remunerative wages." The affidavit went on to say that his homestead could not be considered in the case because the title

The Craig Opera House was the site of Ann's legal trials. She also arranged a post-trial celebration there. *The Museum of NW Colorado–Craig.*

thereof is in the United States, meaning he had not yet proved up on the property and received clear title. He declared that he was without means and unable to pay the excessive alimony asked for by his wife; that she had already received the larger part of the joint property, to wit: seventeen head of cattle valued at $600. He also stated that he had aided and assisted her financially in the late trial in district court by assisting in paying or obligating himself to pay certain attorneys. He denied owning any horses of any description. He accused Ann of disposing of cattle, by giving to her brother, twenty-five head of cattle valued at $35 per head. He alleged that Ann was in as good a financial condition as he.[32]

Affidavit of Non Residence: Hi Bernard alleged that Ann was a non-resident of the state of Colorado because she left on or about October or November of 1911. He said he received only one letter from her mailed from Tucson, Arizona. While he previously heard that his wife was in El Paso, Texas, he hadn't had any communication except from Tucson. He alleged it to be impossible to get service of a summons in the state of Colorado and requested a copy of the summons be sent to Tucson.[33]

Anna Bernard's Answer: Ann admitted leaving but stipulated that she left with his full knowledge, consent, and even with her husband's assistance. She claimed it was mutually agreed that she should depart in order to avert danger and hazard to her life. She replied she would have returned home but she was physically unable and confined to her bed on account of her sickness. At no time did she intend to desert him nor to leave him and live apart from him for a longer period of time than was necessary. She replied that she intended to return and live with him as his wife at such time and as soon as she was in fit physical condition to travel in order to make the journey to her home. If, at which time she was reasonably safe as to her life and well-being, and reasonably secure from personal violence at her home in Moffat County.[34]

Application for Alimony and Suit Money by the Defendant: The application stated that Ann was entirely without means to carry on in the lawsuit and without means to support herself. It alleged that Hi Bernard was an able bodied man and capable of earning a large amount of money and capable of supporting her during the pendency of this action and supplying her with means to carry on this action. Also, that he did own real estate which included an equitable interest in the Douglas Mountain Ranch at about $4000 and his 160-acre homestead adjoining the ranch that was estimated to be worth about $2000. She asked for attorney fees of $250 and maintenance covering board, lodging, transportation, and other necessary items of expense.[35]

Order: The court ordered Hi Bernard to pay Ann $20 for her attorney fees, $30 expense money, and $70 for future lawyer fees.[36]

The divorce trial was held on Saturday, August 23, 1913, before a jury comprised of A.O. Fisher, John Hicks, E.H. Carr, M.C. Pollock, Fred Burns, and W.H. Wood. While the jury couldn't come to an agreement on the alimony, the newspaper reported that by Monday: "the parties to the suit agreed on a compromise and the court granted Mr. Bernard his decree. Mrs. Bernard receives $800 alimony and a part of the household furniture."[37]

Stipulation: "It is hereby stipulated by and between the parties hereto that all question of permanent alimony has been amicably settled by and between the parties hereto out of Court."[38]

Decree: The jury found that the material allegations of Hi Bernard's complaint were sustained. Ann was found guilty of willful desertion of

Ann Bernard, Queen of the Rustlers, was called by the Aurora newspaper, "one of the most beautiful women who has ever lived in northwestern Colorado." *Used by permission. The Museum of NW Colorado–Craig* and *the Uintah County Library Regional History Center. All Rights Reserved.*

more than a year without just reason or cause and therefore Hi Bernard was entitled to a divorce. It was ordered by the court that the bonds of matrimony be dissolved.

The decree also stated: "AND IT IS FURTHER ORDERED ADJUDGED AND DECREED, by the Court, that until the expiration of the full period of one year from and after the date hereof neither of the said parties be permitted to remarry to any other person, and that the plaintiff H.H. Bernard pay the cost of this proceeding, Done in open Court, this the 25th, day of August, A.D. 1913."[39]

The amount of money Hi Bernard agreed to pay Ann was not $800 but $600. While he immediately paid $200 of that, he signed two notes for $200 each to be paid later. Unbeknownst to Ann collecting the money would become an ongoing back and forth of letters and lawyers. She never received the other $400.

Nonetheless, two years had passed since Ann's arrest by a sheriff who came toting a shotgun to her Douglas Mountain Ranch. Now, at age thirty-five, she was finally free. She was free of criminal charges but she was also, suddenly, without a ranch or husband. Local rumors implicated her sister Josie as being complicit in the murder of her fourth husband. Eb was in financial ruin, assisted mightily by the bonds he had so generously given for her and Tom Yarberry. Ann had not been at ease during the past two years while she was away, changing jobs and moving from one place to another. She was unsettled in every sense of the word.

As Queen Ann's expectations were resetting, her fame was finding ways to accentuate itself. A sensationalized article appeared in the *Denver Republican* just after Ann's acquittal. It proved to be an embarrassment to the *Moffat Country Courier* which felt obliged to write a rebuttal. An excerpt from the article in the *Denver Republican* stated:

> Craig, Colo., Aug. 16, – (Special.)–Mrs. Anne Bernard, "Queen Anne of the Escalantes," was acquitted tonight of cattle stealing and Craig is the scene of the most riotous merrymaking in the history of northern Colorado.
>
> When the jury at 7:10 tonight, after being out eight hours, brought in the verdict, cowboy friends of Queen Anne emptied their six shooters in the ceiling of the court room; bands, which had been waiting outside, blared and crowds in the streets cheered the news of the 'Queen's' acquittal. A few minutes after the verdict was read every business house

and place of amusement closed its doors, and young and old joined in the jollification.

Admirers of "Queen Anne" obtained an automobile and, preceded by brass bands, drove her about the city, giving citizens of Craig and the hundreds who had come from the surrounding country to attend the trial a chance to congratulate her.

This ceremony over, a herald went about telling everyone that "Queen Anne" was to be the host to the town and its visitors at the moving picture show.

Three bands playing the catchiest music in their repertoire marched about the city during the interim and later played at a dance given by Mrs. Bernard.

The *Moffat County Courier* ran this rebuttal:

It is sometimes amusing to see the exaggerated "news" reports sent out from the community by the Roberts-Kimball combination [the *Denver Republican*], but the bounds of decency in news exaggeration were overstepped in the reports of the case of Mrs. Anne Bernard in the district court. Any of these matters are easily forgivable until the falsehoods become such as to detract from the moral standing of a community. Craig is a civilized community and a dignified one as well. In our ordinary course of life we are not running a full grown imitation of Buffalo Bill's wild west show nor are our people going hog wild over the acquittal of anyone who has been tried in the district court, no matter how innocent they may have considered the defendant. These reports are disgusting to all decent citizens because they are not only willful fabrications but because they can have greatly injurious effects upon the community that most of us are trying to improve morally as well as develop in a proper way. In order that everyone may know just what we are driving at we will copy below a portion of an article that appeared under a Craig dateline in the *Denver Republican*. It is useless to excuse the writer in this case on the plea that the dailies demand it. To be sure they like sensational stuff, but they also demand a modicum of truth and if their reporters persist in making breaks of this nature we predict that there will be a vacancy in the reportorial staff. While the *Denver Republican* wants the news we are satisfied that they do not want it dished up in the dime novel style.

Of course it is a good "story" and the authors are to be congratulated on their ability to fake, but consider the matter from the standpoint of one totally unfamiliar with the country, and the idea they must get of Craig as a wild west town when in reality it is one of the most law-abiding places west of the Rockies.[40]

Regardless of the effort, the rebuff barely rippled. On the other hand, the sensational, dramatic article joined with others to ride upon enduring winds, winds that gave Ann Bassett the lasting title, "Queen of the Cattle Rustlers."

<hr />

NOTES TO CHAPTER TWENTY-THREE

1. Crawford MacKnight, letter to Edna Haworth, 5 Oct 1961, The Museum of NW Colorado–Craig.
2. Josie Bassett Morris, interview with Messersmith, 7 Jul 1961, The Museum of NW Colorado–Craig.
3. "Brown's Park," *Routt County Republican*, 27 Jan 1911.
4. "Wedding in Browns Park and Other Notes of Interest," *Routt County Courier*, 5 Aug 1909; "Brown's Park," *Routt County Courier*, 26 May 1910.
5. "Brown's Park," *Routt County Republican*, 27 Jan 1911. The article states that Eb and George Bassett moved Sam Bassett's house onto the site of the original ranch house after the original was torn down. However, Josie Bassett Morris stated that a new house was built on the original site. It is likely that Sam's house was actually moved to Eb's homestead adjoining the ranch to the west in order to prove up on the homestead and gain title. Eb received title to his homestead just after that on 11 Jan 1912.
6. Crawford MacKnight, interview with Glade Ross, 5 Mar 1975. The Museum of NW Colorado–Craig.
7. Ann Bassett Willis, from unpublished fragment of her memoir, The Museum of NW Colorado–Craig.
8. "Progress Of District Court," *Moffat County Courier*, 10 Aug 1911.
9. "Queen Ann Is Behind Bars for Rustling," *Cheyenne State Leader*, 29 Mar 1911.
10. "Under Arrest for Cattle Rustling," *Routt County Sentinel*, 31 Mar 1911.
11. "Queen Ann Is Behind Bars," Cheyenne *State Leader*, 29 Mar 1911.
12. "Famed Cattle Queen Hauled Into Courts," *Craig Empire Courier*, 1 Apr 1911.
13. "Brown's Park," *Craig Courier*, 19 Feb 1911.
14. "New Court in Moffat," *Oak Creek Times*, 17 Aug 1911; Moffat County was established in February 1911, from the western part of Routt County.

15. Account of the first trial of Ann (Bassett) Bernard and Thomas Yarberry from the following sources: Court documents including: witness subpoenas; Criminal Complaints; Warrant for arrest of Anna Bernard; Warrant for arrest of Thomas Yarberry; affidavit for change of venue; list of jurors; Certificate of Incorporation of the Haley Livestock and Trading Company, Mar 29, 1908; Colorado Brand and Mark Recording of the state board of stock inspection commissioners registered to Ora Haley, Jun 12, 1899. Newspapers: "Queen Ann is Behind Bars for Rustling," *Cheyenne State Leader*, 29 Mar 1911; "Queen Anne and Tom Yarberry are Arraigned," *Steamboat Pilot*, 9 Aug 1911; "Progress of District Court," *Moffat County Courier*, 10 Aug 1911; "Queen Anne Case," *Routt County Republican*, 11 Aug 1911; "Famed Cattle Queen Hauled Into Courts," *Craig Empire Courier*, 1 Apr 1910; "Jury Disagreed in Queen Ann Trial," *Steamboat Pilot*, (Special to the *Pilot*, 12 Aug 1911); "EXTRA—Jury Disagrees, *Moffat County Courier*," 12 Aug 1911.

16. Surgical spaying is sometimes performed on heifers that are to be supplied to the meat market rather than used for calf production. Spaying removes the ovaries which eliminates estrous cycles and pregnancies.

17. *Steamboat Pilot*, (Special to the *Pilot*, 10 Aug 1911) 16 Aug 1911.

18. Answer: H.H. Bernard Plaintiff v. Anna Bernard Defendant, 8 Aug 1913. The Museum of NW Colorado–Craig.

19. William E. Mullen, *Wyoming Reports, Cases Decided in the Supreme Court of Wyoming From February 13, 1915 to January 25, 1916*, Volume 23, 1916.

20. E.V. Haughey "E.V. Houghy [Haughey] Account," undated transcription by Jay Monaghan, original at the Colorado Historical Society, The Museum of NW Colorado–Craig.

21. Ann (Bassett) Bernard, letter from Sonora, Mexico, 17 Jul 1912, The Museum of NW Colorado–Craig

22. Signed statement from James Vance, M.D., 7 Aug 1912; Affidavit by James Vance, M.D., 26 Sep 1913, submitted to the District Court concerning the People of the State of Colorado v. M.H. Smith, et als, The Museum of NW Colorado–Craig.

23. *Moffat County Courier*, 22 Aug 1912.

24. "Local Mention," *Moffat County Courier*, 5 Jun 1913.

25. "Cattle Queen Facing Divorce," Routt *County Sentinel*, 23 May 1913.

26. "Week's Events in Colorado," *Aurora Democrat*, 15 Aug 1913.

27. "Throng Court Room For Queen Anne Case," *The Craig Empire*, 16 Aug 1913.

28. "Throng Court Room," *The Craig Empire*, 16 Aug 1913.

29. Account of the second trial of Ann (Bassett) Bernard from the following sources: Court records: subpoenas commanding witnesses to testify, list of jurors, Certificate of Incorporation of the Haley Livestock and Trading Company, Mar 29, 1908; Colorado Brand and Marking Recording to the state board of stock inspection commissioners registered to Ora Haley, Jun 12, 1899. Newspapers: "Throng Court Room For Queen Anne Case," *The Craig Empire*, 16 Aug 1913; "Mrs. Bernard Cleared," *Moffat County Courier*, 21 Aug 1913; "August Court Is In Session," *Moffat County Courier*, 14 Aug 1913. All court records provided by The Museum of NW Colorado–Craig.

30. "Moffat County Court News," *Routt County Republican*, 22 Aug 1913. The Novelty Theatre, as it is referred to in the article, was the first place in Craig to show moving pictures but was only called Novelty during June and July of 1913. By August 1913 the name was changed to Movie Theatre. The building was and is at 520 Yampa Avenue and is best known as the Opera House. Dan Davidson, Director, The Museum of NW Colorado–Craig.

31. Complaint, H.H. Bernard, Plaintiff v. Anna Bernard, Defendant, 14 Feb 1913, The Museum of NW Colorado–Craig.

32. Affidavit: H.H. Bernard, Plaintiff vs. Anna Bernard, Defendant, 21 Aug 1913, The Museum of NW Colorado–Craig.

33. Affidavit of Non Residence and For Publication of Summons, H.H. Bernard, Plaintiff v. Anna Bernard, Defendant, 13 May 1913, The Museum of NW Colorado–Craig.

34. Answer: H.H. Bernard, Plaintiff v. Anna Bernard Defendant, 8 Aug 1913.

35. Application for Alimony and Suit Money, H.H. Bernard Plaintiff v. Anna Bernard, Defendant, The Museum of NW Colorado–Craig.

36. Order: H.H. Bernard, Plaintiff v. Anna Bernard, Defendant, 21 Aug 1913 The Museum of NW Colorado–Craig.

37. Moffat County Courier, "Bernard Divorce–Jury Disagrees," 28 Aug 1913.

38. Stipulation: H.H. Bernard, Plaintiff v. Anna Bernard, Defendant, 25 Aug 1913.

39. Decree: H.H. Bernard, Plaintiff v. Anna Bernard, Defendant, 25 Aug 1913.

40. "Craig Featured as Wild West Show," *Moffat County Courier*, 21 Aug 1913.

CHAPTER TWENTY-FOUR

EVERY CEDAR A SYMPHONY

Too often for Ann and her family, more darkness came than light. In the wake of everything, including her trials and divorce, Ann must have searched for her footing. Eb, whom Ann adored, had episodes of a form of anxiety along with painful flair-ups of rheumatism. He was facing financial ruin. Also, while Ann was between cattle rustling trials, Josie suffered the trauma of her fourth husband's death. While support for Ann during her trials was nearly unanimous in Brown's Park, rumors scattered throughout the valley that Josie was guilty of not just sheep stealing, but murder as well. Just after Ann's acquittal, Josie left Brown's Park with a rather uncouth fellow who worked for her. And then, she married him.

Josie was thirty-nine when she moved away from the Davenport place on Willow Creek and married her thirty-four-year-old hired man, M.B. "Ben" Morris, on November 24, 1913. She made her home with him at Jensen, Utah, near Vernal, after leaving behind the rumors and whispered accusations in Brown's Park about the death of her previous husband.

During the late fall of 1912, before Josie's then-husband Nig Wells passed away, Edward D. Samuels, owner of a large sheep operation near Vernal, was driving a huge band of lambs to Rock Springs to be shipped on the railroad. After the Samuels herd crossed Diamond Mountain and dropped down into Brown's Park, the sheep were herded to the Brown's Park Livestock Ranch. A ferryboat was in operation there, at the mouth of Swallow Canyon. An intense operation ensued to get each load of lambs onto the ferry and across the Green River. The lambs were then let loose to graze along the opposite bank and into the meadow along Willow Creek. Stormy weather came and went as the process stretched well into the following day.

Once all the lambs were across, the herders began gathering the sheep to continue the journey to Rock Springs. The owner of the outfit took the time to make a head count. Samuels discovered he was about eighty head short.

It didn't take Samuels and his herders long to find the tracks of the missing lambs for they were plain to see. The lambs had been purposely driven away from the others and herded along Willow Creek through the meadow. The tracks led the men to what was called the Willow Creek lane and a long barn constructed using railroad ties. There they discovered the missing lambs. The brands had already been trimmed and earmarks cut away.

As the sheepmen walked around the corner of the building, they met Nig Wells. Nig's face was pale and his voice shook when he said, "Mr. Samuels, I never had anything to do with this. I want you to know that. I didn't know anything about it and had nothin' to do with it."[1]

The November 29, 1912, *Vernal Express* reported:

> Emerson Wells and Pete Derrick were arrested this week in Brown's park by Sheriff Richard Pope and brought to Vernal.
>
> The charge preferred is the unlawful removing of marks from sheep and the complainant is Edward D. Samuels. The men were placed under $600 bonds to await the preliminary hearing before Justice Massey next Monday.
>
> Mr. Samuels' herd of sheep was being driven to Rock Springs to be loaded on the cars for market. Near the home of Wells, a short distance from the ferry crossing over the Green river, a stop was made during a storm and when the start was made later on the herd was shy about eighty, which were afterward recovered and taken on to the railroad. The earmarks had been removed and the charge is that Wells and Derrick did it. Wells is a rancher and Derrick is a laborer and recently engaged in carrying the mail from Ladore to Bridgeport.[2]

Charges against hired man Peter Derrick were dismissed. However, Emerson "Nig" Wells was bound over on the enhanced charge of grand larceny.[3] Nig was released on bond and allowed to go back home to Brown's Park to await trial.

The exact truth about what happened to Emerson Wells during a New Year's celebration he and Josie attended in Linwood, Utah, remains a mystery. It could very well have simply been alcohol poisoning or heart failure that killed him. However, two very different versions of events surrounding the man's death were recorded by two women who had known each other all their lives. One version was told by Josie and the other by Minnie Crouse. First, Josie's account:

> He was a good man, a good farmer and a good man as ever lived. And he got on those whiskey drunks and went like foolish people. I didn't want to go—but some people—Rifes came, Guy Rife and his people came to our house—and his new wife and his—and another Rife boy, Will Rife's boy, and his wife, and they wanted to go to Linwood. And Minnie Crouse had the hotel there, and we was going to go to Linwood to a dance. I didn't want to go. I thought now if we go there they'll all get drunk. Well I should have knowed it. They'd drink it, and so would the people in Linwood. They were mostly all half-breeds—French and Mexican and Indians. All those mean people were at that time.
>
> So we went over to the dance. And, my husband's name was Wells, Emerson Wells. He was drunk before bedtime. You see, they didn't sell whiskey in Utah and that's right on the line. Folks there in Wyoming—was a regular honky-tonk. And that's why those men proceeded to go to that honky-tonk and get drunk.
>
> Well, there was a dance and I stayed at the hotel with Mrs. Rife. Both Mrs. Rife and I, we had rooms at the hotel. Mrs. Guy Rife wanted me to go with her to the saloon to get the men. Well, I said, "I didn't take them there and I never went to a saloon ever and I'm not going."
>
> An old Mexican, Joe Good, who worked in Brown's Park for the Park Livestock, came over and told me, "I hate to tell you but Wells is terribly drunk and they're running a game. And I stole his watch away from him and his money and brought it to you."
>
> I said, "That was a wonderful thing for you to do; that wasn't stealing at all, you were just protecting him and me, too." He had a hundred dollars in his pocket and a nice watch that the Pierce-Reef Cattle Company gave him.
>
> Well, I didn't know what to do. I couldn't get him away from there. We danced the first night. And I went to the dance and tried to stand it all I could. I couldn't do anything else. I went with Minnie and a whole crowd of women and went to the dance. It was just across the road from the hotel in one of the old log houses. And that was New Year's Eve, the dance; danced all night till sunup. I didn't. I went home and went to bed. The next night they danced again. I went for a little while and went back and went to bed. And the next morning there was a man from Kansas City, was a horse buyer, I forgot his name. He was a very nice man; he was nice to me. And he come to see me and he said, "I think your husband is ready to quit drinking." He said he

hadn't had a thing to eat, not a thing but whiskey. And he said, "He's down in the living room."

It was just a kind of a bunk room—living room. Oh, there's a cot over here and a cot over there and a big stove in the middle. Just a kind of like a bunkhouse. They didn't have room enough for the people that was there.

And I went and he was there. And I said—I said, "Wells I brought you a cup of coffee, do you think you can drink it?"

He said, "I'll try." Said, "I feel like hell this morning."

And I said, "Well don't tell me." And I said, "You did it yourself, I didn't." And now I said, "As soon as it comes sunup, and time, we'll start for home." I said, "I can drive the team."

We had a team; it wasn't very safe. It was kind of a tricky outfit. And I thought, I can drive anything to get out of here. So he drank a little of the coffee and he didn't drink any more, and I helped him get his shoes on and—he had his shoes off and was laying down on that cot—and I helped him get his sweater on, then I got a basin of warm water for him to wash his face, and I said, "Now if you can eat some breakfast, I'll bring it over here." I said, "I haven't had breakfast yet," I said, "I'll bring our breakfast over and eat breakfast right here."

He said, "Alright, I don't want no breakfast." Said, "I feel like hell." Kept saying that to me. And I said, "I'm awful sorry, but I can't help, you did it yourself."

And he kept like he was sick to his stomach, and I said, "Are you going to throw that whiskey up? I wish you would." So I got a slop bucket and set there by him on the bed, and I saw that he was wrong —something was wrong. And while I was fooling around there in the house, getting coffee for Wells and washing his face and those things, Ford DeJournette fell over the stove—drunk, oh, and I found five bottles of whiskey, Red Top Rye, and I thought, what'll I do with them, what'll I do with them. So there was a pair of rubber boots hanging on the wall, and I put the bottles down in those rubber boots.

Well, it got breakfast time pretty soon, and this horse buyer said to me, he said, "If I was in your place I'd give him a drink of whiskey, he needs it."

And I said, "I think he needs anything but a drink of whiskey, but if you think that's alright, I will get it." So I opened one of those pint bottles.

And I said to those fellows, Ford DeJournette, Bill Garrett, and the horse buyer, "Won't you boys have a drink, too?" And they all took a drink out of that bottle.

And, I gave Wells a drink out of it, and he took a drink, too. And then I combed his hair and put the bottle back. I didn't put it in the rubber boot. I put it over back of the lounge in the window. And there was about that much left in it. Well, he kept turning—kind of twisting around like he was in misery somehow, I don't know what. But I knew he was wrong. And finally he just straightened right back and died. And he threw up a little kind of foam. Right from his lungs, of course.

And I said to this horse buyer, "he was full of gas." He said, "Nothing else, nothing else, but you can't help it."

Well, I laid him down and I didn't know what to do. I was stranded. I was just—I might as well have been drunk. I didn't know what in the world—what turn to make. So, there was a fellow there that had been a cowboy in Brown's Park and he had worked for my brother, George. His name was Charley Olmey. And I said, "What am I going to do, Charley?"

He said, "Well I tell you what I'd do. I'd send to Green River City for a casket, right now."

"Alright," I said, "I will. Who will I send?"

He said, "I'll go."

So, he went to Green River. Well he got a team and buggy and went—team and old buckboard. My own team and buckboard, and went and got the coffin. And I stayed there. There was no undertaker; there was nothing. That whiskey done it all; no wonder I hate whiskey.

So, we laid him out and straightened him out and did the best we could. And I waited till the next day noon, till the coffin got there. They just put him in the coffin and Charley Olmey took him home to Brown's Park.

The next day I took him down and buried him by my Uncle Sam, down in that cemetery. It was on the—he died on the third day of the month of January, and was buried on the seventh. And the whole country was there. There were lots of people in Brown's Park then—lots of people.[4]

Minnie Crouse married a man described as "a big Swede," named Knudsen "Knud" Ronholdt. Although she still had her homestead at Spring Creek Gap, during the time of Nig Wells' death, Minnie was running a boarding house in Linwood, Utah. About the incident, Minnie said:

Oren Rife, son of Billy Rife, and Leora came up with Josie and Nig. They came up in a two-wheeled cart to the dance at Linwood and rented a cabin at the boarding house early in the afternoon. They

Minnie Crouse, the daughter of Charlie and Mary Crouse who had known the Bassetts all her life, testified unfavorably about Josie Bassett's actions. *Author's Collection.*

stopped at Spring Creek Gap and had lunch. They made themselves thoroughly at home, I guess, because Josie went through all my stuff and helped herself to jewelry; some onyx pieces that some people had made in the pen and Matt Warner sent to me and my people. She took some cotton embroidery from a baby shirt and my shoe and glove button hook.

By the time the dance was on, Nig was well lit. Then they went down to the dance. Nig was drunk, and they go put him to bed, then Bill Garrett shows up and they give him more drink. They gave him poison! We don't know of course, but Josie wouldn't let Leora give her baby a drink out of that glass.

After midnight Garrett and Josie went to my room in the hotel and locked my door! We hammered and hammered until they had to give in. Then I went in and kicked them out of there. I grabbed up her suitcase and it wasn't latched so it fell all open. That's when I saw my jewelry and a bottle of strychnine. I was so silly, I didn't even say anything about my things, but I grabbed the bottle and kept it. Later I gave it to George Stephens for his private museum in Green River.

The only law around was Justice of the Peace Ed Tolton, a middle-aged man. Josie told him that Nig had fits and seizures, and [Josie] just wrapped Ed around her finger. Everything was in her favor, so she brought Nig back to Brown's Park and said she buried him in the

Lodore Cemetery. But many said the casket was empty, and so, no one knows where he's buried.[5]

Bill Garrett was a good-looking cowboy and skilled roper who worked for the Two-Bar as well as other ranches in the area. Although the sight of him riding his favorite roan gelding caused the teenaged girls of Brown's Park to stare and sigh, it was obvious he only noticed Josie. Talk circulated that Josie and Bill Garrett were lovers.

Not long after the death of Nig Wells, Josie went to Bridgeport where Nina Taylor and her family were now living, having accumulated into their expanding cattle ranch the place just downriver from the remnants of Charlie Crouse's bridge. Josie asked the Taylors to help her convince her other neighbors that she was innocent of any wrongdoing. C.M. Taylor asked Josie, "Mrs. Wells, why in the world didn't you have an examination of the body to prove you were innocent?" Josie looked down at her hands folded in her lap and said, "I didn't know about doing such things."[6]

After Josie left to go home, Nina and C.M. were concerned that Minnie Crouse might be right in her accusations against Josie. They knew Josie to be a much more capable woman than she was acting. Since the incident of the stealing of the lambs, those who knew Josie and Nig had questioned the truth about the incident. Many believed that Josie and Peter Derrick were behind the theft rather than Nig. Nig's trial for the lamb theft would have commenced shortly, had he lived. Soon after Josie's visit to their home, the Taylors saw Bill Garrett ride past and then disappear into the canyon. Garrett never returned.

Sheriff Pope from Vernal stopped by C.M. and Nina Taylor's ranch. He ate supper with the family and stayed the night. After breakfast the next morning he left to conduct an interview with Josie about the circumstances surrounding her husband's death. On his way back through, Sheriff Pope stopped by to tell Nina and C.M. he believed Josie was innocent and there would be no further investigation.[7]

Josie, the supposed steady and serious-minded one of the Bassett girls, was multifaceted in her personality with obvious complications and struggles left unhealed. Neighbors thought her usually genial and cheery, but noted she could also be callous and temperamental.[8] Was she a murderess with the motive of ridding herself of a drunk while making sure he didn't reveal her involvement in the larceny of the sheep? Some of Josie's descendants believe that if Josie gave Nig Wells something that hastened his death, the intention wasn't to harm him but to help the man stop drinking. People could obtain, by mail order or over the counter, bottled home cures of the famed Keeley Cure, and others less well-known, to treat alcohol and drug addiction. These "cures" contained a combination of adverse ingredients that might include morphine, apomorphine, alcohol, strychnine, ammonia, atropine, and cocaine. Some "magical" cure-alls contained doses of opiates and cocaine.

Regardless, Josie McKnight Ranney Williams Wells Morris would, at last, find contentment when she squatted on a lovely place on Cub Creek sixteen miles outside of Jensen. Newly married to Ben, she had a place of her own, where she could plant fruit trees and vegetables and raise some livestock. Her husband built a one room cabin for them and another for Herb when he made his rounds to visit. Although Josie's fifth and final marriage didn't last two years, she was on Cub Creek to stay.

About 1916, Ann decided to follow her sister to Utah. Change was inevitably altering Brown's Park, and Ann found it painful to witness. She wrote about the intensity of her feelings surrounding the evolutions:

> My reaction to the trek of dry farmers with their wire fences and plows, stampeding to Brown's Park and Douglas Mountain, were bitterish. I could see no background among dirt farmers to make up an essence of romance. But they were there for good or evil, seeking and possessing every available spot. Their rights could not be denied. But I could get away and out of vision of the bloodless destruction of my precious native haunts. I would avoid being smothered by fences, and the digging up, where every sage brush, gulch and rock had a meaning of its own, and each blade of grass or scrubby cedar was a symphony. I could make effective my escape. If I had to be hedged in by people I would go away to the crowded cities, to mingle with the human herd and study them from the sidelines, for I had no desire to become a part of their affairs. All I asked of life was to be perpetually let alone, to go my way undisturbed. To Brown's Park and its hills and valleys (the only thing I had ever selfishly loved) I bade goodbye.[9]

Ann acquired a place of her own which was a proved-up homestead on South Fork four or five miles from Josie's place. It had a good spring and some ditches for irrigation but the one room log cabin was not in livable condition. The dirt roof was caved in, windows were broken, and the door was off its hinges and nearly buried beneath cow manure on the dirt floor inside the cabin. Ann lived with Josie while Josie's son, Crawford,

Ann Bassett Bernard moved to a proved-up homestead near Jensen, Utah, not far from Josie's place. *The Museum of NW Colorado–Craig.*

and Crawford's hired man named Dannie Nelson worked under Ann's daily supervision to turn the place into a nice little home with a new set of corrals.[10] The next year in 1917 Ann filed the paperwork to homestead an adjacent 160 acres.

Back in Brown's Park, life for Eb was tough and his hope for happiness dwindling. Apparently he had very little money and a fair amount of debt when he posted the two $1000 bail bonds for Tom Yarberry and Ann. When Eb secured the bonds with his signature, he was signing an indemnity agreement or promissory note obligating him to pay the full amount if Ann and Yarberry, the accused, didn't appear in court. Ultimately, both bonds were deemed forfeit because of non-appearance. In December 1913, notices began appearing in the newspaper about different sheriff's sales to be conducted by Sheriff John Ledford for the amount of certain judgments recently obtained against Elbert Bassett and Anna Bernard.[11]

It had all seemed just a matter of paperwork in 1911 when an error was discovered in the original survey that Herb used as the basis for his homestead filing for the Bassett Ranch in 1884. With the creation of

Moffat County a new survey caught the error. A new claim had to be filed to fix the problem. Since Herb was turning the ranch over to Eb, Eb filed the paperwork in his name for the new patent.

Three years later, on March 14, 1914, in the midst of Eb's financial troubles, a U.S. land patent on the Bassett Ranch was granted to Eb. Nine months later, on December 26, 1914, Eb attempted to deed the ranch to George to save it from forced sale. It didn't work; the law was not sympathetic. Eb's creditors came after him with a vengeance. The agonizing sheriff's sale occurred and the Bassett Ranch fell to, of all people, Ora Haley.

Although George protested and filed suit, he was unsuccessful in the judgment. Conversely, in a breathtaking intervention of the cosmos on Eb's behalf, Eb was able to retain the house, corrals, outbuildings, and the orchard he had so devotedly tended and expanded with new plantings. The new survey had revealed that the land where the ranch headquarters sat was not now or ever had been within the boundary of Herb and Elizabeth's homestead. Therefore, it remained part of the public domain and not deeded ground. Squatter's rights enabled Eb to stay. Having that 28.59 acres and a bit of summer range in Zenobia Basin, Eb could eke out a living.

Just three years later, in 1917, Ora Haley, in ill health, sold out in Brown's Park and liquidated his Colorado holdings. Retired from the cattle business and living in his mansion in Denver, his health steadily declined. The ravages of a series of paralytic strokes took him to the end of his life on December 22, 1919.[12]

It came to this—after all Haley's planning, pushing, plotting, building, and killing that included Isam Dart, Mat Rash, and Chick Bowen—the Two-Bar was sold. It was gone and with it vanished Haley's obsession with growing larger, squeezing out smaller, and dominating every stem of coveted grass. Haley's Colorado operation, including the land that was once the Bassett Ranch, was bought by the Clay Springs Cattle Company, led by its president, W.F. Grounds of Arizona and managed by his son Billy.[13]

During the time when the voluminous transaction was being worked out between Ora Haley and the Clay Springs Cattle Company, Haley made a chillingly callous and revealing statement to Billy Grounds that was in reference to the adage: *The only good rustler is a dead rustler*. After removing five cancelled vouchers from an envelope, Haley threw them

Herb Bassett never claimed to be a cowboy, but was a scholar and a gentleman. This rare photo shows Herb mounted on a horse in his later years. *The Museum of NW Colorado–Craig.*

down on a table and in a low tone said: "Here are the only *good* cattle rustlers I ever knew." Haley then listed five names, two of which Billy later recalled to be Isam Dart and Mat Rash. Three of the checks had been cashed by Hi Bernard. It was understood by Billy Grounds that Bernard had paid the money in cash to the assassin.[14]

The Clay Springs Cattle Company, an enormous operation organized under the laws of Arizona and backed by wealthy owners in Iowa, purchased between 7,000 and 8,000 head of mother cows and around 300 saddle horses from the Haley Live Stock and Trading Company.[15] The Clay Springs Cattle Company retained the Two-Bar brand and name. Now, more than ever, George and Eb Bassett were encircled by Two-Bar cattle. The Bassett meadows now raised hay for Two-Bar herds.

At her new place on South Fork, Ann kept a flock of poultry, seven or eight milk cows that raised that number of calves each year, about ten head of sheep, and four top notch saddle horses. When her father came for an extended stay, he must have been glad to have both his daughters in the same vicinity, tucked into homes on land of their own. He helped

Ann with her place using his skills as a builder and constructed an excellent new outhouse.

By this time, Herb had visited every soldier home in the country, some more than once including the Sawtelle Home for Veterans in Los Angeles and the Illinois Soldiers' and Sailors' Home in Quincy. Herb obviously drew comfort from being with other veterans with whom he shared such life-altering memories.

Herb was living with a melancholy that had certainly been with him since Elizabeth's death but was now more profound. While he loved his daughters with an accepting heart, there is little doubt they caused Herb dismay and probably humiliation. He was eighty-four and in failing health, and he depended on them. Throughout the summer of 1917, and the next winter and spring of 1918, he took turns living with Ann and Josie. In June, something prompted Herb to leave, on his own. Josie said:

> He ran away from us. We didn't know he was going. He told me he was going but he didn't tell me how soon. We didn't know he was going. He had been living with me. And he left on horseback and went up to Mr. Showalter's. He was a great friend of Mr. Showalter. Roy Showalter was a little boy then, and he told Roy Showalter he was going. And Roy Showalter sat down and wrote me a card and he told me he had a talk with my father and said he was running away from me and going to Quincy, Illinois. I got a letter from the captain there at Quincy as soon as Father landed there; and said he was not too well."[16]

A short while after he got to Illinois, Herb wrote a letter to his granddaughter, George's daughter, Edna. Not only do his words reveal the core of his tender being but it explains the roots of his deeply held religious beliefs:[17]

Herbert Bassett
Soldiers Home
    Cottage 8
Quincy, Illinois   June 22nd, 1918

Miss Edna Bassett
My Dear little Grand Daughter,

> I have made all kinds of plans about coming over to visit you people —because you are my people—all of you and circumstances have prevented me from getting started.

I had made up my mind to go over on my pony—and to go part way over the road. I once went to old Ashley [Vernal], to buy flour, a long time ago, and before the city of Vernal was built, and I was riding from Josie's over to Anna's a distance of about four miles. My pony stumbled as he started down a little hill, then went down on his knees, and I pitched off into a ditch on my back, and the pony was in the ditch by the side of me, but got up before I did. I wiggled around and found my right ankle, and my left knee were both injured, so I could not stand up. After some time I got the pony up beside a bank of rocks and I crawled on to him, and went to Ann's. So that settled my going to Ladore for some time—Thus you see that I am going down the journey of life, while you are only getting started up the journey of life.

I am now going to remain here until I am entirely cured of my little kidney trouble, and when I leave this Home I shall come to your place on the "Ab Hughes" line—But for fear of something serious to prevent me from coming at all—I wish to tell you a little story about my dear old stepmother as I write this letter to you.

My own mother died a short time after I was five years old. Father married again, the next year—The stepmother was fine looking, and a good singer, fond of children—And she sang me to sleep many a night—in her lap. As I became 21 years and a voter—I joined a company of young men preparing to follow the advice of Horace Greely of New York City, who said in his newspaper, "Go West Young Man and grow up with the country." I was working for wages preparing to go west. On Sundays I would go home, to my father's house. Mother was always glad to see me, and seemed to encourage me to go west—but would be sorry to see me go. Yet she thought it the best thing for me to do. About the last of September I went home one Sunday—and found the room all dark and the bed out in the middle of the room, and father asleep on a lounge. Mother said—don't try to touch me—The Doctors yesterday said I had the inflammatory Rheumatism, and the putrid Erysipelas, and that I could not get well any more. Don't wake your father, for he has been up with me for three nights. You must help me now. So take off your shoes, coat, and vest, and I will tell you what to do. Mother said she was laying on two heavy linen sheets with knots tied at all four corners. You put your feet on the bed rails, get hold of the knots at the head of bed and settle back and your weight will help me to sit up—then put a pillow to my back—and put your back to the pillow, then I can rest, and talk to you a long time. When she got tired and wanted to lay on her side, I would help her down on to her back and then take hold of two knots and place my feet against the bed rail and pull good and steady, and she would roll from me—Thus I spent the whole night. Mother cried for a long

Address
Herbert Bassett
Soldiers Home
Cottage 8
Quincy Illinois

Soldiers Home
Quincy Illinois
June 22nd 1918

Miss Edna Bassett

My Dear little Grand Daughter.
I have made all kinds of plans about coming
coming over to visit you people—because you are
my people—all of you. and circumstances
have prevented me from getting started.
I had made up my mind to go over on
my pony—and to go part way over the road
I once went to old Ashley, to buy flour. long
time ago. and before the city of Vernal was
built. and I was riding from Josies over to
Annas a distance of about four Miles. my
pony stumbled as he started down a little hill.
then went down on his Knees. and I pitched
off into a ditch on my back. and the pony
was in the ditch by the side of me. but got up
before I did.—I wiggled around and found
my right ankle, and my left Knee were
both injured, so I could not stand up. after
some time I got the pony up beside a bank of rocks
and I crawled on to him. and went to Annas

Herb's letter to his granddaughter was four pages long. This is page one. *The Museum of NW Colorado–Craig.*

time—I asked why she did it. She said she was so sorry that she had neglected to teach us two little children in the way that Jesus said—To wit: Suffer little children to come unto me, and forbid them not, for of such is the kingdom of God. I had heard it read—had read it also myself, but it never affected me as I was affected by Mother telling it to me. She said go and do just the way Jesus says for you to do. Jesus says when you pray—Enter into your closet and when you have shut the door, pray to your Heavenly Father in secret, and He, who heareth in secret, shall reward thee openly—These sayings of Jesus was intended for the old as well as the young.

It is a hard proposition to try to pray without first trying the closet—the Devil will scare it all out of you—but being in the closet with the door shut, you are alone with God—He will protect you from the influence of Satan. And you pray, on and on each day, and you will find the Confession—which is the baptism of the Holy Ghost. A Holy life thus prepares us for death and judgement, and that finally prepares you to have your part in the first Resurrection. Sec. 20 Chapter of Revelations & 6th verse—and when I come to see you we will have lots to talk about. I have not forgotten letter and handkerchief you sent to me.

With love to all—I remain your old Grand Pa

Herbert Bassett[18]

Less than two months later, Herb moved on, beyond his life on Earth. *The Moffat County Courier* printed the following:

PIONEER PASSES AWAY

Word was received recently of the death of A.H. Basset[t], at the Soldiers Home near Quincy, Illinois. He had been with his daughters, Mrs. Morris and Mrs. Bernard of Jensen, Utah the past year. In June he went to the soldiers home in Illinois mainly to be under medical treatment for a while.

On July 20th he had a severe stroke of paralysis and lived only a few hours. Word failed to reach the family in time, so he was given a military burial at the home.

Mr. Basset[t] was one of the first settlers to locate in Brown's Park and his many friends there and elsewhere will regret to learn of his death.

It was not possible for any of his children to be with him when the end came; but it comforts them to know that he was, in every way, prepared to go and was only awaiting the summons that would call him into the life he longed to enter.

He leaves five children, Mrs. Josie Morris, Jensen, Utah, Sam Bassett, Alaska, Mrs. Ann B. Bernard, Jensen, Utah, Elbert and George Bassett, Ladore, Colorado.[19]

The years trickled past and on June 13, 1922, Ann gained clear title to her homestead.[20] She had a strong interest in mining and invested money in mining companies, likely from the time she worked for one in Mexico. The income from investments along with money from her calves, wool, and lambs provided enough so she could make extended trips to visit different locations, sometimes for a couple of months at a time. The place on South Fork gave Ann a home base, but it didn't settle her spirit.

In 1923 at the age of forty-five, Ann married a kind and loving man who'd been a friend to the Bassetts for several years, Frank Willis. Frank was born in Tennessee in 1883 and arrived in Colorado when he was seventeen. He first worked for the Rocky Mountain Fuel Company before going to work for the Two-Bar under Hi Bernard. After Frank quit the Two-Bar he worked on ranches in Wyoming and Nebraska before returning to Brown's Park.[21] After Ann and Hi Bernard divorced, Frank and Hi Bernard lived together for a year or so at the Curtin Ranch in Brown's Park where during downtimes and the long evenings of winter, Hi Bernard told Frank the story of his life, from which Frank later wrote the account he titled "Confidentially Told."

In February 1924, Ann and Frank received word that Hi Bernard was dead. The obituary read:

> Hi Bernard, Browns park ranchman and stock raiser, walked into a restaurant at Rock Springs, Wyo., Thursday after having ridden for several hours, and suddenly collapsed, death being instantaneous. Every old timer in this section knew Hi Bernard. He left his native Texas home at the age of 14, punching cattle on the northward trail. About 50 years ago he was with a cattle outfit at Sweetwater, 15 or 20 years later coming to this section, where he was foreman for the Two-Bar. Hi Bernard was known as the wisest cattleman in Northwestern Colorado, a man absolutely fearless and a leader among men. About 15 years ago he married Miss Anne Bassett, but they separated after a few years. Bernard was about 70 years old. Burial was at Rock Springs Sunday.[22]

In Hi Bernard, Queen Ann had found a partner like no other; together they shared their lives on the ranch, working their cattle while swathed in the mulled fragrance of the range that inspired them both. Reality, however, ended it with a snivel of disappointment for them both.

During the frustrating tussle after the divorce to collect the money he'd promised, Ann finally stopped relying on her lawyer and went to see her ex-husband, the renowned cattleman she'd at first despised and then felt affectionately proud to ride beside. She wrote this letter to her lawyer after her meeting with Hi Bernard:

Jensen Utah
1/29/18

My dear Mr. Pughe,

Just returned from Brown's Park where I went to see Mr Bernard who has been very ill. I find his business affairs in a tangle, and do not consider it advisable at this time to urge payment of our notes. I find Mr. Bernard very feable [feeble], and changed so. I haven't the heart to add to his misfortune just now at least. While as you perhaps know, he did not spare me. Yet it is not my plan to jump on a person when they are down. And I do not see how we can gain any thing in this way.

However, there is some money coming to Mr. B. from Mr. Jones, also some horses to be divided when Mr B. is able to go to Craig. Now Mr B. promises me this. If I will bring the bond to him, also a mortgage note for the ammount [amount] of notes unpaid, to assure him against future payments of same, He says he will pay me. So I wish you would send bond, and fix up a note against my personal property here in Utah to cover the face of notes, 400.00 I can do that, for I am sure those notes cant be collected on again. Send your bill for making out all papers and so on. As I want him to pay that expense. He wishes me to return to Browns Park with those papers and he promises to settle. I do not wish to worry him atal [at all]. And if he will settle this way, alright.[23]

In Frank Willis's commitment to her, Ann found relief and a sense of wellbeing. Frank was honest, outgoing, and witty, played the banjo, and enjoyed sharing stories of his days on the range. Ann was the dominant one in the marriage, and Frank was accepting of her commands. Once when Ann and Frank were visiting Ann's nephew Crawford and his family, Frank made the mistake of coming home a bit drunk. Ann grabbed a broom and hit Frank over the head with it shouting, "You *shall* not behave this way!"[24] During the ongoing molding of Frank, a job Ann took seriously, she would scold her husband roundly before throwing her arms around him and calling him darling. Frank rarely angered but instead took his wife's reprimands to be constructive criticism and the guidance he required in life. Ann wrote to a friend the following: "Now when Frank is in a sarcastic mood he calls me 'Dickie,' a cute short for dictator. It fits nicely."[25]

Within a year after the marriage, Ann and Frank moved to Bakersfield, California, and then on to Huntington Beach, where they purchased the Cooper Hotel. Ann managed the small hotel and Frank was hired by the

Richfield Oil Company.[26] Art Gardner, a Douglas Mountain rancher who was well-known in Brown's Park and Craig, wrote about an incident that happened to Ann and Frank:

> Frank Willis told me about an experience he and Ann Bassett, Queen Ann, his wife at that time, had in California. They were running a rooming house I believe in Santa Fe Springs, just out of Los Angeles. One evening Frank heard a commotion in the lobby and went in to see what was going on. A long, string bean of a fellow and a shorter man were telling one of the roomers that he was to, "Get out right now!"
>
> Frank said, "Here! What goes on here? You're not telling anybody to leave!"
>
> Ann heard the loud voices and she arrived about then, carrying a big revolver. By then the string bean had grabbed Frank under one arm and was holding him tight against his body. Ann swung her revolver at the big man but he ducked and Ann hit Frank in the head, dazing him for a few seconds. At this point Frank pulled out a small caliber hand gun, pressed it into String Bean's side and pulled the trigger twice. That put the big guy out, and the little one was standing there like he didn't know what to do. Someone called the police and Frank turned his gun over to the officer.
>
> It turned out that these two characters who were handing out orders were Ku Klux Klan and they decided that California didn't need one of Frank and Ann's roomers. After the would-be tough guy was on the way to the hospital and the law officer was taking Frank in to book him, the officer handed Frank his gun, saying that the fellow he shot might have a pal lurking around who might try to waylay them and Frank would need a gun.
>
> The KKK man was not injured too badly and soon was able to appear in court. Frank was found innocent. The KKK man got a little time in the penitentiary. Frank was a quiet, mild acting little guy but wasn't going to take any pushing around.[27]

Josie's grandson, Frank, named after Ann's husband was the son of Crawford and Flossie MacKnight. When young Frank was five years old, Ann and Frank asked to adopt him and raise him as their own. Of course the proposal was turned down by Crawford and Flossie. Ann never became a mother. Instead, Frank and Ann's nomadic way of life continued and satisfied Ann's need to stay on the move. Their routine was to move with Frank's work in the oil industry, start a business, and hold onto it until they could sell for a profit, and then move on to something else.[28]

Through the years, tales were spun about the mysterious Ann Bassett and her time at her ranch on South Fork. The ranch came to be described as a way station for rustled cattle and a hideaway for outlaws and rustlers where numbers of night riders congregated. From this operation, some declared, Queen Ann had made her money. No matter that the small valley where Ann lived wasn't that secluded nor in any way capable of supporting very many cattle.[29] Such narratives fit with the image of the captivating cattlewoman who continued her journey into legend.

NOTES TO CHAPTER TWENTY-FOUR

1. Jesse Taylor, interviews with author, 1981-1982.

2. "Removed Marks From Sheep In Charge," Vernal *Express*, 29 Nov 1912.

3. "Local and Personal," *Vernal Express*, 20 December 1912.

4. Josie Bassett Morris, interview with G.E. Untermann, A.R. Mortensen, and E.L. Cooley, 1959, The Museum of NW Colorado–Craig.

5. Minnie Crouse Ronholdt Rasmussen, interview with Marie Taylor Allen, circa 1970, Author's Collection.

6. Jesse Taylor, interviews with author, 1981-1982.

7. Jesse Taylor, interviews with author, 1981-1982.

8. Jesse Taylor, interviews with author, 1981-1982.

9. Ann Willis, "Queen Ann of Brown's Park," *The Colorado Magazine,* Jan 1953 76.

10. Frank McKnight, *A Family Remembered*, 99.

11. "Sheriff's Sale," *The Craig Empire*, 20 Dec 1913 and 13 Dec 1913.

12. "Little Hope Held Out for His Recovery," The *Laramie Republican*, 8 Sep 1919.

13. "Ora Haley Sells Cattle Holdings," *The Routt County Sentinel*, 20 Apr 1917.

14. John Cureton Grounds, *Trail Dust of the Southwest*, 220.

15. John Cureton Grounds, *Trail Dust of the Southwest*, 220.

16. Josie Bassett Morris, interview with Untermann, etc., 1959.

17. Minor changes were made during the transcription of the letter for clarity.

18. Herb Bassett, letter written to his granddaughter Edna Bassett, 22 Jun 1918.

19. "Pioneer Passes Away," *Moffat County Courier*, 29 Aug 1918.

20. Warren G. Harding, President of the United States, The United State of America Patent, Secure Homestead Claim of Anna B. Bernard, Number 867916, Vernal, Utah Land Office, 13 Jun 1922.

21. "Graveside Services Held Sunday for Frank Willis," *The Empire-Courier,* 25 Jul 1963.

22. "Three Early Pioneers Pass Out Suddenly Within the Past Week," *Craig Empire*, 6 Feb 1924.

23. Ann (Bassett) Bernard, letter to her attorney Pughe, Jan 29, 1918, Courtesy of University of Colorado Boulder through The Museum of NW Colorado –Craig.

24. Grace McClure, *The Bassett Women*, 140.

25. Ann Willis, letter to Duward and Esther Campbell, 25 Feb 1950, Museum of the West through The Museum of NW Colorado–Craig.

26. Frank McKnight, *A Family Remembered*, 100.

27. Art Gardner, excerpt from Art Gardner's notes, courtesy of his grandson, James "Jim" Gardner.

28. Frank McKnight, *A Family Remembered*, 100.

29. Frank McKnight, *A Family Remembered*, 102.

CHAPTER TWENTY-FIVE

EB

When Queen Ann wrote tenderly about her brother Eb, she referenced a verse in Corinthians: And now abideth faith, hope, charity, these three; but the greatest of these is charity.[1] Then she said, "Elbert Bassett maintained a free home at the old Bassett Ranch, a spot where the birds and the beasts, homeless, travel-wearied mankind all found a refuge, food and shelter, given in kindness and without reservation."[2]

Eb lived his life getting by and running a few head of cattle. He had the 28.59 acres on the home place and his homestead filing in Zenobia Basin. The still handsome cowboy enjoyed attending rodeos and being among his friends. He may have, as his nephew Crawford MacKnight believed, pined for a woman he could not have, possibly Avvon (Leath) Chew. Whether or not that was true, Avvon was now grown and married to someone else. Eb and George continued to be close in much of their daily lives with George accepting Eb's failings. George and his family provided stability for Eb, although George's wife Ruby may have found it difficult at times to be patient with her husband's brother. However, Ruby was often away in the winter months when her daughter attended school in Missouri.

Both Eb and George were well acquainted with C.M. and Nina Taylor's son, Jess. As a youngster, Jess boarded with George and Ruby Bassett when going to the Lodore School at the new schoolhouse located nearby. Ruby's sister, Willa McClure, was Jess's teacher, and she also lived with George and Ruby. As Jess grew into a young man, he worked for Hi Bernard when Hi was foreman for Charles Sparks who then owned the Willow Creek Ranch, and Jess also rode for the Two-Bar. During the early 1920s George Bassett hired Jess Taylor to do some work for him.

Jess ended up spending a lot of time riding and working with Eb; the two became friends. Jess admired Eb's remarkable ability to handle a lariat and compared the skill to that of the professional trick ropers. Throughout the fall, Eb and Jess worked together cutting cedar posts to build fence for George, and they rode together, gathering the Bassett cattle from Zenobia Basin and trailing them to George's ranch in Brown's Park. Because cattle prices happened to be low George held back shipping in the hope that prices would trend upward. By the last of November, George concluded he could wait no longer because he did not have enough hay and pasture to hold the herd any longer. He gave Eb and Jess the job of trailing the cattle to the stockyards at Bitter Creek, Wyoming, to ship them on the railroad.

Little snow had fallen in Brown's Park, but beyond the valley, ten or twelve inches had sifted and settled. The sky was clear when the herd started, but it was miserably cold. The cows balked at being trailed from the valley into such conditions. Throughout the day, moving the cattle forward was exhausting. That night, Eb and Jess bunked at rancher Charlie Sparks's place. Sparks instructed his hired man, Guy McNurlen, an old Two-Bar cowboy, to take provisions and accompany the Bassett herd with a chuckwagon. The cowboys and wagon were on the trail by daylight.

The constant breeze was bitter. The snow crunched and squeaked beneath the hooves of cattle and horses. While there was a semblance of a road to follow, the cattle constantly veered from it. Snow had blown and drifted, filling many of the gullies and washes. Time and again cows and saddle horses stepped off into the camouflaged cavities, causing the animals to flounder and struggle to get away from the trap of crust and powder. After Eb's horse took a head-first tumble into a wash, Eb suggested to Jess that they take their stirrups off to stay clear and not get hung up during a fall. At midnight, the two cowboys finally pushed the cattle through the gate of an isolated wild horse corral.

When they headed out the next morning at dawn, the cowboys had another seventeen hours on the trail before the beleaguered herd and men arrived at the railroad. Guy McNurlen had the gate open into the pens and Eb and Jess believed they were nearly finished with the job. But, every time the cattle were about to start through the gate, a train or lone engine would clank and rumble along the tracks, causing the cattle to startle and scatter.

By the time Guy McNurlen borrowed a horse and came to help, both Eb and Jess were fully fatigued and their voices hoarse from yelling. Well after midnight the herd was finally corralled in the stockyard. After the

Left to right: Hayes Hughes, Slats Humphreys, "Whitie," "Red," Eb Bassett (with high-crowned light hat), Dutch H. (in the background), Earl Gadd (horse with blaze), Clark (in background), Cary Mann (in high-crowned black hat), Duke or Ike Kellog, Bob Brown, Stanley Crouse. *Used by permission, Uintah County Library Regional History Center. All Rights Reserved.*

train cars were spotted (the doors brought even with the loading chute) and the floors covered in sand, the cattle were loaded. When the last boxcar door slid shut, Jess murmured to Eb, "That was a helluva trip for fifty bucks a month."[3]

During the ride back to Brown's Park the two cowboys confided in each other. Jess opened up to Eb about how he had never been able to get over a feeling of loneliness since scarlet fever took the life of his little sister, Nancy. In turn, Eb told Jess about the way the lynching of John Bennett affected him; he was tormented by that incident years ago at the Bassett Ranch. Eb could not forgive himself for the part he played in entrapping Bennett; inviting him, as a friend, into an ambush. Watching and hearing the man beg for his life before being hoisted to his death haunted Eb in nightmares. He was emotional when he told Jess, "I see that man's face every night; every single night in my sleep."[4]

On February 8, 1925, Eb was nostalgic when he penned an answer to a letter from an old friend who had inquired about some of the cowboys he'd known in years past. Eb wrote to his "Friend Joe" [Joe Martin Blansit]:

> Your letter just recd. and will ans. at once. Was glad to hear from you. Your letter recalled to me so many that I knew and had not thot [thought] of for so long.

Ed Rife has been dead about seven years the Rife out fit is still run by his son Guy. Lou Fisher has been dead for years. He went back to Texas. The Heards are all dead but Al. Lou was kicked by a horse last spring and killed. Mrs Heard has been dead about five yrs. Ben Morgan left long ago and went to Evanston, Wyo. Joe Sainsbury was in Salt Lake the last I knew of him. Jim McKnight is also in Salt Lake. Tim Kinney lives in Calif. Pierce sold the ranch on Bear River and the // [Two-Bar] owns it now. The Templetons Bill and Henry are still on the old place. [Longhorn] Thompson is dead. Went to Vernal Utah and died there.

I still live on the same place and run cattle. This country is settling up but they cant seem to thrive much on the dry land. All springs are taken. You are sure heavier than I remember you. Sam weighs 216, or did not long ago. I am the small one. I only weigh 130 and am 5 ft 8. Also the only one of the family not married and am too old to try any new tricks now. Will be 45 next June.

Ab Hughes is living between here and Snake [River] at what we call Willow Spgs I guess you know where it is. He has about fourteen kids all sizes and ages. His sister who was Mattie Hughes and now Mrs Dave Edwards is visiting them this winter and as gay as when young.

I thot I told you in my other letter that my father was dead. He has been dead six years. Had a stroke and lived but a few hours.

Well I guess my letter is about long enough to tire you so will quit. Write anytime I am always glad to hear from the old timers. Some way I cant get used to the new comers. But the old timers are getting scarce here. With best luck and good wishes to you I am

Your friend

Eb Bassett[5]

Mattie Hughes Edwards, who was visiting her brother Ab and family during the winter of 1924-1925, was widowed. She and Eb grew close. Whether or not there was a romance, it was a tender relationship, and they spent time together and came to care for each other.

It was difficult as ever, for Eb to graze his cattle alongside the Two-Bar herds. Billy Grounds, then managing the Two-Bar, had the same old mindset about coveting the range and was heard making the brag that he would graze out other ranchers trying to summer their cattle on the Douglas Mountain range.[6]

Regrettably, in the fall of 1925, Eb's life began a serious turning when he purchased an insurance policy on his cabin located in Zenobia Basin. In September, a short time later, the cabin caught fire. Just after the blaze

Jess Taylor confided that he could never get over the death of his little sister. *Author's Collection.*

took the mountain cabin, Earl Gadd, a Brown's Parker who was working for the Two-Bar and riding with his nephew Delbert Ducey, went to look at Eb's burned cabin. The two had been instructed by Billy Grounds to bring in a certain Two-Bar cow that had been left ranging in Zenobia Basin. She was a large, dry cow that was held back to be butchered for beef. Gadd and Ducey found relatively fresh cow tracks but they couldn't find any other trace of the animal. After scrutinizing Eb's burned cabin, they grew suspicious. Not only did the burning show some signs of being staged but, deep tracks made by what was presumed to be a loaded wagon led away from where the front entrance of the cabin had been.

Earl Gadd and Delbert Ducey followed the wagon tracks to a rock point and up a wash. Then, beneath a red rock ledge they found a stash of items obviously saved from the cabin. Some of the things they found included windows and a door along with their casings, also a stove and some furniture pieces. According to John Cureton Grounds, son of Billy Grounds, stretched out on some sawed lumber in plain sight, Gadd and Ducey discovered a Two-Bar cow hide.

Billy Grounds was accompanied by Sheriff Tom Blevins when the men drove in to Eb's place in Brown's Park. Eb had just mounted a horse and had ridden a short distance away when he saw the car arrive and pull to a stop just below the corrals. Eb reined his horse around, dismounted, and tied his horse to the hitching rail. Then he went to greet his visitors.

Just after daylight that morning, the sheriff and Billy Grounds had arrived at William Sweet's place in Brown's Draw which is located near Douglas Mountain. There they discovered portions of the quarters of a freshly dressed beef hanging at the front of the cabin off the extending roof logs. When William Sweet was confronted about how he came by the meat, Sweet said he got it from Eb Bassett. When asked about the whereabouts of the hide, Sweet said he guessed Eb had it.

Grounds immediately asked Eb if he had any meat on hand and Eb replied, "I always do." After Eb took the men to the cellar and removed the canvas from his provision of beef, Grounds said, "All right, Eb, now let's see the hide."[7]

Eb was placed under arrest along with William Sweet and Eb's hired man from Jensen, Ed Ainge. They were all taken to jail in Craig. Word spread that an insurance adjuster met with Sheriff Blevins about having another charge preferred against Eb.[8] Friends in Craig soon posted bail for the three men. A hearing before Justice of the Peace Wash Held was scheduled for Tuesday, November 17, 1925.

In anticipation of the hearing, Eb and his dog Jack arrived at Frank Lawrence's farm on lower Big Gulch about twelve miles away from Craig. Eb and Frank Lawrence had known each other ever since the man moved there, about fifteen years earlier. Eb and Jack traveled in the company of William Sweet, Sweet's wife Lillie, and twenty-two-year-old Ed Ainge.

Charged with stealing and killing a cow, Eb, William Sweet, and Ed Ainge appeared before Justice of the Peace Held on Tuesday, November 17 and were bound over to district court for a preliminary hearing to take place two days later on Thursday, November 19.[9] The men returned to Frank Lawrence's place to await the hearing.

Early Thursday morning, as the household awakened, Eb's friends realized Eb was nowhere in the house. During the night, no one heard when Eb left his bed and dressed. No one awoke when he went into the kitchen and placed a note on the table. No one knew when Eb, in silence, stepped out into the night.

Later that day, an unforeseen coroner's inquest was held instead of the scheduled hearing in District Court. Witnesses concerned with the inquest were interrogated by Deputy District Attorney T.P. Fahey before a jury composed of six men.

The following is constructed from the actual testimony recorded in the document: FINDINGS AND TESTIMONY RE CAUSE OF DEATH IN THE CASE OF E.B. BASSETT, DECEASED, CRAIG COLORADO, NOVEMBER 19, 1925. The original twenty page inquest is entirely dialogue in a question and answer format. In the narrative below, direct quotes from the testimony are noted, while the remainder of the document is condensed and paraphrased:

Frank A. Lawrence testified that he would soon be fifty-three, that his house was two rooms having a kitchen and bedroom, and that he was a farmer. When Lawrence was asked to state in his own way what he knew about the case, he answered, "I don't know anything for sure about it, but I know some circumstances that make me believe it is true. Night before last I went over across the creek to get a chicken to cook for dinner yesterday, and Bassett said, 'I will go with you,' and we had been talking about killing coyotes, and going over he asked me what kind of strychnine I had been using, and I said the last I got was crystallized, and he said that he had never seen any that was in crystals. He asked if he could see it, and I said 'Yes' it was there at the house. When we got back I opened that box you have, but the light was too dim, and I said 'you can look at it in the morning,' and I am sure that I never closed that box, and this morning when Mr. Sweet found him I looked at the box and the box was covered."

Lawrence described the sleeping arrangements that night and said Mr. and Mrs. Sweet slept in the kitchen by the stove and that Eb slept with him in the bed and Ed Ainge slept on the floor across the room near the window. Also that Eb made a bed on the floor for his dog. Lawrence said the last thing he remembered was Eb sitting up on the side of the bed and smoking a cigarette. The next morning, Lawrence got up before daylight and built a fire in the stove. He said to William Sweet, "Eb isn't here. Does he have any trouble?"

Lillie Sweet took the stand and during questioning said, "Well, first Frank got up and built a fire. My husband got up to get breakfast, and then something was said before then, and then I started to dress, and then he came back in and—my husband had gone out to look around for Mr. Bassett—and came back in a while, I was dressing, and told us what he had found, and he told me to get breakfast just as soon as I could, just some coffee. Then while they went out there again I found the note on the table."

William Sweet took the stand and responded that he was twenty-nine and had lived in the area five or six years and had known Eb for about two years. He said, "Well, my wife and I slept in the room where the stove was in the kitchen, and they slept in another room right off from it. I went to bed about 10:30. We talked about what time we would get up, what time we would start to town, and one thing and another, and Eb fixed his dog a bed in our room, and the last I saw of him was sitting on the edge of the bed where he slept, smoking."

When Sweet was asked what frame of mind Eb was in he said, "Well, Eb was worried yesterday." Asked if the deceased said anything about what he wanted done if anything happened to him, Sweet answered, "I heard him mention his dog. He told my wife in case he didn't come back home with us, he wanted us to keep his dog."

William Sweet was asked to state the way he found Mr. Bassett and the conditions of things. Sweet said, "Well, I went out to hunt Eb this morning just about daylight, and I went on out to the granary, and the first thing I saw was his shoes, and I thought there was something wrong, and I opened the door and called to him, but didn't hear anything, and I went in. There are two rooms in the granary, and there he was lying in the other room of the granary on his stomach. I called to him, and he didn't answer, so I took hold of his arm, and he was dead; so I went back and told Mr. Ainge and Lawrence and my wife, and we got a blanket and had just got out of the house and she (indicating wife) called to us and said she had found a note."

When Lillie Sweet was questioned about the conversation she had with Eb about taking care of his dog she answered, "That if they gypped him, for me to keep his dog Jack, and never to part with him. He said they were after him and would try to railroad him."

Ed Ainge testified he had known Mr. Bassett for about seven years and had been living with him since July. When asked to state what he knew about the case he said, "Well, I know I heard Mr. Lawrence holler and ask Mr. Sweet this morning if he knew where his bed partner was, and he said 'No' and he came in and looked, and Sweet went out to see if he could see anything of him." When Ainge was asked if Bassett ever complained of illness, Ainge said, "All I ever heard him say anything about, was that he had spells of rheumatism."

After Ed Ainge was asked if he'd had any discussion about what was going to take place in Craig since giving bond he replied, "The only thing was; he said they didn't have anything on us." Asked if the deceased at any time made any statement that would lead him to believe that he contemplated suicide, he said, "The only thing he ever said was you had arrested him for a blind, and that you were going to get him in court and get him."

When Ainge was asked about the strychnine he said, "Well Sir, Mr. Bassett said to me, 'This is the first time I have ever seen crystallized strychnine.'" Ainge explained that the strychnine was on the dresser when he saw it and that the lid was off the box and the paper was pulled up.

Next, Eb's brother George was called to testify. When George received the news about Eb he had immediately driven to the Lawrence farm. He told the jury, "Well, we found him right in the granary at the left of the door. When we went in he was covered up with a grey blanket, lying face down and his hands crossed something like this [*gesture*]. As I remember one hand was shut, and we examined the body. Didn't find anything only what was in his pockets. We didn't see any marks on his body. We never stripped it or anything like that though. Then we went to the house and got this box of poison setting in the corner on a little dresser, and I looked through his jacket pocket, and there was nothing in it except a pair of gloves. We went back and got the body and brought it to town. We got this note. It was on the kitchen table."

When questioned about the note, George responded, "That is his writing and signature, yes, Sir, I could swear to that anywhere in the United States." George was asked if he'd ever heard his brother say anything about contemplating self-destruction and George responded, "No, Sir. He never seemed to be of that mind. Not any more than I am right now."

Dr. Clayton was called to the stand and he said he'd known Eb for ten or twelve years. He had examined the body at the granary. "I went in with Mr. French [Clarence French, Deputy Coroner] and the body had on a woolen shirt and a pair of pants and underwear. He wanted me to examine it, so we undressed the body, and I think there were socks on him. When we undressed him his arms were very stiff. That the jaw was

Ruby McClure Bassett overlooks the Bassett Cemetery in 1926. *Author's Collection.*

set and wouldn't move and the legs were so still that if you took hold of them and lifted, the whole body would lift up."

A nearly empty bottle, with a ginger ale label and a cork stopper, was discovered by Deputy Coroner French. He testified, "Well, when we first got there, we went down to the granary and backed in, and I believe the shoes were setting on the outside at that time, anyway, they picked the shoes up, and went up to the house. We came back and searched the pockets for evidence. When we came back out I saw a bottle. I was standing facing the door and it was on the outside. I picked it up and pulled the cork and smelled it, and said 'White Mule,' and set it back down. Then we went back to the house and got the note that was left."

Prohibition, which had gone into effect five years earlier in 1920, was a nationwide constitutional ban on the production, importation, sale, and transportation of alcohol. The liquid remnant in the ginger ale bottle was discerned by the coroner to be moonshine when he described it as White Mule. Deputy Coroner French testified that if sitting down in the granary door, the bottle would have been three or four feet away.

William and Lillie Sweet, Frank Lawrence, and Ed Ainge all agreed in their testimony that they had never seen the bottle before and that no liquor had been consumed that they knew of by anyone while they were at the Lawrence farm. Lawrence said that if he'd been offered a drink of it, he would have taken it.

The final verdict following the autopsy and testimony was that Elbert Bassett died from taking poison into his stomach. Because the doctor didn't have the facilities in Craig to prove conclusively that Eb took strychnine, the doctor left open the possibility Eb could have died from drinking poison liquor. However, it was agreed that the most likely conclusion with all things considered, including the note and condition of the body, was that Eb drank the liquor when he swallowed crystalized strychnine. The combination, the doctor stated, would have caused the poison to react quickly, resulting in Eb falling face first without a sign of struggle.[10]

❧ ❧ ❧

Obviously, Eb intended to protect his friends. His suicide note said: *No one but me knows or suspects what I am going to do, no one. Eb Bassett*

Without Eb, there was no case of cattle theft to be made against William Sweet and Ed Ainge. The charges were dismissed.

Eb's funeral in Brown's Park drew a very large crowd. His casket was carried to the hilltop and buried in the family cemetery. His grave overlooks the place where he spent his entire life.

When Ann and Josie sat in George's home and talked with George about Eb, they decided to leave Eb's house as it was and allow Eb's close friend, Mattie Edwards, to live there. Anyway, that's the way George understood it. He was stunned when a moving truck arrived and packed up Eb's entire household and took it to Jensen.[11] That was just the beginning of four years of hurt, anger, mismanagement, correspondence, and legal back and forth that ensued in settling Eb's affairs.

Eb's entire estate was valued at $1,452.80 and consisted of nineteen head of cattle, fourteen horses, a $500 note, and the $24.80 Eb had on him when he died.[12] Eb's homestead in Zenobia Basin had not been fully proved up on, and George's efforts to get it approved were unsuccessful, thus the homestead claim was dissolved and removed from Eb's estate.

Eb had made out a handwritten will on September 15, 1909, that said: "In case of death to me all my property real estate and all other property goes to Geo. and Ruby Bassett. Elbert Bassett." On June 24, 1911, he added: "All outstanding debts owing me to be collected by Ann Bernard. E.B. Thompson owes me $600 Due Dec. 1, 1911. Eb Bassett."[13] Eb did not realize that in order for the will to be valid, he needed two witnesses to sign the will in the presence of each other.

Apparently, neither Ann nor Josie knew about the requirement of witnesses. In 1928, three years after Eb's death, they presented a will to the attorney dated 1918 which they said Eb made out when he thought he was going to be drafted during World War I. This will declared that Eb left everything to Ann and Josie. While this will did have signatures of two witnesses, Ann's husband Frank and Longhorn Thompson's son Lyman, the witnesses had not signed in the presence of each other while witnessing Eb's execution of the will. The attorney for the estate, George Pughe, was dubious about the will from the beginning;[14] once he discerned the witnesses had not properly subscribed their signatures to the will, he informed the heirs that the will was void and wouldn't be presented to the court.[15] The estate was not settled until August 1929, nearly four years after Eb's death.[16]

Mattie Hughes Edwards did move into Eb's house shortly after his death, and there she made her home. Although Mattie apparently purchased the buildings,[17] the 28.59 acres of the old ranch headquarters still stood on public domain, and Mattie settled there as a squatter as had Eb. She purchased a large headstone and had it placed at the head of Eb's grave. On it she had words of endearment carved in the stone that read, "Dear Old Pal."

Avvon Chew Hughel was devastated by Eb's death. She could not bear to let her memory of him slip away with the passing of time. In longhand she wrote her remembrance. Unable to cope with Eb's suicide, she refused to make it in any way part of her story of him:

EB BASSETT

Eb's name was Elbert. His nickname originated when very young with Queen Ann and she called him Ebbert and then Eb and the name stuck.

Eb was the shortest of the three Bassett boys, being 5 foot 9 inches, while Sam and George were each 6 feet.

Eb had coal black hair and large expressive gray eyes set rather wide apart. He was always smooth shaven and a very handsome man, urbane, distinguished, agreeable and an excellent dancer—at home in any company. Children adored him. The small, weak, or helpless aroused his instant compassion. His shoulder was always available for most anyone's hard-luck story. However, I have no recollection of Eb being played for a sucker by anyone. He possessed a keen human insight. Rarely offered or asked advice, but somehow always said the consoling

Avvon Chew Hughel refused to accept Eb's suicide. *Courtesy of Jo Semotan.*

words. He had a keen wit—was an excellent raconteur—good company anytime under any conditions.

He was a splendid horseman. His riding string was well broken, well trained, and, exceedingly well cared for.

Many women loved him, but he promised a very young girl, a child really, of thirteen to wait for her and this he did, until he died.

Eb was not even a good average business man. One might say he was inept. He was two years younger than Queen Ann, her pal and confidant. His death was a serious blow to her. He was thrown from a bucking bronco and struck his head on a rock. Seven months later he died suddenly from a blood clot on the brain, at the age of 44.

Avvon Hughel[18]

Thus, the life of Queen Ann's pal and confidant passed into memory. The women who loved him, the surviving old timers who rode beside him, and the newcomers Eb found difficult to get used to all held their individual beliefs about the intricate composite that was the Brown's Park cowboy, Eb Bassett. When Ann wrote about her brother's generosity and kindness, she attached the following thought:[19]

Out yonder in the corral is the horse you used to ride. The heart of him's gone with you, pard, across the great divide.

NOTES TO CHAPTER TWENTY-FIVE

1. 1 Corinthians 13:13 King James Version (KJV).

2. Ann Bassett Willis, *The Colorado Magazine,* "Queen Ann of Brown's Park," Jan 1953, 70.

3. Jesse Taylor, interviews with author 1981-1982.

4. Jesse Taylor, interviews with author, 1981-1982.

5. Eb Bassett, letter to Joe Martin Blansit, 28 Feb 1925, The Museum of NW Colorado–Craig.

6. Ruby Bassett, letter to George A. Pughe, 30 Apr 1928, Special Collections and Archives, University of Colorado Boulder Libraries.

7. John Grounds, *Trail Dust of the Southwest,* (Marysvale, UT: J.C. Grounds, 1977) 260-261.

8. John Grounds, *Trail Dust of the Southwest,* 261.

9 "Ladore Rancher Suicides," *The Moffat County Bell,* 29 Nov 1925.

10. Elbert Bassett, report of inquest hearing: Findings and Testimony Re Cause of Death in the Case of E.B. Bassett, Deceased, Craig, Colorado, 19 Nov 1925, The Museum of NW Colorado–Craig.

11. Ruby Bassett, letter to attorney George A. Pughe, 30 Apr 1928.

12. Final Report of Administratrix of the Estate of Elbert Bassett, 5 Dec 1925 to 22 Jul 1929, Special Collections and Archives, University of Colorado Boulder Libraries.

13. Eb Bassett, handwritten will, 15 Sep 1909, The Museum of NW Colorado–Craig.

14. George Pughe, letter to George Bassett, 14 Dec 1928, Special Collections and Archives, University of Colorado Boulder Libraries.

15. George Pughe, letter to Frank Willis, 9 Nov, 1928.

16. George Pughe, letter to Josie Bassett Morris, 7 Aug 1929.

17. *Craig Empire Courier,* 29 Sep 1926.

18. "Eb Bassett," Avvon Hughel, handwritten story given to Evelyn P. Semotan, courtesy of Jo Semotan.

19. Ann Bassett Willis, from a working copy of her memoir, The Museum of NW Colorado–Craig.

CHAPTER TWENTY-SIX

THE EVANESCENCE

Ann's life with Brown's Park, the valley with which she was so inter-woven, was layered in dapples of sunlight and shadow. She remained as complex as ever, and it showed in her emotions. Ann was heartbroken on a level that perhaps wasn't reasonable or explainable, even if she tried. She had a sadness sometimes masking as anger which may have come from her separation from the place that so defined her. She had nothing there; owned nothing of the Bassett Ranch. George, her little brother and the youngest in the family, and his wife, Ruby, a girl from Missouri, had everything that was left. She loved George and was no doubt glad and proud that he'd remained steady and been successful in building a ranch. He had even managed to buy back the land Eb lost, from Billy Grounds of the Clay Springs Cattle Company. That the land was once again Bassett ground was wonderful news and she must surely have been happy, but she was also hurt and resentful. Ann saw the place that held her heart disappear, like the waning of a mist.

Ann naturally longed for the comfort of her youth, when her sister and all her brothers were untroubled fledglings; when the Bassett Ranch blos-somed and cowhands in the bunkhouse sang the ballads telling of storms and stampedes and broncs. Back there . . . in her mother's dominion.

Life in different cities in California made Ann weary, and she yearned to once again feel a good horse beneath her. She wrote:

> Surrounded by so many things I did not like, I felt docile and questioned my judgement in the selection of a camp site. Soft life in the cities had encumbered me with pounds of suet, and left me wob-bling about like a bowl of jelly.
>
> In the city corrals as I stumbled along pavements to ponder over the cluttered surroundings where my feet went milling around in a more or less pleasant by-play, my heart was always in the open far from the hurly-burly world I traveled in, for I still, in memory, had

George Bassett was proud of the Hereford bulls he raised. *Courtesy of Tracy MacKnight.*

recourse to scenes of exceptional beauty of open spaces and the re-membrance of watching the moon and the stars in their appointed visitations carrying with them a new mystery, strange and lovely, and I became tired of many things useless, and pined for those simple levels of satisfaction left behind, and with a desire to keep my peace of mind reasonably intact I determined to go back to the world I loved so well. To engage in the cattle business on the range, to hear again the bells of a horse cavy hazed in by the nighthawk when day was just breaking with a faint glow of pink in the east.[1]

By 1931, Ann's longing to be back on the range carried her and her husband Frank to the Hualapai Valley in northwest Arizona, the very place where the Clay Springs Cattle Company originated. The Blizzard of 1927-1928 had taken a large toll on the Two-Bar cattle in Colorado and the Great Depression hit in 1929. It was then that George was able to make a deal on the land Eb lost, as the Clay Springs Land and Cattle Company continued a downward slide. Remarkably, in 1930 the mighty Two-Bar outfit in Brown's Park was let go for taxes. The ranch was taken up by the Brown's Park Livestock Company owned by W.H. and Carrie Gottsche[2] and operated by Charlie Crouse's son, Stanley.

Ann and Frank bought a ranch near Hackberry, Arizona, where they built a home and went into the cattle business, building their herd up to 1,200 head.[3] Ann was comforted to not only be back on a ranch but also that she was once again near the Indian people. She found the Hualapai to be both noble and modern. Josie's son Chick, with whom Ann had always been close, joined them in Arizona with his wife Edith. While the two couples owned individual ranches, they worked in tandem.

She found the daily tasks, while fulfilling, more exhausting now; the days were dry and hot. Ann said, "A cow business on the desert, where water is desperately scarce is not a gem of simplicity." One day when Ann was trailing stray cattle many miles from home, she was tired, overheated, and very thirsty when she stopped at a neighboring ranch to ask for a drink of water. Ann so appreciated the charming ranch woman, Mrs. Gaddis, who invited her inside to share the noontime meal. Mrs. Gaddis served what was to Ann, "a most heavenly dessert with a spicy goodness blended with perfection." Ann's thirst and tiredness, and Mrs. Gaddis's kind and generous offerings, caused Ann to decide that of all her experiences in Arizona she counted Mrs. Gaddis's rice pudding to be the most memorable.[4]

Mrs. Gaddis was just one of the ranch women with whom Ann found a place of refuge. Throughout her life she found women to be her symbols of grace and strength. Referring to her cattle rustling trials Ann admitted she was guilty, but of exactly what, she did not say:

> Let men brag about their brute strength, yet when they get mired up to the ankles, they invariably SOS the women, exactly as I do, knowing when one's knees get to wobbling, they can back up against the supporting cast of woman's strength. For despite several errors, women are still a length ahead in this human race, two years old or over.
>
> My best friends and guides have always been women, the wives, sisters and mothers of the men who were clamoring to see my shatter-proof hide neatly drying on a corral fence. These noble women—and I salute them—were standing by, giving a hand of helpful encouragement, irradiating wisdom and patience during the staging of those elaborate tournaments where men enjoyed the pastime sport of having me arrested and dragged through the courts for various alleged crimes against the lordly Two-Bar—many of which I was as guilty as hell! They charged to my rescue and went over the top with financial and moral support.[5]

J.S. Hoy said Ann admitted her guilt to him. In 1920, J.S. had left Brown's Park and was living in Denver. He wrote to his step-daughter to tell her that he had finished writing a manuscript on the history of Brown's Park. At the end of the letter he referenced Ann: "The heroine of my book wrote me lately that she trapped 30 coyotes and wild cats this winter which she sold for $300 dollars. In conversation she calls a spade a spade and pleads guilty to being a cattle rustler. I call her 'Ann of Douglas Mountain.' She is a terror and considerable of a wild cat herself."[6]

In 1936 while working her Arizona ranch, Ann learned that Pablo Springs and so much more was at last truly gone from the Bassett family. Her brother George sold his house and 650 acres which included his BLM allotments, to Greek immigrants, Steve and Georgia Simos, a fine and aspiring couple. George retained just a few acres in the northwest corner of the property on which he and Ruby could retire and live out their years.

When the monumental Taylor Grazing Act was enacted in 1934 it was the first federal effort to regulate grazing on public lands. The Act established grazing districts and used a permitting system to manage the grazing of livestock within those districts "to stop injury to public grazing lands by preventing overgrazing and stabilize the livestock industry dependent upon the public range."[7]

The Great Depression, having started in 1929, made all things tough. Then Chick was seriously injured in a car accident which necessitated a long recovery for a broken neck. Chick and his wife sold out before long and went back to live in Nevada. Ann and Frank sold their ranch in 1937 and returned to Colorado. Frank first found work with the Humphrey Gold Mining Company headquartered in Denver, before being hired as sampler foreman for the U.S. Bureau of Mines. Once again, Ann and Frank stayed on the move, living in different places in Wyoming, Colorado, and California as they shared an interest in mining.[8]

Ann, in the company of her grown niece Edna Haworth, went to visit George and Ruby in Brown's Park. While there Ann saw something at the old place where Mattie Edwards was living that apparently distressed her. In a letter to Edna, Ann said that when she viewed the "disturbing situation" her mind was made up. After Ann began acting on that decision, everything appeared to start easing into place for her. She began writing letters to see if the Bassett home place, which was still possessed only through squatters' rights, could be purchased from the government through the division of grazing in the manner that her ranch in Arizona had. That was just her first of many steps to follow. Ann had put the process in motion: she would do her best to get the old Bassett head-quarters back, for the family. The application process for the patent was tedious and slow-moving, but she was not deterred.

In March 1939, George's original two-story house in Brown's Park caught fire and burned. The six-room log home, then belonging to Steve Simos was occupied by local cowboy Sam Carr and his wife, who were hired to oversee the place. Although no one was in the house at the time, the Carrs arrived shortly and were able to get a few of their belongings out before the fire's intensity took the building down. The fire appeared to have started either on the roof or in the attic; no one knew for sure. According to the Craig newspaper, Steve and Georgia Simos had the house insured for $2,000 but the Carrs had no insurance to claim on their possessions.[9]

Ann wanted Mattie Hughes Edwards to move out of Eb's house and off the Bassett place and expressed her wishes to Mattie. Mattie had lived there for over ten years and was in every way part of the Brown's Park community. She had no intention of leaving. Then, just nine months after the Simos fire, on December 21, 1939, Mattie left home to spend some time in Craig. Later that night her house caught fire. *The Craig Empire-Courier* reported in the "Locals" column:

> A letter received this week from Mrs. George Bassett of Grey-stone[10] states that the home on the old A.H. Bassett ranch in Brown's park was completely destroyed by fire on the night of December 21st. This was the second house built on the homestead filing made by Mr. Bassett in the 1870s. Mrs. Edwards had been living there the last 10 years. She was away from home at the time of the fire. Cause of the fire was unknown but presumably it started from faulty stove flues and burned late at night.[11]

Not only did the house burn, so did all of Mattie's belongings and most of the outbuildings, including Herb's old post office. The community had a benefit dance and basket supper for Mattie at the Lodore School and over one hundred people attended. A little over $70 was made from the sale of the baskets and was applied to a fund to help Mattie.

Many suspected Ann had burned Mattie out, but made no formal ac-cusations. Not long after the fire, though, Ann's letter from Oakland, California, to her niece Edna Haworth was, perhaps, revealing.

First, Ann explained to Edna the long process she'd been through in applying for the patent while presenting her case including that her father built the place believing the ground was part of his homestead, had planted an orchard there and cultivated the land, Bassett family members were buried there, and that the place had been occupied by the family for sixty years. Then in her letter to Edna, Ann wrote something that could surely raise eyebrows:

> Now while final patent has not been issued and I did not hasten that part of it until after the fire and fireworks. Geo hasn't a thing to worry. House being gone, so is the tenant. Strike one. His best bet, she is off, keep her off.[12]

Some months later, on December 3, 1940, Ann wrote another letter to Edna Haworth, and Edna's son Bill. Apparently Ann and Frank had recently, and happily, spent some time on the old place in Brown's Park, staying in Paul and Edna's camper accompanied by Edna's little boy, Bill. Much of the letter is written tongue-in-cheek and reveals Ann's humor and new-found lightheartedness. It reads:

> Greystone Dec 3—40
> Dear Edna and Bill,
>
> You surely found the trailer in good shape. Well it is to be expected when you leave your things to trash [like me] from Arkansas. We did expect to get back and fix the thing up. Paul was so disgusted he would not even let the little red curtains hang up and I wanted them to stay in trailer, I thot they were cute even if one wasn't hemmed. I got you a new broom. Willie the work horse ate that one to pieces. He couldn't find another thing to chew on this summer.
>
> And those quilts. You must let me know cleaning charges. I am surely going to make that right. I let Bill do a little painting with kalsomine and one of the quilts got in his way. They were dusty and when Ed came in with his smelly feet; that was enough. I intended to slip them to cleaners before you saw them.
>
> My desire to protect from outside invasion this spot mentioned has caused the enclosed brain child to be born. [Ann enclosed a document she was having prepared to keep the Bassett home site and its 28.59 acres in the Bassett family in perpetuity.]
>
> Papers are signed and delivered by [from] Sam's family. Now ready for Geo. and Josie.
>
> Please suggest any thing to be added or taken away from my form letter. I intend to have it put in shape and recorded soon as

patent is issued. Nice smelly job for the future generations of Bassetts? I would say. None of you can kick off the burden, just another yoak [yoke] for having been born a Bassett.

One never knows when they may get swept up into the dust pan, when they start out in the mad scramble of people and things. And I wish to add most people are things. Anything can happen. So, if, and but, you will have a clue to my desire in the matter of this spot.

I am not expecting to ripen and drop off like an apple. Windfalls do come down green sometimes. I should get patent when Josie's signature is in. Of course it all depends on Sect. [Secretary of the Interior] Ickes. When he sees fit to have one of his several hundred under things take the matter up.

The signs seem to be pointing southward, road maps are out and I notice a slight stirring, and pawing over stuff. So I presume the tramps are starting, "Oakies and Arkies" [speaking of herself and Frank] getting under way, next week. Then when the swallows come back from Capistrano, we may limp back [to Brown's Park.]

It would please me to slip the Haworth family in the little trailer and drag it to some warm sunny spot south then wake up and find Bill in it. Now isn't that an idea. Paul said, quote and unquote, I am full of the most brilliant ideas. I know what that word brilliant meant.

It's nice here now after freezing us to death a while back. Geo and Ruby seem quite pert for old folks. They will be cackling and licking themselves, if this sunshine lasts. Spitzie is fine; she killed a sparrow, mouse, and chipmunk a few nights ago. My ink got spilled so until I make contact with another bottle, it will be pencil.

Your cold would vanish into air if you got out of Craig's climate for a few months.

We may go your way and hope to when journeying to the Holy Land.   Ann[13]

Ann was eventually successful in acquiring the patent[14] on the original Bassett homeplace and drew up her will in a manner that would keep her beloved acreage evermore under Bassett ownership. The knowing of it was sweet balm to her inner anguishes. Now, her active mind was free to concentrate more on the writing that called to her, day and night. Ann was driven to preserve the days she'd lived among the pioneers who now rode in her thoughts. She wanted to share, and therefore hold close, her life as a cowhand on the open range.

The years passed and retirement beckoned. By then Ann and Frank had their cabin built; it sat very near where the original Bassett house lived out its days. They purchased a home in Leeds, Colorado, where they spent their winters. Summers belonged to Brown's Park. When she wrote about first coming home, she said:

> Many years went by before I returned to my "sacred cow," Brown's Park. I was lured by curiosity, as people will go back in mental morbidness to view the ravishing and despoliation by human hands. I was surprised to find so many pretty little homes tucked away in the hills. Just puncturing the landscape here and there, yielding fine dividends to their owners, a friendly folk who make up our traditional rural life in America.[15]

Ann detested certain books written about Brown's Park; the pretenders of history that fictionalized Ann, her family, and the people of Brown's Park into sensationalized caricatures. The two books that she despised most were *Outskirt Episodes* by William G. Tittsworth and *The Outlaw Trail* written by Charles Kelly.[16] Both books were published as nonfiction. Ann likely recognized that among the most insidious treatments in these two books was that of Isam Dart. Ned Huddleston, an imaginary character very loosely based on Isam Dart first emerged in *Outskirt Episodes* and then continued his exploits in *The Outlaw Trail*. It is greatly unfortunate that, perhaps unknowingly, writers and researchers carried forward and magnified the fictional Ned Huddleston to be the real man while treating Isam Dart as an alias.

Through the years, truth morphed into legend in accounts of Ann's mother. Cattlewoman Elizabeth Bassett was deemed the leader of the notorious Bassett gang and a commander of rustlers. The chronicle expanded from a 1919 newspaper account of when, in 1888, Valentine Hoy swore complaints against Elizabeth, Herb, and other Brown's Parkers. In the article written thirty-one years after the fact, Elizabeth was described as being involved in altering brands on a large number of Hoy cattle. The article, while mostly well-researched, has its points of sensationalism. It states that the rustlers, fearing they were about to be caught with the stolen animals "rounded up the cattle near Zenobia Peak and corralled them on the brink of a cliff that reared itself like a wall a thousand feet above Green River. The cattle were shot and hurled over a cliff and were carried away by that swift current of that turbulent stream and it was supposed that the evidence was lost, as in fact it was, to a large extent."[17] Later accounts say that Elizabeth Bassett stampeded five hundred head

Ann Bassett Willis in 1949 was still a mesmerizing horsewoman. *The Museum of NW Colorado–Craig.*

of stolen cattle off a cliff leaving behind stacks of bleached bones below in Lodore Canyon. No photos, eye witnesses, or other evidence of such a reprehensible deed ever surfaced.

A tantalizing myth arose that Ann Bassett and the famed Etta Place, the girlfriend of the Sundance Kid, were the same person. While the two were similar in age, lovely, and knew some of the same people, extensive documentation proves the two women lived contrasting lives in separate locations. For instance, Ann married Hi Bernard in Colorado in April 1904. At that time Etta Place, according to Pinkerton files, lived with the Sundance Kid and Butch Cassidy at their ranch in South America. That summer, while Ann ranched at her new husband's side, Etta Place and the Sundance Kid barely escaped capture at the St. Louis World's Fair and soon returned to South America.[18]

Josie Bassett has been mischaracterized by some as Butch Cassidy's girlfriend and lover. While Ann and Josie knew Butch Cassidy's friend and partner Elzy Lay very well, they had only a few encounters with Butch Cassidy. Josie's young romance was not with Butch Cassidy but revolved around the Bassett Ranch foreman, Jim McKnight.

In 1948, Ann wrote a letter to Cora Templeton in Maybell. In the letter she told Cora that she and Josie were double-crossed by *Life Magazine* in a write-up about Josie and that it was a "foul representation."

Norma Gardner riding Croppy on Douglas Mountain at about the time she watched Queen Ann expertly handle a wild cow. *Courtesy of Norma Gardner Snow.*

Ann also said that she had submitted her own writings on the history of Brown's Park to agents in New York. "They changed my script to the most stupid, wild fairy tales you ever saw. I would not go for it. When it was in book form and ready to sign, I shut it down."[19]

As Queen Ann authored her own stories, she wrote with great charm. Somehow, though, and surprisingly so, she never quite realized that her true life stories were so magnificently compelling that there was absolutely no need, ever, to alter or exaggerate them, as she sometimes did.[20] During the selective moments when Ann allowed her heart to be revealed, she did so in lines both moving and poetic. Describing the three-room cabin her father built on Zenobia Peak she wrote: "The logs for this were dragged from the timber by horse. Door and window facings were hewed by hand. This cabin still stands intact high on a point above scenic Zenobia Basin, an untouched spot, serenely dreaming in an enchanting loveliness of peaks and space."[21]

In 1950, Ann was visiting her brother George when Art Gardner and Art's seven-year-old daughter Norma arrived in their pickup. Art had purchased a large Hereford cow from George and came to pick the cow up and take her back to his ranch located on Douglas Mountain. George already had the cow in the corral, and he and Ann were standing nearby.

Norma was mesmerized by the sight of Queen Ann, the woman who up to then she had only heard about. At seventy-two Ann was still a very beautiful woman. She was wearing a dress, two-inch heels, and earrings and a necklace made of pearls. Ann's hair had now lightened with age to a tinge of chestnut. Her entire manner and way of speaking matched her appearance. Queen Ann was the image of refinement.[22]

Norma's father soon had the pickup backed up to the loading chute and the gate on the pickup rack opened. Norma perched herself on the top pole of the corral to watch as her dad went in the corral with the cow. The big Hereford was feisty and she was having none of it. The cow took after Art sending him scrambling over the corral fence.

The adults decided the safest place for Norma would be in the cab of the truck. Once inside the truck the little girl got on her knees so she could better watch the action. Moments later George and Art, working together, had the saliva-slinging cow headed up the loading chute. However when the cow hit the bed of the pickup she never slowed her momentum. Instead, she jumped up and over the rack, landing on the cab of the truck and bending it to bump the top of Norma's head before sliding down the side of the truck, taking off the rear view mirror as she went. As soon as the Hereford's feet hit the ground, she was on the run. So was Queen Ann, sprinting in her heels to the house.

George had his and Ann's horses saddled by the time Ann emerged from the cabin. Once again Norma was awestruck. Queen Ann was transformed. Wearing Levis, denim shirt, boots, spurs, and a light-colored wide-brimmed hat, the cattlewoman swung into her saddle and she and George went side by side after the cow in a gallop. While Art strung a lariat across the top of the rack to prevent another escape, Norma hustled out of the truck and hurried up the corral fence. The cab, she decided, was not the safest place to be.

Soon Ann, George, and the cow were heading toward the corral in a dust. Ann, with her form being one with the horse, and her rope in hand and swinging, was a glorious forever-remembered sight for the little

LAST WILL AND TESTAMENT

I, Ann Bassett Willis, being of sound mind and disposing memory, do declare this to be my Last Will and Testament.

I am the sole owner of the land and improvements on same, herein described: Lots in Sec. 34, T. 10, R. 102 W, 6 P.M. in Moffat County, Colorado. Said land is free of all encumbrances and it shall remain so.

At my death the property shall be under the control of Frank M. Willis who has full right to live on the land and receive proceeds from same during his life time.

Said land cannot be sold, traded, mortgaged or given away.

At the death of Frank M. Willis complete control of said land goes to George Emerson Bassett who, under the same clause, is to have control and benefit of said property during his life time.

Title of the property herein described shall remain in the control of a direct descendant of Amous Herbert and Mary E. Bassett. Direct descentants now eligible are: Edna Bassett Haworth; Bill Haworth; Roy Bassett; Clark Bassett; Sam Bassett; Jr. and Frank N. MacKnight. A wife or husband of such decendant cannot control or have control of any interest in said property. Said wife or husband shall not control same for a minor child.

Should any devisee in control of said land fail to pay taxes on same the county treasurer of Moffat County, Colorado shall appoint an agent to pay such taxes by sale of produce from the land and notify the next of kin who is eligible, who may pay such taxes and take a life control of said property.

All improvements placed upon said land shall become the property of the land and cannot be removed.

The place shall be kept in good clean condition, ditches, fences, etc.

All the rest of my property shall become the property of Frank M. Willis.

Dated this 1 day of March 1952.

D. Glenn Beal
Witness

Mayme E. Beal Colbath
Witness

Hilma Beal

Ann Bassett Willis
Ann Bassett Willis

In 1952, Ann rewrote her will to specify that her land stay in control of a direct descendant of her parents and that it be well kept up. Her other property was to go to her husband Frank Willis. *The Museum of NW Colorado–Craig.*

ranch girl on the corral fence. Once inside the corral George and Ann stayed on their horses. After roping the cow around the horns and then positioning their horses so there was one on each side of the cow, they bent the big cow's path toward the chute. Up the chute and into the back of the pickup the Hereford went. As the truck went on its way carrying the new cow home, Norma watched out the window for as long as she could before the sight of Queen Ann faded into the distance.[23]

Two years later and two days before Christmas on December 23, 1952, George died at home at the age of sixty-seven. Ruby, being in ill health, had not lived at the ranch with George for some time. After George's funeral in Craig, he was buried on the hill, in the family cemetery. Ann and Frank had worked at maintaining Herb's white steel fence around the cemetery including applying a coat of fresh paint and doing repairs to the corner walls of concrete and native rock.[24]

When Ann and Frank returned to Brown's Park in the spring of 1953, the place must have felt lonesome, indeed, without George nearby. Still, Ann was at home in her place of reassurance. Throughout the summer, she breathed in the air her parents had so long ago gifted to her when they chose a remote and rugged land on which to homestead. The fragrant breezes came off the mountains of her valley to be stirred into the scent of a river's flow. As the weeks passed, though, Ann felt fatigued and unwell.

Ten-year-old Norma Gardner was sad when she heard Queen Ann was ill. Ann was lying in bed when Norma went with her mother to visit Ann and take her and Frank some food for meals. Then in September, Norma was in the little white schoolhouse nearby when an airplane buzzed overhead before landing on the road. The young girl watched as Queen Ann, in the clutches of a heart attack, was carried to the plane that would fly her to the hospital in Craig.

Although Ann survived the attack, heart disease steadily drained her. In the spring of 1954 she wrote to her dear niece Edna, the daughter she never had, from her home in Leeds: "It is hard for me to be on the helpless list after a life of so much activity. I write so poorly because I got out of bed in Salt Lake and fell on my face and hands. What a shiner I had for a week and I can't use my right hand yet, I did not think I could get so weak."[25]

Four days before Ann's seventy-eighth birthday, the golden threads of her life story wove silently to the end. Queen Ann's words, though, of being home among the memories she shared with her beloved valley linger still:

> Brown's Park brought back a poignant yearning, to dash away and drive an avalanche of Two Bar cattle back across the divide. Then I would awaken from my dream to discover that I had been peeping into a past that cannot return. Live Two Bar cattle are conspicuously absent. The winds have buried all the dead ones.
>
> The roundup days are over, and so are most of the old knee-sprung, saddle-marked punchers over—over there. Just snare old Tommy horse in the ropes for me boys. I'll be riding him, at our next bunch ground.[26]
>
> SO LONG![27]

The warm seasons of Brown's Park bring the nighthawks. At dusk and dawn they fly in graceful spirals and loops, flashing glimpses of white as they hunt on the wing for insects. The booming sounds of their flight and lilt of their songs are reminders of the night herders and of Queen Ann Bassett riding the trails of her valley at the dimming of the day.

NOTES TO CHAPTER TWENTY-SIX

1. Ann Bassett Willis, "Arizona," unpublished account, The Museum of NW Colorado–Craig.

2. William H. and Carrie Gottsche became highly successful sheep ranchers, butchers, and bankers in Rock Springs. The Gottsche Foundation was incorporated March 1954 as a foundation providing diagnosis and treatment of crippling conditions for children and adults. The nonprofit foundation is renowned for its rehabilitation health facility.

3. "Graveside Services Held Sunday for Frank Willis," *The Craig-Empire Courier,* 25 Jul 1963.

4. Ann Bassett Willis, "Arizona," unpublished account.

5. Ann Bassett Willis, excerpt from Evelyn Semotan tape, a portion of Ann Bassett's writings, The Museum of NW Colorado–Craig.

6. Catherine Sevenau and Gordon Clemens, "Lore, Libel, & Lies: A Family History," 106, The Museum of NW Colorado–Craig. After J.S. Hoy's death, when his unpublished manuscript was gathered together, the sections about Ann and her trials were missing and have never been found.

7. Taylor Grazing Act, 48 Stat 1269, "Act of Jun 28, 1934" codified at 43 U.S.C. 315 et seq.

8. "Graveside Services for Frank Willis," The Craig Empire-Courier, 25 Jul 1963.

9. "Fire Destroys House On Old Bassett Ranch," The Craig Empire-Courier, 29 Mar 1939.

10. Greystone is a small establishment southeast of Brown's Park that served as the local post office.

11. "Locals," The Craig Empire-Courier, 10 Jan 1940.

12. Ann Bassett Willis, letter sent from Oakland, California, to Edna Haworth, 1939, The Museum of NW Colorado–Craig.

13. Ann Bassett Willis, letter to Edna Haworth, 3 Dec 1940, The Museum of NW Colorado–Craig.

14. United States of America General Land Office, Denver 051518, 27 Nov 1944, Record of Patent: Patent Number 1119228, Grant to Ann B. Willis, 28.59 acres.

15. Ann Bassett Willis, "Queen Ann of Brown's Park," The Colorado Magazine, Jan 1953, 76.

16. Ann Bassett Willis, letter to Duward and Esther Campbell, 2 Dec 1952, The Museum of the West through The Museum of NW Colorado–Craig. Ann wrote in the letter that she sued Charles Kelly and received a judgment that tied up his publishing house. She said that in 1942 Kelly begged her to let the judgment go by default. She wrote: "I am a pushover and did it." Outskirts Episodes was finished and published after the death of William G. "Billy Tittsworth." It is possible that Tittsworth never intended the book to be considered nonfiction but rather a work of fiction loosely based on events and people he knew.

17. "Tales of Early Days," Moffat County Bell, 5 Dec 1919, The Museum of NW Colorado–Craig.

18. Dan Buck and Ann Meadows, "Etta Place: A Most Wanted Woman;" "Who are those guys?;" "Neighbors on the Hot Seat: Revelations"; Bill Betenson, Butch Cassidy, My Uncle.

19. Ann Bassett Willis, letter to Cora Templeton, 8 Mar 1948. This was most likely Ann's memoir, "Scars and Two Bars."

20. Ann was first published in the spring of 1943. A memoir she titled "Scars and Two Bars" ran in the *Moffat County Mirror* in a series. In April, July, and Oct 1952, and January 1953 her memoir "Queen Ann of Brown's Park," was published in *The Colorado Magazine* by The State Historical Society of Colorado.

21. Ann Bassett Willis, "Queen Ann of Brown's Park," 97.

22. Norma Gardner Snow, interview with author, 10 May 2013.

23. Norma Gardner Snow, interview 10 May 2013.

24. Josie Bassett Morris, interview with Untermann, Mortensen, and Cooley, 1959, The Museum of NW Colorado – Craig.

25. Ann Bassett Willis, letter to Edna Haworth, 14 Apr 1954, The Museum of NW Colorado – Craig.

26. A term for the gathering grounds of a roundup.

27. Ann Bassett Willis, taken from her working copy of her memoir before certain lines were edited out, The Museum of NW Colorado – Craig.

.

BIBLIOGRAPHY

Books

Ball, Larry D. *Tom Horn In Life and Legend*. Norman: University of Oklahoma Press, 2014.

Betensen, Bill. *Butch Cassidy, My Uncle*. Glendo, WY: High Plains Press, 2012.

Burroughs, John R. *Where the Old West Stayed Young*. New York: Bonanza Books, 1962.

Carson, Kit. *Kit Carson's Autobiography*, edited by Milo Milton. Chicago: R.R. Donnelly and Sons, 1935.

Carlson, Chip. *Tom Horn Blood on the Moon*. Glendo, WY: High Plains Press, 2001.

Chivington, L. H. "Doc." *Last Guard: The True Story of Cowboy Life, from actual experiences of L. H. "Doc" Chivington*. Minneapolis: Celebrations of Life Services, Inc., 2015.

DeJournette, Dick and Daun. *One Hundred Years of Brown's Park and Diamond Mountain*. Vernal: DeJournette Enterprises, 1996.

Ellison, Douglas W. *David Lant—The Vanished Outlaw*. Aberdeen: Midstates Printing, 1988.

Farnham, Thomas J. *Travels in the Great Western Prairies, The Anahuac and Rocky Mountains, and the Oregon Territory*. Poughkeepsie: Killey and Lossing Printers, 1841.

Grounds, John Cureton. *Trail Dust of the Southwest*. Marysvale: J.C. Grounds, 1977.

Hamilton, William T. *My Sixty Years on the Plains: Trapping, Trading, and Indian Fighting*. New York: Forest and Stream Publishing Company, 1905.

Horn, Tom. *Life of Tom Horn: Government Scout and Interpreter*. Norman: University of Oklahoma Press, Reprint edition, 1964.

Hughel, Avvon. *The Chew Bunch of Brown's Park*. San Francisco: Scrimshaw Press, 1970.

Jameson, W. C. *Billy The Kid: Beyond The Grave*. Lanham: Taylor Trade Publishing, 2005.

Larson, T. A. *The History of Wyoming*. Lincoln: University of Nebraska Press, 1965.

McClure, Grace. *The Bassett Women*. Athens: Ohio University Press, 1985.

McKnight, Frank. *A Family Remembered*. Salt Lake City: Ponderosa Printing, 1996.

Mullen, William E. *Wyoming Reports, Cases Decided In The Supreme Court of Wyoming From February 13, 1915 To January 25, 1916*. Laramie: The Laramie Republican Company Printers and Binders, 1916.

Murdock, Harvey Lay. *The Educated Outlaw: The Story of Elzy Lay of the Wild Bunch*. Bloomington: Author House, 2009.

Nelson, Richard. *Lincoln's Loyalists: Union Soldiers from the Confederacy*. Lebanon: Northeastern University Press, 1992.

Parent, Laurence. *Scenic Driving Wyoming*. Helena: Falcon Press, 1997.

Progressive Men of Western Colorado. Chicago: A.W. Bowen and Co., 1905;.

Rhode, Robert B. *Booms and Busts on Bitter Creek: A History of Rock Springs, Wyoming*. Boulder: Pruett Publishing Company, 1987.

Rockwell, Wilson. *The Utes A Forgotten People*. Denver: Sage Books, 1956.

Sage, Rufus B. *Rocky Mountain Life Or, Startling Scenes and Perilous Adventures in the Far West, During an Expedition of Three Years*. Lincoln: University of Nebraska Press, 1982.

Sprague, Marshall. *Massacre: The Tragedy at White River*. Lincoln: University of Nebraska Press Bison Books, 1980.

Stegner, Wallace. *Beyond the Hundredth Meridian John Wesley Powell and the Second Opening of the West*. Boston: Houghton Mifflin Company, The Riverside Press, 1954.

Stoddard, C. A; edited by Dan Davidson, Janet Gerber, Shannan Koucherik. *Tales of the Old West: Retold Early Stories of Northwestern Colorado*. Montrose: Lifetime Chronicle Press, 2007.

Warner, Matt; Murray E. King. *The Last of the Bandit Riders*. New York: Bonanza Books, 1940.

Warner, Matt: Murray E. King, updated by Joyce Warner and Dr. Steve Lacy. *Last of the Bandit Riders… Revisited*. Salt Lake City: Big Moon Traders, 2000.

Wilson, Rockwell. *The Utes—A Forgotten People*. Lake City, Western Reflections Publishing Company: 2003.

Articles and Internet Sources

"10 Surprising Civil War Facts." History.com. history.com/news/10-surprising-civil-war-facts. Accessed 15 Jun 2017.

"Army Bands." Goarmy.com. goarmy.com/band/about-army-bands/history.html. Accessed 12 Jan 2015.

"Battle of The Wilderness." History.com. history.com/topics/american-civil-war/battle-of-the-wilderness. Accessed 2 May 2015.

Bowers, Carol L. "School Bells and Winchesters: The Sad Saga of Glendolene Myrtle Kimmell;" Glendolene Kimmell sworn Affidavit, 10 Nov 1902; uwacadweb.uwyo.edu/robertshistory/school_bells_and_winchesters.htm. Accessed 6 Oct 2016.

Buck, Daniel and Annie Meadows. "Etta Place: A Most Wanted Woman;" *WOLA Journal,* Vol III, No 1, Spring/Summer 1993.

———— "Neighbors on the Hot Seat: Revelations: From The Long-Lost Argentine Police File," *WOLA Journal,* Vol V, No 2, Spring/Summer, 1996.

————. "Who are those Guys?" *True West Magazine*.

"Californians and the Military: Major-General Harrison Gray Otis, U.S.V., Publisher of the *Los Angeles Times*," californiamilitaryhistory.org/Otis. Accessed 24 Jan 2017.

"Chamberlain, Ewell." Ancestry.com. Accessed 28 Jun 2017.

Correia, David. "Retribution Will Be Their Reward: New Mexico's Las Gorras Blancas and the Fight for the Las Vegas Land Grant Commons." *Radical History Review,* Issue 108 (Fall 2010).

Davis, John W. "The Johnson County War: 1892 Invasion of Northern Wyoming." Wyohistory.org, A project of the Wyoming State Historical Society. wyohistory.org/encyclopedia/johnson-county-war-1892-invasion-northern-wyoming. Accessed 5 Jan 2017.

Find A Grave Index. 1600-Current. findagrave.com

Hoy, Valentine Shade (1848-1898). Find A Grave Memorial.

"Indian Territory." Columbia University Press, *The Columbia Electronic Encyclopedia,* www.infoplease.com/encyclopedia, Accessed 17 Jun 2016.

Larson, T.A. "Wyoming Statehood," *Annals of Wyoming*, Vol. 12, No. 4, (1940).

"Marriage Age." True West Historical Society. truewest.ning.com/forum/topics/marriage-age. Accessed 15 Jul 2017.

"Meeker Massacre." *Utah Genealogy Trails.* Delta County, Colorado, Genealogy and History. Genealogytrails.com/colo/delta. Accessed 15 Jan 2015.

"Meet General Otis and His Los Angeles Times," latimesbomb.com/2010/09/meet-general-otis-his-los-angeles-times. Accessed 25 Jan 2017.

National Archives and Records Administration, *Civil War Pension Index: General Index to Pension Files, 1861-1934.* Ancestry.com. Accessed 11 Nov 2015).

Nieto-Philips, John. *Encyclopedia of the Great Plains.* "Herrera, Juan Jose (ca. 1840s-1902)." plainshumanities.unl.edu/encyclopedia/doc/egp.ha.019. Accessed 11 Nov 2015.

"Panic of 1893-Saylor Academy." Saylor.org. saylor.org/site/wp-content/uloads/hist312-1a-2-panic-of-1893.pdf. Accessed 5 Feb 2017

Parker, James B. Wm Pulaski Chamberlain Family Facts Part 1. Ancestry.com. Accessed 12 Feb 2014.

Patent Detail. U.S. Department of the Interior, Bureau of Land Management, General Land Office Records. hppts://glorecords.blm.gov.

"Reconstruction Plans Under Lincoln." Education.com. education.com/study-help/article/us-history-reconstruction-civil-war-lincoln-johnson. Accessed 15 Sep 2014.

Rutherford, David Rennnow. Ancestry.com. Accessed 28 Jun 2017.

Salt Lake County, Utah. Death Register, in the Salt Lake County, Utah, Death Records, 1908-1949. Ancestry.com.

"Settlement Of Ashley Valley." *Utah Genealogy Trails, History and Genealogy of Uintah County, Utah.* genealogytrails.com/Utah. Accessed 23 Jan 2015.

State of Colorado Division of Vital Statistics Marriage Record Report. Film Number 001690141. Ancestry.com. Accessed 4 Feb 2017.

Steamboat Springs Pro Rodeo Series, steamboatprorodeo.com, steamboatprorodeo.com/history/. Accessed 14 May 2017.

"The Battle." Totallyhistory.com. totallyhistory.com/battle-of-the-wilderness/. Accessed 5 Jun 2015.

"Uinta vs. Uintah." *The Edge Magazine*. Neola, Utah, www.theedgemagazine.gldgspot.com/2010/uinta-vs-uintah.html. Accessed 25 Mar 2018.

U.S. National Park Service. The Civil War Soldiers and Sailors System: Soldiers Database, nps.gov, nps.gov/civilwar/index.htm. 11 Nov 2015.

"History and Genealogy for Uintah County, Utah, Settlement of Ashley Valley, The Hard Winter." *Utah Genealogy Trails*. genealogytrails.com/utah/.

"Watson, Ellen Liddy 'Ella'." findagrave.com. Accessed 16 Jan 2017.

"Were Causes of Depression—1893," *reference.com,* reference.com/history/were-causes-depression-1893-62d1353f9e7b10b1. Accessed 5 Feb 2017.

Western States Marriage Record Index. ID No. 267157. Ancestry.com.

"What is a Ute?" University of Utah, utefans.net/home/ancient_ute/utetribe.html. Accessed 29 Jul 2016.

"Who was Nicholas Senn?, sennfriendsforever.org/Who-is-Nicholas-Senn-html, accessed 30 Mar 2016.

Willis, Ann Bassett. "Queen Ann of Brown's Park," *Colorado Magazine: The State Historical Society of Colorado.* Apr 1952; Jul 1952; Oct 1952; Jan 1953.

Census Records

Colorado Census. 1885.

Twelfth Census of the U.S. Schedule No. 1–Population. State of New Mexico, County: San Miguel, Precinct: Las Vegas Precinct No. 26. 30 Jun 1900.

United States Federal Census. 1870, 1880, 1900.

Newspapers

Aspen Evening Chronicle. Colorado. 30 Sep 1890.

Aspen Weekly Times. Colorado. 28 Feb 1885.

Aurora Democrat. "Week's Events in Colorado." 15 Aug 1913.

Bangor Daily Whig and Courier. Maine. 20 Jul 1880.

Carbon County Journal. Wyoming, 17 Nov 1888, 8 Nov 1879.

Cheyenne Daily Leader. Wyoming, 14 Oct 1879, 18 Jul 1880, 27 Nov 1903, 6 Jan 1903.

The Cheyenne Daily Sun. Wyoming, 30 Jul 1889, 10 Jan 1892, 8 Dec 1897.

Cheyenne State Leader. Wyoming, 13 Oct 1902, 29 Mar 1911.

The Chicago Tribune. Illinois, 25 Jul 1897.

Craig Courier. Colorado, 16 Dec 1892, 26 Dec 1896, 9 Jan 1897, 16 Jan 1897, 6 Nov 1897, 4 Dec 1897, 19 Mar 1898, 20 Jan 1900, 14 Apr 1900, 2 Jun 1900,

16 Jun 1900, 13 Oct 1900, 20 Oct 1900, 3 Nov 1900, 23 Nov 1900, 8 Dec 1900, 5 Jan 1901, 26 Jan 1901, 9 Feb 1901, 8 Nov 1901, 24 May 1902, 16 Oct 1903, 30 Nov 1905, 29 Mar 1939, 10 Jan 1940, 25 Jul 1963.

Craig Empire. Colorado, 1 Apr 1910, 1 Apr 1911, 16 Aug 1913, 13 Dec 1913, 20 Dec 1913, 17 Aug 1921, 29 Sep 1926, 6 Feb 1924, 26 Aug 1931, 31 May 1933, 25 Jul 1963.

Colorado Daily Chieftain. Colorado, 6 Nov 1879, 8 Jan 1880, 8 Sep 1893, 16 Sep 1893.

Colorado Miner. Georgetown, 15 Nov 1879.

Colorado Transcript. Denver, 17 Dec 1879.

Denver Post. Colorado, 5 Mar 1961.

Fremont Clipper, Wyoming, 31 Dec 1887.

The Frontier Index. Nebraska, 11 Sep 1868.

Laramie Boomerang. Wyoming, 19 Aug 1897, 1 Aug 1889, 22 Aug 1889, 3 Nov 1903, 5 Nov 1903, 28 Nov 1903.

Laramie Republic. Wyoming, 18 Dec 1900, 8 Sep 1919.

Laramie Sentinel. Wyoming, 18 Oct 1879.

Moffat County Bell. Colorado, 29 Nov 1925, 5 Dec 1919.

Moffat County Courie., Colorado, 18 Feb 1911, 10 Aug 1911, 12 Aug 1911, 17 Aug 1913, 21 Aug 1913, 28 Aug 1913, 29 Aug 1918.

Moffat County Jubilee. 1908-1958 Historical Booklet.

Moffat County Mirror. Colorado, Spring 1943, Apr, Jul, Oct 1952.

New York Daily Tribune. New York, 31 Dec 1882.

Ogden Standard. Utah, 13 May 1890.

Oak Creek Times. Colorado, 17 Aug 1911.

Rifle Reveille. Colorado, 18 Mar 1898.

Rock Springs Miner. Wyoming, 14 Sep 1892, 16 Sep 1897,18 Aug 1894, 1 Jun 1892, 10 Dec 1896, 31 Dec 1896, 18 Nov 1897, 13 Jul 1899, 14 Sep 1899, 26 Mar 1903, 31 Mar 1904.

Rock Springs Independent. Wyoming, 13 Apr 1906.

Rock Springs Rocket. Wyoming, 5 Apr 1900, 4 Apr 1929, 5 Apr 1929.

Routt County Courier. Colorado, 14 Apr 1904, 20 Oct 1904, 1 Dec 1904, 4 Apr 1907, 7 Jul 1907, 19 Sep 1907, 31 Dec 1908, 14 Jan 1909, 15 Jul 1909, 22 Jul 1909, 29 Jul 1909, 5 Aug 1909, 2 Sep 1909, 22 Aug 1913.

Routt County Republican. Colorado, 11 Aug 1911, 27 Jan 1911, 22 Aug 1913.

Routt County Sentinel. Colorado, 31 Mar 1911, 23 May 1913, 20 Apr 1917.

Saguache Chronicle. Colorado, 10 Jan 1880, 8 May 1880.

Salida Mail. Colorado, 8 Sep 1893.

Salt Lake Herald. Utah, 13 May 1892, 18 Aug 1897, 27 Oct 1897, 2 Dec 1897.

Silver Cliff Rustler. Colorado, 16 Mar 1898.

Silver Standard. Colorado, 16 Sep 1893

Solid Muldoon Weekly. Colorado, 7 Nov 1879.

Steamboat Pilot. Colorado, 9 Mar 1898, 25 Jul 1900, 1 Aug 1900, 29 Aug 1900, 17 Oct 1900, 6 Nov 1900, 14 Nov 1900, 5 Dec 1900, 9 Aug 1911, 10 Aug 1911, 12 Aug 1911, 16 Aug 1911, 23 Oct 1918, 13 Nov 1947.

Vernal Express. Utah, 14 Sep 1893, 23 Nov 1893, 28 Oct 1897, 4 Nov 1897, 18 Nov 1897, 3 Mar 1898, 21 Apr 1898, 21 Jul 1900, 11 Aug 1900, 12 Jul 1902, 14 Jul 1909, 29 Nov 1912, 20 Dec 1912, 9 Oct 1941.

Western Newspaper Union. Utah, 20 Nov 1898.

Wheatland World. Wyoming, 10 Dec 1897.

Wyoming Tribune. 23 Dec 1900.

The Yakima Herald. Washington, 6 Apr 1893.

U.S. Government Documents

46th Congress, House of Representatives, 2d Session, No. 38, May 1, 1880. Testimony in Relation to the Ute Indian Outbreak. Taken By The Committee On Indian Affairs Of The House Of Representatives.

46th Congress, House of Representatives, 2d Session, No. 83, May 1, 1880. Testimony in Relation to the Ute Indian Outbreak. Taken By The Committee On Indian Affairs Of The House Of Representatives.

Adjutant General of the State of Illinois. (1900) Report of the Adjutant General of the State of Illinois, Vol VI, containing reports for the years 1861-1866. Springfield, Ill: Journal Company, Printers and Binders.

Annual Reports of the Department of the Interior for the Fiscal Year Ended Jun 30, 1898, Indian Affairs. Washington: Government Printing Office 1898 of the Commissioner of Indian Affairs, "Killing of Utes in Colorado."

Iowa, Adjutant General Office. *"Roster and Record of Iowa Soldiers in the War of the Rebellion, Together with Historical Sketches of Volunteer Organizations, 1861-1866."* Des Moines: E.H. English, State Printer, E.D. Chassell, State Binder.

National Park Service. *U.S. Civil War Soldiers, 1861-1865*. Provo, UT, USA: Ancestry.com Operations Inc., 2007.

Taylor Grazing Act. (48 Stat 1269, "Act of Jun 28, 1934" codified at 43 U.S.C. 315 et seq).

Tennent, William L. *John Jarvie of Brown's Park*. Cultural Resource Series No. 7, 1981.

United States of America, General Land Office, Denver 051518. 27 Nov 1944, Record of Patent: Patent Number 1119228. Grant to Ann B. Willis, 28.59 acres.

Court Documents

Brand and Mark Recording (Colorado), Statement and Affidavit by James Vance, M.D., 13 Aug 1913.

"Estate of H.H. Bernard." 1924. Museum of NW Colorado–Craig.

"Estate of Isham Dart." Affidavit of Decease sworn by William H. Blair, 20 Nov 1900; Creditor Claim by Henry Lang, 6 Nov, 1900.

"H.H. Bernard, Plaintiff v. Anna Bernard, Defendant." Divorce, Affidavit of Non Residence For Publication of Summons, affidavit, answer, Application for Alimony and Suit Money, Complaint, Decree, Order, Stipulation, 25 Aug 1913.

"Inquest Hearing of Elbert Bassett." Findings And Testimony Re Cause Of Death In The Case Of E.B. Bassett, Deceased, Craig, Colorado," 19 Nov 1925.

"Inquest Testimony," for Wiliam Strang, deceased, 1898.

"Sweetwater County Court Records."

"Isham [sic] Dart, Plaintiff v. Elroy Philbreck."

"Territory of Wyoming, v. Isahm [sic] Dart," Affidavit of charged offense filed by Tom Horn, 24 Sep 1888.

"The State of Colorado, County of Routt, Estate of Madison M. Rash," 28 Jul 1900; Samuel A. Rash Petition for Letters of Administration to Judge, 9 Aug 1900; Judge statement denying petition of Anna M. Bassett, 24 Sep 1900.

"The State of Colorado v. Isham Dart," 26 Sep 1900.

"The State of Colorado, Plaintiff v. Anna Bernard and Thomas Yarberry, Defendants," Witness subpoenas, criminal complaints, warrant for arrest of Anna Bernard, warrant for arrest of Thomas Yarberry, affidavit for change of venue, list of jurors, certificate of incorporation of Haley Livestock and Trading Company, Colorado Brand and Mark Recording , 9 Aug 1911.

"The State of Colorado, Plaintiff v. Anna Bernard and Thomas Yarberry, Defendants," Subpoenas commanding witnesses to testify, list of jurors, certificate of incorporation of Haley Livestock and Trading Company, Colorado

"The State of Colorado, Routt County, First Judicial District Court. County Attorney William Wiley File. Documents on the case of The People of the State of Colorado v. Madison M. Rash, 20 Mar 1894.

"W.B. McClelland, Plaintiff v. Annie M. Bassett, Defendant," Transcript of Judgement, 5 Oct 1903.

Letters

Ashley, William Henry letter to General Atkinson, From St. Louis, Dec 1825, pp 28 and 29, C1939, Folder1. The State Historical Society of Missouri: St. Louis, Missouri.

Bassett, Ann, letter to Eb Bassett. 8 Nov 1901.

Bassett, Eb, handwritten will. 15 Sep 1909.

Bassett, Eb, letter to Friend Joe Martin Blansit. 28 Feb 1925.

Bassett, Herb, letter. 30 May 1903.

Bassett, Herb, letter written to his granddaughter Edna Bassett. 22 Jun 1918.

Bassett, Sam, letter written to J.M. Blansit. 25 Aug 1900.

Bechdolt, Lizzie Delaney, letter written 21 Jul 1886, describing Willow Creek Canyon.

Bernard, Ann, letter from Sonora, Mexico. 17 Jul 1912.

Bernard, Ann, letter to her attorney Pughe. 29 Jan 1918.

Chew, Enola, letter to her niece Kristy Wall. 17 Feb 1972.

Crouse, Mary, letter to Billy Tittsworth.

Delaney, Lizzie, letters to Hattie Reals. 2 Apr 1885, 8 Sep 1885, 11 Jan 1886.

Duncan, Tap, letter to Ann Willis. 15 Mar 1941.

Hoy, J.S. letter published in the *Routt County Courier.* Volume 11, Number 1, 20 Jul 1905.

Hoy, Valentine, letter, 20 Feb 1898.

Kimmell, Glendolene, to Mr. H. Zimmerman. 7 Nov 1903, Rec. Group 001.16.

MacKnight, Crawford, letter to Cary Stif. 12 Nov 1968.

MacKnight, Crawford (Josie's son Crawford used the Scottish spelling of McKnight), letter written to his cousin, Edna Haworth. Oct 1961.

Rash, Mat, letter written to Joe Martin. 13 Nov 1898.

Taylor, Jesse G., letters to Author. 3 Aug 1981, 21 Sep 1981, 10 May 1982.

Willis, Ann, letter to Cora Templeton. 8 Mar 1948.

Willis, Ann, letters to Duward and Esther Campbell. 25 Feb 1950, 23 Apr 1950, 2 Mar 1951, 2 Dec 1952, 3 Mar 1953.

Willis, Ann, letter to Edna Haworth. 1939 from Oakland, California, 3 Dec 1940 and 14 Apr 1954.

Unpublished Manuscripts

Bassett, Edna, "Besieged." Unpublished manuscript, 17 April 1896. The Museum of Northwest Colorado–Craig.

Hoy, J.S. "The J.S. Hoy Manuscript." Unpublished manuscript, undated. Photocopy of original. Author's Collection.

Hughel, Avvon. "Eb Bassett." Handwritten unpublished manuscript, undated. Private collection of Jo Semotan.

Willis, Ann, "Arizona." Unpublished manuscript, undated. Author's collection.

Willis, Ann Bassett. "Scars and Two Bars." Unpublished segments of manuscript, undated. The Museum of Northwest Colorado–Craig

Willis, Ann, handwritten account of "Wild Bunch Dinner." Museum of the West , Grand Junction, Colorado; The Museum of NW Colorado–Craig.

Willis, Ann, "The Gray Wolves. Unpublished manuscript, undated. Author's Collection.

Willis, Frank [attributed], "Confidentially Told." Unpublished Manuscript, 1924. The Museum of Northwest Colorado–Craig.

Interviews

Allen, William "Bill." Interview with author. Brown's Park, 6 Jun 1981.

MacKnight, Crawford. Interview with Glade Ross, 5 Mar 1975.

Miller, Patty Vaughn. Telephone interview with author, 27 Apr 2015.

Morris, Josie. Interview with G.E. Untermann, A.R. Mortensen and E.L. Cooley, 25 Sep 1959.

Morris, Josie Bassett. Interview with Murl Messersmith, 18 Jul 1960 and 7 Jul 1961.

Overy, Hazel Teters. Interviews with author. 15 Jul 1981, 10 Oct 1981.

Rasmussen, Minnie Crouse Ronholdt. Interview with Marie Taylor Allen. circa 1970.

Snow, Norma Gardner. Interview with author, May 10, 2013.

Taylor, Jesse. Interviews with author, 26 May 1981, 27 May 1981, 10 Oct 1981, 11 Oct 1981, 30 Mar 1982.

Taylor, Nina. Her story to author, circa 1960.

Tittsworth, William Daniel. Interview with C.A. Stoddard Jr., 1998.

Collections

George A. Pughe Collection, Letters : Bassett, Ruby, letter to attorney George A. Pughe, 30 Apr 1928; Bassett, Ruby, letter to George A. Pughe, 30 Apr 1928; Pughe, George, letter to Frank Willis, 9 Nov 1928; Pughe, George, letter to George Bassett, 14 Dec 1928; Pughe, George, letter to Josie Morris, 7 Aug 1929, Court Documents : "Estate of Elbert Bassett," 1927; Final report of Administratrix of the Estate, 5 Dec 1925 to 22 Jul 1929, Special Collections and Archives, University of Colorado Boulder Libraries.

Frederick Krueger Collection, Roslyn Bank Robbery Papers, 1892-1893, *archiveswest. orbiscascade.org,* Archives West Orbis Cascade Alliance, archiveswest.orbiscascade.org/ark:/80444/xv45370. Accessed 1 Feb 2017.

Statement of George Banks, undated, Folder 4, George Banks papers, 1898-2005, Collection Number 11450, American Heritage Center, University of Wyoming.

Thomas, D.G., letter to attorney with the Sweetwater County Office of the County and Prosecuting Attorney to U.S. Marshal Frank Hadsell, 12 Aug 1899.

Wyoming Stock Growers Association (1887). *Wyoming Brand Book. Digitalcollections.uwyo,* Cheyenne, Wyoming. American Heritage Center Digital Collections, Wyoming Stock Growers Association Records, University of Wyoming. digitalcollections.uwyo.edu.

Miscellaneous Sources

Bennion, Mary Goodman, "Frank Goodman." A one-page typescript about her father, undated. The Museum of Northwest Colorado–Craig.

1 Corinthians 13:13 King James Version (KJV).

American Bar Association, (1898), Report of the Twenty-First Annual Meeting of the American Bar Association, Volume 21, Part 1898, Pages 715-717. Dando Printing and Publishing Company, 34 South Third Street, Philadelphia, Pennsylvania, 1898.

Athearn, Frederic J., "An Isolated Empire: A History of Northwest Colorado", BLM Cultural Resource Series, 1977.

Craig: Moffat Golden Jubilee, Inc., 1908-1958 Historical Booklet.

Daisy Dowden Autograph Booklet.

Gardner, Art, excerpt from Art Gardner's notes.

Harding, Warren G., President of the United States, The United State of America Patent, Secure Homestead Claim of Anna B. Bernard, Number 867916, Vernal, Utah Land Office, 13 Jun 1922.

Haughey, E. V., "E. V. Houghy [Haughey] Account," Oral history transcribed by Jay Monaghan. Colorado Historical Society through The Museum of NW Colorado–Craig.

Homestead Proof–Testimony of Claimant, James F. McKnight, Glenwood Springs Land Office; Testimony of Witness, E.A. Farnham, 5 Sep 1900.

Jarvie, John, "Eulogy for Mary Crouse."

Josephine Meeker's Obituary, Smithsonian.

Marriage records in Sweetwater County Court House, Green River, Wyoming.

Red Creek Ranch abstracts. Author's Collection.

Sevenau, Catherine and Clemens, Gordon, *Lore, Libel, & Lies: A Family History.* Spiral-bound typescript, 5 April 2006. The Museum of NW Colorado–Craig.

Toliver Family Members. *Descendants of John Toliver.* Informally printed digital script. Provided by descendant Frank Hall.

The Heritage, "Rockport, Second Oldest Post Office In Arkansas," Hot Springs County Historical Society, Jul 1974.

Willis, Ann, excerpt from Evelyn Semotan tape, a portion of Ann Bassett's writings.

Yost, Nellie Snyder. Untitled and undated typescript. The Museum of Northwest Colorado–Craig.

INDEX

ACKNOWLEDGMENTS

My love and thankfulness are infinite for my husband, Mike Kouris. Mike immersed himself in my world of historical research after retiring from a stellar career in education. He tirelessly assisted me in giving this book life. My every request for obscure information was fulfilled by him, each of my torturous anxieties was soothed by him, every chapter was critiqued by him, and each of my successes was celebrated by him. He designed the maps with loving care. This book would not be if not for Mike.

To Dan Davidson, Director of the Museum of Northwest Colorado, I express my profound admiration and gratitude. I thank him for the way he honors history with a devotion to seek and preserve the truth. I will forever be grateful for the countless hours Dan spent in support of this book, not only in supplying a treasure trove of archived research but in tracking down a substantial amount of exciting new material and rare photographs. He generously shared much of his valuable time and expertise to help me assure that the book's historical details were precisely accurate. His assistance in creating this biography was invaluable. Dan's dedicated staff made many contributions to the benefit of this book. I'm deeply grateful to retired Assistant Director Jan Gerber, Assistant Director Paul Knowles, Registrar Linda Herschberg, and Assistant Registrars Kristi Hankins and Misty Watson.

I wish to express my profound gratefulness to my son, Nick, who long ago taught me that a mystical realm exists where grace and nobility live. Thank you to Ashley, our sweet angel and Nick's wife, for her love of family and the artistic contribution to the cover of this book.

Thank you to my sister Nonie Allen whose loving encouragement is a substantial part of my bedrock as well as my writing life. I'm deeply thankful to Jim Gardner for his kindhearted support and for the story about Ann that had been told to him by his grandfather, Art Gardner.

To the late Norma Gardner Snow, I want to express my affection and heartfelt appreciation for her firsthand accounts about Ann Bassett. Those stories were of great importance to the ending of this book.

My sincere thank you goes to Bassett/MacKnight descendants Tracy MacKnight, Dan Christensen, and Pat Christensen for their contributions and for entrusting me with the telling of their family's story.

I owe years of gratitude to accomplished author Betty Starks Case who is my loving friend and confidant. Her belief in the importance of my work is awe-inspiring and her words strengthen my commitment.

Immense appreciation goes to High Plains Press for its devotion to excellence and for its unwavering determination to bring this book forward as a significant contribution to history.

DIANA ALLEN KOURIS is an award-winning author of nonfiction articles and books. She grew up a Brown's Park cowgirl in the famed region where Colorado, Wyoming, and Utah converge. Decades of research and writing have rendered Kouris an authority on the spellbinding history of the area. Her previous books are *The Romantic and Notorious History of Brown's Park* and *Riding the Edge of an Era: Growing Up Cowboy on the Outlaw Trail.*

Nighthawk Rising serves as the apex of her work as a historian.

NOTES ON THE PRODUCTION OF THE BOOK

This book was simultaneously released in two editions.

A *limited edition hardcover* of only 300 copies
with headbands of blue and gold,
bound in Midnight Navy Arrestox B,
embossed with Sundance Gold foil,
and wrapped in a full-color dustjacket.
Each copy is hand-numbered and signed by the author.

The *softcover trade edition* is covered with ten-point stock,
printed in four colors, and coated with a ultra-gloss finish.

The text of both editions is from the Adobe Garamond Family
and Oldbook from ITC.
Display type is Nelson by Laura Worthington.

The book is printed on sixty-pound white Kateroo,
an acid-free, recycled paper, by Versa.